This is

Key themes from the Bible

Acknowledgments

The editor gratefully wishes to thank the Consultants of the *NIV Thematic Study Bible*: Alister McGrath, Donald J. Wiseman, J. I. Packer, Stephen Travis, Gordon McConville, and all those who compiled and edited the Thematic Section of the *NIV Thematic Study Bible*, on which this work is based.

THIS IS LIFE IN
CHRIST

*Key themes
from the Bible*

Edited by Martin H. Manser

Hodder & Stoughton
LONDON SYDNEY AUCKLAND

Scripture quotations taken from the HOLY BIBLE, NEW
INTERNATIONAL VERSION. Copyright © 1973, 1978,
1984 by International Bible Society. First published in Great
Britain 1979. Inclusive language version 1995, 1996. Used by
permission of Hodder & Stoughton, a member of the Hodder
Headline Group.

10 9 8 7 6 5 4 3 2 1

A CIP catalogue record for this title is
available from the British Library

ISBN 0 340 65651 4

Typeset by Hewer Text Composition Services, Edinburgh
Printed and bound in Great Britain by
Clays Ltd, St Ives plc

Hodder & Stoughton Ltd
A Division of Hodder Headline PLC
338 Euston Road
London NW1 3BH

Contents

Introduction

The study of Scripture lies at the heart of the Christian faith. It is therefore important that readers of Scripture are given every means of help so that they will derive as much benefit and enjoyment as possible out of reading the Bible. *This is Life in Christ* is a selection of some 250 themes from the acclaimed *NIV Thematic Study Bible* published by Hodder and Stoughton.

Thematic study of the Bible is important because it draws together from different parts of the Bible what Scripture says on a particular subject. *This is Life in Christ* is a selection of themes relating to Christian living, particularly from the viewpoint of the individual believer. You will find here answers from the Bible to such questions as: How do we grow in faith and love? What is discipleship? How do we receive God's guidance? What is the importance of witnessing? How do we cope in times of temptation? What is meant by sanctification? What is revival? Why is spiritual growth important? Practically, how does our faith work out in terms of the use of money and the giving of our possessions, talents and time? But our life in Christ is not only individual; so such themes as *fellowship*, *the church* and *ministry* are also included.

A thematic study is different from a lexical study in that the former is based on related ideas, the latter on individual words. The difference between them can be appreciated by considering the theme of "guidance". A word-based approach would be limited to identifying biblical passages in which the word "guidance" appears and these are very few and only in the Old Testament. A thematic approach, however, goes far beyond this and explores all the various elements of the theme. It identifies its basic concepts, its background and its consequences, in order that the theme in its fulness can be unfolded to the reader. For example the material that deals with guidance covers the *need for guidance, God's promises of guidance*, the *ways in which God's guidance is received* (e.g., through the truth and counsel of God, to those who are humble and willing to obey him, by the Holy Spirit, through Scripture) and *examples of God's guidance*.

In this selection the actual text of key verses is quoted from the inclusive-language (gender-neutral) NIV Bible text. Many other verse references are also included to provide a wealth of biblical material.

A thorough system of cross-references allows the interrelationship of biblical themes to be understood and explored. For example, from "discipleship" the reader is referred to the following: abiding in Christ; Christlikeness; commitment; discipleship; faithfulness; fellowship; guidance; holiness; hope; knowing God; life, of faith; obedience; peace; persecution; sanctification; self-denial; spiritual growth.

Martin H. Manser
Aylesbury 1998

How to study a theme

Themes in this edition are arranged alphabetically by title. Each theme consists of a precise summary of the nature and importance of the theme, followed by a detailed analysis of its main parts. The text of Scripture for the main references appears in full, and many other scriptural references document each of the theme's aspects. At the end of the themes cross-references are provided to related themes included in this book.

Theme name ——————→ **Holy Spirit, indwelling**
The Holy Spirit dwells within Jesus Christ and his

Introduction gives a concise definition of the theme →
to show its contents and importance
disciples. Recognisable results in believers' lives include Christlikeness and the fruit of the Spirit.

Major headings set out clearly the key aspects of →
the theme
The indwelling of the Holy Spirit in the OT
Ge 41:38 So Pharaoh asked them [his

Main verse reference printed in bold type
(e.g., Ge 41:38)
officials], "Can we find anyone like this man [Joseph], one in whom is the spirit of God?"
Ex 35:31 ". . . and he [the Lord] has filled him

Scripture text given for main references ——→
[Bezalel] with the Spirit of God, with skill, ability and knowledge in all kinds of crafts—" *See also* **Nu** 27:18; **1Sa** 10:6–7; **Isa** 59:21; **Hag** 2:5

Comment or explanation is in reduced type. If it
relates to a single verse reference it follows it; if
it relates to a group of references it precedes
them
The Holy Spirit indwells believers
2Ti 1:14 . . . the Holy Spirit who lives in us.
→ Believers are described as the temple of the Holy Spirit:

If there are further secondary references after
such a group, they start on a new line
1Co 3:16; 6:19
Eph 2:22; **1Jn** 2:27; 3:24

Parallel passages are preceded by "pp" and are not →
in bold type
Results of the Holy Spirit's indwelling in believers
→ Preaching and public testimony is aided **Mt**

Subheadings
10:20→pp Mk 13:11 pp Lk 12:12; **Ac** 4:8–12; 5:29–32
The fruit of the Spirit is displayed

Secondary verses support the main verse, preceded
by See also. The Bible book name only is
printed in bold type
(e.g., **Ro** 5:5)
Gal 5:22–23 . . . the fruit of the Spirit is love, joy, peace, patience, kindness, goodness, faithfulness, gentleness and self-control . . .
→ *See also* **Ro** 5:5; 14:17; 15:13,30

Cross-references to other themes are in italics.
These enable you to look up related material
Those without the Holy Spirit's indwelling are not Christlike
Gal 5:17; **Jude** 18–19 *See also* Christlikeness; *Holy Spirit in life of Jesus Christ; Holy Spirit, filling with;*

Abbreviations

A.D.	since the birth of Jesus Christ
B.C.	before the birth of Jesus Christ
c.	about
fn	footnote
NT	New Testament
OT	Old Testament
pp	parallel passage

The Old Testament

Genesis	**Ge**	2 Chronicles	**2Ch**	Daniel	**Da**
Exodus	**Ex**	Ezra	**Ezr**	Hosea	**Hos**
Leviticus	**Lev**	Nehemiah	**Ne**	Joel	**Joel**
Numbers	**Nu**	Esther	**Est**	Amos	**Am**
Deuteronomy	**Dt**	Job	**Job**	Obadiah	**Ob**
Joshua	**Jos**	Psalms	**Ps**	Jonah	**Jnh**
Judges	**Jdg**	Proverbs	**Pr**	Micah	**Mic**
Ruth	**Ru**	Ecclesiastes	**Ecc**	Nahum	**Na**
1 Samuel	**1Sa**	Song of Songs	**SS**	Habakkuk	**Hab**
2 Samuel	**2Sa**	Isaiah	**Isa**	Zephaniah	**Zep**
1 Kings	**1Ki**	Jeremiah	**Jer**	Haggai	**Hag**
2 Kings	**2Ki**	Lamentations	**La**	Zechariah	**Zec**
1 Chronicles	**1Ch**	Ezekiel	**Eze**	Malachi	**Mal**

The New Testament

Matthew	**Mt**	Ephesians	**Eph**	Hebrews	**Heb**
Mark	**Mk**	Philippians	**Php**	James	**Jas**
Luke	**Lk**	Colossians	**Col**	1 Peter	**1Pe**
John	**Jn**	1 Thessalonians	**1Th**	2 Peter	**2Pe**
Acts	**Ac**	2 Thessalonians	**2Th**	1 John	**1Jn**
Romans	**Ro**	1 Timothy	**1Ti**	2 John	**2Jn**
1 Corinthians	**1Co**	2 Timothy	**2Ti**	3 John	**3Jn**
2 Corinthians	**2Co**	Titus	**Tit**	Jude	**Jude**
Galatians	**Gal**	Philemon	**Phm**	Revelation	**Rev**

BIBLE THEMES

abiding in Christ

The NT stresses the need for believers to remain in Christ. The reality of this close personal relationship with Jesus Christ is expressed in obedience to his word and is essential to effective discipleship.

Jesus Christ tells his disciples to abide in him

Jn 15:4–9 "Remain in me, and I will remain in you . . ." *See also* **Mt** 24:10–13; **Lk** 9:62; **Jn** 6:67

NT writers exhort believers to abide in Christ

Col 2:6 . . . as you received Christ Jesus as Lord, continue to live in him, *See also* **Gal** 4:9; 5:5–6; **Col** 3:1–3; **Heb** 12:1–3

Abiding in Christ depends upon holding on to his teaching

1Jn 2:24 See that what you have heard from the beginning remains in you. If it does, you also will remain in the Son and in the Father. *See also* **Jn** 8:31; **2Th** 2:15; **2Ti** 3:14; **2Jn** 9; **3Jn** 3–4

It depends on obedience to him
Jn 15:10 "If you [disciples] obey my [Jesus'] commands, you will remain in my love, just as I have obeyed my Father's commands and remain in his love." *See also* **Mt** 7:24–25; **Jn** 14:23; **Jas** 1:25; **1Jn** 3:24

It requires living like Jesus Christ
1Jn 2:6 Whoever claims to live in him must walk as Jesus did.

Aids to abiding in Christ
Eating his flesh and drinking his blood
Jn 6:56 "Those who eat my [Jesus'] flesh and drink my blood remain in me, and I in them."

The Spirit's anointing
1Jn 2:27 . . . the anointing you [believers] received from him [the Holy One] remains in you, and you do not need anyone to teach you . . . *See also* **Jn** 14:17,23; **Ro** 8:9; **1Jn** 3:24

Jesus Christ abides in believers
Jn 15:4 "Remain in me [Jesus], and I will remain in you [disciples] . . ." *See also* **Jn** 17:23; **Col** 1:27; **1Jn** 3:24; **Rev** 3:20

By his Spirit Jn 14:17; **Ro** 8:9–10; **1Co** 3:16; **1Jn** 2:27
By faith Eph 3:17–19; **Gal** 2:20

Results of abiding in Christ
Fruitfulness
Jn 15:4–5 ". . . I [Jesus] am the vine; you are the branches. If you remain in me and I in you, you will bear much fruit . . ." *See also* **Gal** 5:22–23

Answered prayer Jn 15:7,16
Freedom from persistent sin
1Jn 3:6–9 No-one who lives in him [Jesus] keeps on sinning . . .

Relationship with God the Father Jn 14:23; **2Jn** 9
Confidence in the face of the last day 1Jn 2:28

Warnings to those who fail to abide in Christ

Mt 24:12–13; **Jn** 15:2,6; **1Co** 15:2; **Heb** 6:4–6 *See also discipleship; obedience; peace, experience; perseverance; prayer; union with Christ.*

adoption, privileges and duties

As adopted members of the family of God, believers receive both the privileges and responsibilities of being children of God.

The privileges received by believers through adoption

Believers are given the Spirit of adoption
Gal 4:6 Because you are his children, he sent the Spirit of his Son into our hearts, the Spirit who calls out, "Abba, Father."　*See also* **Ro** 8:15

Believers have access to their heavenly Father
Eph 2:18 For through him we both have access to the Father by one Spirit.　*See also* **Eph** 3:12; **Heb** 4:16

Believers become heirs with Christ of heaven
Ro 8:17 Now if we are children, then we are heirs—heirs of God and co-heirs with Christ . . .　*See also* **Gal** 3:29; 4:7; **Col** 1:12; **1Pe** 1:4

The benefits God gives to those he adopts

Believers are pitied by him
Ps 103:13 As a father has compassion on his children, so the LORD has compassion on those who fear him;

Believers are protected
Pr 14:26 Those who fear the LORD have a secure fortress, and for their children it will be a refuge.

Believers are provided for
Mt 6:31–33 "So do not worry, saying, 'What shall we eat?' or 'What shall we drink?' or 'What shall we wear?' For the pagans run after all these things, and your heavenly Father knows that you need them. But seek first his kingdom and his righteousness, and all these things will be given to you as well."

Believers receive loving discipline
Heb 12:6 "because the Lord disciplines those he loves, and he punishes everyone he accepts as a child."

Believers are never forsaken
Ps 94:14 For the LORD will not reject his people; he will never forsake his inheritance.

Believers are assured by the Spirit
Ro 8:16 The Spirit himself testifies with our spirit that we are God's children.

The responsibilities of God's adopted children

Believers are to walk in the light Jn 12:35–36; Eph 5:8; 1Th 5:4–5
Believers are to shun evil 2Co 6:17–18; Php 2:15
Believers are to purify themselves 2Co 7:1; 1Jn 3:2–3
Believers are to live obediently Mt 12:50; 1Pe 1:14; 1Jn 5:2–3
Believers are to live in peace Mt 5:9; Ro 14:19
Believers are to live in love Gal 5:13; 1Pe 4:8; 1Jn 3:18
Believers are to be watchful 1Th 5:5–6
See also obedience.

apostasy, personal

Individual believers can fall away from faith and be restored. Scripture gives examples of such falling away, and offers advice on how such people should be dealt with pastorally.

Warnings of the dangers of personal apostasy
2Co 11:2–3 I [Paul] am jealous for you with a godly jealousy. I promised you to one husband, to Christ, so that I might present you as a pure virgin to him. But I am afraid that just as Eve was deceived by the serpent's cunning, your minds may somehow be led astray from your sincere and pure devotion to Christ.　*See also* **Ps** 125:4–5; **Lk** 9:59–62; **Gal** 3:1–3; 4:8–10

Warnings against leading others into apostasy
Mt 18:6 "But if any of you causes one of these little ones who believe in me to sin, it would be better for you to have a large millstone hung around your neck and to be drowned in the depths of the sea."　*See also* **Pr** 28:10; **Gal** 5:7–10

Encouragements to guard against personal apostasy
1Co 10:12–13 So, if you think you are standing firm, be careful that you don't fall! No

temptation has seized you except what is common among people. And God is faithful; he will not let you be tempted beyond what you can bear. But when you are tempted, he will also provide a way out so that you can stand up under it.
Heb 3:12–14 See to it, brothers and sisters, that none of you has a sinful, unbelieving heart that turns away from the living God. But encourage one another daily, as long as it is called Today, so that none of you may be hardened by sin's deceitfulness. We have come to share in Christ if we hold firmly till the end the confidence we had at first.   *See also* **Ps** 85:8; **Mt** 24:10–13,24–25 pp **Mk** 13:22–23; **Col** 1:21–23; **1Ti** 6:20–21; **Heb** 10:35–39; 12:1–8; **2Pe** 3:17–18; **Rev** 13:5–10

Dealing with apostate believers
Gal 6:1 Brothers and sisters, if someone is caught in a sin, you who are spiritual should restore that person gently. But watch yourself, or you also may be tempted.   *See also* **1Co** 5:4–5; **Jas** 5:19–20; **1Jn** 5:16–17

Examples of those who were restored from apostasy
Samson: **Jdg** 16:20,28–30
David: **Ps** 51:1–17
Peter: **Mt** 26:74 pp **Mk** 14:72 pp **Lk** 22:61–62 pp **Jn** 18:27; **Jn** 21:15–17
John Mark: **Ac** 15:37–38; **2Ti** 4:11

The punishment of apostates
Isa 65:12–15; **Eze** 3:20; 18:24–26; **2Th** 2:11–12; **2Pe** 2:17
Punishment through misfortune Dt 28:63; **Am** 2:4–6
Punishment through defeat Nu 14:43; **Jdg** 2:12–15
Punishment through rejection 2Ch 24:20; **Hos** 4:6   *See also church; leadership; repentance; temptation.*

---

assurance, and life of faith
The completeness of conviction and confidence expressed in the life of the believer, worked by

the Holy Spirit. It derives from a reliance upon God and his promises alone, and results in boldness and steadfastness in service and in the face of difficulties.

Assurance and faith
Dt 9:3 But be assured today that the LORD your God is the one who goes across ahead of you [Israel] like a devouring fire. He will destroy them; he will subdue them [the Anakites] before you. And you will drive them out and annihilate them quickly, as the LORD has promised you.
Heb 10:22 let us draw near to God with a sincere heart in full assurance of faith, having our hearts sprinkled to cleanse us from a guilty conscience and having our bodies washed with pure water.   *See also* **Dt** 1:21; **Jos** 1:9; **2Ch** 20:17; **Jn** 17:8; **Heb** 11:1; 12:5

Assurance and hope
Heb 6:11 We want each of you to show this same diligence to the very end, in order to make your hope sure.   *See also* **Pr** 23:18; **Heb** 6:19

Assurance expressed by believers
Assurance in adversity
Heb 13:6 So we say with confidence, "The Lord is my helper; I will not be afraid. What can human beings do to me?"   *See also* **Ps** 118:6–7; 3:6; 27:3–5; 46:1–3; 71:5–6; 73:26; **Ro** 8:38–39; **2Co** 4:16
Assurance of God's promises
Jos 23:14 "Now I [Joshua] am about to go the way of all the earth. You know with all your heart and soul that not one of all the good promises the LORD your God gave you has failed. Every promise has been fulfilled; not one has failed."   *See also* **1Ki** 8:56; **Ro** 4:20–21; **2Co** 1:20
Assurance in ministry
Ro 1:16 I [Paul] am not ashamed of the gospel, because it is the power of God for the salvation of everyone who believes: first for the Jew, then for the Gentile.
1Ti 3:13 Those who have served well gain an excellent standing and great assurance in their faith in Christ Jesus.   *See also* **2Co** 3:4; 4:1; 5:14; **1Th** 1:5; **2Pe** 1:12

Assurance in prayer
1Jn 5:14 This is the confidence we have in approaching God: that if we ask anything according to his will, he hears us. *See also* **1Jn** 3:21–22

Assurance of God's will
Ro 14:5 Some consider one day more sacred than another; others consider every day alike. Everybody should be fully convinced in their own minds. *See also* **Ro** 14:14,23; **1Co** 8:9–11

Assurance may be strengthened
Examples of believers asking for assurance Ge 15:8; **Ex** 33:16; **Jdg** 6:17; **Lk** 1:18
Assurance through understanding
Col 2:2 My [Paul's] purpose is that they may be encouraged in heart and united in love, so that they may have the full riches of complete understanding, in order that they may know the mystery of God, namely, Christ,
Assurance through waiting on God
Ps 46:10 "Be still, and know that I am God; I will be exalted among the nations, I will be exalted in the earth." *See also* **Ps** 27:14; 33:20; **Isa** 30:15; 32:17–18
Assurance strengthened by others 2Ch 32:6–8; **2Ti** 3:14; **Col** 4:12; **1Th** 3:2–3
False teaching weakens assurance 2Th 2:2; **2Ti** 2:18

The delusion of false assurance
The danger of self-assurance Lk 18:9–14; **2Co** 10:12; **Php** 3:3–4
Such assurance proved false by conduct
1Jn 1:6 If we claim to have fellowship with him yet walk in the darkness, we lie and do not live by the truth. *See also* **1Jn** 2:9–11; 3:6; 4:20; **2Jn** 9; **3Jn** 11 *See also doubt, dealing with; faith; hope; life, of faith; obedience; peace, experience.*

baptism
A washing with water, which symbolises the cleansing of believers from the stain and dirt of sin through the grace of God. Jesus Christ submitted to baptism as an example to believers. Through the work of the Holy Spirit, baptism is linked with union with the risen Jesus Christ.

baptism, practice
Baptism is associated with repenting of sin, believing the gospel message and becoming a member of Christ's body.

Baptism is ordained by Jesus Christ himself
Mt 28:19 "Therefore go and make disciples of all nations, baptising them in the name of the Father and of the Son and of the Holy Spirit." *See also* **Ac** 9:17–18; 16:14–15

Baptism is linked with repentance
Ac 2:38 Peter replied, "Repent and be baptised, every one of you, in the name of Jesus Christ for the forgiveness of your sins . . ." *See also* **Heb** 6:1–2

Baptism follows the decision to believe
Ac 2:41 Those who accepted his [Peter's] message were baptised . . .
Ac 18:8 . . . many of the Corinthians who heard him [Paul] believed and were baptised. *See also* **Ac** 8:12–13; 16:31–33

Baptism in the name of God or Jesus Christ
Baptism in or into the name of Jesus Christ
Ac 19:5 . . . they [a group of believers] were baptised into the name of the Lord Jesus. *See also* **Ac** 2:38; 8:16; 10:48
Baptism in the name of the Trinity Mt 28:18–20

Baptism was by immersion
Ro 6:4 We were therefore buried with him [Christ] through baptism . . . *See also* **Ac** 8:38

Baptism is linked with the gift of the Holy Spirit
Mk 1:8 "I [John the Baptist] baptise you with water, but he [Jesus] will baptise you with the Holy Spirit."
Ac 1:5 ". . . in a few days you [the apostles] will be baptised with the Holy Spirit." *See also* **Ac** 2:4; 11:16

1Co 12:13 . . . we were all baptised by one Spirit into one body . . .

Manifestations of the Holy Spirit may follow or precede water baptism
Ac 8:12–17; 9:17–18; 10:44–48

The person who baptises is of little importance
1Co 1:14 I [Paul] am thankful that I did not baptise any of you [members of the church at Corinth] except Crispus and Gaius,

Baptism "for the dead"
1Co 15:29 Now if there is no resurrection, what will those do who are baptised for the dead? . . .

Passages which may imply infant baptism
The "households" (not merely individuals) may well have included children: Ac 16:15,33; 18:8; 1Co 1:16
Mk 10:13–16; 1Co 7:14; Col 2:11–12

Passages apparently negating infant baptism
Ac 2:38–41; Gal 3:7   *See also repentance.*

---

baptism, with Holy Spirit
A divine act, promised by John the Baptist and by Jesus Christ, whereby the Holy Spirit initiates Christians into realised union and communion with the glorified Jesus Christ, thus equipping and enabling them for sanctity and service.

Baptism with the Holy Spirit promised
John the Baptist anticipates baptism with the Spirit
Jn 1:33 ". . . The man on whom you see the Spirit come down and remain is the one who will baptise with the Holy Spirit.'" pp Mt 3:11 pp Mk 1:8 pp Lk 3:16
Jesus Christ promises baptism with the Spirit
Ac 1:4–5 . . . ". . . wait for the gift my Father promised, which you have heard me speak about. For John baptised with water, but in a few days you will be baptised with the Holy Spirit."   *See also* Lk 24:49; Ac 1:8

The gift of the Holy Spirit followed Jesus Christ's glorification
Ac 2:33 "Exalted to the right hand of God, he [Jesus] has received from the Father the promised Holy Spirit and has poured out what you now see and hear."   *See also* Jn 7:39

Instances of baptism with the Holy Spirit
Ac 2:2–4
After Pentecost: Ac 8:15–17; 10:44–47; 19:6
A work of God recognised by Jewish Christians as experienced by Gentiles: Ac 10:46–47; 11:15–17; 15:8

The gift of the Holy Spirit is for all believers at the outset of their Christian lives
Ac 2:38–39 . . . "Repent and be baptised, every one of you, in the name of Jesus Christ for the forgiveness of your sins. And you will receive the gift of the Holy Spirit. The promise is for you and your children and for all who are far off—for all whom the Lord our God will call."
See also Ac 2:16–18; Joel 2:28–29; Gal 3:2–5

This gift of the Holy Spirit links believers together in the one body of Christ
1Co 12:13 For we were all baptised by one Spirit into one body—whether Jews or Greeks, slave or free—and we were all given the one Spirit to drink.   *See also baptism; equipping, spiritual; union with Christ.*

Christlikeness
The process by which believers are conformed to the likeness of Jesus Christ, especially in relation to obedience to and trust in God. Through the Holy Spirit, God refashions believers in the image of his Son, who is set before them as a model of the form of the redeemed life.

Believers are to become Christlike
1Co 11:1 Follow my [Paul's] example, as I follow the example of Christ.

Php 2:5 Your attitude should be the same as that of Christ Jesus: *See also* **Jn** 13:15; **Ro** 8:29; **Eph** 4:11–13; **Php** 3:8–11,20–21; **1Jn** 2:6

The Holy Spirit makes believers Christlike

2Co 3:18 And we, who with unveiled faces all reflect the Lord's glory, are being transformed into his likeness with ever-increasing glory, which comes from the Lord, who is the Spirit. *See also* **Ro** 8:5–9; **Gal** 5:22–23; **1Th** 1:6

Christlikeness is the aim of discipleship

Mt 10:25 "It is enough for students to be like their teachers, and the servants like their masters . . ." *See also* **Lk** 6:40; **1Jn** 2:6

Christlikeness is based on total commitment to Jesus Christ

Lk 9:57–62 As they were walking along the road, someone said to him [Jesus], "I will follow you wherever you go." Jesus replied, "Foxes have holes and birds of the air have nests, but the Son of Man has nowhere to lay his head." He said to another man, "Follow me." But he replied, "Lord, first let me go and bury my father." Jesus said to him, "Let the dead bury their own dead, but you go and proclaim the kingdom of God." Still another said, "I will follow you, Lord; but first let me go back and say good-bye to my family." Jesus replied, "No-one who takes hold of the plough and looks back is fit for service in the kingdom of God." *See also* **Mt** 9:9 pp **Mk** 2:14 pp **Lk** 5:27; **Mt** 19:21 pp **Lk** 18:22; **Jn** 1:43; 10:27; 12:26; 15:10; **2Jn** 9

The demonstration of Christlikeness
In costly sacrifice

Mk 8:34–35 Then he [Jesus] called the crowd to him along with his disciples and said: "Those who would come after me must deny themselves and take up their cross and follow me. For those who want to save their lives will lose them, but those who lose their lives for me and for the gospel will save them." pp **Mt** 16:24 pp **Lk** 9:23–24

1Pe 2:21–23 To this you were called, because

Christ suffered for you, leaving you an example, that you should follow in his steps. "He committed no sin, and no deceit was found in his mouth." When they hurled their insults at him, he did not retaliate; when he suffered, he made no threats. Instead, he entrusted himself to him who judges justly. *See also* **Mt** 10:38; **Lk** 14:26–27; **Jn** 12:26; 21:19; **Php** 3:10; **1Pe** 4:1

In humility and service

Mt 20:26–28 [Jesus said] " . . . whoever wants to become great among you must be your servant, and whoever wants to be first must be your slave—just as the Son of Man did not come to be served, but to serve, and to give his life as a ransom for many." pp **Mk** 10:43–45 *See also* **Mt** 11:29; **Mk** 9:35; **Lk** 22:24–26; **Jn** 13:14–15; **Php** 2:4–5

In love for other believers

Jn 15:12 [Jesus said] "My command is this: Love each other as I have loved you."

1Jn 3:16 This is how we know what love is: Jesus Christ laid down his life for us. And we ought to lay down our lives for one another. *See also* **Jn** 13:34; 15:17; **Eph** 5:2,25

In a readiness to forgive others

Col 3:13 Bear with each other and forgive whatever grievances you may have against one another. Forgive as the Lord forgave you. *See also* **Mt** 6:12 pp **Lk** 11:4

In sharing Jesus Christ's mission to the world

Mt 4:19 "Come, follow me," Jesus said, "and I will make you fishers of men and women." pp **Mk** 1:17 *See also* **Jn** 20:21

By following godly examples that imitate Jesus Christ

1Co 11:1 Follow my [Paul's] example, as I follow the example of Christ. *See also* **Eph** 5:1; **1Th** 1:5–6; 2:14; **Heb** 6:12; 13:7–8; **3Jn** 11

Christlikeness is part of God's re-creation

Ge 1:26–27 Then God said, "Let us make human beings in our image, in our likeness, and let them rule over the fish of the sea and the birds of the air, over the livestock, over all the earth, and over all the creatures that move along the ground." So God created human beings in his own image, in the image of God he created them; male and female he created them.

2Co 4:4 The god of this age [the devil] has blinded the minds of unbelievers, so that they cannot see the light of the gospel of the glory of Christ, who is the image of God.

Eph 4:24 and to put on the new self, created to be like God in true righteousness and holiness.

Col 3:10 and have put on the new self, which is being renewed in knowledge in the image of its Creator.

The process of becoming Christlike
It is the purpose for which believers are saved

Ro 8:28–29 And we know that in all things God works for the good of those who love him, who have been called according to his purpose. For those God foreknew he also predestined to be conformed to the likeness of his Son, that he might be the firstborn among many brothers and sisters.   *See also* **Eph** 2:10; **2Pe** 1:4

It continues in the experience of believers

2Co 3:18 And we, who with unveiled faces all reflect the Lord's glory, are being transformed into his likeness with ever-increasing glory, which comes from the Lord, who is the Spirit.

It will be complete when believers finally share Jesus Christ's glory

1Jn 3:2–3 Dear friends, now we are children of God, and what we will be has not yet been made known. But we know that when he appears, we shall be like him, for we shall see him as he is. All who have this hope in them purify themselves, just as he is pure.   *See also* **Ps** 17:15; **Jn** 17:24; **1Co** 15:49–53; **Gal** 4:19; **Php** 3:20–21; **Col** 3:4; **1Jn** 4:17   *See also discipleship; faith; holiness; maturity; spiritual; obedience; sanctification; self-denial; spiritual growth.*

church

The community of faithful believers, of whom Jesus Christ is the head, called out from the world to serve God down the ages. Scripture emphasises that the church is the body of Christ whose members are intended to be filled with the Holy

Spirit. Scriptural understanding of the church is corporate, rather than solitary or individual.

---

church, leadership

Jesus Christ is the absolute head of the church. He sets leaders in the church to enable the whole church to grow into maturity. Christ's authority in the church is acknowledged more by the church's obedience to God than through any particular form of government.

Jesus Christ alone is head of the church
Col 1:18 And he [Christ] is the head of the body, the church; he is the beginning and the firstborn from among the dead, so that in everything he might have the supremacy.
See also **Mt** 23:8–10; **Eph** 1:22; 4:15; 5:23; **Col** 2:19; **Heb** 3:3

The Holy Spirit directs the church
Ac 13:2 While they [prophets and teachers] were worshipping the Lord and fasting, the Holy Spirit said, "Set apart for me Barnabas and Saul for the work to which I have called them."
See also **Ac** 15:28; 16:6–7; 20:28; **Ro** 8:14; **1Co** 12:11; **Rev** 2:7,11

The appointment of leaders in the church
God calls and equips leaders

Eph 4:11 It was he [Christ] who gave some to be apostles, some to be prophets, some to be evangelists, and some to be pastors and teachers,   *See also* **Mt** 16:18; **Ac** 1:24–26; 9:15–16; 20:28; 26:16–18; **1Co** 12:28; **Gal** 1.15–17

Delegated leadership Ac 6:3–6; 14:23; **Tit** 1:5
The appointment of apostles

Mk 3:13–19 . . . He [Jesus] appointed twelve—designating them apostles—that they might be with him and that he might send them out to preach and to have authority to drive out demons . . . pp **Mt** 10:1–4 pp **Lk** 6:12–16

As founders of the church: **1Co** 9:1–2; **2Co** 3:3; **Eph** 2:20; **Rev** 21:14

As leaders of the church: **Ac** 2:42; 15:6,22–23; **1Th** 2:6; **2Pe** 3:2; **Jude** 17

Prophets as leaders
Ac 15:32 Judas and Silas, who themselves were prophets, said much to encourage and strengthen the believers.   *See also* **Ac** 11:27–30; 13:1–2; **Ro** 12:6; **1Co** 12:28; 14:29–30; **Eph** 3:5

Evangelists as leaders
Ac 21:8 Leaving the next day, we reached Caesarea and stayed at the house of Philip the evangelist, one of the Seven.   *See also* **Eph** 4:11; **2Ti** 4:5

Pastors and teachers as leaders
Ac 20:28 "Keep watch over yourselves and all the flock of which the Holy Spirit has made you overseers. Be shepherds of the church of God, which he bought with his own blood."   *See also* **Jn** 21:15–17; **Ac** 13:1; **Ro** 12:7; **1Co** 12:28; **1Ti** 3:2; **Tit** 1:9; **Jas** 3:1; **1Pe** 5:2

Elders as leaders
1Ti 3:1 Here is a trustworthy saying: Whoever aspires to be an overseer desires a noble task.
See also **Ac** 11:30; 14:23; 15:2,22; 20:17; **1Ti** 5:17; **Tit** 1:5; **Jas** 5:14; **2Jn** 1

Deacons as leaders
Php 1:1 Paul and Timothy, servants of Christ Jesus, To all the saints in Christ Jesus at Philippi, together with the overseers and deacons:
See also **Ac** 6:5–6; **1Ti** 3:8

Qualifications for church leadership
The first apostles were witnesses of Jesus Christ's life and resurrection: **Ac** 1:21–22; 10:41; **1Co** 9:1–2; 15:7–8; **2Pe** 1:16
Qualifications for elders and deacons: **Ac** 6:3; **1Ti** 3:1–12; 5:17; **Tit** 1:6–9; **1Pe** 5:1–4

Responsibilities of church leaders
To preach the gospel **Ro** 1:15; **1Co** 1:17; **Gal** 2:8; **Eph** 3:8; **1Ti** 2:7
To teach sound doctrine **1Ti** 4:6,13; 5:17; **Heb** 13:7
To give direction in church life **Ac** 15:2,6,22–23; 16:4; 20:28–31; **1Ti** 5:17; **1Pe** 5:2
To be an example in loving service **Mt** 20:26–28 pp **Mk** 10:43–45; **Mk** 9:35; **Jn** 13:13–15; **Heb** 13:7; **1Pe** 5:3
To train and appoint other leaders **Ac** 14:23; **1Ti** 4:14; **2Ti** 2:2; **Tit** 1:5

To pray for the sick **Jas** 5:14
To exercise discipline in the church **2Co** 13:10; **1Th** 5:12; **1Ti** 1:20; 5:20; **Tit** 3:10; **3Jn** 10

The church's responsibilities to its leaders
Ac 16:4
To respect and submit to its leaders **1Th** 5:12–13; **1Ti** 5:19; **Heb** 13:17
To pray for its leaders **Eph** 6:19; **1Th** 5:25
To support its leaders financially **1Co** 9:7–14; **Php** 4:15–19; **1Ti** 5:17–18

The corporate government of the church
In choosing leaders **Ac** 6:3–6
In implementing decisions **Ac** 15:22–29
In building up the church **Ro** 12:4–8; **1Co** 12:4–12,27; **Eph** 4:3,7–16; **1Pe** 4:10–11
In discerning true and false teachings **1Jn** 4:1–3; **2Jn** 10; **Rev** 2:2
In exercising discipline **Mt** 18:15–20; **1Co** 5:4–5; **2Co** 2:6–8; **2Th** 3:14–15

The structure of the church
The pattern of church life
Ac 2:42 They devoted themselves to the apostles' teaching and to the fellowship, to the breaking of bread and to prayer.   *See also* **Ac** 2:46; 5:42
The house church Ac 1:13–14; 12:12; 16:40; **Ro** 16:5; **1Co** 16:19; **Col** 4:15; **Phm** 2
The local church Ac 13:1; **Ro** 16:1; **1Co** 1:2; **1Th** 1:1
Churches in a region Ac 9:31; 15:41; **1Co** 16:1; **2Co** 8:1; **Gal** 1:2,22; **Rev** 1:4
The universal church
Mt 16:18 "And I [Jesus] tell you that you are Peter, and on this rock I will build my church, and the gates of Hades will not overcome it."
Referring to the local as well as the universal church: **1Co** 12:28; **Eph** 1:22; 3:10; 5:25   *See also* ministry.

church, life of
The church lives its life in union with Christ and in

the power of the Holy Spirit. It is called to mutual love, holy living, and to worship.

The church lives its life in union with Christ
The church lives in Christ and Christ lives in the church
1Co 1:30 It is because of him [God] that you are in Christ Jesus . . .   *See also* **Mt** 18:20; **Jn** 15:5; 17:21; **1Co** 8:6; **Gal** 2:20; **Col** 1:27; 2:6; **1Jn** 4:13
Believers are united with Christ in baptism
Gal 3:27 for all of you who were baptised into Christ have clothed yourselves with Christ. *See also* **Ac** 2:38; 19:5; **Ro** 6:3–4; **Col** 2:12

The church lives its life in the power of the Holy Spirit
The church lives in the Spirit, and the Spirit lives in the church
Ro 8:9–11 You, however, are controlled not by the sinful nature but by the Spirit, if the Spirit of God lives in you. And if anyone does not have the Spirit of Christ, that person does not belong to Christ . . .   *See also* **1Co** 3:16; **Gal** 5:16,25; **Eph** 2:22; **2Ti** 1:14; **1Jn** 2:27
The Spirit is given to the church
Ac 1:4–5 ". . . Do not leave Jerusalem, but wait for the gift my [Jesus'] Father promised, which you have heard me speak about. For John baptised with water, but in a few days you will be baptised with the Holy Spirit."   *See also* **Jn** 20:22; **Ac** 2:4; 15:8; **Ro** 7:6; 15:16; **1Co** 6:11; **Gal** 3:3; **1Pe** 1:1–2
The Spirit seals the church
Eph 1:13 . . . Having believed, you were marked in him [Christ] with a seal, the promised Holy Spirit,   *See also* **2Co** 1:22; 5:5; **Eph** 4:30
The Spirit guides the church
Rev 2:7 "Those who have ears, let them hear what the Spirit says to the churches . . ."
See also **Ac** 8:29; 10:19; 11:12; 13:2; 20:23; 21:4
The Spirit teaches the church
1Co 2:13 . . . we speak, not in words taught us by human wisdom but in words taught by the Spirit . . .   *See also* **Jn** 16:13; **Eph** 1:17

The Spirit sanctifies the church
Ro 15:16 . . . so that the Gentiles might become an offering acceptable to God, sanctified by the Holy Spirit.   *See also* **1Co** 6:11; **2Th** 2:13; **1Pe** 1:2
The Spirit endows the church with gifts
1Co 12:7 Now to each one the manifestation of the Spirit is given for the common good. *See also* **Ro** 12:6–8; **1Co** 12:8–11,28; **Eph** 4:11

The church as a fellowship
As a fellowship of mutual love
1Th 5:11 Therefore encourage one another and build each other up, just as in fact you are doing.   *See also* **Ro** 15:2; **1Co** 14:12; **Gal** 6:10; **1Th** 4:18; **Heb** 10:25
As a fellowship of ordinary people
1Co 1:26–27 . . . But God chose the foolish things of the world to shame the wise; God chose the weak things of the world to shame the strong.   *See also* **Lk** 6:20; **Jas** 2:5

The distinctiveness of the church
The church as a chosen people
1Pe 2:9 But you are a chosen people, a royal priesthood, a holy nation, a people belonging to God . . .   *See also* **Eph** 1:4; **Col** 3:12
The church as a holy people
Heb 12:14 Make every effort . . . to be holy; without holiness no-one will see the Lord.   *See also* **Ro** 11:16; 15:16; **1Co** 1:2; **Eph** 2:21; 5:3; **1Th** 3:13; **Heb** 2:11; **1Pe** 1:15–16; **2Pe** 3:11
The church as a people set apart
2Co 7:1 Since we have these promises, dear friends, let us purify ourselves from everything that contaminates body and spirit, perfecting holiness out of reverence for God.   *See also* **1Co** 5:9–12; **2Co** 6:14–18; **Eph** 5:7; **2Th** 3:14; **2Ti** 3:1–5; **Tit** 3:10–11
The church as a heavenly people
Jn 17:14–16 ". . . They [the disciples] are not of the world, even as I [Jesus] am not of it."   *See also* **Lk** 10:20; **1Co** 15:48; **Gal** 4:26; **Eph** 2:6; **Php** 3:20; **Col** 3:1–4; **Heb** 11:16; 12:22–23

The church and worship
Praise in the life of the church
Heb 13:15 Through Jesus, therefore, let us continually offer to God a sacrifice of praise—the fruit of lips that confess his name. *See also* **Ac** 2:47; **1Co** 14:26; **Eph** 5:18–20; **Php** 3:3; **Col** 3:16
Prayer in the life of the church
Corporate prayer in the church: **Ac** 1:14; 2:42; 4:24–31; 12:5,12; 20:36; 21:5

Prayer for church leaders: **Ro** 15:30; **Eph** 6:19–20; **Col** 4:2–4; **1Th** 5:25; **2Th** 3:1; **Heb** 13:18 **Eph** 6:18; **1Ti** 2:1–2

Baptism in the life of the church
Ac 2:38; **1Co** 1:13; **Gal** 3:26–27; **Eph** 4:4–5; **Col** 2:11–12; **1Pe** 3:21
The Lord's Supper in the life of the church
1Co 10:16–17 Is not the cup of thanksgiving for which we give thanks a participation in the blood of Christ? And is not the bread that we break a participation in the body of Christ? Because there is one loaf, we, who are many, are one body, for we all partake of the one loaf. *See also* **Ac** 2:42,46; 20:7; **1Co** 10:21; 11:17–34

The suffering of the church
Suffering persecution from a hostile world
Jn 16:33 "I [Jesus] have told you these things, so that in me you may have peace. In this world you will have trouble. But take heart! I have overcome the world." *See also* **Mt** 5:10–12; **1Co** 4:12; **2Co** 4:9; **1Th** 3:4; **2Ti** 3:12
Sharing in the sufferings of Christ
Php 3:10 I [Paul] want to know Christ and the power of his resurrection and the fellowship of sharing in his sufferings, becoming like him in his death, *See also* **Jn** 15:20; **Ro** 8:17; **2Co** 4:10–11; **1Pe** 4:13
Suffering as the road to glory
Jas 1:12 Blessed are those who persevere under trial, because when they have stood the test, they will receive the crown of life that God has promised to those who love him. *See also* **Ro** 5:3; 8:18; **2Co** 4:17; **2Ti** 2:11–12; **1Pe** 5:10
See also holiness; life, spiritual; praise; prayer, in the church; spiritual gifts; worship.

church, nature of
The church is the people called by God, who are united by their faith in Christ and by their common life in him. Various descriptions and metaphors emphasise the continuity between the people of God in the OT and NT.

NT images of the church
The body of Christ
Ro 12:4–5 Just as each of us has one body with many members, and these members do not all have the same function, so in Christ we who are many form one body, and each member belongs to all the others. *See also* **1Co** 12:12,27; **Eph** 3:6; 5:23; **Col** 1:18,24; 2:19; 3:15
God's building or temple
1Co 3:16–17 Don't you know that you yourselves are God's temple and that God's Spirit lives in you? . . . *See also* **1Co** 3:10; **2Co** 6:16; **Eph** 2:21–22; **Heb** 3:6; 10:21; **1Pe** 2:5
A plant or vine
Jn 15:1–8 ". . . I [Jesus] am the vine; you [the disciples] are the branches . . ." *See also* **Ro** 11:17–24; **1Co** 3:6–8
Jesus Christ's flock
Jn 10:14–16 "I [Jesus] am the good shepherd; I know my sheep and my sheep know me . . . there shall be one flock and one shepherd." *See also* **Mt** 25:33; **Lk** 12:32; **Ac** 20:28–29; **1Pe** 5:2–4
The bride of Christ
Rev 21:2 I [John] saw the Holy City, the new Jerusalem, coming down out of heaven from God, prepared as a bride beautifully dressed for her husband. *See also* **Eph** 5:25–27,31–32; **Rev** 19:7; 22:17
God's household or family
Eph 2:19 . . . you [Gentile believers] are no longer foreigners and aliens, but fellow-citizens with God's people and members of God's household, *See also* **Jn** 8:35–36; **Gal** 6:10; **Eph** 3:15; **1Ti** 3:15; **Heb** 2:11; **1Pe** 2:17; 4:17

NT descriptions of the church
Emphasising continuity with the OT church
Abraham's offspring: **Ro** 4:16; **Gal** 3:7,29

The people of God: **Ro 9:25; 2Co 6:16; Heb 13:12; 1Pe 2:9-10**

The new Jerusalem: **Gal 4:26; Heb 12:22; Rev 3:12; 21:2,9-10**

the Israel of God: **Gal 6:16**

Emphasising God's call and authority in the church

Children of God: **Mt 5:9; Jn 1:12; Ro 8:15-16; 2Co 6:18; Gal 3:26; 4:5-6; 1Jn 3:10**

The elect: **Mt 24:22; Ro 11:7; 2Ti 2:10; 1Pe 1:1**

Heirs of God and God's inheritance: **Ro 8:17; Gal 3:29; 4:7; Tit 3:7; Heb 1:14; 6:17; 1Pe 1:4**

A priesthood: **1Pe 2:5,9; Rev 1:6; 5:10; 20:6**

Descriptions applied to the church by outsiders

Followers of the Way: **Ac 9:2; 19:9,23; 22:4; 24:14**

Christians: **Ac 11:26**

"the Nazarene sect": **Ac 24:5**

Descriptions used by Christians

The believers. All these titles are seldom in the singular, emphasising the corporateness of Christian life: **Ac 1:15; 2:44; 5:12; Gal 6:10; 1Ti 4:12; 1Pe 2:17**

The disciples: **Ac 6:1-2; 9:19; 11:26; 14:22; 20:1**

The "saints" is the most frequently used NT term for Christians. It means "set apart for God", "made holy": **Ro 1:7; 15:25; 1Co 6:1; 14:33; Eph 1:1; Php 4:21; Col 1:12; Jude 3**

Other NT descriptions of the church **1Ti 3:15; Heb 12:23**

The foundation of the church

Jesus Christ as the church's foundation-stone

1Co 3:11 For no-one can lay any foundation other than the one already laid, which is Jesus Christ.   *See also* **Mt 7:24-25; 21:42 pp Mk 12:10 pp Lk 20:17; Ac 4:11; Eph 2:20; 1Pe 2:6; Isa 28:16; 1Pe 2:7; Ps 118:22**

Apostles and prophets as founders of the church

Eph 2:19-20 . . . God's household, built on the foundation of the apostles and prophets, with Christ Jesus himself as the chief cornerstone. *See also* **Mt 16:18-19; Rev 21:14**

The church as God's people

A people chosen by God

1Pe 2:9 But you are a chosen people, a royal priesthood, a holy nation, a people belonging to God, that you may declare the praises of him who called you out of darkness into his wonderful light.   *See also* **Jn 15:16; Ro 8:33; Eph 1:4; Col 3:12; 2Th 2:13; Jas 2:5; 1Pe 1:2**

A people called by God

Ro 1:6 And you also [Christians in Rome] are among those who are called to belong to Jesus Christ.   *See also* **Ac 2:39; 1Co 1:2,9; Gal 1:6; 2Th 2:14; 2Ti 1:9; Jude 1**

A people loved by God

1Pe 2:10 Once you were not a people, but now you are the people of God; once you had not received mercy, but now you have received mercy.   *See also* **Eph 2:1-5; Tit 3:4-7**

God's covenant people

Heb 8:8-10 . . . ". . . This is the covenant I will make with the house of Israel after that time, declares the Lord. I will put my laws in their minds and write them on their hearts. I will be their God, and they will be my people."

See also **Ro 11:27; Isa 59:20-21; Heb 10:16; Jer 31:31-33**

---

church, purpose

The church is called to praise and glorify God, to establish Jesus Christ's kingdom, and to proclaim the gospel throughout the world.

God's purposes for the church

To praise God

1Pe 2:9 But you are a chosen people, a royal priesthood, a holy nation, a people belonging to God, that you may declare the praises of him who called you out of darkness into his wonderful light.   *See also* **Eph 1:5-6,11-12,14; Heb 13:15; 1Pe 2:5**

To share God's glory

Ro 8:29-30 For those God foreknew he also predestined to be conformed to the likeness of his Son, that he might be the firstborn among many brothers and sisters. And those he predestined, he also called; those he called, he also justified; those he justified, he also glorified.   *See also* **Mt 13:43; Jn 17:24; Ro 9:23; 1Co 2:7; Php 3:21; Col 3:4; 2Th 2:14; Rev 2:26-27; 3:4-5,21**

God will build his church

Mt 16:18-19 "And I [Jesus] tell you that you

are Peter, and on this rock I will build my church, and the gates of Hades will not overcome it. I will give you the keys of the kingdom of heaven; whatever you bind on earth will be bound in heaven, and whatever you loose on earth will be loosed in heaven." *See also* **Mt** 27:40 pp **Mk** 15:29; **Jn** 2:19–22; **1Co** 3:9; **Eph** 2:21–22; 4:11–13; **Heb** 3:3–6; **1Pe** 2:5

To challenge Satan's dominion
Eph 3:10–11 His [God's] intent was that now, through the church, the manifold wisdom of God should be made known to the rulers and authorities in the heavenly realms . . .
See also **Mt** 16:18; **Eph** 6:12; **1Jn** 2:14

To go into the world in mission
2Co 5:18 All this is from God, who reconciled us to himself through Christ and gave us the ministry of reconciliation: *See also* **Mt** 5:13–16; 28:19–20; **Mk** 16:15; **Lk** 24:48; **Jn** 20:21; **Ac** 1:8; **Php** 2:15–16; **Col** 1:27

The church's mission
To preach the gospel to the world
Mk 13:10 "And the gospel must first be preached to all nations." pp Mt 24:14 *See also* **Mt** 28:19; **Lk** 24:47; **Jn** 10:16; **Ac** 13:47

To do good to all
Gal 6:10 Therefore, as we have opportunity, let us do good to all people, especially to those who belong to the family of believers. *See also* **Mt** 25:37–40; **Lk** 6:35; **Ac** 9:36; **Eph** 2:10; **1Ti** 6:18; **Jas** 1:27; **1Pe** 2:12

Images of the church's mission
Mt 5:13–16 "You are the salt of the earth . . . You are the light of the world . . ."
Jn 15:5–8 "I [Jesus] am the vine; you are the branches. If you remain in me and I in you, you will bear much fruit . . ."
A fruitful plant in a fruitless world: **Mt** 7:18–19; **Ro** 7:4; **Eph** 5:9–10; **Php** 1:11; **Col** 1:6,10; **Jas** 3:17
Salt in an insipid world: **Mk** 9:50; **Lk** 14:34–35
Light in a dark world: **Ro** 13:12–14; **Eph** 5:8; **Php** 2:15; **1Th** 5:5–6

The growth of the church
Numerical growth among the first Christians
Ac 11:21 The Lord's hand was with them, and a great number of people believed and turned to the Lord. *See also* **Ac** 2:41,47; 4:4; 5:14; 6:1,7; 9:31,42; 11:24; 12:24; 13:49; 16:5; 17:4; 18:8; 19:20

The church is to grow to maturity
Eph 4:12–13 . . . so that the body of Christ may be built up until we all reach unity in the faith and in the knowledge of the Son of God and become mature, attaining to the whole measure of the fulness of Christ. *See also* **Php** 1:6; 3:13–15; **2Th** 1:3

Aspects of growth
Growth in character: **1Co** 9:10; **1Th** 3:12
Growth into Christ: **Eph** 4:15; **Col** 1:10; **2Pe** 3:18; **Heb** 6:1

Prayers for the growth of the church
Eph 3:14–19 . . . And I [Paul] pray that you, being rooted and established in love, may have power, together with all the saints, to grasp how wide and long and high and deep is the love of Christ, and to know this love that surpasses knowledge—that you may be filled to the measure of all the fulness of God. *See also* **Eph** 1:17–19; **Php** 1:9–11; **Col** 1:9–12; **1Th** 3:11–13; **2Th** 1:11–12

Visions of the church's final destiny
Rev 7:9–10 After this I looked and there before me was a great multitude that no-one could count, from every nation, tribe, people and language, standing before the throne and in front of the Lamb . . . *See also* **Mt** 24:31; **Jn** 10:16; **Eph** 1:10; **1Th** 4:16–17; **Heb** 12:22–23; **Rev** 21:2 *See also evangelism; good works; maturity; mission, of church; preaching; spiritual growth; spiritual warfare.*

church, unity
The church is one in essence, because it is founded on one gospel, united to one Lord and indwelt by one Spirit. Its unity is under constant threat because of the tendency to division that is inherent in fallen humanity, and needs to be continually maintained and actively expressed in fellowship.

The unity of the church
The church is one
Ro 12:5 . . . in Christ we who are many form one body, and each member belongs to all the others.   *See also* **1Co** 12:12,20; **Eph** 4:25

The church transcends all barriers
Col 3:11 Here there is no Greek or Jew, circumcised or uncircumcised, barbarian, Scythian, slave or free, but Christ is all, and is in all.
See also **Jn** 10:16; **Ac** 10:28–29,47; 15:8–9; **Gal** 3:28; **Eph** 2:14–16; 3:6

The church's unity reflects the unity within the Trinity
Eph 4:4–6 There is one body and one Spirit— just as you were called to one hope when you were called—one Lord, one faith, one baptism; one God and Father of all, who is over all and through all and in all.   *See also* **Jn** 17:11; **Ro** 3:29–30; 10:12–13; **Gal** 3:27–28

The church's unity is the work of the Trinity
Eph 2:16–18 . . . in this one body to reconcile both of them to God through the cross, by which he [Christ] put to death their hostility . . . For through him we both have access to the Father by one Spirit.   *See also* **Jn** 11:52; **Ac** 10:45–47; **1Co** 12:13; **Eph** 2:22; 4:3

The purpose of the church's unity
To lead others to faith
Jn 17:23 ". . . May they [all believers] be brought to complete unity to let the world know that you sent me [Jesus] and have loved them even as you have loved me."   *See also* **Jn** 17:21

To lead believers to maturity
Eph 4:13 until we all reach unity in the faith and in the knowledge of the Son of God and become mature, attaining to the whole measure of the fulness of Christ.

The nature of the church's unity
Php 2:1–2 . . . then make my [Paul's] joy complete by being like-minded, having the same love, being one in spirit and purpose.   *See also* **2Co** 13:11; **Php** 1:27; **Col** 2:2

Appeals for unity in the church
Eph 4:3 Make every effort to keep the unity of the Spirit through the bond of peace.   *See also* **Ro** 12:10; 15:5,7; **1Co** 12:25; **Col** 3:14; **1Pe** 3:8

The church's unity is expressed in fellowship
Fellowship with God
1Co 1:9 God, who has called you into fellowship with his Son Jesus Christ our Lord, is faithful.
See also **2Co** 13:14; **Php** 2:1; **2Pe** 1:4; **1Jn** 1:3,6–7

Fellowship expressed by meeting together
Ac 2:46 Every day they continued to meet together in the temple courts. They broke bread in their homes and ate together with glad and sincere hearts,   *See also* **Ac** 2:1,42; 5:12; 6:2; **1Co** 14:26; **Heb** 10:25

Fellowship expressed through sharing resources
Ac 2:44–45 All the believers were together and had everything in common. Selling their possessions and goods, they gave to anyone who had need.   *See also* **Ac** 4:32,34–37; 11:27–30; **Ro** 15:26; **1Co** 16:1–2; **2Co** 8:2–5,13–14; 9:13; **Php** 4:14–18

Fellowship through suffering
Rev 1:9 I, John, your brother and companion in the suffering and kingdom and patient endurance that are ours in Jesus . . .   *See also* **Ro** 8:17; **2Co** 1:7; **Php** 3:10; 4:14; **Heb** 10:33–34; 13:3

Fellowship through shared spiritual blessings
1Co 9:23 I [Paul] do all this for the sake of the gospel, that I may share in its blessings.
See also **Ro** 11:17; **Php** 1:7; **2Th** 2:14; **1Pe** 5:1; **Jude** 3

Specific actions which express fellowship and unity in the church
Sharing in the Lord's Supper
1Co 10:16–17 Is not the cup of thanksgiving for which we give thanks a participation in the blood of Christ? And is not the bread that we break a participation in the body of Christ? . . .   *See also* **Ac** 2:46; 20:7; **1Co** 11:33

Baptism as an expression of unity
Eph 4:4–6 There is one body and one Spirit—

just as you were called to one hope when you were called—one Lord, one faith, one baptism; one God and Father of all, who is over all and through all and in all.   *See also* **1Co** 12:13

Extending hospitality Ac 28:7; **Ro** 12:13; 16:23; **1Ti** 5:10; **Tit** 1:8; **1Pe** 4:9; **3Jn** 8

Greeting one another Ac 18:27; **Ro** 16:3–16; **1Co** 16:19–20; **Col** 4:10; **Phm** 17

Welcoming former opponents Ac 9:26–27; **Gal** 2:9; **2Co** 2:5–8

Divisions in the church
Causes of division in the NT church
Personal ambition: **Mk** 9:34; 10:35–41 pp Mt 20:20–24
Ethnic tension: **Ac** 6:1
Differences of opinion: **Ac** 15:37–40; **Php** 4:2
Troublesome heretical leaders: **Ro** 16:17; **Jude** 19
Partisan spirit: **1Co** 1:11–12; 3:3–4
1Co 6:1–6
Greed: **1Co** 11:18,20–21; **Jas** 4:1–3
Warnings against divisions in the church
1Co 1:10 I [Paul] appeal to you, brothers and sisters, in the name of our Lord Jesus Christ, that all of you agree with one another so that there may be no divisions among you and that you may be perfectly united in mind and thought.
See also **Ro** 12:16; 16:17; **2Co** 12:20; **Eph** 4:31; **Jas** 4:11
Acceptable differences in the church
In secondary matters of conscience, Christians are to respect rather than judge each other. These things need not impair the essential unity that is in Christ: **Ro** 14:1–3,5–6; **1Co** 8:9–13
In varieties of spiritual gifts: **1Co** 12:4–6,14–25; **Gal** 2:7
Necessary divisions in the church
Between the true gospel and heretical alternatives: **2Co** 11:2–6,13–15; **Gal** 1:6–9; **Col** 2:8,16–19; **1Ti** 4:1–6; **1Jn** 2:18–19; **2Jn** 9–11; **Jude** 18–20
Between those truly committed to Jesus Christ, and those apparently part of the church but living sinful lives: **1Co** 5:9–10; **2Th** 3:6; **1Ti** 6:3–5; **2Ti** 3:2–9; **2Pe** 1:20–21; 2:1–3; **Rev** 2:20,24; 3:1,4
Over essential gospel principles: **Ac** 15:2,5–6,19; **Gal** 2:11   *See also commitment, to God's people; fellowship; love; union with Christ.*

commitment
A state of personal dedication to something or someone, which results in actively promoting and working for their good and well-being.

commitment, to Christ
Commitment to Jesus Christ is grounded in the knowledge of his saving power and divinity, and expresses itself in adoration and obedience to Jesus Christ.

Jesus Christ commanded people to make the commitment to follow him
Mt 4:19 "Come, follow me," Jesus said [to Peter and Andrew], "and I will make you fishers of men and women." pp Mk 1:17
Mt 9:9 . . . Jesus . . . saw a man named Matthew sitting at the tax collector's booth. "Follow me," he told him . . . pp Mk 2:14 pp Lk 5:27   *See also* **Mt** 19:21–22; **Jn** 1:43; 21:19,22; **Ro** 15:5; **1Co** 1:12

Jesus Christ frequently spelt out the cost of commitment to him
Mt 10:37–38 [Jesus said] "Anyone who loves father or mother more than me is not worthy of me; anyone who loves son or daughter more than me is not worthy of me. Those who do not take up their cross and follow me are not worthy of me." pp Lk 14:26–27
Mt 16:24 Then Jesus said to his disciples, "Those who would come after me must deny themselves and take up their cross and follow me." pp Mk 8:34 pp Lk 9:23
Jn 12:25–26 [Jesus said] "Those who love their lives will lose them, while those who hate their lives in this world will keep them for eternal life. Whoever serves me must follow me . . ."
See also **Mt** 8:22; 10:39 pp Mk 8:35 pp Lk 17:33; **Mt** 19:21 pp Mk 10:21 pp Lk 18:22; **Lk** 14:28–33; **1Pe** 2:21

Jesus Christ's demand for commitment was sometimes met with a refusal
Lk 9:59 He [Jesus] said to another man,

"Follow me." But he replied, "Lord, first let me go and bury my father."   *See also* **Lk** 9:61

Sometimes people followed Jesus Christ without being truly committed to him
Jn 6:2 . . . a great crowd of people followed him [Jesus] because they saw the miraculous signs he had performed on the sick.

Some committed themselves wholeheartedly to his invitation
Jn 6:66; **Mt** 4:20 pp Mk 1:18; **Mt** 4:22 pp Mk 1:20; **Mt** 9:9 pp Mk 2:14 pp Lk 5:28; **Jn** 1:40

Secret commitment to Jesus Christ
Jn 12:42 Yet at the same time many even among the leaders believed in him [Jesus]. But because of the Pharisees they would not confess their faith for fear they would be put out of the synagogue;   *See also* **Jn** 3:1–2

True commitment to Jesus Christ is seen in love and obedience to him
Jn 14:21 [Jesus said to his disciples] "Those who have my commands and obey them are the ones who love me . . ."
Php 2:12 Therefore, my dear friends, as you have always obeyed — not only in my [Paul's] presence, but now much more in my absence—continue to work out your salvation with fear and trembling,   *See also* **Jn** 8:31; 14:15,23–24; **1Co** 11:1; 16:22; **Eph** 6:5–6,24; **1Jn** 2:3; 3:22–24; **Rev** 14:4   *See also abiding in Christ; discipleship; nature of; obedience; perseverance; self-denial.*

---

commitment, to God

Commitment to God arises from faith in his promises, is expressed in worship and adoration and leads to obedience to his commands.

Commitment to God commanded
Dt 27:10 "Obey the LORD your God and follow his commands and decrees that I give you today."
Jos 24:14 "Now fear the LORD and serve him with all faithfulness. Throw away the gods your

ancestors worshipped beyond the River and in Egypt, and serve the LORD."
Ro 12:1–2 Therefore, I urge you, brothers and sisters, in view of God's mercy, to offer your bodies as living sacrifices, holy and pleasing to God—this is your spiritual act of worship. Do not conform any longer to the pattern of this world, but be transformed by the renewing of your mind. Then you will be able to test and approve what God's will is—his good, pleasing and perfect will.   *See also* **Dt** 6:13; 10:12–13; 13:4; **Jos** 22:5; **Jdg** 6:10; **1Sa** 7:3; 12:24; **1Ch** 28:9; **2Ch** 19:9; **Jer** 38:20; **1Th** 4:1; **2Ti** 2:22

Obedience to God's commands as a sign of commitment
Dt 7:9 Know therefore that the LORD your God is God; he is the faithful God, keeping his covenant of love to a thousand generations of those who love him and keep his commands.
Jos 24:24 And the people said to Joshua, "We will serve the LORD our God and obey him."
Ro 6:17 But thanks be to God that, though you used to be slaves to sin, you wholeheartedly obeyed the form of teaching to which you were entrusted.   *See also* **Ex** 19:8; **Dt** 11:22; **1Ki** 8:61; **Ne** 10:29; **Ps** 40:6–8; **Jer** 7:23; 11:3; 38:20; 42:6; **Hag** 1:12; **Zec** 6:15
Jesus Christ equates obedience with love: **Jn** 14:15; 15:10
Ac 5:29; **Ro** 2:13

Love for God and worship of him are hallmarks of commitment
Dt 30:6 The LORD your God will circumcise your hearts and the hearts of your descendants, so that you may love him with all your heart and with all your soul, and live.
Jn 21:15 . . . Jesus said to Simon Peter, "Simon son of John, do you truly love me more than these?" . . .   *See also* **Dt** 6:5; 10:12; 11:1,13,22; **Jos** 23:11; **Ne** 1:5; **Isa** 56:6–7; **Jer** 20:12; **Da** 9:4; **Mt** 6:24 pp Lk 16:13; **Mt** 22:37 pp Mk 12:30

Benefits of commitment to God
Dt 30:20 . . . that you may love the LORD

your God, listen to his voice, and hold fast to
him. For the LORD is your life, and he will give
you many years in the land he swore to give to
your fathers, Abraham, Isaac and Jacob.
2Ch 16:9 "For the eyes of the LORD range
throughout the earth to strengthen those whose
hearts are fully committed to him . . ."
Pr 16:3 Commit to the LORD whatever you do,
and your plans will succeed.
Rev 2:10 ". . . Be faithful, even to the point
of death, and I [Jesus] will give you the crown
of life." *See also* **Ex** 19:5–6; 20:6; **Dt** 28:1;
1Sa 12:14; **1Ki** 2:2–4; **Ps** 97:10; **Pr** 2:7–8; **Isa**
1:19; **Jer** 26:13

Examples of commitment to God
Abraham: **Ge** 22:17–18; **Heb** 11:8
Nu 12:7; **Jos** 22:2; **1Ki** 15:5,14 pp 2Ch 15:17
Hezekiah: **2Ki** 20:3; **2Ch** 31:20
2Ki 23:25; **Ne** 13:14; **Jn** 13:37

**God's commitment of gifts and tasks to
his people**
God's commitment of gifts 1Co 9:17
God's commitment of the faith to believers
Jude 3 *See also faithfulness; love.*

---

commitment, to God's people
Commitment to God means a commitment to his
people. Believers are meant to be nourished and
supported by the church, and to work towards its
edification.

Commitment to the church
Ac 2:42 They [the first Christian believers]
devoted themselves to the apostles' teaching and
to the fellowship, to the breaking of bread and to
prayer.
Eph 4:3–4 Make every effort to keep the unity
of the Spirit through the bond of peace. There is
one body and one Spirit . . .
Col 3:15 Let the peace of Christ rule in your
hearts, since as members of one body you were
called to peace . . .
Paul uses the picture of the body to describe the
interdependence of believers: **Ro** 12:4–10; **1Co**
12:12–27

Commitment to other Christians is an expression of love made known in Christ
Jn 13:34–35 [Jesus said] "A new command I
give you: Love one another. As I have loved you,
so you must love one another. By this everyone
will know that you are my disciples, if you love
one another."
Col 3:13–14 Bear with each other and forgive
whatever grievances you may have against one
another. Forgive as the Lord forgave you. And
over all these virtues put on love, which binds
them all together in perfect unity.
1Pe 1:22 Now that you have purified yourselves
by obeying the truth, so that you have sincere
mutual affection, love one another deeply, from
the heart. *See also* **Jn** 15:12,17; **Ro** 12:10,16;
13:8; **Gal** 5:13; **Eph** 4:32–5:2; **1Th** 3:12; 4:9; **2Th**
1:3; **Heb** 13:1; **1Pe** 2:17; **1Jn** 3:11,23; 4:7,21; 5:2

Such commitment is expressed in mutual responsibility and concern
Gal 6:2 Carry each other's burdens, and in this
way you will fulfil the law of Christ.
Heb 10:24–25 And let us consider how we
may spur one another on towards love and good
deeds. Let us not give up meeting together, as
some are in the habit of doing, but let us
encourage one another—and all the more as you
see the Day approaching.
1Pe 3:8 Finally, all of you, live in harmony with
one another; be sympathetic, love one another, be
compassionate and humble. *See also* **Ro** 14:13;
15:7,14; **1Co** 1:10; **Eph** 5:21; **Col** 3:13,16; **1Ti**
5:11; **Heb** 3:13; **Jas** 4:11; **1Pe** 4:9; 5:5

For its leaders, commitment to the church may prove a joy and a burden
Ac 20:28 "Keep watch over yourselves and all
the flock of which the Holy Spirit has made you
overseers. Be shepherds of the church of God,
which he bought with his own blood."
2Co 11:28 Besides everything else, I [Paul]
face daily the pressure of my concern for all the
churches. *See also* **Col** 1:24; **1Th** 2:8; 5:12–13;
1Ti 3:1; **Heb** 13:17; **1Pe** 5:1–3 *See also church;
fellowship.*

confession of sin

An admission of sin on the part of individuals or groups of people. Genuine repentance and confession herald divine forgiveness.

Confession of sin leads to divine forgiveness
Under the old covenant

Pr 28:13 Those who conceal their sins do not prosper, but those who confess and renounce them find mercy.   *See also* **Lev** 16:21; 26:40–42; **1Ki** 8:33–36 pp 2Ch 6:24–27; **1Ki** 8:46–52 pp 2Ch 6:36–39; **Ps** 32:3–5

Under the new covenant

1Jn 1:8–10 If we claim to be without sin, we deceive ourselves and the truth is not in us. If we confess our sins, he [God] is faithful and just and will forgive us our sins and purify us from all unrighteousness. If we claim we have not sinned, we make him out to be a liar and his word has no place in our lives.   *See also* **Jas** 5:13–16

Confession of sin accompanied by acts appropriate to repentance

Nu 5:5–8 The LORD said to Moses, "Say to the Israelites: 'When a man or woman wrongs another in any way and so is unfaithful to the LORD, such people are guilty and must confess the sin they have committed. They must make full restitution for the wrong they have done, add one fifth to it and give it all to the person they have wronged . . . '"   *See also* **Lev** 5:5–6; **Ezr** 10:10–11; **Ne** 9:1–3; **Lk** 19:8; **Ac** 19:18–19

Examples of confession of sin
On behalf of the nation

Ne 1:5–7 Then I [Nehemiah] said: "O LORD, God of heaven, the great and awesome God, who keeps his covenant of love with those who love him and obey his commands, let your ear be attentive and your eyes open to hear the prayer your servant is praying before you day and night for your servants, the people of Israel. I confess the sins we Israelites, including myself and my family, have committed against you. We have acted very wickedly towards you. We have not obeyed the commands, decrees and laws you gave your servant Moses."   *See also* **Ezr** 9:5–15; **Isa** 59:12–13; 64:6–7; **Jer** 14:7,20; **Da** 9:4–14

By the people as a whole

1Sa 7:5–6 Then Samuel said, "Assemble all Israel at Mizpah and I will intercede with the LORD for you." When they had assembled at Mizpah, they drew water and poured it out before the LORD. On that day they fasted and there they confessed, "We have sinned against the LORD." . . .   *See also* **Ezr** 9:4–7,10–15; **Ne** 9:33–35; **Ps** 106:6; **Jer** 3:24–25

By individuals

Ps 51:1–5 . . . For I [David] know my transgressions, and my sin is always before me. Against you, you only, have I sinned and done what is evil in your sight, so that you are proved right when you speak and justified when you judge. Surely I was sinful at birth, sinful from the time my mother conceived me.   *See also* **2Sa** 24:10 pp 1Ch 21:10; **2Sa** 24:17 pp 1Ch 21:17; **Job** 7:20; 42:5–6; **Isa** 6:5

Confession of sin to other people

Jos 7:20–21 Achan replied, "It is true! I have sinned against the LORD, the God of Israel. This is what I have done: When I saw in the plunder a beautiful robe from Babylonia, two hundred shekels of silver and a wedge of gold weighing fifty shekels, I coveted them and took them. They are hidden in the ground inside my tent, with the silver underneath."   *See also* **Lk** 15:17–24; **Jas** 5:16   *See also baptism; forgiveness; prayer, God's promises; repentance; sin; worship, acceptable attitudes.*

conversion

Turning or returning to God in repentance, faith and obedience by those who do not know God or who have turned from him. Although conversion can be seen as a human act or decision, Scripture stresses that the work of God lies behind this human decision, guiding and motivating it. True repentance results in a turning from sin and an inner renewal which can only be brought about by God, who draws people to himself and who, through Jesus Christ, gives forgiveness and new life.

Conversion as turning to God
Turning back to God
Dt 4:30–31 When you [the people of Israel] are in distress and all these things have happened to you, then in later days you will return to the LORD your God and obey him . . .
Lk 1:16–17 "Many of the people of Israel will he [John the Baptist] bring back to the Lord their God . . ."   *See also* **Dt** 30:2–3,10; **Lk** 22:32; **Jas** 5:19–20
Turning from idolatry
Ac 14:15 ". . . We [Barnabas and Paul] are bringing you [people of Lystra] good news, telling you to turn from these worthless things to the living God, who made heaven and earth and sea and everything in them."   *See also* **1Sa** 7:3; **Jer** 3:12–13; 4:1–2; **1Th** 1:9–10
Turning from sinful ways
2Ki 17:13–14 The LORD warned Israel and Judah through all his prophets and seers: "Turn from your evil ways. Observe my commands and decrees, in accordance with the entire Law that I commanded your ancestors to obey and that I delivered to you through my servants the prophets." . . .
Isa 55:6–7 . . . Let the wicked forsake their ways and the unrighteous their thoughts. Let them turn to the LORD, and he will have mercy on them, and to our God, for he will freely pardon.   *See also* **2Ki** 13:11; 14:24; 15:9; **Jer** 18:11; 25:5; **Eze** 18:23; **Da** 9:13

Conversion as a turning away from unbelief to faith
It is linked to repentance
Ac 3:19 "Repent, then, and turn to God, so that your sins may be wiped out, that times of refreshing may come from the Lord,"   *See also* **Eze** 14:6; 18:30; **Ac** 26:20
It is linked to coming to faith
Ac 11:21 The Lord's hand was with them [believers from Cyprus and Cyrene], and a great number of people believed and turned to the Lord.

Conversion brings new life
It results in a transformed life
2Co 5:17 Therefore, if anyone is in Christ, there is a new creation: the old has gone, the new has come!   *See also* **Ro** 12:2; **2Co** 3:18; **Gal** 6:14–15
It is symbolised in baptism
Ro 6:3–4 . . . We were therefore buried with him through baptism into death in order that, just as Christ was raised from the dead through the glory of the Father, we too may live a new life.   *See also* **Col** 2:12; 3:1–3
It demands a new lifestyle
Hos 12:6 But you must return to your God; maintain love and justice, and wait for your God always.
Mt 18:3–4 And he [Jesus] said: "I tell you the truth, unless you change and become like little children, you will never enter the kingdom of heaven . . ."   *See also* **Gal** 5:22–24; **Eph** 4:1; 5:8–11; **1Pe** 2:11–12

Conversion brings a new relationship with God
It brings a new status
Gal 4:7 So you are no longer slaves, but God's children; and since you are his children, he has made you also heirs.   *See also* **Gal** 3:26–29; **1Jn** 3:1; **1Pe** 2:9–10
It brings a new understanding
2Co 3:15–16 . . . whenever anyone turns to the Lord, the veil is taken away.   *See also* **Jer** 31:34; **Heb** 8:11

Conversion is a work of God
God turns people to himself
Jer 24:7 "'I will give them a heart to know me, that I am the LORD. They will be my people, and I will be their God, for they will return to me with all their heart.'"
La 5:21 Restore us to yourself, O LORD, that we may return; renew our days as of old   *See also* **1Ki** 8:58; **Jer** 31:18; **Eze** 36:26–27; **Jn** 6:44; 15:16; **Eph** 2:12–13
God gives new birth
Jas 1:17–18 . . . He [God] chose to give us birth through the word of truth, that we might be

a kind of firstfruits of all he created.   *See also*
Jn 3:3–6; **Tit** 3:4–5; **1Pe** 1:23   *See also baptism,
practice; faith; grace; knowing God, nature of; renewal;
repentance.*

coveting

Coveting, desiring to possess something at the
expense of the legitimate owner, is forbidden by
God and can lead to terrible consequences. It
occasionally refers to a commendable earnest
desiring.

Coveting is forbidden by God
In the Ten Commandments
Ex 20:17 "You [Israel] shall not covet your
neighbour's house. You shall not covet your
neighbour's wife, or his male or female servant,
his ox or donkey, or anything that belongs to
your neighbour." pp Dt 5:21
Ro 7:7–8 . . . For I [Paul] would not have
known what coveting really was if the law had
not said, "Do not covet." But sin, seizing the
opportunity afforded by the commandment,
produced in me every kind of covetous
desire . . .   *See also* **Ro** 13:9–10
Through the prophets Isa 5:8; 57:17; **Eze** 33:31;
Am 2:6; 5:11–12; 8:5–6; **Mic** 2:2
In Jesus Christ's teaching
Mt 6:19–21 "Do not store up for yourselves
treasures on earth, where moth and rust destroy,
and where thieves break in and steal. But store
up for yourselves treasures in heaven, where moth
and rust do not destroy, and where thieves do
not break in and steal. For where your treasure
is, there your heart will be also."   *See also* **Lk**
12:15

Coveting has some terrible
consequences
2Sa 11:2–4; **1Ki** 21:18–19
Failure to enter the kingdom of heaven: **Mt** 18:1–3;
Mk 9:33–35 pp Lk 9:46–48; **1Co** 6:9–10
Ac 5:3–10

Further examples of coveting
Jos 7:21 "When I [Achan] saw in the plunder

a beautiful robe from Babylonia, two hundred
shekels of silver and a wedge of gold weighing
fifty shekels, I coveted them and took them. They
are hidden in the ground inside my tent, with the
silver underneath."   *See also* **Dt** 7:25; **Jos**
22:20; **1Sa** 2:12–15; 8:3; 15:9–10; **Pr** 30:16; **Jer**
6:13; 8:10; **Hab** 2:5; **Ac** 8:13–23

Believers may pray to be free from
coveting
Ps 119:36

Godly people claim not to have
coveted
Samuel 1Sa 12:3–5
Paul
Ac 20:33 "I [Paul] have not coveted anyone's
silver or gold or clothing."   *See also* **1Co** 9:12;
2Co 7:2; 11:9; 12:14–18; **1Th** 2:5

Coveting as a commendable earnest
desiring
A desire for the greater spiritual gifts: **1Co** 12:31;
14:1,39
1Ti 3:1

discernment

The sound judgment which makes possible the
distinguishing of good from evil, and the
recognition of God's right ways for his people. It
is necessary for the understanding of spiritual
realities and, on a practical level, for right
government and the avoidance of life's pitfalls.
Discernment is given by God, through his Holy
Spirit. It is received through God's word and
through the insight of a renewed mind. Discerning
believers seek to grow in their understanding and
knowledge of God's truth.

Discernment as sound judgment
Judging the right course
Pr 15:21 Folly delights those who lack
judgment, but those who have insight keep a
straight course.
Php 1:9–10 . . . that you may be able to
discern what is best and may be pure and

blameless until the day of Christ,   *See also* **Pr** 3:21–23; 8:8–9; 10:21; 11:12; 18:1; 24:30; **Hos** 14:9

Distinguishing good from evil
2Sa 14:17 "And now your servant says, 'May the word of my lord the king bring me rest, for my lord the king is like an angel of God in discerning good and evil . . .'"   *See also* **Ge** 3:22; **Job** 6:30; 34:3–4; **Isa** 7:15

Distinguishing holy from common Lev 10:10; 11:47; **Eze** 22:26; 44:23

Seeing through outward appearances
Pr 28:11 The rich may be wise in their own eyes, but the poor who have discernment see how deluded they are.   *See also* **1Sa** 16:7; **Isa** 11:3

Understanding the significance of events
Dt 32:29–30 If only they [the Israelites] were wise and would understand this and discern what their end will be! How could one chase a thousand, or two put ten thousand to flight, unless their Rock had sold them, unless the LORD had given them up?   *See also* **1Ch** 12:32; **Est** 1:13; **Mt** 24:32–33 pp **Mk** 13:28–29; **Lk** 12:54–56

Exercising judgment to rule
1Ki 3:9 "So give your servant [Solomon] a discerning heart to govern your people and to distinguish between right and wrong. For who is able to govern this great people of yours?" *See also* **Pr** 8:14–16; 28:2,16; **Jer** 23:5

Discernment as insight into spiritual realities
Distinguishing between spirits
1Co 12:10 . . . to another distinguishing between spirits . . .   *See also* **1Ki** 22:19–23 pp 2Ch 18:18–22; **1Ti** 4:1; **1Jn** 4:1–3

Discerning true and false prophecy Dt 13:1–3; 18:21–22; **1Co** 14:29

Characteristics of discerning people
The discerning grow in wisdom
Pr 1:5 let the wise listen and add to their learning, and let the discerning get guidance. *See also* **Pr** 9:9; 10:14; 14:6; 15:14; 17:24; 18:15

The discerning accept rebuke Pr 17:10; 19:25

The discerning keep God's law 1Ch 22:12; **Ps** 119:34; **Pr** 28:7

The source of discernment
Discernment is given by God
Da 2:21 "He [God] changes times and seasons; he sets up kings and deposes them. He gives wisdom to the wise and knowledge to the discerning."   *See also* **Pr** 9:10; **Da** 2:27–28; **1Co** 2:12–15

Discernment through God's word
Heb 5:14 But solid food is for the mature, who by constant use have trained themselves to distinguish good from evil.   *See also* **Ps** 19:7; 119:98–100,130; **Ro** 2:18

Discernment through a renewed mind
Ro 12:2 Do not conform any longer to the pattern of this world, but be transformed by the renewing of your mind. Then you will be able to test and approve what God's will is—his good, pleasing and perfect will.   *See also* **Jer** 31:33; **1Co** 2:16

Asking for discernment
Ps 119:66 Teach me knowledge and good judgment, for I believe in your commands. *See also* **Ps** 119:27,125; **Jas** 1:5   *See also spiritual gifts; understanding.*

discipleship
The process of becoming a committed follower of Jesus Christ, with all the spiritual discipline and benefits which this brings.

discipleship, benefits
Joy, peace and happiness result from following Jesus Christ, together with the hope of being like him and with him in heaven. This is anticipated in the OT, which stresses the importance of obedience to the LORD.

Blessings result from obedient discipleship
Lk 11:28 He [Jesus] replied, "Blessed rather are those who hear the word of God and obey it."   *See also* **Pr** 8:32; **Mt** 7:24–25 pp **Lk** 6:47–48; **Jn** 13:17; 14:21; **Jas** 1:25

Joy results from discipleship
Jn 15:10–11 "If you obey my [Christ's]

commands, you will remain in my love, just as I have obeyed my Father's commands and remain in his love. I have told you this so that my joy may be in you and that your joy may be complete."   *See also* **Ps** 119:14; **Ac** 13:52; 16:34; **Ro** 14:17; 15:13; **Gal** 5:22; **Php** 1:25; **1Th** 1:6; **Heb** 10:34; **1Pe** 1:6,8; **Jude** 24

Peace results from discipleship
Jn 14:27 "Peace I [Jesus] leave with you; my peace I give you . . ."   *See also* **Nu** 6:26; **Ps** 4:8; 29:11; 37:11; **Isa** 26:3; **Mt** 11:28–29; **Lk** 2:14 Jesus Christ's greeting to his disciples when he first appeared to them after his resurrection: **Lk** 24:36; **Jn** 20:19
Jn 16:33; 20:21,26; **Ro** 2:10; 5:1; **Php** 4:7; **Col** 3:15

True happiness results from discipleship
Happiness flows from doing God's will
Ps 1:1 Blessed are those who do not walk in the counsel of the wicked or stand in the way of sinners or sit in the seat of mockers.
Ps 119:1–2 Blessed are those whose ways are blameless, who walk according to the law of the LORD. Blessed are those who keep his statutes and seek him with all their heart.   *See also* **Ps** 94:12; 112:1; 128:1; **Pr** 29:18
Disciples are truly happy
Mt 5:3–12 "Blessed are the poor in spirit, for theirs is the kingdom of heaven. Blessed are those who mourn, for they will be comforted. Blessed are the meek, for they will inherit the earth. Blessed are those who hunger and thirst for righteousness, for they will be filled. Blessed are the merciful, for they will be shown mercy. Blessed are the pure in heart, for they will see God. Blessed are the peacemakers, for they will be called children of God. Blessed are those who are persecuted because of righteousness, for theirs is the kingdom of heaven. Blessed are you when people insult you, persecute you and falsely say all kinds of evil against you because of me. Rejoice and be glad, because great is your reward in heaven, for in the same way they persecuted the prophets who were before you." pp **Lk** 6:20–23   *See also* **Rev** 1:3; 22:14

Disciples are abundantly recompensed in this life
Mk 10:29–30 "I tell you the truth," Jesus replied, "no-one who has left home or brothers or sisters or mother or father or children or fields for me and the gospel will fail to receive a hundred times as much in this present age (homes, brothers, sisters, mothers, children and fields . . ." pp **Mt** 19:29 pp **Lk** 18:29–30   *See also* **Pr** 15:16; 16:8; **Mt** 7:7–11 pp **Lk** 11:9–13; **Jn** 8:12; 10:27; 12:26; **Ro** 8:31–39; **1Ti** 6:6

Disciples are blessed by being united with Jesus Christ in the family of God
Mt 12:46–50 While Jesus was still talking to the crowd, his mother and brothers stood outside, wanting to speak to him. Someone told him, "Your mother and brothers are standing outside, wanting to speak to you." He replied to him, "Who is my mother, and who are my brothers?" Pointing to his disciples, he said, "Here are my mother and my brothers. For whoever does the will of my Father in heaven is my brother and sister and mother." pp **Mk** 3:31–35 pp **Lk** 8:19–21   *See also* **Gal** 6:10; **Eph** 2:19; 3:15

Disciples will be blessed with eternal life
Mt 19:29 "And everyone who has left houses or brothers or sisters or father or mother or children or fields for my sake will receive a hundred times as much and will inherit eternal life." pp **Mk** 10:30 pp **Lk** 18:30   *See also* **Mt** 25:46; **Ro** 2:7; **Gal** 6:8; **1Jn** 1:2; 5:11,13,20

Disciples have the hope of being like Jesus Christ and being with him in heaven
1Jn 3:2 Dear friends, now we are children of God, and what we will be has not yet been made known. But we know that when he appears, we shall be like him [Christ] . . .
See also **Jn** 12:26; 14:3; **Ro** 8:29; **1Co** 15:49; **2Pe** 1:4   *See also eternal life; fellowship; guidance; hope; knowing God; peace; spiritual growth.*

discipleship, cost

The denial of self-interests and desires, and a total commitment to do the will of God, even to the point of death.

The cost of discipleship involves a denial of self-interests and desires
The cost involves self-denial

Mt 16:24 Then Jesus said to his disciples, "Those who would come after me must deny themselves and take up their cross and follow me." pp Mk 8:34 pp Lk 9:23   *See also* **Mt 10:38; Lk 14:27**

Self-denial means not living for oneself
Ro 14:7 For we do not live to ourselves alone . . .   *See also* **2Co 5:15; Gal 2:20; 1Pe 4:2**

The cost of discipleship is to be carefully considered

Lk 14:28–32 "Suppose one of you wants to build a tower. Will you not first sit down and estimate the cost to see if you have enough money to complete it? For if you lay the foundation and are not able to finish it, everyone who sees it will ridicule you, saying, 'This person began to build and was not able to finish.' Or suppose a king is about to go to war against another king. Will he not first sit down and consider whether he is able with ten thousand men to oppose the one coming against him with twenty thousand? If he is not able, he will send a delegation while the other is still a long way off and will ask for terms of peace."

The cost of discipleship means total commitment to the will of God
Total surrender is required

Lk 14:33 ". . . those of you who do not give up everything you have cannot be my [Christ's] disciples." *See also* **Php 3:7–8**

The security of the world is to be resisted
Mt 8:19–20 Then a teacher of the law came to him and said, "Teacher, I will follow you wherever you go." Jesus replied, "Foxes have holes and birds of the air have nests, but the Son of Man has nowhere to lay his head." pp Lk 9:57–58

Jesus Christ must have first priority

Lk 9:59–60 He [Jesus] said to another man, "Follow me." But he replied, "Lord, first let me go and bury my father." Jesus said to him, "Let the dead bury their own dead, but you go and proclaim the kingdom of God." pp Mt 8:21–22   *See also* **Mt 19:16–21 pp Mk 10:17–21 pp Lk 18:18–22; Col 1:18**

Jesus Christ must come before family ties

Lk 9:61–62 Still another said, "I will follow you, Lord; but first let me go back and say good-bye to my family." Jesus replied, "No-one who takes hold of the plough and looks back is fit for service in the kingdom of God."   *See also* **Mt 10:37; Lk 14:26**

The cost of discipleship is constant

Lk 9:23 . . . "Those who would come after me [Christ] must deny themselves and take up their cross daily and follow me."

The cost of discipleship includes persecution

Jn 15:20 "Remember the words I [Christ] spoke to you: 'Servants are not greater than their masters.' If they persecuted me, they will persecute you also . . ."   *See also* **Ac 14:22; 2Ti 3:12**

The cost of discipleship includes willingness to suffer and die for Jesus Christ's sake

Mt 10:38–39 "Those who do not take up their cross and follow me [Christ] are not worthy of me. Those who find their lives will lose them, and those who lose their lives for my sake will find them." *See also* **Mt 16:24–25 pp Mk 8:34–35 pp Lk 9:23–24; Jn 12:25**   *See also* *faithfulness; persecution; self-denial.*

discipleship, nature of

The state of following Jesus Christ, and serving and obeying him. The NT stresses the privileges, joys and cost of this calling.

Discipleship involves learning
Learning from God
Jn 6:45 "It is written in the Prophets: 'They will all be taught by God.' Everyone who listens to the Father and learns from him comes to me [Christ]." *See also* **Isa** 54:13; **Lev** 11:44–45; 19:2; 20:7; **Eph** 5:1–2; **1Pe** 1:15–16

Learning from Jesus Christ
Mt 11:29 "Take my [Christ's] yoke upon you and learn from me . . ." *See also* **Jn** 13:15; **Eph** 4:20–21; **Php** 2:5; **1Pe** 2:21; **1Jn** 2:6

Learning from the Holy Spirit
Jn 14:26 "But the Counsellor, the Holy Spirit, whom the Father will send in my name, will teach you all things and will remind you of everything I have said to you." *See also* **Lk** 12:12; **Jn** 16:13; **1Co** 2:13; **Eph** 1:17; 3:16–19; **1Pe** 1:12

Learning from other people
Php 4:9 Whatever you have learned or received or heard from me [Paul], or seen in me—put it into practice . . . *See also* **Dt** 4:10; 5:1; 31:12; **1Co** 4:6,16; 11:1; **Php** 3:17; **2Th** 3:7,9; **1Ti** 2:11; 5:4; **2Ti** 3:14

Learning to do what is good
Tit 3:14 Our people must learn to devote themselves to doing what is good, in order that they may provide for daily necessities and not live unproductive lives. *See also* **Ps** 34:14; 37:27; **Isa** 1:17; 26:9; **3Jn** 11

Jesus Christ calls people to be his disciples
Mt 4:19 "Come, follow me," Jesus said, "and I will make you fishers of men and women." pp **Mk** 1:17 *See also* **Mt** 4:21 pp **Mk** 1:20; **Mt** 8:21–22 **Lk** 9:59–60; **Mt** 9:9 pp **Mk** 2:14 pp **Lk** 5:27; **Mt** 19:21 pp **Mk** 10:21 pp **Lk** 18:22; **Jn** 1:43; 21:19

The consequences of discipleship
Following Jesus Christ
Mt 10:38 "Those who do not take up their cross and follow me [Christ] are not worthy of me." *See also* **Mt** 16:24 pp **Mk** 8:34 pp **Lk** 9:23; **Lk** 14:27; **Jn** 10:27; 12:26; **Rev** 14:4

Serving Jesus Christ
Col 3:24 . . . It is the Lord Christ you are serving. *See also* **Mt** 20:25–28 pp **Mk** 10:42–45; **Ro** 12:11; **1Th** 1:9

Obeying Jesus Christ
Jn 8:31 . . . Jesus said, "If you hold to my teaching, you are really my disciples." *See also* **Jn** 14:21,23–24; 15:10,14; **1Jn** 2:3; 3:22,24; 5:3

Responding immediately to Jesus Christ's commands
Mt 8:21–22 Another disciple said to him, "Lord, first let me go and bury my father." But Jesus told him, "Follow me, and let the dead bury their own dead." *See also* **Mt** 4:20 pp **Mk** 1:18; **Mt** 4:22 pp **Mk** 1:20 pp **Lk** 5:11

Living for Jesus Christ and not for oneself
2Co 5:15 . . . those who live should no longer live for themselves but for him [Christ] who died for them and was raised again. *See also* **Ro** 14:7–8; **1Pe** 4:2

Loving others
Jn 13:12–17 When he had finished washing their feet, he put on his clothes and returned to his place. "Do you understand what I have done for you?" he asked them. "You call me 'Teacher' and 'Lord', and rightly so, for that is what I am. Now that I, your Lord and Teacher, have washed your feet, you also should wash one another's feet. I have set you an example that you should do as I have done for you. I tell you the truth, servants are not greater than their masters, nor are messengers greater than those who sent them. Now that you know these things, you will be blessed if you do them." *See also* **Jn** 15:9–14; **1Jn** 4:7–21

Total commitment is required of Jesus Christ's disciples
Mt 10:37–39 "Anyone who loves father or mother more than me [Christ] is not worthy of me; anyone who loves son or daughter more than me is not worthy of me. Those who do not take up their cross and follow me are not worthy of me. Those who find their lives will lose them, and those who lose their lives for my sake will find them." *See also* **Mt** 16:24–25 pp **Mk** 8:34–35 pp **Lk** 9:23–24; **Mk** 6:8; **Lk** 14:26–27; 17:33; **Jn** 12:25

The purpose of discipleship is to become Christlike

Eph 4:22–24 You were taught, with regard to your former way of life, to put off your old self, which is being corrupted by its deceitful desires; to be made new in the attitude of your minds; and to put on the new self, created to be like God in true righteousness and holiness.   *See also* **Mt** 5:48; **Lk** 6:40; **Ro** 8:29; 12:1–2; 13:14; **2Co** 3:18; 7:1; **Eph** 1:4; **Col** 1:28; 3:12; **2Ti** 3:17; **1Pe** 1:14–15; **2Pe** 1:5–7; **1Jn** 3:2–3

Examples of secret discipleship

Jn 3:1–2 Now there was a Pharisee named Nicodemus, a member of the Jewish ruling council. He came to Jesus at night and said, "Rabbi, we know you are a teacher who has come from God. For you could not perform the miraculous signs you are doing if God were not with you."   *See also* **Jn** 7:50; 12:42; 19:38–39   *See also abiding in Christ; Christlikeness; commitment; holiness; life, of faith; obedience; sanctification.*

discipline

Loving and corrective training that leads to maturity and responsibility on the part of those who experience it.

discipline, divine

God disciplines his people through his word, through their experiences and through punishment, so that they may live in ways pleasing to him.

The nature of God's discipline
It is a sign of God's love

Heb 12:6 ". . . the Lord disciplines those he loves . . ."   *See also* **Pr** 3:12; **Ps** 119:75; **Rev** 3:19

It is a sign of belonging to God's family

Heb 12:6 ". . . he [the Lord] punishes everyone he accepts as a child."   *See also* **Pr** 3:12; **Dt** 8:5; **2Sa** 7:14; **Heb** 12:7

It trains God's people

Heb 12:11 . . . it [God's discipline] produces a harvest of righteousness and peace for those who have been trained by it.

The means of God's discipline
The use of Scripture

2Ti 3:16 All Scripture is God-breathed and is useful for teaching, rebuking, correcting and training in righteousness,   *See also* **Dt** 4:36; 29:29; **Isa** 8:11

The knowledge of God's grace

Tit 2:11–12 For the grace of God that brings salvation has appeared to all people. It teaches us to say "No" to ungodliness and worldly passions, and to live self-controlled, upright and godly lives in this present age,

Instructive experiences Dt 8:1–5; 11:2–7; **Ps** 90:12; **Isa** 48:17

Painful experiences

Heb 12:7 Endure hardship as discipline; God is treating you as children . . .   *See also* **2Co** 12:7–10; **Heb** 12:5,11; **1Pe** 1:6–7

Punishment

Heb 12:6 ". . . he [the Lord] punishes everyone he accepts as a child."   *See also* **Pr** 3:12; **Lev** 26:18,21,23–24,27–28; **2Sa** 7:14; **Ps** 73:14; **Jer** 32:19; **Hos** 5:2; 7:15–16; **1Co** 11:32

God disciplines all and only his children

Heb 12:8 If you are not disciplined (and everyone undergoes discipline), then you are illegitimate and not true children.   *See also* **Heb** 12:6

The goals of God's discipline
Respectful submission to God

Heb 12:9 . . . How much more should we submit to the Father of our spirits and live!

The good of God's people

Heb 12:10 . . . God disciplines us for our good, that we may share in his holiness.   *See also* **Job** 5:17–18; **Ps** 94:12; 119:67,71,75

Spiritual growth

Heb 12:11 . . . it [God's discipline] produces a harvest of righteousness and peace for those who have been trained by it.   *See also* **Pr** 1:2–3

Preparation for heaven

2Co 4:17–18 For our light and momentary troubles are achieving for us an eternal glory that far outweighs them all. So we fix our eyes not on what is seen, but on what is unseen. For what is seen is temporary, but what is unseen is eternal. *See also* **Ro** 8:18; **Jas** 1:12

Believers should not despise God's discipline
Job 5:17 ". . . do not despise the discipline of the Almighty." *See also* **Heb** 12:5; **Pr** 3:11

Divine discipline in the church
By reproof 2Co 7:8; 13:2; **2Th** 3:15
For the benefit of sinners Mt 18:15; **1Co** 5:1–7; **2Th** 3:14
As a warning to others 1Ti 5:20
To be exercised with kindness 2Co 2:6; **Gal** 6:1
The role of witnesses Mt 18:16; **1Ti** 5:19
See also holiness; sanctification; spiritual growth; suffering.

---

discipline, family
Parents' loving, corrective training of their children, by verbal instruction and punishments, so that they grow up in the way God wants.

Parents are to discipline their children
Heb 12:7 . . . For what children are not disciplined by their parents? *See also* **Dt** 8:5; **Heb** 12:9–11

Parents discipline out of love for their children
Pr 13:24 Those who spare the rod hate their children, but those who love them are careful to discipline them. *See also* **Pr** 3:12

The means of parental discipline
Training
Pr 22:6 Train children in the way they should go, and when they are old they will not turn from it. *See also* **Ge** 18:19; **Dt** 6:7; **Pr** 29:17; **Eph** 6:4; **Col** 3:21
Correction
Pr 22:15 Folly is bound up in the heart of a child, but the rod of discipline will drive it far away. *See also* **Pr** 19:18; 23:13–14; 29:15
Verbal instruction
Eph 6:4 Fathers, do not exasperate your

children; instead, bring them up in the training and instruction of the Lord. *See also* **Dt** 4:9; 6:7,20–25; 11:19; 31:13; **Ps** 78:5; **Pr** 1:8; 6:20; **2Ti** 3:15
Punishment
Pr 23:13–14 Do not withhold discipline from children; if you punish them with the rod, they will not die. Punish them with the rod and save their souls from death. *See also* **Pr** 22:15; 29:15

The purpose of parental discipline is to impart wisdom
Pr 29:15 The rod of correction imparts wisdom, but children left to themselves disgrace their mothers. *See also* **Pr** 19:18; 22:15; 29:17; **Heb** 12:9,11

Examples of parents who neglected discipline
Eli
1Sa 3:13 "For I [the Lord] told him [Eli] that I would judge his family for ever because of the sin he knew about; his sons made themselves contemptible, and he failed to restrain them."
David
1Ki 1:5–6 Now Adonijah, whose mother was Haggith, put himself forward and said, "I will be king." So he got chariots and horses ready, with fifty men to run ahead of him. (His father [David] had never interfered with him by asking, "Why do you behave as you do?" . . .)

---

disobedience
The refusal to obey someone, especially someone in a position of authority. Scripture insists on the need to obey God at all times.

Disobedience enters people's hearts for various reasons
Disobedience comes through greed and lust
Ge 3:6 When the woman [Eve] saw that the fruit of the tree was good for food and pleasing to the eye, and also desirable for gaining wisdom, she took some and ate it . . . *See also* **Ge** 3:11–12; **Ex** 16:19–20; **Jos** 7:20–21; **2Sa** 11:2–4

Disobedience arises from impatience
Ex 32:23 "They said to me [Aaron], 'Make us gods who will go before us. As for this fellow Moses who brought us up out of Egypt, we don't know what has happened to him.'"   *See also* **Nu** 20:10–11; **1Sa** 13:8–14
Disobedience comes through fear Jer 43:2–7; **Jn** 7:13; 12:42; **Gal** 2:12
Disobedience results from pride and arrogance
Lev 10:1 Aaron's sons Nadab and Abihu took their censers, put fire in them and added incense; and they offered unauthorised fire before the LORD, contrary to his command.   *See also* **Ex** 5:2; **2Ch** 26:16

Unbelief is disobedience
Heb 3:12 See to it, brothers and sisters, that none of you has a sinful, unbelieving heart that turns away from the living God.   *See also* **Jer** 7:23–28; **Ro** 11:30–32; **Heb** 3:18–19; 4:2,6

Lack of love is disobedience
Jn 14:24 "Anyone who does not love me [Jesus] will not obey my teaching . . ."   *See also* **1Jn** 2:9; 3:15

Disobedience to God leads to punishment
Punishment is applied to individuals
Ge 3:17–19 To Adam he [God] said, "Because you listened to your wife and ate from the tree about which I commanded you, 'You must not eat of it,' . . . By the sweat of your brow you will eat your food until you return to the ground, since from it you were taken; for dust you are and to dust you will return."   *See also* **Ge** 3:23–24; **Lev** 10:1–2; **Nu** 20:12; **1Sa** 28:18; **2Sa** 12:14; **Jnh** 1:10–12; **Eph** 5:5–6
Punishment for the disobedience of unbelief
2Th 1:8–9 He will punish those who do not know God and do not obey the gospel of our Lord Jesus . . .   *See also* **Heb** 2:2–3
Nations are also punished
Ge 15:14 "But I [the LORD] will punish the nation they serve as slaves, and afterwards they will come out with great possessions."   *See also* **Ac** 7:7

Dt 11:26–28 See, I am setting before you today a blessing and a curse—the blessing if you obey the commands of the LORD your God that I am giving you today; the curse if you disobey the commands of the LORD your God and turn from the way that I command you today by following other gods, which you have not known.
1Sa 12:15 "But if you do not obey the LORD, and if you rebel against his commands, his hand will be against you, as it was against your ancestors." *See also* **Ex** 32:35; **Dt** 28:15; **Isa** 13:11
Disobedience, like all sin, can be forgiven
Ro 5:19 For just as through the disobedience of the one man the many were made sinners, so also through the obedience of the one man the many will be made righteous.   *See also* **Eph** 2:1–5   *See also obedience.*

---

doubt
Uncertainty about the truth and reality of spiritual things, as seen especially in a lack of faith in and commitment to God.

---

doubt, dealing with
Uncertainty may be remedied by gaining assurance from God's word, remembering God's past goodness, reflecting on his power and appealing to his unfailing love. Believers should help the weak with the patience and encouragement that reflects God's own compassion.

Doubt dealt with by holding on to God's truth
Gaining assurance from God's word
Ps 119:147 I rise before dawn and cry for help; I have put my hope in your word.
1Jn 5:13 I [John] write these things to you who believe in the name of the Son of God so that you may know that you have eternal life. *See also* **Ps** 119:116; **Jn** 20:31; **Ro** 15:4; **2Pe** 1:19
Receiving correction and understanding through God's word
2Ti 3:14–17 But as for you, continue in what you have learned and have become convinced of . . . All Scripture is God-breathed and is useful for teaching, rebuking, correcting and training in

righteousness . . .   *See also* **Ps** 119:130; **Pr** 6:23; **1Co** 10:11

Avoiding idle speculation Eph 4:14; **1Ti** 6:20–21; **2Ti** 2:16,23; **Tit** 3:9

Doubt dealt with by meditating on God's works

Remembering God's past deeds

Ps 77:10–20 . . . I will remember the deeds of the LORD; yes, I will remember your miracles of long ago. I will meditate on all your works and consider all your mighty deeds . . .   *See also* **Dt** 7:17–19; **1Ch** 16:8–12 pp Ps 105:1–6; **Ps** 22:4–5; 74:12–17; 143:5; **Isa** 46:9; **Mt** 16:9–10

Commemorating God's deeds

Ex 12:14 "This [Passover] is a day you are to commemorate; for the generations to come you shall celebrate it as a festival to the LORD—a lasting ordinance."   *See also* **Dt** 16:1; **Lk** 22:19; **1Co** 11:24–25

Reflecting on divine power Mt 11:4–6; **Jn** 10:38; 14:11

Doubt dealt with by trusting

Trusting in God's unfailing love

Ps 6:2–4 . . . Turn, O LORD, and deliver me; save me because of your unfailing love.   *See also* **Ps** 42:8; **Isa** 49:15–16; 54:10; **Jer** 31:3–4

Trusting in God's presence

Ge 28:15 "I [the LORD] am with you [Abraham] and will watch over you wherever you go, and I will bring you back to this land. I will not leave you until I have done what I have promised you."   *See also* **Ex** 3:12; **Dt** 20:1; **2Ch** 20:15–17; **Ps** 42:11; 73:23–26

Trusting in God's strength

Isa 41:10 "So do not fear, for I am with you; do not be dismayed, for I am your God. I will strengthen you and help you; I will uphold you with my righteous right hand."   *See also* **1Ki** 19:6–8; **Isa** 40:28–31; 43:2

Remembering God's concern for the weak

God's compassion for the weak

Eze 34:16 " 'I [the LORD] will search for the lost and bring back the strays. I will bind up the injured and strengthen the weak . . .' "   *See also* **Isa** 42:3

God's grace to those with doubts

Ex 5:22–6:1 . . . Then the LORD said to Moses, "Now you will see what I will do to Pharaoh: Because of my mighty hand he will let them go; because of my mighty hand he will drive them out of his country."   *See also* **Nu** 11:21–23; **Jdg** 6:39–40; **Jn** 20:27

Pastoral concern for those who doubt

Being patient with doubters

Jude 22 Be merciful to those who doubt; *See also* **Ro** 14:1–4,15–17; 15:1

Encouraging those with doubts

Jdg 20:22 But the Israelites encouraged one another and again took up their positions where they had stationed themselves the first day.

Job 4:3–4 "Think how you [Job] have instructed many, how you have strengthened feeble hands. Your words have supported those who stumbled; you have strengthened faltering knees."   *See also* **2Ch** 32:6–8; **Isa** 35:3–4; 40:1; **1Th** 3:2; **Heb** 10:23–25; 12:12   *See also faith, growth in.*

doubt, nature of

Doubt leads to insecurity and lack of trust concerning God's willingness and ability to deliver his people. It also leads to a fear of people and situations.

Doubting God's truth

Doubt as a questioning of God's words

Ge 3:1 Now the serpent was more crafty than any of the wild animals the LORD God had made. He said to the woman, "Did God really say, 'You must not eat from any tree in the garden'?"
See also **Ge** 3:4; **Isa** 5:19; **Jer** 17:15; **2Pe** 3:4

Doubt as lack of faith

Mt 21:21–22 Jesus replied, "I tell you the truth, if you have faith and do not doubt, not only can you do what was done to the fig-tree, but also you can say to this mountain, 'Go, throw yourself into the sea,' and it will be done . . ." pp Mk 11:23–24   *See also* **Mt** 17:20; **Mk** 6:6; 16:14; **Lk** 17:6

Doubt as wavering

Jas 1:6 But when you ask, you must believe and not doubt, because the one who doubts is like a wave of the sea, blown and tossed by the wind.　*See also* **1Ki** 18:21; **Ro** 4:20; **Eph** 4:13–14

Doubt as double-mindedness

Jas 1:8 they [who doubt] are double-minded and unstable in all they do.　*See also* **2Ki** 17:40–41; **Lk** 16:13; **1Co** 10:21; **Jas** 4:8

Doubt as insecurity about relationship with God

Doubting God's compassion

Ps 77:7–9 "Will the Lord reject for ever? Will he never show his favour again? Has his unfailing love vanished for ever? Has his promise failed for all time? Has God forgotten to be merciful? Has he in anger withheld his compassion?" . . .
See also **Ps** 90:13; **Heb** 12:5–6

Doubting God's concern

Job 30:20 "I [Job] cry out to you, O God, but you do not answer; I stand up, but you merely look at me."

Isa 49:14 But Zion said, "The LORD has forsaken me, the Lord has forgotten me."
See also **Ps** 13:1–2; 22:1–2; 35:17; **Isa** 40:27; **Jer** 8:18–22; **La** 3:8; **Hab** 1:2

Doubting God's desire to deliver

Jer 45:3 "You [Baruch] said, 'Woe to me! The LORD has added sorrow to my pain; I am worn out with groaning and find no rest.'"　*See also* **Ex** 5:22–23; **La** 2:1–9; 3:13–20

Doubting God's ability to deliver

Ps 78:18–22 . . . They [the people of Israel] spoke against God, saying, "Can God spread a table in the desert? . . ." . . .　*See also* **Ex** 14:10–12; **Ps** 78:41–43; **Mt** 8:26 pp **Mk** 4:39–40 pp **Lk** 8:24–25

Doubting God's justice

Jer 12:1 You are always righteous, O LORD, when I [Jeremiah] bring a case before you. Yet I would speak with you about your justice: Why does the way of the wicked prosper? Why do all the faithless live at ease?　*See also* **Job** 9:23; **Ps** 73:13–16; 82:2; **Jer** 15:16–18; **Hab** 1:13

Doubt as fear of people and situations

Mt 14:30–31 But when he [Peter] saw the wind, he was afraid and, beginning to sink, cried out, "Lord, save me!" Immediately Jesus reached out his hand and caught him. "You of little faith," he said, "why did you doubt?"　*See also* **Ge** 12:12–13; 19:30; 26:7; **Jos** 7:5; **1Sa** 17:11; **Isa** 51:12–13　*See also* **faith, nature of; prayer, doubts.**

doubt, results of

Doubt results in uncertainty and ineffectiveness in the spiritual life of individual believers and of the believing community. God appeals to those who waver to make a clear choice.

Doubt results in spiritual uncertainty

Uncertainty about commitment

Lk 9:57–62 . . . Jesus replied, "No-one who takes hold of the plough and looks back is fit for service in the kingdom of God." pp **Mt** 8:19–22　*See also* **Ge** 19:17,26; **Ex** 16:2–3; **Mt** 6:24 pp **Lk** 16:13; **Heb** 11:15

Uncertainty about God's power

Nu 13:31 But the men who had gone up with him [Caleb] said, "We can't attack those people; they are stronger than we are."　*See also* **Dt** 1:29–33

Uncertainty about God's love

Isa 40:27 Why do you say, O Jacob, and complain, O Israel, "My way is hidden from the LORD; my cause is disregarded by my God"?
See also **Dt** 1:27; **Job** 9:16–18; 30:21

Uncertainty about the meaning of life

Job 3:16 "Or why was I [Job] not hidden in the ground like a stillborn child, like an infant who never saw the light of day?"　*See also* **1Ki** 19:3–4; **Ps** 42:3–4; **Jer** 20:14–18; **Jnh** 4:3

Uncertainty about teaching

Eph 4:14 Then we will no longer be infants, tossed back and forth by the waves, and blown here and there by every wind of teaching and by the cunning and craftiness of people in their deceitful scheming.　*See also* **1Ti** 6:20–21

Uncertainty about the will of God

Jdg 6:17 Gideon replied, "If now I have found favour in your [the LORD's] eyes, give me a sign that it is really you talking to me." *See also* **Jdg** 6:36–40; **Jn** 20:25; **2Co** 13:3

Doubt may result in a spiritual decline
Doubt may result in drifting from faith
Heb 2:1 We must pay more careful attention, therefore, to what we have heard, so that we do not drift away. *See also* **2Ch** 36:12–13; **Ne** 9:16–17; **Ps** 95:8–9; **La** 5:20; **Heb** 3:12–13; 6:4–6; **2Pe** 2:20–21
Doubt may result in faithless action
Isa 31:1 Woe to those who go down to Egypt for help, who rely on horses, who trust in the multitude of their chariots and in the great strength of their horsemen, but do not look to the Holy One of Israel, or seek help from the Lord.
Ro 14:23 . . . everything that does not come from faith is sin. *See also* **Ge** 12:13; 16:2–3; **Ex** 32:1; **Nu** 20:11–12; **Ac** 7:40; **Ro** 14:14
Doubt brings the risk of God's judgment
Nu 20:12 But the Lord said to Moses and Aaron, "Because you did not trust in me enough to honour me as holy in the sight of the Israelites, you will not bring this community into the land I give them." *See also* **Nu** 11:1; 14:37; **Heb** 6:7–8

Doubt leads to ineffectiveness in prayer
Jas 1:6–7 But when you ask, you must believe and not doubt, because the one who doubts is like a wave of the sea, blown and tossed by the wind. Those who doubt should not think they will receive anything from the Lord; *See also* **Mt** 17:20; 21:21 pp Mk 11:23

Doubt spreads
Dt 1:28 "Where can we [Israelites] go? Our brothers have made us lose heart. They say, 'The people are stronger and taller than we are; the cities are large, with walls up to the sky. We even saw the Anakites there.'" *See also* **Nu** 13:32; **2Ki** 17:14

God's appeal for a clear decision
1Ki 18:21 Elijah went before the people and said, "How long will you waver between two opinions? If the Lord is God, follow him; but if

Baal is God, follow him." But the people said nothing. *See also* **Dt** 30:15–17; **Jos** 24:15; **Jn** 20:27; **Jas** 4:8

---

equipping, spiritual
Scripture provides examples of individuals who have been equipped to carry out tasks or responsibilities of a spiritual nature.

Jesus Christ was equipped for his work
Isa 61:1–2 The Spirit of the Sovereign Lord is on me, because the Lord has anointed me to preach good news to the poor. He has sent me to bind up the broken-hearted, to proclaim freedom for the captives and release from darkness for the prisoners, to proclaim the year of the Lord's favour and the day of vengeance of our God, to comfort all who mourn, *See also* **Ps** 72:1; **Isa** 50:4–7; **Mt** 12:18; **Isa** 42:1; **Lk** 4:18–19; 19:31; **Jn** 3:34; **Ac** 10:38; **Heb** 10:5

God's people are equipped for service
In the OT
Ex 4:10–12 Moses said to the Lord, "O Lord, I have never been eloquent, neither in the past nor since you have spoken to your servant. I am slow of speech and tongue." The Lord said to him, "Who gave human beings their mouths? Who makes them deaf or mute? Who gives them sight or makes them blind? Is it not I, the Lord? Now go; I will help you speak and will teach you what to say."
Bezalel and Oholiab: **Ex** 31:1–6; 35:30–36:2
Lev 8:7–9; **Jdg** 3:10
Gideon: **Jdg** 6:14,34
Jdg 11:29; 14:19; **1Sa** 10:10
Solomon: **1Ki** 3:7–9; **2Ch** 2:12
2Ki 2:9; **Ne** 13:9; **Isa** 6:6–7; **Jer** 1:9; **Eze** 1:1; 3:23
In the NT
2Ti 2:20–21 In a large house there are articles not only of gold and silver, but also of wood and clay; some are for noble purposes and some for ignoble. Any who cleanse themselves from the latter will be instruments for noble purposes, made holy, useful to the Master and prepared to do any

good work. *See also* **Mt** 4:19; **Lk** 1:15,41,67; **Lk** 12:33; **Ac** 4:8; 6:3; 9:17; 11:24; **Ro** 13:12; **Eph** 4:12; 6:11–18; **Php** 4:19; **2Ti** 3:16–17; **Heb** 13:20–21; **1Pe** 3:15

Believers are equipped for spiritual tasks
By the call of Jesus Christ
Mt 4:19 "Come, follow me," Jesus said, "and I will make you fishers of men and women." pp **Mk** 1:17 *See also* **Mk** 10:24–31; **Lk** 9:1–2; 10:1–3; **Jn** 1:35–42
By spiritual gifts
1Co 12:7 Now to each one the manifestation of the Spirit is given for the common good. *See also* **Ac** 6:3–6; **Ro** 12:6–8; **1Co** 12:8–11, 27–31; **Eph** 4:7,11–12
By the word of God
2Ti 2:15 Do your best to present yourself to God as one approved, a worker who does not need to be ashamed and who correctly handles the word of truth. *See also* **Col** 3:16; **2Ti** 3:16–17; **2Pe** 1:19; **1Jn** 2:14
By the empowering of the Holy Spirit **Ac** 2:4; 4:31; 13:9; **Eph** 5:18
For spiritual conflict
Eph 6:11 Put on the full armour of God so that you can take your stand against the devil's schemes. *See also* **Ro** 13:12; **Eph** 4:20–24; 6:12–18; **Col** 3:12–15; **1Th** 5:8; **1Ti** 6:12; **Heb** 13:21; **1Pe** 3:15 *See also spiritual gifts; spiritual warfare.*

eternal life
The state of being in a permanent living relationship with God, through Jesus Christ, begun in this life and consummated at the resurrection of believers with triumph over death and infinitely extended life. It also means a unique quality of life, knowing God in this life and sharing the life of Christ. Its source is God himself.

Eternal life is knowing God and enjoying his eternal blessings
Jn 17:3 "Now this is eternal life: that they may know you, the only true God, and Jesus Christ, whom you have sent."
Ps 16:11 You have made known to me the path of life; you will fill me with joy in your presence, with eternal pleasures at your right hand. *See also* **Ps** 21:4–6; **Eph** 1:3–14
Eternal glory is the believer's inheritance
2Co 4:17 For our light and momentary troubles are achieving for us an eternal glory that far outweighs them all. *See also* **Da** 12:3; **2Ti** 2:10; **1Pe** 5:4,10
Contrasted with eternal judgment and rejection
Mt 25:46 "Then they [the "goats"] will go away to eternal punishment, but the righteous to eternal life." *See also* **Da** 12:2; **Mt** 25:46; **Jn** 3:16; **2Th** 1:8–9
The work of helping others come to eternal life **Jn** 4:35–36

Eternal life as endless life
The guarantee of the resurrection
1Co 15:20–22 . . . Christ has indeed been raised from the dead, the firstfruits of those who have fallen asleep . . . *See also* **Ps** 49:15; **Isa** 26:19; **1Th** 4:14
Death will be vanquished
Rev 21:4 "He [God] will wipe every tear from their eyes. There will be no more death or mourning or crying or pain, for the old order of things has passed away." *See also* **Isa** 25:8; **1Co** 15:26,50–57
Believers will live for ever
Jn 11:25–26 Jesus said to her [Martha], "I am the resurrection and the life. Those who believe in me will live, even though they die; and whoever lives and believes in me will never die . . ." *See also* **Lk** 20:34–36; **Jn** 6:51,54,58; 8:51; **1Jn** 2:17

Eternal life as a quality of life
Jn 10:10 ". . . I [Jesus] have come that they may have life, and have it to the full." *See also* **Jn** 4:14
One of the blessings associated with the kingdom of God **Mt** 19:29 pp **Mk** 10:30 pp **Lk** 18:30; **Lk** 18:18
Life with Christ **Jn** 6:67–69; 15:5; **Col** 3:4; **1Th** 5:10

Eternal life as experiencing Jesus Christ's life
Gal 2:20 I have been crucified with Christ and I no longer live, but Christ lives in me . . . *See also* **2Co** 4:10–11; **Ro** 6:4,8; 8:10–11

God is the source and giver of eternal life
God the Father
Jn 17:3 "Now this is eternal life: that they may know you, the only true God, and Jesus Christ, whom you have sent." *See also* **Dt** 5:26; **Ps** 36:9; 42:2; 56:13; **Mt** 22:32 pp **Mk** 12:27; **Lk** 20:38; **1Ti** 6:13
God the Son
Jn 14:6 Jesus answered, "I am the way and the truth and the life. No-one comes to the Father except through me." *See also* **Jn** 1:4; 11:25–26; 17:3; **1Jn** 1:1–2; 5:20
God the Holy Spirit
Jn 6:63 "The Spirit gives life . . ." *See also* **2Co** 3:6; **Gal** 6:8 *See also knowing God; life, spiritual.*

---

eternal life, experience
Eternal life is a present possession, to be experienced here and now, but it also offers rich and joyful future prospects.

Eternal life as a present possession
Jn 5:24 "I tell you the truth, those who hear my word and believe him who sent me [Jesus] have eternal life and will not be condemned; they have crossed over from death to life." *See also* **Ro** 6:22; **Gal** 2:20; **Eph** 2:4–5; **Col** 2:13; 3:1–4; **1Ti** 6:12
The Holy Spirit as a sign of new life **Ro** 8:9; **1Co** 3:16; 6:19; **Eph** 1:13–14; **2Ti** 1:14
Eternal life as a future hope
1Pe 1:3–5 Praise be to the God and Father of our Lord Jesus Christ! In his great mercy he has given us new birth into a living hope through the resurrection of Jesus Christ from the dead . . .
Present experience the basis for future hope
Col 1:27; **2Th** 2:16–17
Eternal life contrasted with present suffering
Ro 8:18 I [Paul] consider that our present sufferings are not worth comparing with the glory that will be revealed in us. *See also* **Mt** 5:11–12; **Lk** 18:28–30 pp **Mt** 19:29 pp **Mk** 10:29–30; **Jas** 1:12
The life to come
1Ti 4:8 For physical training is of some value, but godliness has value for all things, holding promise for both the present life and the life to come. *See also* **Ro** 2:7; **2Co** 5:4; **Col** 1:5; **Jude** 21
Being with Christ for ever
2Co 5:8 We are confident, I say, and would prefer to be away from the body and at home with the Lord. *See also* **Lk** 23:43; **Jn** 14:2–3; 17:24; **1Th** 4:15–17

Assurance of eternal life
The keeping power of God
Jn 10:28–29 "I [Jesus] give them eternal life, and they shall never perish; no-one can snatch them out of my hand. My Father, who has given them to me, is greater than all; no-one can snatch them out of my Father's hand." *See also* **Ro** 8:38–39; **1Pe** 1:3–5
The believer's confidence in God
Jn 17:2–3 "For you granted him authority over all people that he might give eternal life to all those you have given him. Now this is eternal life: that they may know you, the only true God, and Jesus Christ, whom you have sent." *See also* **Ps** 73:26; **Job** 19:25; **1Jn** 5:11–13
The sure and certain hope **Tit** 1:2; 3:5–7; **2Pe** 1:10–11 *See. also hope; suffering, of believers.*

---

evangelism
The proclamation of the good news of Jesus Christ, which arises naturally from believers' love for God and appreciation of all that God has done for them. The NT stresses the importance of evangelism, and provides guidance as to how it should be carried out.

---

evangelism, kinds of
Scripture recognises that evangelism takes place in a variety of contexts, and offers models for evangelism in today's church.

Public evangelism
Preaching in synagogues
Ac 14:1 At Iconium Paul and Barnabas went as usual into the Jewish synagogue. There they spoke so effectively that a great number of Jews and Gentiles believed.

In Pisidian Antioch: **Ac** 13:14–16,42–44 **Ac** 17:2,10,17; 18:4; 19:8

Preaching in recognised meeting-places
Ac 17:19–23 . . . Paul then stood up in the meeting of the Areopagus and said: "People of Athens! I see that in every way you are very religious . . ."   *See also* **Ac** 5:25; 10:27–28; 16:13; 19:9

Making a public defence to accusers
Ac 21:37–22:1 . . . Paul answered, "I am a Jew, from Tarsus in Cilicia, a citizen of no ordinary city. Please let me speak to the people." . . .   *See also* **Ac** 4:7–12; 7:1–2; 24:10; 26:1

Personal evangelism
Giving personal testimony
1Jn 1:1–3 . . . We proclaim to you what we have seen and heard, so that you also may have fellowship with us. And our fellowship is with the Father and with his Son, Jesus Christ.   *See also* **Mk** 5:19; **Jn** 4:39; **Ac** 26:9–18; **1Co** 7:16; **1Pe** 3:1–2

Evangelism in homes
Ac 10:24–25 The following day he [Peter] arrived in Caesarea. Cornelius was expecting them and had called together his relatives and close friends. As Peter entered the house, Cornelius met him and fell at his feet in reverence.

Believers invite others into their homes: **Lk** 5:29; **Ac** 18:26; 28:30–31

Believers visit the homes of others: **Ac** 9:17 pp Ac 22:12; **Ac** 16:32–34

Evangelism in strategic areas
Going to major centres Ac 16:12; 17:1,15; 18:1,19

Rome: **Ac** 23:11; 28:14

Going into new territories Ro 15:20,23–24; **2Co** 10:15–16

Evangelism among strategic people
Speaking to prominent people
Ac 18:8 Crispus, the synagogue ruler, and his entire household believed in the Lord; and many of the Corinthians who heard him believed and were baptised.   *See also* **Ac** 13:7; 24:24; 25:8–9,11–12; 26:2–3; 28:7–8

Evangelising households
Ac 16:34 The jailer brought them [Paul and Silas] into his house and set a meal before them; he was filled with joy because he had come to believe in God—he and his whole family.
See also **Jn** 4:53; **Ac** 11:14; 18:8

Using literature in evangelism
Jn 20:30–31 Jesus did many other miraculous signs in the presence of his disciples, which are not recorded in this book. But these are written that you may believe that Jesus is the Christ, the Son of God, and that by believing you may have life in his name.   *See also* **Lk** 1:1–4; **Ac** 1:1–2

Appealing to Scripture in evangelism
Ac 26:22–23 ". . . I [Paul] stand here and testify to small and great alike. I am saying nothing beyond what the prophets and Moses said would happen . . ."   *See also* **Ac** 8:35; 10:43; 13:22–23; **Ro** 1:2–3; 16:25–26; **1Co** 15:3–4

Signs and wonders in evangelism
Miracles confirm the message
Ac 8:6 When the crowds heard Philip and saw the miraculous signs he did, they all paid close attention to what he said. *See also* **Mk** 16:17–20; **Ac** 4:14; 19:10–12; **1Co** 2:4–5; **Heb** 2:3–4

Miracles give opportunity for preaching
Ac 3:9–16 . . . While the beggar held on to Peter and John, all the people were astonished and came running to them in the place called Solomon's Colonnade. When Peter saw this, he said to them: "People of Israel, why does this surprise you? Why do you stare at us as if by our own power or godliness we had made this man walk? . . ."   *See also* **Ac** 2:5–14; 14:8–11; 16:26–31

Miracles result in people believing
Ac 9:40–42 . . . He [Peter] took her [Tabitha]

by the hand and helped her to her feet. Then he called the believers and the widows and presented her to them alive. This became known all over Joppa, and many people believed in the Lord.
See also **Jn** 7:31; 11:45; **Ac** 9:33–35; 13:10–12

The response to evangelism
Acceptance of the message
Ac 2:37–41 . . . Those who accepted his [Peter's] message were baptised, and about three thousand were added to their number that day.
See also **Ac** 4:4; 17:4,34; 19:17–20; **1Th** 2:13
Rejection of the message
Heb 4:2 For we also have had the gospel preached to us, just as they did; but the message they heard was of no value to them, because those who heard did not combine it with faith.
See also **Ro** 10:16; **Ac** 13:50–51; 17:32; 18:6

---

evangelism, motivation
Evangelism arises from a natural response to the grace of God, a concern for those who have yet to hear the good news and a desire to be faithful to the great commission to bring the good news to the ends of the earth. Evangelism is guided and directed by the Holy Spirit.

Motives for evangelism
Recognising God's call
2Ti 1:11 And of this gospel I [Paul] was appointed a herald and an apostle and a teacher. *See also* **Isa** 6:8–9; **Jnh** 1:1–2; **Ac** 22:14–15; **2Co** 4:1; **1Ti** 2:7
A divine compulsion
1Co 9:16–17 Yet when I [Paul] preach the gospel, I cannot boast, for I am compelled to preach. Woe to me if I do not preach the gospel! . . . *See also* **Jer** 20:9; **Am** 3:8; **Ac** 4:20
A God-given responsibility
Eze 3:17–20 ". . . When I [the LORD] say to the wicked, 'You will surely die,' and you do not warn them or speak out to dissuade them from their evil ways in order to save their lives, those wicked people will die for their sins, and I will hold you accountable for their blood . . ."
See also **Eze** 33:7–9; **1Co** 3:10–15; **2Co** 5:10–11

A desire to win the lost
Ro 10:1 Brothers and sisters, my [Paul's] heart's desire and prayer to God for the Israelites is that they may be saved.
1Co 9:19–23 . . . To the weak I [Paul] became weak, to win the weak. I have become all things to all people so that by all possible means I might save some . . . *See also* **Ac** 20:19–20; **Ro** 1:14–15; 9:1–3; 11:14; 15:17–20; **2Co** 5:20
A recognition of coming judgment
Jude 23 snatch others from the fire and save them . . . *See also* **Jas** 5:20; **2Pe** 3:9
Responding to God's grace
2Co 5:14–15 For Christ's love compels us, because we are convinced that one died for all, and therefore all died . . . *See also* **2Co** 5:18–19; **Eph** 3:7; **1Ti** 1:12–16
Confidence in the gospel
Ro 1:16–17 I [Paul] am not ashamed of the gospel, because it is the power of God for the salvation of everyone who believes: first for the Jew, then for the Gentile . . . *See also* **Isa** 55:10–11; **1Co** 1:17–18; **2Co** 10:4–5; **2Ti** 1:8–9

God directs and guides evangelism
Divine guidance in evangelism
Ac 8:26–29 . . . The Spirit told Philip, "Go to that chariot and stay near it."
Ac 16:6–10 . . . After Paul had seen the vision, we got ready at once to leave for Macedonia, concluding that God had called us to preach the gospel to them. *See also* **Ac** 5:19–20; 9:10–11; 10:19–20; 11:12; 13:2; 18:9–11
God opens the door for evangelism
2Co 2:12 Now when I [Paul] went to Troas to preach the gospel of Christ and found that the Lord had opened a door for me, *See also* **Ac** 14:27; **1Co** 16:9; **Col** 4:3; **Rev** 3:8
Areas of ministry assigned by God
Gal 2:7–9 . . . For God, who was at work in the ministry of Peter as an apostle to the Jews, was also at work in my [Paul's] ministry as an apostle to the Gentiles . . . *See also* **Ac** 9:15

The Holy Spirit empowers evangelism
Ac 1:8 "But you will receive power when the

Holy Spirit comes on you; and you will be my [Jesus'] witnesses in Jerusalem, and in all Judea and Samaria, and to the ends of the earth." See also **Mt** 10:19–20 pp **Mk** 13:11 pp **Lk** 12:11–12; **Jn** 15:26–27; **1Th** 1:5

Evangelism as a result of persecution
Ac 8:4–5 Those who had been scattered preached the word wherever they went . . .
See also **Ac** 11:19–21; 13:50–51; 14:6–7; 18:2
See also *guidance; persecution; witnessing.*

---

evangelism, nature of

Evangelism focuses on the proclaiming of the good news of the coming of the kingdom of God in Christ, including the forgiveness of sins and the hope of eternal life, through the death and resurrection of Jesus Christ.

Evangelism as the proclamation of good news

Isa 52:7 How beautiful on the mountains are the feet of those who bring good news, who proclaim peace, who bring good tidings, who proclaim salvation, who say to Zion, "Your God reigns!"
Mk 16:15 He [Jesus] said to them [the disciples], "Go into all the world and preach the good news to all creation." See also **2Sa** 18:31; **2Ki** 7:9; **Isa** 40:9; 41:27; **Na** 1:15; **Ac** 14:7,15; **Ro** 10:15; 15:16; **1Ti** 2:7; **2Ti** 1:11

Jesus Christ as the focus of evangelism
The gospel message is revealed by God
Gal 1:11–12 . . . I [Paul] did not receive it [the gospel] from any human source, nor was I taught it; rather, I received it by revelation from Jesus Christ. See also **Ro** 16:25–26; **Gal** 1:15–16; **Eph** 3:3–6
The gospel message centres on Jesus Christ
Mk 1:1 The beginning of the gospel about Jesus Christ, the Son of God.
Eph 3:8 Although I [Paul] am less than the least of all God's people, this grace was given me: to preach to the Gentiles the unsearchable riches of Christ, See also **Lk** 1:19; 2:10; 3:16–18; **Ac** 11:20; **Ro** 1:9; **2Co** 4:4

The announcement of God's kingdom
Ac 28:31 Boldly and without hindrance he [Paul] preached the kingdom of God and taught about the Lord Jesus Christ. See also **Mt** 24:14; **Mk** 1:14–15; **Lk** 4:43; 8:1; 9:2; **Ac** 8:12
God's promises are fulfilled in Jesus Christ
Lk 4:18–19 "The Spirit of the Lord is on me [Jesus], because he has anointed me to preach good news to the poor. He has sent me to proclaim freedom for the prisoners and recovery of sight for the blind, to release the oppressed, to proclaim the year of the Lord's favour."
See also **Isa** 61:1–2; **Mt** 11:3–5 pp **Lk** 7:20–22; **Ac** 5:42; 8:35; 9:22; 13:32–33; **Ro** 1:2–4
Jesus Christ's death and resurrection
1Co 15:3–4 For what I [Paul] received I passed on to you as of first importance: that Christ died for our sins according to the Scriptures, that he was buried, that he was raised on the third day according to the Scriptures, See also **Ac** 2:22–24; 3:15; 17:18; **1Co** 15:14; 1:23; **2Ti** 2:8
The announcement of God's salvation
Ro 1:16–17 I [Paul] am not ashamed of the gospel, because it is the power of God for the salvation of everyone who believes: first for the Jew, then for the Gentile . . . See also **Ps** 40:10; 96:2–3 pp **1Ch** 16:23–24; **1Co** 1:21; 15:1–2; **Eph** 1:13; **2Th** 2:13–14
The call to repentance for the forgiveness of sins
Lk 24:47 "and repentance and forgiveness of sins will be preached in his [Jesus'] name to all nations, beginning at Jerusalem." See also **Mt** 4:17; 12:41 pp **Lk** 11:32; **Mk** 1:4 pp **Mt** 3:2 pp **Lk** 3:3; **Ac** 2:38
The announcement of peace with God
Ac 10:36 "You know the message God sent to the people of Israel, telling the good news of peace through Jesus Christ, who is Lord of all." See also **Eph** 2:17–18; 6:15

Evangelism and miracles
Mt 4:23 Jesus went throughout Galilee, teaching in their synagogues, preaching the good news of the kingdom, and healing every disease and sickness among the people.

1Co 2:4–5 My [Paul's] message and my preaching were not with wise and persuasive words, but with a demonstration of the Spirit's power, so that your faith might not rest on human wisdom, but on God's power. *See also* **Mt** 9:35; 10:7–8; **Lk** 9:6; 11:20; **Ro** 15:18–19; **1Th** 1:5; **Heb** 2:3–4 *See also church, purpose; forgiveness; peace; preaching.*

experience

The direct personal knowledge of people and situations which comes from a firsthand encounter with life. To experience God is to encounter and know him directly, rather than merely to know facts about him.

experience, of God

Scripture stresses the importance and also the possibility of a true experience of the living God. This is contrasted with the more academic knowledge about him. Experiential knowledge of God comes through personal encounter, through the witness of the Holy Spirit, through reflection on his past goodness and through the shared experiences of others.

Personal experience of God
Contrasted with academic knowledge
Job 42:5 "My [Job's] ears had heard of you [the LORD] but now my eyes have seen you." *See also* **Jer** 31:34; **Jn** 4:42; 5:39–40; **Jas** 2:19
Experience of God's blessing
Ps 34:8 Taste and see that the LORD is good; blessed are those who take refuge in him. *See also* **1Pe** 2:3; **Heb** 6:4–5
Experiencing God through Scripture **Mt** 22:29; **Jn** 5:39–40; **Ac** 17:11–12; **2Ti** 3:15–17
Knowing God through the Spirit
Ro 8:15–16 . . . The Spirit himself testifies with our spirit that we are God's children. *See also* **Jn** 14:16–17,26; 16:14–15; **1Co** 2:9–10; **Isa** 64:4
Examples of personal encounter with God
Dt 11:2–7 Remember today that your [the Israelites'] children were not the ones who saw and experienced the discipline of the LORD your

God: his majesty, his mighty hand, his outstretched arm . . . But it was your own eyes that saw all these great things the LORD has done. *See also* **Dt** 5:3–4; **Ge** 32:30; **Ex** 3:3–4; **Isa** 6:1; **Ac** 9:3–6; **2Co** 12:2–4; **Rev** 1:17

Sharing experience of God
Experience of God through his people
Zec 8:23 This is what the LORD Almighty says: "In those days ten people from all languages and nations will take firm hold of one Jew by the hem of his robe and say, 'Let us go with you, because we have heard that God is with you.'" *See also* **Isa** 45:14; **1Co** 14:24–25
Leaders with experience of God
Jos 24:31 Israel served the LORD throughout the lifetime of Joshua and of the elders who outlived him and who had experienced everything the LORD had done for Israel. *See also* **Nu** 12:8; **Jdg** 6:22; **Ac** 1:21–22; **1Co** 15:3–7; **2Pe** 1:16–18
Speaking to future generations
Dt 4:9–10 Only be careful, and watch yourselves closely so that you [the Israelites] do not forget the things your eyes have seen or let them slip from your heart as long as you live. Teach them to your children and to their children after them . . . *See also* **Ex** 10:2; **Dt** 6:20–21; **Job** 8:8–9; **Ps** 71:18
Speaking from personal experience: OT
Dt 7:18–19 . . . You [the Israelites] saw with your own eyes the great trials, the miraculous signs and wonders, the mighty hand and outstretched arm, with which the LORD your God brought you out. The LORD your God will do the same to all the peoples you now fear. *See also* **1Sa** 17:34–37
The exiles' confidence is based upon God's deliverance in the past: **Isa** 43:14–17; 51:9–11
Jer 16:14–15
Speaking from personal experience: NT
Jn 3:11 "I [Jesus] tell you [Nicodemus] the truth, we speak of what we know, and we testify to what we have seen, but still you people do not accept our testimony." *See also* **Jn** 20:18; **Ac** 4:13; **1Jn** 1:1–3
Jn 9:25 He [the man born blind] replied, "Whether he is a sinner or not, I don't know.

One thing I do know. I was blind but now I see!"   *See also* **Mk** 5:19–20 pp Lk 8:39; **Jn** 4:28–29

Confidence based on past experience
Mt 16:9–10 pp Mk 8:18–20; **2Ti** 4:17–18
See also eternal life, experience; grace; knowing God; peace, experience; witnessing; importance.

experience, of life
Experience of life comes with increasing age and through observation, reflection and the application of lessons learned. Experience in a craft or profession comes through training and practice.

Experience associated with advancing years
Job 12:12 "Is not wisdom found among the aged? Does not long life bring understanding?"   *See also* **Job** 32:6–7; **1Ki** 12:6–7 pp 2Ch 10:6–7; **Ps** 37:25; **Pr** 4:1–4

Dissatisfaction with life's experiences
Ecc 2:11 Yet when I surveyed all that my hands had done and what I had toiled to achieve, everything was meaningless, a chasing after the wind; nothing was gained under the sun.
See also **Ecc** 1:13–17; 2:1–8; 3:11
Ecc 2:24–26 People can do nothing better than to eat and drink and find satisfaction in their work. This too, I see, is from the hand of God . . .   *See also* **Ecc** 3:12–14; 12:13–14

Learning from life's experiences
Pr 24:32 I applied my heart to what I observed and learned a lesson from what I saw:
See also **Job** 4:8–9; 5:3; **Ps** 107:43
Sympathy resulting from personal experience
Ex 23:9 "Do not oppress an alien; you yourselves know how it feels to be aliens, because you were aliens in Egypt."   *See also* **Ex** 22:21; **Dt** 15:12–15; **2Co** 1:3–4; **Heb** 10:32–34
Growing through experiences
Ro 5:3–4 Not only so, but we also rejoice in our sufferings, because we know that suffering produces perseverance; perseverance, character; and character, hope.   *See also* **Heb** 5:8; **Jas** 1:2–4

Learning from everyday experiences
Mt 24:32 "Now learn this lesson from the fig-tree: As soon as its twigs get tender and its leaves come out, you know that summer is near." pp Mk 13:28   *See also* **Mt** 16:2–3; **Lk** 12:54–55; **Mt** 6:28–31 pp Lk 12:27–29

Jesus Christ shared human experience
Heb 4:15 For we do not have a high priest who is unable to sympathise with our weaknesses, but we have one who has been tempted in every way, just as we are—yet was without sin.
See also **Heb** 2:17–18; **Php** 2:8; **Heb** 2:9

Experience in a craft or profession
Skilled workers
2Ch 2:7 "Send me [Solomon], therefore, a man skilled to work in gold and silver, bronze and iron, and in purple, crimson and blue yarn, and experienced in the art of engraving, to work in Judah and Jerusalem with my skilled workers, whom my father David provided."   *See also* **2Ch** 2:13–14; **1Ki** 7:13–14; **Ex** 36:1–2; **1Ch** 22:15–16
Experienced soldiers
2Ch 17:12–13 . . . [Jehoshaphat] had large supplies in the towns of Judah. He also kept experienced fighting men in Jerusalem.   *See also* **1Sa** 17:33; **2Sa** 17:8; **1Ch** 12:33; **SS** 3:7–8
Other competent people 1Sa 12:2; **Est** 1:13; **Mt** 2:4; **Ac** 18:2–3   *See also joy, experience; life, believers' experience; understanding.*

faith
A constant outlook of trust towards God, whereby human beings abandon all reliance on their own efforts and put their full confidence in him, his word and his promises.

faith, and blessings
Confidence in the ability and willingness of God to act in supernatural power to advance his kingdom, and a commitment, expressed in prayer and action, to being the means by which he does so.

God's power is released through faith
Mt 17:20 He [Jesus] replied, "Because you

have so little faith. I tell you the truth, if you have faith as small as a mustard seed, you can say to this mountain, 'Move from here to there' and it will move. Nothing will be impossible for you." *See also* **Mk** 9:23; **Lk** 17:6

Praying in faith
Mt 21:21–22 Jesus replied, "I tell you the truth, if you have faith and do not doubt, not only can you do what was done to the fig-tree, but also you can say to this mountain, 'Go, throw yourself into the sea,' and it will be done. If you believe, you will receive whatever you ask for in prayer." pp Mk 11:22–24   *See also* **Jas** 1:5–7; 5:14–15

Praying in Jesus Christ's name
Jn 14:12–14 "I [Jesus] tell you the truth, all who have faith in me will do what I have been doing and they will do even greater things than these, because I am going to the Father. And I will do whatever you ask in my name, so that the Son may bring glory to the Father. You may ask me for anything in my name, and I will do it."

In the OT, faith in God's power
Heb 11:32–34 . . . who through faith conquered kingdoms, administered justice, and gained what was promised; who shut the mouths of lions, quenched the fury of the flames, and escaped the edge of the sword; whose weakness was turned to strength; and who became powerful in battle and routed foreign armies.   *See also* **Heb** 11:11–12; **Jos** 14:6–14; **1Sa** 14:6; 17:32–47; **2Ch** 20:20; 32:7–8; **Da** 6:23

In the NT, healing in response to faith
Mt 9:22 Jesus turned and saw her [the woman with a severe haemorrhage]. "Take heart, daughter," he said, "your faith has healed you." And the woman was healed from that moment. pp Mk 5:34 pp Lk 8:48   *See also* **Mt** 9:29–30; **Mk** 10:52 pp Lk 18:42; **Lk** 17:19; **Ac** 3:16; 14:8–10

Powerful ministries marked by faith
Ac 11:24 He [Barnabas] was a good man, full of the Holy Spirit and faith, and a great number of people were brought to the Lord.   *See also* **Ac** 6:5–10; **1Co** 12:9

Faith and spiritual warfare
Eph 6:16 In addition to all this, take up the shield of faith, with which you can extinguish all the flaming arrows of the evil one.   *See also* **1Th** 5:8; **1Jn** 5:4–5

The importance of love accompanying faith
1Co 13:2 . . . if I have a faith that can move mountains, but have not love, I am nothing.
See also commitment; prayer, and faith; spiritual warfare.

---

faith, and salvation

Both in the OT and in the NT faith is the only basis of salvation. Faith is the means by which God's grace in Christ, and with him the blessings of salvation, are received. Paul's doctrine of justification by faith emphasises the centrality of faith in the Christian life.

Salvation by faith in the OT
Hab 2:4 ". . . the righteous will live by their faith – "

The faith of Abraham and other individuals
Ge 15:6 Abram believed the LORD, and he credited it to him as righteousness.   *See also* **Ro** 4:9–16; **Heb** 11:4–5,7

Salvation by faith in the NT
Ro 1:16–17 . . . in the gospel a righteousness from God is revealed, a righteousness that is by faith from first to last, just as it is written: "The righteous will live by faith."   *See also* **1Co** 1:21; **Php** 3:8–9

Salvation through faith alone
Eph 2:8–9 For it is by grace you have been saved, through faith—and this not from yourselves, it is the gift of God—not by works, so that no-one can boast.   *See also* **Ro** 3:27–28; 4:1–8; **Ps** 32:1–2; **Ro** 9:30–32; **Gal** 3:10–14; **Dt** 27:26

Salvation is by faith in Jesus Christ
Jn 3:14–16 "Just as Moses lifted up the snake in the desert, so the Son of Man must be lifted

up, that everyone who believes in him may have eternal life. For God so loved the world that he gave his one and only Son, that whoever believes in him shall not perish but have eternal life."
Ro 10:9–10 . . . if you confess with your mouth, "Jesus is Lord," and believe in your heart that God raised him from the dead, you will be saved . . .   *See also* **Jn** 8:24; **Ac** 8:37 fn; 13:38–39; **Ro** 3:21–26; 4:24; **2Co** 4:13–14; **Gal** 3:22

Salvation is for all who believe
Ro 10:4 Christ is the end of the law so that there may be righteousness for everyone who believes.   *See also* **Ac** 15:7–9; **Ro** 3:29–30

Salvation is for those who persevere in their faith
Col 1:21–23 . . . if you continue in your faith, established and firm, not moved from the hope held out in the gospel . . .   *See also* **Heb** 3:14; 6:11–12

Saving faith shows itself in action
Jas 2:14 What good is it, my brothers and sisters, if people claim to have faith but have no deeds? Can such faith save them?

Blessings of salvation received through faith
Justification and peace with God Ro 5:1–2; **Gal** 2:15–16; 5:5
Forgiveness Lk 7:48–50; **Ac** 10:43
Adoption into God's family Jn 1:12; **Gal** 3:26
The gift of the Holy Spirit Jn 7:38–39; **Gal** 3:2; **Eph** 1:13
Jesus Christ in the heart Eph 3:17
Protection through God's power 1Pe 1:5
Access to God Eph 3:12; **Heb** 10:22
Sanctification Ac 26:17–18
New life Gal 2:20
Eternal life Jn 3:16,36; 5:24; 6:40,47
Victory over death Jn 11:25–27   *See also conversion; eternal life; forgiveness; sanctification.*

faith, growth in
Christians are called to have a growing faith, built up by prayer and the encouragement of others, and also through testing.

Examples of growing faith
2Th 1:3 We [Paul, Silas and Timothy] ought always to thank God for you [the Christians at Thessalonica], brothers and sisters, and rightly so, because your faith is growing more and more, and the love every one of you has for each other is increasing.   *See also* **Ac** 16:5; **2Co** 10:15; **Rev** 2:19

Weak faith
Weak faith rebuked
Mt 6:28–30 "And why do you worry about clothes? See how the lilies of the field grow. They do not labour or spin . . . If that is how God clothes the grass of the field, which is here today and tomorrow is thrown into the fire, will he not much more clothe you, O you of little faith?" pp Lk 12:27–28   *See also* **Mt** 8:26 pp Mk 4:40 pp Lk 8:25; **Mt** 14:31; 16:8; 17:20
Other examples of weak faith Jn 12:42–43; 19:38; **Ro** 14:1–23; **1Co** 8:1–13

Strong faith
Strong faith commended and encouraged
Heb 10:22 let us draw near to God with a sincere heart in full assurance of faith, having our hearts sprinkled to cleanse us from a guilty conscience and having our bodies washed with pure water.   *See also* **Mt** 8:10 pp Lk 7:9; **Mt** 9:20–22 pp Mk 5:25–34 pp Lk 8:43–48; **Mt** 15:28 pp Mk 7:29
The faith of OT leaders 1Ki 18:3; **2Ki** 18:5 pp 2Ch 31:20

The faith of Christian leaders
1Ti 4:12 Don't let anyone look down on you [Timothy] because you are young, but set an example for the believers in speech, in life, in love, in faith and in purity.
Heb 13:7 Remember your leaders, who spoke the word of God to you. Consider the outcome of their way of life and imitate their faith.
See also **Ac** 6:5; 11:24; **2Ti** 3:10
Paul's encouragements to Timothy: **1Ti** 6:11; **2Ti** 2:22
Other examples of strong faith
Hab 3:17–18 Though the fig-tree does not bud and there are no grapes on the vines, though the olive crop fails and the fields produce no food,

though there are no sheep in the pen and no cattle in the stalls, yet I [Habakkuk] will rejoice in the LORD, I will be joyful in God my Saviour. *See also* **Job** 13:15; 19:25–27; **Mt** 14:35–36 pp **Mk** 6:56; **2Co** 8:7; **Col** 2:5–7

The growth of faith
Praying for more faith
Lk 17:5 The apostles said to the Lord, "Increase our faith!" *See also* **Mk** 9:24
The encouragement of others
2Ch 32:7–8 "Be strong and courageous. Do not be afraid or discouraged because of the king of Assyria and the vast army with him, for there is a greater power with us than with him. With him is only the arm of flesh, but with us is the LORD our God to help us and to fight our battles." And the people gained confidence from what Hezekiah the king of Judah said.
1Th 3:10 Night and day we [Paul, Silas and Timothy] pray most earnestly that we may see you [the Christians in Thessalonica] again and supply what is lacking in your faith. *See also* **Nu** 14:6–9; **1k** 22:32; **Ac** 14:22; **Ro** 1:11–12; **1Th** 3:2–3; **Jude** 20
Faith strengthened through testing
Ro 4:18–21 . . . Without weakening in his faith, he [Abraham] faced the fact that his body was as good as dead—since he was about a hundred years old—and that Sarah's womb was also dead. Yet he did not waver through unbelief regarding the promise of God, but was strengthened in his faith and gave glory to God . . . *See also* **Ge** 15:5; **Jas** 1:2–4; **1Pe** 1:6–7 *See also faithfulness; perseverance; prayer, for others; spiritual growth; suffering, encouragements in.*

---

faith, nature of
Confidence in and commitment to God and Jesus Christ. These attitudes remain sure even though the objects of faith are unseen. True faith is seen in obedient action, love and continuing good works.

The object of faith
God as the object of faith
Heb 11:6 And without faith it is impossible to

please God, because anyone who comes to him must believe that he exists and that he rewards those who earnestly seek him. *See also* **Ps** 25:1–2; 26:1; **Pr** 29:25; **1Pe** 1:21
Jesus Christ as the object of faith
Jn 14:1 "Do not let your [the disciples'] hearts be troubled. Trust in God; trust also in me [Jesus]." *See also* **Jn** 3:16,18,36; 6:68–69
False objects of faith
Human resources: **Ps** 20:7; **Hos** 10:13
Ps 118:9; **Pr** 28:26; **Isa** 42:17

Faith is personal trust in God
2Sa 22:31 "As for God, his way is perfect; the word of the LORD is flawless. He is a shield for all who take refuge in him." *See also* **Ps** 18:2–6; 27:13–14; **1Pe** 2:23
True faith cannot be second-hand
2Ti 1:5 I [Paul] have been reminded of your [Timothy's] sincere faith, which first lived in your grandmother Lois and in your mother Eunice and, I am persuaded, now lives in you also. *See also* **Jn** 4:42

Faith and assurance
Assurance accompanies faith
Heb 11:1 Now faith is being sure of what we hope for and certain of what we do not see. *See also* **Ro** 4:19–21; **1Ti** 3:13; **Heb** 10:22
Faith may be mixed with doubt Mt 14:31; **Mk** 9:24; **Jn** 20:24–28

Faith and sight
2Co 5:7 We live by faith, not by sight.
Faith as trust in what is unseen
Jn 20:29 Then Jesus told him [Thomas], "Because you have seen me, you have believed; blessed are those who have not seen and yet have believed." *See also* **2Co** 4:18; **Heb** 11:1–3,7,27
Faith looks towards an unseen future
Heb 11:13–14 All these people [Abel, Enoch, Noah, Abraham] were still living by faith when they died. They did not receive the things promised; they only saw them and welcomed them from a distance. And they admitted that they were aliens and strangers on earth. People

who say such things show that they are looking for a country of their own.   *See also* **Heb** 11:8–10,20–22,24–26

Faith and obedience
True faith is demonstrated in obedience
Ro 1:5 Through him and for his name's sake, we received grace and apostleship to call people from among all the Gentiles to the obedience that comes from faith.

Heb 4:2 For we also have had the gospel preached to us, just as they did; but the message they heard was of no value to them, because those who heard did not combine it with faith. *See also* **Ro** 16:26; **2Co** 9:13; **1Pe** 1:2

Examples of obedient faith
Noah builds the ark: **Ge** 6:22; **Heb** 11:7

Abraham leaves Haran: **Ge** 12:4; **Heb** 11:8

Abraham offers Isaac: **Ge** 22:1–10; **Heb** 11:17

Ex 14:15–16

Caleb and Joshua: **Nu** 13:30; 14:8–9

Jos 3:5–13

Joshua at Jericho; **Jos** 6:2–5; **Heb** 11:30

Jn 21:4–6; **Ac** 26:19

Faith and works
True faith is demonstrated in good deeds
Jas 2:14–26 . . . faith by itself, if it is not accompanied by action, is dead. But someone will say, "You have faith; I have deeds." Show me your faith without deeds, and I will show you my faith by what I do . . . *See also* **Php** 2:17; **1Th** 1:3; **Tit** 1:1; **2Pe** 1:5

True faith issues in love
Gal 5:6 For in Christ Jesus neither circumcision nor uncircumcision has any value. The only thing that counts is faith expressing itself through love. *See also* **Eph** 1:15; 6:23; **1Th** 3:6; 5:8; **1Ti** 1:5,14; 4:12

True faith is constantly productive
Lk 8:15 "But the seed on good soil stands for those with a noble and good heart, who hear the word, retain it, and by persevering produce a crop." pp **Mt** 13:23 pp **Mk** 4:20 *See also* **Jn** 15:1–5 *See also commitment; doubt, nature of; good works; hope; life, of faith; love; obedience, to God.*

faith, necessity
A fundamental duty for all people and the necessary response to God's self-revelation. The only channel through which God's blessings may be received, and the only means by which life may be made meaningful, in relationship with God.

The call to faith
In the OT
Ps 37:3–5 Trust in the Lord and do good; dwell in the land and enjoy safe pasture. Delight yourself in the Lord and he will give you the desires of your heart. Commit your way to the Lord; trust in him and he will do this: *See also* **Pr** 3:5–6; **Isa** 26:4; 50:10
In the NT
Jn 6:28–29 . . . Jesus answered, "The work of God is this: to believe in the one he has sent." *See also* **Mk** 1:15; **Ac** 16:30–31; 19:4; 20:21; **Ro** 1:5; **1Jn** 3:23

God's self-revelation leaves no excuse for unbelief
Jn 14:8–11 . . . Jesus answered: "Don't you know me, Philip, even after I have been among you such a long time? Anyone who has seen me has seen the Father. How can you say, 'Show us the Father'? . . ."

Ro 10:17–18 Consequently, faith comes from hearing the message, and the message is heard through the word of Christ. But I ask: Did they not hear? Of course they did: "Their voice has gone out into all the earth, their words to the ends of the world." *See also* **Ps** 19:4; **Jn** 1:10–12; **Ro** 1:18–21; 3:1–4; **Ps** 51:4; **Ro** 16:25–27

The need for faith in God
The Lord is the only true God
Hab 2:18–20 "Of what value is an idol, since someone has carved it? Or an image that teaches lies? For those who make them trust in their own creations; they make idols that cannot speak . . . But the Lord is in his holy temple; let all the

earth be silent before him." *See also* **Ps** 115:2–11

God alone can be trusted absolutely
Ps 9:10 Those who know your name will trust in you, for you, LORD, have never forsaken those who seek you. *See also* **Ps** 91:1–4; **Isa** 12:2; **Na** 1:7

Faith in God is the basis for peace
Isa 26:3 You will keep in perfect peace those whose minds are steadfast, because they trust in you. *See also* **Ps** 42:11; **Jn** 14:1; **Ro** 15:13; **2Pe** 1:1–2

Faith is necessary to receive God's blessing
Heb 11:6 And without faith it is impossible to please God, because anyone who comes to him must believe that he exists and that he rewards those who earnestly seek him. *See also* **Ps** 40:4; **Jer** 17:7–8; **Jn** 5:24

Faith is necessary to avoid God's judgment
Jn 3:36 "Those who believe in the Son have eternal life, but those who reject the Son will not see life, for God's wrath remains on them."
See also **Jn** 3:18; **2Th** 2:12; **1Pe** 2:6–8; **Isa** 28:16; **Ps** 118:22; **Isa** 8:14

Actions not springing from faith are sinful
Ro 14:23 . . . and everything that does not come from faith is sin. *See also* **Ro** 14:5–8,14

Unbelief challenged
Heb 3:12–18; **Ps** 95:7–8; **Isa** 7:9; **Jer** 17:5–6; **Mk** 16:14 *See also eternal life; repentance.*

faith, testing of

The means through which the genuineness of faith is proved and Christian character developed. God promises to help his people during times of testing.

God allows faith to be tested
Testing proves the genuineness of faith
1Pe 1:6–7 In this you greatly rejoice, though now for a little while you may have had to suffer grief in all kinds of trials. These have come so that your faith—of greater worth than gold,

which perishes even though refined by fire—may be proved genuine and may result in praise, glory and honour when Jesus Christ is revealed. *See also* **Mt** 13:20–21 pp **Mk** 4:16–17 pp **Lk** 8:13

Testing develops Christian character
Jas 1:2–4 Consider it pure joy, my brothers and sisters, whenever you face trials of many kinds, because you know that the testing of your faith develops perseverance. Perseverance must finish its work so that you may be mature and complete, not lacking anything. *See also* **Ro** 5:3–4

Testing purifies God's people
Isa 48:10 "See, I [the LORD] have refined you, though not as silver; I have tested you in the furnace of affliction." *See also* **Ps** 66:10–12; **Jer** 9:7; **Zec** 13:9; **Mal** 3:2–3; **1Pe** 4:17

Examples of God testing faith
Abraham is told to sacrifice Isaac: **Ge** 22:1–2; **Heb** 11:17–19
Dt 8:2–5; **Jdg** 7:1–8; **Mt** 15:21–28 pp **Mk** 7:24–30; **Jn** 11:1–6

Means by which faith is tested
God allows Satan to test faith
Job 2:7 So Satan went out from the presence of the LORD and afflicted Job with painful sores from the soles of his feet to the top of his head. *See also* **Lk** 22:31; **1Th** 3:4–5; **Rev** 2:10
Difficult circumstances test faith **1Ki** 17:17–18; **2Ki** 4:1,27–28; **Ac** 14:22; **2Co** 11:25–27
Persecution tests faith **Da** 6:10–12; **Ac** 8:1–4; **Heb** 11:35–38
Discouraging people test faith **2Ki** 18:19–25 pp 2Ch 32:10–15 pp Isa 36:4–10; **Mk** 5:35–36 pp Lk 8:49–50; **Mk** 5:40 pp Mt 9:24 pp Lk 8:53

God's promise of help during testing
Isa 43:2 "When you pass through the waters, I [the LORD] will be with you; and when you pass through the rivers, they will not sweep over you. When you walk through the fire, you will not be burned; the flames will not set you ablaze."
Lk 22:32 ". . . I [Jesus] have prayed for you, Simon, that your faith may not fail. And when you have turned back, strengthen your brothers." *See also* **Ps** 91:14–15; **1Co** 10:13; **2Co** 12:7–9; **1Pe** 5:10; **2Pe** 2:9

God's help through the encouragement of others
1Th 3:2–3 We [Paul and Silas] sent Timothy, who is our brother and God's fellow-worker in spreading the gospel of Christ, to strengthen and encourage you in your faith . . .   *See also* **2Co** 7:5–7

The response to trials
Rejoicing at sharing Jesus Christ's suffering
1Pe 4:12–13
Praying for God's help Heb 4:14–16; **1Pe** 4:19
Persevering
Jas 1:12 Blessed are those who persevere under trial, because when they have stood the test, they will receive the crown of life that God has promised to those who love him.   *See also* **2Th** 1:4; **Heb** 12:1–3; **Jas** 5:11; **Rev** 2:3,19

Examples of faith victorious through testing
Ge 22:9–12; **2Ki** 6:15–17; **Job** 1:22; **Da** 3:16–27; **Ac** 5:27–29; 7:59–60; **2Co** 4:7–9   *See also persecution; prayer, asking God; suffering, of believers; temptation.*

---

faithfulness

Commitment to a relationship with God or fellow human beings; seen in that loyalty, devotion and service which is a reflection of God's own faithfulness.

---

faithfulness, relationships

Loyalty and commitment within human relationships is important in the life of God's people. It is seen particularly in fidelity within marriage, fulfilling family obligations, honouring vows, dutiful service and trustworthy speech and conduct.

Faithfulness within society
It is important in the life of God's people
Hos 12:6 But you must return to your God; maintain love and justice, and wait for your God always.   *See also* **Mic** 6:8; **Mt** 23:23 pp Lk 11:42

It is a reflection of God's faithfulness to his people
Ps 89:14 Righteousness and justice are the foundation of your [the LORD's] throne; love and faithfulness go before you.   *See also* **Dt** 32:4; **Isa** 11:4–5

Faithfulness in marriage
Heb 13:4 Marriage should be honoured by all, and the marriage bed kept pure, for God will judge the adulterer and all the sexually immoral.   *See also* **Mal** 2:11,14–15; **Mt** 5:27–28; **Ex** 20:14; **Eph** 5:33; **1Ti** 5:9

Faithfulness in family relationships
1Ti 5:4 But if a widow has children or grandchildren, these should learn first of all to put their religion into practice by caring for their own family and so repaying their parents and grandparents, for this is pleasing to God.
1Ti 5:8 Anyone who does not provide for relatives, and especially for immediate family members, has denied the faith and is worse than an unbeliever.   *See also* **Ge** 24:47–51; 47:28–31
Ruth's faithfulness to Naomi: **Ru** 1:16–18; 2:11–12
1Sa 2:19
The wife of noble character provides for her family: **Pr** 31:15,21,27–28
Jn 19:25–27

Faithfulness to vows and covenants
Nu 30:2 "When a man makes a vow to the LORD or takes an oath to bind himself by a pledge, he must not break his word but must do everything he said."
Jacob and Laban: **Ge** 29:18,30
The sons of Israel and Joseph: **Ge** 50:25; **Ex** 13:19
The Israelites and Rahab: **Jos** 2:14; 6:25
Jos 9:15–20
David and Jonathan: **1Sa** 18:3; 20:8,42; 23:16
1Ki 20:34

Faithfulness in speech
In carrying messages
Pr 13:17 A wicked messenger falls into trouble, but a trustworthy envoy brings healing.   *See also* **Pr** 25:13

In telling the truth Pr 12:17; 14:5
In bringing God's word
Jer 23:28 "Let the prophets who have dreams tell their dreams, but let the one who has my word speak it faithfully. For what has straw to do with grain?" declares the LORD. *See also* **2Co** 2:17; 4:2; **2Ti** 2:15

Faithfulness in conduct
In serving others
3Jn 5 Dear friend, you are faithful in what you are doing for the believers, even though they are strangers to you. *See also* **Ro** 16:1–2; **Gal** 6:10; **1Pe** 4:10
In intercession Ro 1:9–10; **Eph** 6:18; **Col** 4:2–4
In giving
2Co 8:7–11 But just as you excel in everything—in faith, in speech, in knowledge, in complete earnestness and in your love for us—see that you also excel in this grace of giving . . . *See also* **2Ch** 31:5–10; **Php** 4:15–18
In handling money
2Ki 12:13–15 The money brought into the temple . . . was paid to the workers, who used it to repair the temple. They did not require an accounting from those to whom they gave the money to pay the workers, because they acted with complete honesty. *See also* **2Ki** 22:7; **2Ch** 31:12–15; **Mt** 25:21; **Lk** 16:10; 19:17

The rarity of true faithfulness
Pr 20:6 Many claim to have unfailing love, but a faithful person who can find? *See also* **Ps** 12:1–2; **Isa** 57:1; **Jer** 17:9 *See also commitment, to God's people; giving.*

faithfulness, to God

The proper response to God by his covenant people; seen in a steadfast commitment which reflects God's own faithfulness to the covenant. Encouraged in all believers, it is especially important in leaders.

Faithfulness is the proper response to God by his covenant people
God's covenant with his people requires faithfulness
1Ki 2:3–4 ". . . observe what the LORD your God requires: Walk in his ways, and keep his decrees and commands, his laws and requirements, as written in the Law of Moses, so that you may prosper in all you do and wherever you go, and that the LORD may keep his promise to me [Solomon]: 'If your descendants watch how they live, and if they walk faithfully before me with all their heart and soul, you will never fail to have a successor on the throne of Israel.'" *See also* **Ex** 19:5; **Dt** 5:32–33; 10:12–13; 29:9; **Isa** 1:26

Faithfulness to God seen as marital fidelity
Hos 2:20 "I [the LORD] will betroth you [Israel] in faithfulness, and you will acknowledge the LORD." *See also* **Isa** 54:5; **Jer** 2:2; **Eze** 16:8; **Eph** 1:1; 5:22–25
Faithfulness to God reflects God's faithfulness
Dt 7:9 Know therefore that the LORD your God is God; he is the faithful God, keeping his covenant of love to a thousand generations of those who love him and keep his commands. *See also* **1Sa** 2:35; **1Co** 10:12–13; **Heb** 4:14–16; 10:23; **1Pe** 4:19

Faithfulness is seen as steadfast commitment to God
In unwavering devotion
Mic 4:5 All the nations may walk in the name of their gods; we will walk in the name of the LORD our God for ever and ever. *See also* **Jos** 24:14–15; **Lk** 9:62; **Rev** 2:10
In obedience Dt 11:13; **Eze** 18:9
In service 1Sa 12:24; **2Ch** 19:9; 34:10–12 pp 2Ki 22:4–7; **Eze** 44:15; 48:11; **1Ti** 1:12
In giving 2Ch 31:12; **2Co** 8:1–5
In prayer Ro 12:12; **1Th** 5:17
In patient endurance 2Ti 2:11–13; **Heb** 10:36; **Rev** 13:10; 14:12
In fulfilling vows Nu 30:2; **Dt** 23:21–23; **Ps** 22:25; 61:8; **Ecc** 5:4; **Jnh** 2:9

Faithfulness is especially important in leaders
1Co 4:1–2 So then, you ought to regard us [the apostles] as servants of Christ and as those entrusted with the secret things of God. Now it is

required that those who have been given a trust must prove faithful.

3Jn 3 It gave me [John] great joy to have some believers come and tell about your faithfulness to the truth and how you continue to walk in the truth.   *See also* **Ex** 18:21; **1Ti** 4:13–16; 6:20; **2Ti** 1:13–14; 2:2,15; 4:1–2

Encouragements to faithfulness
The call to faithfulness
1Co 15:58 Therefore, my dear brothers and sisters, stand firm. Let nothing move you. Always give yourselves fully to the work of the Lord, because you know that your labour in the Lord is not in vain.   *See also* **Pr** 3:5–6; **Isa** 26:4; **Jn** 14:1; **1Co** 16:13; **Gal** 5:1; **Eph** 6:13
God watches over the faithful
Ps 97:10 Let those who love the LORD hate evil, for he guards the lives of his faithful ones and delivers them from the hand of the wicked.   *See also* **Ps** 31:23; 37:28; 86:2; **Pr** 2:8
God rewards faithfulness
1Sa 26:23 "The LORD rewards everyone for their righteousness and faithfulness . . ."
Mt 25:21 "His master replied, 'Well done, good and faithful servant! You have been faithful with a few things; I will put you in charge of many things. Come and share your master's happiness!'"   pp **Lk** 19:17   *See also* **Ps** 101:6; **Pr** 28:20; **Mt** 24:45–47 pp **Lk** 12:42–44; **2Ti** 4:6–8; **Rev** 17:14; 20:4

Lack of faithfulness
Hos 4:1 Hear the word of the LORD, you Israelites, because the LORD has a charge to bring against you who live in the land: "There is no faithfulness, no love, no acknowledgment of God in the land."   *See also* **Ps** 12:1; 78:8,37; **Hos** 1:2; 5:7; 9:1   *See also commitment, to God; discipleship; obedience; perseverance.*

---

fasting
Abstaining from food, and possibly drink, for a limited period of time as a mark of religious commitment and devotion or as an expression of repentance for sins.

---

fasting, nature of
Scripture frequently refers to individuals fasting and describes the different kinds of fast which may be undertaken.

Kinds of fasting
Abstaining from food and drink
Ezr 10:6 Then Ezra withdrew from before the house of God . . . he ate no food and drank no water, because he continued to mourn over the unfaithfulness of the exiles.   *See also* **Da** 9:3; **Ac** 23:12
Abstaining from food only
1Sa 1:7 . . . Whenever Hannah went up to the house of the LORD, her rival provoked her till she wept and would not eat.   *See also* **Da** 6:18

The duration of fasting
One day: the normal fast period Lev 23:32; **Jdg** 20:26; **2Sa** 1:12
Three days Est 4:16; **Ac** 9:9
Seven days 1Sa 31:13 pp **1Ch** 10:12; **2Sa** 12:16–20
Forty days
These 40–day fasts are all in unique circumstances and are not prescribed: **Ex** 34:28; **1Ki** 19:8; **Mt** 4:2 pp **Lk** 4:2

Regular observances of fasting
Those prescribed by the Law
Lev 16:29–31 ". . . On the tenth day of the seventh month you must deny yourselves and not do any work—whether native-born or an alien living among you—because on this day atonement will be made for you, to cleanse you. Then, before the LORD, you will be clean from all your sins. It is a sabbath of rest, and you must deny yourselves; it is a lasting ordinance."   *NIV footnote at verse 29.*   *See also* **Lev** 23:26–32; **Nu** 29:7; **Ac** 27:9fn
Those observed in Jewish tradition
Zec 8:19 This is what the LORD Almighty says: "The fasts of the fourth, fifth, seventh and tenth months will become joyful and glad occasions and happy festivals for Judah. Therefore love truth and peace."   *See also* **Est** 9:30–31; **Zec** 7:2–5
Those observed by the Pharisees Lk 18:11–12

Involuntary fasts
Those imposed by decree
2Ch 20:3 Alarmed, Jehoshaphat resolved to enquire of the LORD, and he proclaimed a fast for all Judah.   *See also* 1Sa 14:24
A special instance of an individual instructed by God to fast: **1Ki** 13:8–9,16
1Ki 21:9; **Jer** 36:9
Those imposed by circumstances Ac 27:33; **2Co** 6:5; 11:27

Voluntary fasts
Ne 1:4 When I [Nehemiah] heard these things, I sat down and wept. For some days I mourned and fasted and prayed before the God of heaven.   *See also* **Lk** 2:37   *See also self-denial.*

fasting, practice
Although fasting is a negative practice, it is not an end in itself but is to be undertaken for a positive purpose.

Fasting is not an end in itself
Fasting as empty ritual is condemned
Jer 14:11–12 Then the LORD said to me, "Do not pray for the well-being of this people. Although they fast, I will not listen to their cry; though they offer burnt offerings and grain offerings, I will not accept them. Instead, I will destroy them with the sword, famine and plague."   *See also* **Isa** 58:1–7; **Zec** 7:4–7
Fasting as mere show is condemned
Mt 6:16–18 "When you fast, do not look sombre as the hypocrites do, for they disfigure their faces to show others they are fasting . . . But when you fast, put oil on your head and wash your face, so that it will not be obvious to others that you are fasting, but only to your Father . . ."   *See also* **Mt** 9:14–15 pp **Mk** 2:18–20 pp **Lk** 5:33–35
Fasting imposed for false motives 1Sa 14:24–30

Attitudes appropriate to fasting
Humility
Ps 35:13 Yet when they were ill, I put on sackcloth and humbled myself with fasting . . .
See also **1Ki** 21:27–29; **Ezr** 8:21; **Ps** 69:10

Repentance
1Sa 7:6 . . . On that day they [Israel] fasted and there they confessed, "We have sinned against the LORD." . . .   *See also* **Ne** 9:1–3; **Joel** 1:13–14; 2:12–15

Fasting and prayer
Ne 1:4 When I [Nehemiah] heard these things, I sat down and wept. For some days I mourned and fasted and prayed before the God of heaven.   *See also* **Ezr** 8:21–23; **Ps** 35:13; **Da** 9:3; **Mt** 17:20 fn pp **Mk** 9:29 fn; **Lk** 2:37; 5:33; **Ac** 13:3; 14:23; **1Co** 7:3–5

Fasting and worship
Ac 13:2 While they [church leaders at Antioch] were worshipping the Lord and fasting . . .
See also **Lk** 2:37   *See also prayer, practicalities; repentance; worship.*

fasting, reasons
Scripture identifies a number of situations in which fasting is appropriate.

Situations in which fasting is appropriate
Bereavement
1Ch 10:11–12 When all the inhabitants of Jabesh Gilead heard of everything the Philistines had done to Saul, all their valiant men went and took the bodies of Saul and his sons and brought them to Jabesh. Then they buried their bones under the great tree in Jabesh, and they fasted seven days. pp 1Sa 31:11–13   *See also* **2Sa** 1:11–12; 3:31–35
Distress
Est 4:3 In every province to which the edict and order of the king came, there was great mourning among the Jews, with fasting, weeping and wailing. Many lay in sackcloth and ashes.
See also **1Sa** 1:7; 20:34; **1Ki** 21:4–6; **Ps** 109:24; **Da** 6:18; **Ac** 27:33
Penitence
1Sa 7:5–6 Then Samuel said, "Assemble all Israel at Mizpah and I will intercede with the LORD for you." When they had assembled at Mizpah, they drew water and poured it out before

the LORD. On that day they fasted and there they confessed, "We have sinned against the LORD." . . .   *See also* **Ne** 9:1–3; **Da** 9:3–6,20; **Joel** 1:13–14; 2:12–15; **Jnh** 3:5–9

Seeking God's intervention
2Sa 12:15–17 After Nathan had gone home, the LORD struck the child that Uriah's wife had borne to David, and he became ill. David pleaded with God for the child. He fasted and went into his house and spent the nights lying on the ground. The elders of his household stood beside him to get him up from the ground, but he refused, and he would not eat any food with them.   *See also* **2Ch** 20:2–4; **Ezr** 8:21; **Est** 4:15–16; **Ps** 35:13–14

Seeking guidance
Jdg 20:26–28 Then the Israelites, all the people, went up to Bethel, and there they sat weeping before the LORD. They fasted that day until evening and presented burnt offerings and fellowship offerings to the LORD. And the Israelites enquired of the LORD . . . "Shall we go up again to battle against the Benjamites our fellow Israelites, or not?" The LORD responded, "Go, for tomorrow I will give them into your hands." *See also* **Dt** 9:9; **Da** 9:1–3,20–23; 10:1–2,12; **Ac** 13:1–3

Indicating earnestness Ac 23:12–13   *See also confession of sin; guidance; humility.*

---

fellowship
Association based upon the sharing of something in common. Believers have fellowship with one another on the basis of their common fellowship with God, their participation in the blessings of the gospel and their common task of mission. True fellowship is demonstrated in concern for, and practical commitment to, one another.

fellowship, among believers
The fellowship that believers share as a result of their common union with God through Jesus Christ is expressed in life together. It is evident in worship together, in a love for one another which reflects God's own love and in a practical commitment to one another which is demonstrated

in concern for the weak and readiness to share with the poor and needy.

Sharing in the fellowship of God's love
1Jn 4:10–12 . . . Dear friends, since God so loved us, we also ought to love one another . . .   *See also* **Jn** 13:34; 15:12; **Eph** 5:1–2; **1Jn** 3:10

Sharing in the fellowship of a common devotional life
Ac 2:42 They [the believers] devoted themselves to the apostles' teaching and to the fellowship, to the breaking of bread and to prayer.

Worshipping together
Ps 55:14 with whom I once enjoyed sweet fellowship as we walked with the throng at the house of God.   *See also* **Ps** 42:4; **1Co** 14:26; **Eph** 5:19; **Col** 3:16

Praying together
Ac 1:14 They [the believers] all joined together constantly in prayer, along with the women and Mary the mother of Jesus, and with his brothers.   *See also* **Ac** 4:24; 12:12; **Jas** 5:16
Breaking bread together 1Co 10:16–17; **2Pe** 2:13; **Jude** 12

True fellowship means sharing with those in need
Heb 13:16 And do not forget to do good and to share with others, for with such sacrifices God is pleased.   *See also* **Ac** 20:34–35; **Eph** 4:28

Showing hospitality
Ro 12:13 Share with God's people who are in need. Practise hospitality.   *See also* **Isa** 58:7; **Heb** 13:1–2; **1Pe** 4:9; **3Jn** 8

Sharing money and possessions
Dt 15:10–11 . . . There will always be poor people in the land. Therefore I command you to be open-handed towards those of your people who are poor and needy in your land.
Ac 2:44–45 All the believers were together and had everything in common. Selling their possessions and goods, they gave to anyone who had need.   *See also* **Dt** 10:18–19; **Mt** 25:35–36; **Lk** 3:11; **Ac** 4:32–35; **2Co** 8:13–15; **1Ti** 6:17–18; **Jas** 1:27; 2:15–16

Examples of sharing with the needy Job
31:16–20; **Ac** 6:1; 9:36

The collection for believers in Judea: **Ac** 11:29–30; **Ro**
15:26; **2Co** 8:3–4

Strengthening one another in fellowship together

Bearing with the weak

Gal 6:1–2 . . . Carry each other's burdens, and
in this way you will fulfil the law of Christ.
See also **Isa** 42:3; **Ro** 14:1; 15:1; **1Th** 5:14

Strengthening the weak

Isa 35:3–4 Strengthen the feeble hands, steady
the knees that give way . . .   *See also* **Job**
4:3–4

Encouraging one another

Heb 10:24–25 And let us consider how we
may spur one another on towards love and good
deeds. Let us not give up meeting together, as
some are in the habit of doing, but let us
encourage one another—and all the more as you
see the Day approaching.   *See also* **1Sa** 23:16;
Ro 1:12; **1Th** 5:11; **Heb** 13:3

Putting the needs of others first

Ro 15:2 We should all please our neighbours for
their good, to build them up.   *See also* **1Co**
10:24,32–33

True fellowship means living in harmony

1Pe 3:8 Finally, all of you, live in harmony with
one another; be sympathetic, love one another, be
compassionate and humble.   *See also* **Ro** 12:16;
Eph 4:2–3; **Php** 2:1–4; **Col** 3:12–14

Showing equal concern for all **Ac** 10:34; **1Co**
12:25; **Jas** 2:1–4

Examples of fellowship Nu 10:31–32; **1Sa** 18:3;
2Ki 10:15–16

Failure to exhibit true fellowship 1Sa 30:22;
1Co 1:11–12; 11:17–22   *See also church, life of;
church, unity; love, for one another; peace, experience;
prayer; suffering, encouragements in; worship.*

---

fellowship, in gospel

A mutual participation in the blessings of God's
grace. Believers are united with one another on
the basis of their common reception of the
benefits of salvation.

Fellowship and the community of God's people

God calls out a community of people, for fellowship with himself

Dt 7:6 For you [Israel] are a people holy to the
LORD your God. The LORD your God has chosen
you out of all the peoples on the face of the
earth to be his people, his treasured
possession.   *See also* **Ex** 19:5–6; **1Pe** 2:5,9–11

God will bless a people united in fellowship

Mt 18:19–20; **2Ch** 7:14; **Jer** 31:23–25; **1Co**
11:29–34

God will restore fellowship with his scattered people

Mic 2:12 "I [the LORD] will surely gather all of
you, O Jacob; I will surely bring together the
remnant of Israel. I will bring them together like
sheep in a pen, like a flock in its pasture; the
place will throng with people."   *See also* **Isa**
11:12–13; **Jer** 3:18; 31:1; 50:4–5

Sharing in God's grace

Fellowship in a common blessing

Ps 106:4–5 . . . that I may enjoy the
prosperity of your chosen ones, that I may share
in the joy of your [the LORD's] nation and join
your inheritance in giving praise.   *See also* **Nu**
10:32; **Jos** 22:19

Fellowship in a common salvation

Jude 3 Dear friends, although I was very eager
to write to you about the salvation we share, I
felt I had to write and urge you to contend for
the faith that was once for all entrusted to the
saints.   *See also* **1Co** 9:23; **Php** 1:7; **Tit** 1:4;
Heb 3:1; **1Pe** 5:1; **2Pe** 1:4; **1Jn** 1:7

Fellowship in a common inheritance

Col 1:12 giving thanks to the Father, who has
qualified you to share in the inheritance of the
saints in the kingdom of light.   *See also* **Ro**
8:17; **1Pe** 3:7

Fellowship in God's family

Heb 2:11 Both the one who makes people holy
and those who are made holy are of the same
family. So Jesus is not ashamed to call them
brothers and sisters.   *See also* **Mal** 2:10; **Mt** 6:9
pp Lk 11:2; **Mt** 12:49–50 pp Mk 3:34–35 pp Lk
8:21; **Mt** 23:8–9

Fellowship between Jew and Gentile
Eph 3:6 This mystery is that through the gospel
the Gentiles are heirs together with Israel,
members together of one body, and sharers
together in the promise in Christ Jesus.   *See also*
Ro 11:17; 15:27; **Eph** 2:16–18

Fellowship in holding a common truth
2Th 2:15 So then, brothers and sisters, stand
firm and hold to the teachings we passed on to
you, whether by word of mouth or by letter.
See also **Ps** 119:63; **1Co** 11:2; 15:2–3; **2Ti** 2:2;
3:14; **Tit** 2:15

Fellowship in union with Christ
1Co 10:16–17 Is not the cup of thanksgiving
for which we give thanks a participation in the
blood of Christ? And is not the bread that we
break a participation in the body of Christ?
Because there is one loaf, we, who are many, are
one body, for we all partake of the one loaf.
Eph 2:19–22 . . . And in him [Christ Jesus]
you too are being built together to become a
dwelling in which God lives by his Spirit.   *See
also* **Ro** 12:5; **1Co** 12:12,27; **Eph** 4:4–5; **Col** 1:15;
1Pe 2:4–5

Fellowship through the Holy Spirit
1Co 12:13 For we were all baptised by one
Spirit into one body—whether Jews or Greeks,
slave or free—and we were all given the one
Spirit to drink.   *See also* **Eze** 36:27–28; **2Co**
13:14; **Eph** 4:3; **Php** 2:1   *See also baptism; Lord's
Supper; sanctification; union with Christ.*

---

fellowship, in service
Partnership in a common enterprise. God's people
are called to work together especially in the task
of mission, to recognise one another's gifts and to
give support to one another's ministries.

Fellowship in mission
Partnership in preaching the gospel
Gal 2:9 James, Peter and John, those reputed
to be pillars, gave me [Paul] and Barnabas the
right hand of fellowship when they recognised the
grace given to me. They agreed that we should

go to the Gentiles, and they to the Jews.
See also **Mk** 10:7; **Lk** 10:1–2; **Php** 1:5
Supporting the work of others
Ac 14:26 From Attalia they [Paul and Barnabas]
sailed back to Antioch, where they had been
committed to the grace of God for the work they
had now completed.
Php 4:14–16 . . . as you Philippians know, in
the early days of your acquaintance with the
gospel, when I [Paul] set out from Macedonia,
not one church shared with me in the matter of
giving and receiving, except you only . . .
See also **Ac** 13:2–3; 15:40; **2Co** 11:9; **3Jn** 5–8
Standing together in adversity
Heb 10:32–34 . . . Sometimes you [Hebrew
Christians] were publicly exposed to insult and
persecution; at other times you stood side by side
with those who were so treated . . .   *See also*
2Co 1:7; **Php** 1:27–30; 4:14; **Heb** 11:25
Fellowship between Paul and his co-workers
Php 4:3 . . . I [Paul] ask you, true companion,
help these women [Euodia and Syntyche] who
have contended at my side in the cause of the
gospel, along with Clement and the rest of my
co-workers, whose names are in the book of life.
Barnabas: **Ac** 11:26–30; 13:42–50; 14:1–23;
15:22–29
Ro 16:3,9,21; **2Co** 8:23; **Php** 2:25; **Phm** 1,24

**In fellowship different gifts are
combined for effective service**
1Co 12:12 The body is a unit, though it is
made up of many parts; and though all its parts
are many, they form one body. So it is with
Christ.   *See also* **1Co** 12:4–6
Spiritual gifts are given to all to share
1Co 12:7 Now to each one the manifestation
of the Spirit is given for the common good.
See also **Ro** 12:4–8; **1Co** 12:14–20; **1Pe** 4:10
Recognising one another's gifts
1Co 12:21–26 The eye cannot say to the
hand, "I don't need you!" And the head cannot
say to the feet, "I don't need you!" . . .
Accepting one another's ministries
Gal 2:7–8 . . . For God, who was at work in
the ministry of Peter as an apostle to the Jews,
was also at work in my [Paul's] ministry as an

apostle to the Gentiles.　*See also* **1Co** 12:27–31; 16:15–18; **2Pe** 3:15–16

Examples of sharing in different roles
Ne 4:16–22 From that day on, half of my men did the work, while the other half were equipped with spears, shields, bows and armour . . .

1Co 3:5–8 . . . The one who plants and the one who waters have one purpose, and they will each be rewarded according to their own labour.　*See also* **Ex** 4:15–16; 17:10–13; **1Co** 12:8–11

Examples of working together in fellowship
Ecc 4:9–12 Two are better than one, because they have a good return for their work: If they fall down, one can help the other up. But pity those who fall and have no friend to help them up . . .　*See also* **Dt** 3:18–20; **Jdg** 20:11; **Ezr** 3:8–10; **Ne** 4:6; **Lk** 5:7–10　*See also evangelism; mission, of church; persecution; spiritual gifts; witnessing.*

fellowship, with God

The relationship with God, disrupted by sin yet established through Jesus Christ, which provides the only proper basis for true human fellowship. God's desire for fellowship with humanity is made known through his calling of a people to be his own and to reflect his holiness and love.

God's fellowship with his people is shown by his presence
God's presence with Israel
Lev 26:12 " 'I will walk among you [Israel] and be your God, and you will be my people.' "　*See also* **Ex** 33:14; **Isa** 63:9; **Hag** 1:13

God's presence in the tabernacle
Ex 25:8 "Then have them [the Israelites] make a sanctuary for me, and I [the LORD] will dwell among them."　*See also* **Ex** 29:45–46; 40:34–36; **Lev** 26:11; **Dt** 12:11

God's presence in the temple
1Ki 6:12–13 ". . . I [the LORD] will live among the Israelites and will not abandon my people Israel."　*See also* **1Ki** 8:29 pp 2Ch 6:20; **2Ch** 7:1–2; **Isa** 6:1

God's presence in the new Jerusalem
Zec 2:10–13 "Shout and be glad, O Daughter of Zion. For I am coming, and I will live among you," declares the LORD . . .　*See also* **Eze** 37:26–28; 43:4–7; 48:35; **Rev** 21:3

The church's fellowship with God
Fellowship with the Father, Son and Holy Spirit
Jn 14:23 Jesus replied, "Those who love me will obey my teaching. My Father will love them, and we will come to them and make our home with them."　*See also* **Jn** 14:7,16–17

Fellowship is made possible through Jesus Christ
Eph 2:18–19 For through him [Christ Jesus] we both have access to the Father by one Spirit . . .　*See also* **Ro** 5:10; **2Co** 5:18–19; **Col** 1:20–22; **Heb** 10:19–22

Fellowship with Jesus Christ
1Co 1:9 God, who has called you into fellowship with his Son Jesus Christ our Lord, is faithful.　*See also* **Mt** 28:20; **Jn** 15:4–5; **Ro** 6:4–5; **1Co** 10:15–16; **Php** 3:10

Fellowship with God is inseparable from fellowship with one another
1Jn 1:3 We [the apostles] proclaim to you what we have seen and heard, so that you also may have fellowship with us. And our fellowship is with the Father and with his Son, Jesus Christ.　*See also* **Mt** 18:20; **Mk** 9:37; **Jn** 17:21; **2Co** 13:11

The demands of fellowship with God
Holiness
Lev 20:26 " 'You [Israel] are to be holy to me because I, the LORD, am holy, and I have set you apart from the nations to be my own."

2Co 6:14–18 . . . What agreement is there between the temple of God and idols? For we are the temple of the living God. As God has said: "I will live with them and walk among them, and I will be their God, and they will be my people." "Therefore come out from them and be separate, says the Lord. Touch no unclean thing, and I will receive you." . . .　*See also* **Ex** 34:12–14; **Ezr** 6:21; **1Co** 5:11; **Eph** 5:8–11; **Jas** 4:4

Obedience to God's will

1Jn 3:24 Those who obey his [God's] commands live in him, and he in them. And this is how we know that he lives in us: We know it by the Spirit he gave us.   *See also* **Isa** 57:15; **Mt** 12:49–50 pp Mk 3:34–35 pp Lk 8:21; **Jn** 14:21

Sin separates people from fellowship with God

Isa 59:2 But your iniquities have separated you from your God; your sins have hidden his face from you, so that he will not hear.

1Jn 1:5–6 . . . If we claim to have fellowship with him [God] yet walk in the darkness, we lie and do not live by the truth.   *See also* **Ge** 3:8; **Eze** 39:23

Examples of fellowship with God

Ge 5:22; 6:9; **2Ch** 20:7

Moses: **Ex** 33:11; **Nu** 12:3

Jos 1:9; **Mal** 2:6   *See also abiding in Christ; forgiveness; friendship with God; holiness; sin.*

flesh, sinful nature

The physical aspect of human beings, which distinguishes them from God and is therefore frequently used in the NT as a symbol of human sinful nature in contrast with God's perfection. (The Greek word for "flesh" is sometimes translated by other words and phrases in the passages cited in this theme.)

Flesh as the bodily substance of human beings

As individuals or in relation to others

Ps 84:2 My soul yearns, even faints, for the courts of the LORD; my heart and my flesh cry out for the living God.   *See also* **Ge** 2:23–24; 29:14; **1Co** 15:39

The following two examples from Paul, where the normal word for "flesh" underlies the translation "body", make clear that to live "in the flesh" is normal human experience; the phrase does not necessarily imply that human nature is sinful, even though in many other instances a specific connection between "flesh" and "sin" is intended: **Gal** 2:20; **Php** 1:22–24

As the means by which Jesus Christ identified with the human race to bring salvation

Jn 1:14 The Word became flesh and made his dwelling among us. We have seen his glory, the glory of the One and Only, who came from the Father, full of grace and truth.   *See also* **Eph** 2:15; **Heb** 10:20; **1Jn** 4:2

As subject to mortality

Isa 40:6–7 A voice says, "Cry out." And I said, "What shall I cry?" "All people are like grass, and all their glory is like the flowers of the field. The grass withers and the flowers fall, because the breath of the LORD blows on them. Surely the people are grass."   *See also* **Ps** 78:39; **Ac** 2:31; **1Co** 15:50

As subject to weakness

2Ch 32:8 "With him [Sennacherib, the king of Assyria] is only the arm of flesh, but with us is the LORD our God to help us and to fight our battles." And the people gained confidence from what Hezekiah the king of Judah said.   *See also* **Ps** 73:26; **Mt** 26:41 pp Mk 14:38

Flesh as contrasting human nature with God's perfection

The powerlessness of human beings contrasted with God's eternal power

Isa 31:3 But the Egyptians are mortals and not God; their horses are flesh and not spirit. When the LORD stretches out his hand, those who help will stumble, those who are helped will fall; both will perish together.   *See also* **Jn** 3:6; 6:63

Human or worldly standards contrasted with God's standards

Jn 8:15 "You [Pharisees] judge by human standards; I [Jesus] pass judgment on no-one." *See also* **1Co** 1:26; **2Co** 5:16; 10:3–4

Flesh as denoting the sinful nature of human beings

The tendency to sin

Ro 7:18 I [Paul] know that nothing good lives in me, that is, in my sinful nature. For I have the desire to do what is good, but I cannot carry it out.   *See also* **Jer** 17:5

The conflict in human experience between the sinful nature and the Spirit of God

Gal 5:17 For the sinful nature desires what is contrary to the Spirit, and the Spirit what is contrary to the sinful nature. They are in conflict with each other, so that you do not do what you want. *See also* **Ro** 8:4–9; **Gal** 5:19–25

The sinful nature is opposed to God and his will

This opposition finds expression in a range of acts and attitudes

Gal 5:19–21 The acts of the sinful nature are obvious: sexual immorality, impurity and debauchery; idolatry and witchcraft; hatred, discord, jealousy, fits of rage, selfish ambition, dissensions, factions and envy; drunkenness, orgies, and the like. I warn you, as I did before, that those who live like this will not inherit the kingdom of God. *See also* **Ro** 7:14–25; 8:7; 13:13–14; **1Co** 6:9–11; **Eph** 5:5; **Jas** 1:14–15; **1Pe** 2:11; **2Pe** 2:10,18; **1Jn** 2:16

Confidence in the law is futile

Ro 8:3 . . . what the law was powerless to do in that it was weakened by the sinful nature . . .
Gal 3:3 Are you so foolish? After beginning with the Spirit, are you now trying to attain your goal by human effort? *See also* **Ro** 7:25; **Php** 3:3–9

The sinful nature controls human behaviour in ways which run counter to God's purpose

Ro 8:8 Those controlled by the sinful nature cannot please God. *See also* **Ro** 7:5

The sinful nature therefore makes people subject to God's judgment and to death

Ro 8:13 For if you live according to the sinful nature, you will die; but if by the Spirit you put to death the misdeeds of the body, you will live,
Eph 2:3 All of us also lived among them at one time, gratifying the cravings of our sinful nature and following its desires and thoughts. Like the rest, we were by nature objects of wrath.
See also **Gal** 6:8

Believers are not controlled by the sinful nature

Through Jesus Christ's entering into human flesh, God delivers from the power and consequences of human sinfulness

Ro 8:3 For what the law was powerless to do in that it was weakened by the sinful nature, God did by sending his own Son in the likeness of sinful humanity to be a sin offering. And so he condemned sin in our sinful nature, *See also* **Eph** 2:15

Believers have crucified the sinful nature

Ro 7:5–6 For when we were controlled by the sinful nature, the sinful passions aroused by the law were at work in our bodies, so that we bore fruit for death. But now, by dying to what once bound us, we have been released from the law so that we serve in the new way of the Spirit, and not in the old way of the written code.
See also **Ro** 8:8–9; **Gal** 5:24; **Col** 2:11

The power of God's Spirit enables believers to continue to resist the sinful nature

Ro 8:13 . . . if by the Spirit you put to death the misdeeds of the body, you will live, *See also* **Ro** 13:14; **Gal** 5:13; **Col** 3:5–6; **1Pe** 2:11

God's provision of church discipline in eliminating the sinful nature

1Co 5:5 hand this man over to Satan, so that the sinful nature may be destroyed and his spirit saved on the day of the Lord. *See also freedom; sin; temptation.*

---

forgiveness

The freeing of a person from guilt and its consequences, including punishment; usually as an act of favour, compassion or love, with the aim of restoring a broken personal relationship. Forgiveness can involve both the remission of punishment and the cancellation of debts.

---

forgiveness, application

God's forgiveness of believers' sins leads them to pray for his forgiveness of others and to be forgiving in their dealings with other people.

Prayers for forgiveness on behalf of others

For God's own people

Ex 32:30–32 The next day Moses said to the people, "You have committed a great sin. But now I will go up to the LORD; perhaps I can make atonement for your sin." So Moses went back to the LORD and said, "Oh, what a great sin these people have committed! They have made themselves gods of gold. But now, please forgive their sin—but if not, then blot me out of the book you have written."   *See also* **Ne** 1:4–11; **Da** 9:4–19; **Am** 7:1–6

For other human beings

Ge 18:20–33 . . . but Abraham remained standing before the LORD. Then Abraham approached him and said: "Will you sweep away the righteous with the wicked? What if there are fifty righteous people in the city? Will you really sweep it away and not spare the place for the sake of the fifty righteous people in it? Far be it from you to do such a thing—to kill the righteous with the wicked, treating the righteous and the wicked alike. Far be it from you! Will not the Judge of all the earth do right?" . . .

For one's persecutors

Lk 23:33–34 When they came to the place called the Skull, there they crucified him, along with the criminals—one on his right, the other on his left. Jesus said, "Father, forgive them, for they do not know what they are doing." . . .
See also **Mt** 5:43–44; **Ac** 7:59–60

Prayers for forgiveness for oneself

Lk 11:4 " 'Forgive us our sins, for we also forgive everyone who sins against us . . .' "
pp **Mt** 6:12   *See also* **Ne** 9:1–3; **Ps** 51:1–17

Examples of forgiveness given

Ps 32:1–5 Blessed are those whose transgressions are forgiven, whose sins are covered. Blessed are those whose sin the LORD does not count against them and in whose spirit is no deceit. When I kept silent, my bones wasted away through my groaning all day long. For day and night your hand was heavy upon me; my strength was sapped as in the heat of summer. *Selah* Then I

acknowledged my sin to you and did not cover up my iniquity. I said, "I will confess my transgressions to the LORD"—and you forgave the guilt of my sin.   *See also* **Isa** 6:1–7; **Jn** 8:3–11

The call to exercise forgiveness

As a principle of life

Lk 6:37 "Do not judge, and you will not be judged. Do not condemn, and you will not be condemned. Forgive, and you will be forgiven."
See also **Mt** 5:38–48 pp **Lk** 6:27–36

Within the church

Col 3:12–13 Therefore, as God's chosen people, holy and dearly loved, clothe yourselves with compassion, kindness, humility, gentleness and patience. Bear with each other and forgive whatever grievances you may have against one another. Forgive as the Lord forgave you.
See also **2Co** 2:5–11; **Eph** 4:32; **1Pe** 3:8–9
Forgiving enemies Pr 24:17; 25:21–22; **Mt** 5:44; **Ro** 12:20

Being forgiven is dependent on forgiving others

Mk 11:25 "And when you stand praying, if you hold anything against anyone, forgive them, so that your Father in heaven may forgive you your sins."   *NIV footnote at verse 26.   See Also* **Mt** 6:12; pp **Lk** 11:4; **Mt** 6:14–15; 18:21–35; **Lk** 6:37

Forgiveness is to be without limits

Lk 17:3–4 ". . . Rebuke a brother or sister who sins, and if they repent, forgive them. If anyone sins against you seven times in a day, and seven times comes back to you and says, 'I repent,' you must forgive them."   *See also* **Mt** 18:21–22

Examples of human forgiveness

Ac 7:59–60 While they were stoning him, Stephen prayed, "Lord Jesus, receive my spirit." Then he fell on his knees and cried out, "Lord, do not hold this sin against them." When he had said this, he fell asleep.   *See also* **Ge** 50:15–21; **2Sa** 16:5–11   *See also confession of sin; neighbours, duty to; prayer, for others; sin, forgiveness of.*

forgiveness, divine

God forgives the sins of believers on the basis of the once for all sacrifice offered by Jesus Christ on the cross. Believers' sins are no longer held against them, on account of the atoning death of Jesus Christ.

God's nature and forgiveness

Ex 34:5-7 Then the LORD came down in the cloud and stood there with him and proclaimed his name, the LORD. And he passed in front of Moses, proclaiming, "The LORD, the LORD, the compassionate and gracious God, slow to anger, abounding in love and faithfulness, maintaining love to thousands, and forgiving wickedness, rebellion and sin . . ."   *See also* **Nu** 14:17-20; **Ne** 9:16-17; **Ps** 103:1-18; **Isa** 43:25; **Mic** 7:18-20; **1Jn** 1:8-9

God's promise of forgiveness

Jer 31:31-34 "The time is coming," declares the LORD, "when I will make a new covenant with the house of Israel and with the house of Judah. It will not be like the covenant I made with their ancestors when I took them by the hand to lead them out of Egypt, because they broke my covenant, though I was a husband to them," declares the LORD. "This is the covenant that I will make with the house of Israel after that time," declares the LORD. "I will put my law in their minds and write it on their hearts. I will be their God, and they will be my people. No longer will they teach their neighbours, or say to one another, 'Know the LORD,' because they will all know me, from the least of them to the greatest," declares the LORD. "For I will forgive their wickedness and will remember their sins no more."   *See also* **2Ch** 7:14; **Isa** 55:6-7; **Heb** 8:8-12

People's need of forgiveness

1Jn 1:8-10 If we claim to be without sin, we deceive ourselves and the truth is not in us. If we confess our sins, he is faithful and just and will forgive us our sins and purify us from all unrighteousness. If we claim we have not sinned, we make him out to be a liar and his word has no place in our lives.   *See also* **Ps** 51:1-5; **Isa** 6:1-5; **Ro** 3:9,23

The means of forgiveness

Under the old covenant

Heb 9:22 In fact, the law requires that nearly everything be cleansed with blood, and without the shedding of blood there is no forgiveness. *See also* **Lev** 4:27-31; 5:17-18

Under the new covenant

Mt 26:27-28 Then he [Jesus] took the cup, gave thanks and offered it to them, saying, "Drink from it, all of you. This is my blood of the covenant, which is poured out for many for the forgiveness of sins."   *See also* **Jn** 1:29; **Eph** 1:7-8; **Col** 2:13-15

The assurance of forgiveness

1Jn 1:8-9 If we claim to be without sin, we deceive ourselves and the truth is not in us. If we confess our sins, he is faithful and just and will forgive us our sins and purify us from all unrighteousness.   *See also* **Ps** 51:7; 103:8-12; 130:3-4; **Pr** 28:13; **Isa** 1:18; **Ac** 2:38; **Jas** 5:13-16; **1Jn** 2:1-2   *See also conversion; grace; repentance.*

forgiveness, Jesus Christ's ministry

A central feature of Jesus Christ's ministry was his declaration that believers' sins were forgiven through their faith in him.

Jesus Christ's ministry of forgiveness was foretold

Mt 1:20-21 . . . "Joseph son of David, do not be afraid to take Mary home as your wife, because what is conceived in her is from the Holy Spirit. She will give birth to a son, and you are to give him the name Jesus, because he will save his people from their sins."

Jn 1:29 The next day John saw Jesus coming towards him and said, "Look, the Lamb of God, who takes away the sin of the world!"

Jesus Christ's exercise of forgiveness

Lk 23:33–34 When they came to the place called the Skull, there they crucified him, along with the criminals—one on his right, the other on his left. Jesus said, "Father, forgive them, for they do not know what they are doing." . . . *See also* **Jn** 8:3–11

Jesus Christ has authority on account of his divinity to forgive sins

Mt 9:5–8 . . . "Which is easier: to say, 'Your sins are forgiven,' or to say, 'Get up and walk'? But so that you may know that the Son of Man has authority on earth to forgive sins. . . ." Then he [Jesus] said to the paralytic, "Get up, take your mat and go home." And the man got up and went home. When the crowd saw this, they were filled with awe; and they praised God, who had given such authority to human beings. pp Mk 2:1–12 pp Lk 5:17–26

People's offence at Jesus Christ's exercise of forgiveness

Mk 2:5–7 When Jesus saw their faith, he said to the paralytic, "Son, your sins are forgiven." Now some teachers of the law were sitting there, thinking to themselves, "Why does this fellow talk like that? He's blaspheming! Who can forgive sins but God alone?" pp Mt 9:2–3 pp Lk 5:20–21

Parables of forgiveness

Mt 18:23–35; **Lk** 7:36–50; 15:11–32

The church's ministry of forgiveness in Jesus Christ's name

Jn 20:21–23 Again Jesus said, "Peace be with you! As the Father has sent me, I am sending you." And with that he breathed on them and said, "Receive the Holy Spirit. If you forgive the sins of anyone, their sins are forgiven; if you do not forgive them, they are not forgiven." *See also* **Ac** 2:38; 13:38; 26:15–18   *See also sin, forgiveness of.*

freedom

The state of liberty that results from not being oppressed or in bondage. Scripture stresses that human beings lack freedom on account of sin, but that faith in Jesus Christ brings freedom from the power of sin and the law.

freedom, abuse

Although Christians have been set free from condemnation by grace, they remain under an obligation to be obedient to God. Abuses of Christian freedom result from a failure to take responsibilities towards God seriously.

Christian freedom can be abused

Believers are freed from condemnation

Ro 8:1 Therefore, there is now no condemnation for those who are in Christ Jesus.   *See also* **Isa** 50:8–9; **Ro** 8:33–39; **Col** 1:22; **Rev** 1:5

Sin need not enslave believers

Jn 8:34–36 Jesus replied, "I tell you the truth, everyone who sins is a slave to sin. Now a slave has no permanent place in the family, but a son belongs to it for ever. So if the Son sets you free, you will be free indeed."   *See also* **Ro** 6:16–18; 7:14–25; **1Co** 7:22–23; **2Pe** 2:19

Believers must resist sin

Ro 6:12 Therefore do not let sin reign in your mortal body so that you obey its evil desires. **Ro 6:14** For sin shall not be your master, because you are not under law, but under grace.   *See also* **Heb** 12:1–2; **1Jn** 5:16–18

The false idea that grace gives believers the freedom to sin

Ro 6:1–2 What shall we say, then? Shall we go on sinning, so that grace may increase? By no means! We died to sin; how can we live in it any longer?

Ro 6:15 What then? Shall we sin because we are not under law but under grace? By no means!   *See also* **Ro** 3:5–8; **1Co** 10:23; **Gal** 2:17–21

The dangers of abusing Christian freedom

Becoming a stumbling-block to others

1Co 8:9–12 Be careful, however, that the exercise of your freedom does not become a stumbling-block to the weak. For if anyone with a weak conscience sees you who have this knowledge eating in an idol's temple, won't such a person be emboldened to eat what has been sacrificed to idols? So this weak brother or sister, for whom Christ died, is destroyed by your knowledge. When you sin against other believers in this way and wound their weak conscience, you sin against Christ.   *See also* **Ro** 15:1–3

Indulging oneself

Gal 5:13 You, my brothers and sisters, were called to be free. But do not use your freedom to indulge the sinful nature; rather, serve one another in love.   *See also* **Ro** 14:1–18

Using freedom to cover up evil

1Pe 2:16 Live as free persons, but do not use your freedom as a cover-up for evil; live as servants of God.

Examples of abuse of Christian freedom

Falling back into deliberate sin Ro 6:1–2; **Heb** 12:1; **1Jn** 3:6; 5:16–18

Disobedience towards God 1Jn 3:4; **2Co** 10:6; **Eph** 5:6

Selfishness

1Jn 3:17 If anyone of you has material possessions and sees a brother or sister in need but has no pity on them, how can the love of God be in you?   *See also* **Lk** 6:32–34

Eating food sacrificed to idols 1Co 8:1–13; **Rev** 2:14,20   *See also grace; holiness; believers' growth in; love, for one another; perseverance; spiritual warfare.*

---

freedom, through Jesus Christ

Jesus Christ, the promised deliverer, sets his people free from the present effects of sin and from the power of sin and will finally deliver them completely from its presence.

The OT points ahead to a new and greater freedom and to a new deliverer

The OT predicts Jesus Christ as the deliverer

Isa 61:1 . . . He [the Sovereign Lord] has sent me to bind up the broken-hearted, to proclaim freedom for the captives and release from darkness for the prisoners,   *See also* **Isa** 42:6–7

The redemption of the exodus foreshadows the redemption achieved by Jesus Christ

Col 1:13–14 For he [the Father] has rescued us from the dominion of darkness and brought us into the kingdom of the Son he loves, in whom we have redemption, the forgiveness of sins.   *See also* **1Co** 10:1–4

Jesus Christ fulfils the OT predictions of him as deliverer

Lk 4:18–19 ". . . He [the Lord] has sent me to proclaim freedom for the prisoners and recovery of sight for the blind, to release the oppressed . . ."   *See also* **Ro** 11:26; **Isa** 59:20

The freedom that comes through Jesus Christ

Jn 8:32–36 . . . ". . . So if the Son sets you free, you will be free indeed."   *See also* **Mt** 1:21

Jesus Christ sets his people free from the penalty of sin

1Th 1:10 . . . Jesus, who rescues us from the coming wrath.   *See also* **Jn** 3:36; **Ro** 8:1–2; **Heb** 9:15; **Rev** 1:5

Jesus Christ sets his people free from the spiritual death that accompanies sin

Ro 6:1–7 . . . because anyone who has died has been freed from sin.   *See also* **Eph** 2:1–5; **Heb** 9:14

Jesus Christ sets his people free from the fear of death

Heb 2:14–15 Since the children have flesh and blood, he too shared in their humanity so that by his death he might destroy him who holds the power of death—that is, the devil—and free those who all their lives were held in slavery by their fear of death.

Jesus Christ will finally set his people free from death itself

1Co 15:22–23 For as in Adam all die, so in Christ all will be made alive. But in this order: Christ, the firstfruits; then, when he comes, those who belong to him.   *See also* **Ro** 5:12–17; 7:24

Jesus Christ sets his people free from the power of sin

Ro 6:11–14 In the same way, count yourselves dead to sin but alive to God in Christ Jesus.

Therefore do not let sin reign in your mortal body so that you obey its evil desires. Do not offer the parts of your body to sin, as instruments of wickedness, but rather offer yourselves to God, as those who have been brought from death to life; and offer the parts of your body to him as instruments of righteousness. For sin shall not be your master, because you are not under law, but under grace.   *See also* **Ro** 6:22–23

Jesus Christ sets his people free from the pollution of sin

2Pe 1:2–4 . . . Through these [God's glory and goodness] he has given us his very great and precious promises, so that through them you may participate in the divine nature and escape the corruption in the world caused by evil desires. *See also* **Gal** 1:3–4

Jesus Christ sets his people free from the power of Satan

Col 1:13–14 . . . he [the Father] has rescued us from the dominion of darkness and brought us into the kingdom of the Son he loves, in whom we have redemption, the forgiveness of sins. *See also* **Mk** 3:27; **Ac** 26:17–18

Jesus Christ will set his people free from the presence of sin

Php 3:21 who [the Lord Jesus Christ], by the power that enables him to bring everything under his control, will transform our lowly bodies so that they will be like his glorious body.   *See also* **Eph** 5:27; **Col** 1:22; **1Th** 3:13; 5:23; **Rev** 21:4

Freedom as the result of being rescued from trials by Jesus Christ

2Ti 3:11 persecutions, sufferings—what kinds of things happened to me in Antioch, Iconium and Lystra, the persecutions I endured. Yet the Lord rescued me from all of them.   *See also* **Ac** 26:17; **2Ti** 4:18; **2Pe** 2:9   *See also sin, deliverance from.*

friendship with God

A relationship of love and faithfulness into which God calls all people through faith.

Examples of friendship with God
Abraham
Jas 2:23 And the scripture was fulfilled that says, "Abraham believed God, and it was credited to him as righteousness," and he was called God's friend.   *See also* **2Ch** 20:7; **Isa** 41:8
Moses
Ex 33:11 The LORD would speak to Moses face to face, as one speaks to a friend . . . *See also* **Nu** 12:8; **Dt** 34:10
Job
Job 29:4–5 "Oh, for the days when I [Job] was in my prime, when God's intimate friendship blessed my house, when the Almighty was still with me and my children were around me, *See also* **Job** 16:20–21

Examples of friendship with Jesus Christ
Mary, Martha and Lazarus
Jn 11:5 Jesus loved Martha and her sister and Lazarus.   *See also* **Jn** 11:3,11,35–36; 12:1–2
The beloved disciple
Jn 13:23 One of them, the disciple whom Jesus loved, was reclining next to him.   *See also* **Jn** 19:26; 20:2; 21:7,20
The disciples
Jn 15:14–15 ". . . I [Jesus] no longer call you [the disciples] servants, because servants do not know their master's business. Instead, I have called you friends, for everything that I learned from my Father I have made known to you."

The ministry of Jesus Christ is an expression of friendship to sinners
In his life on earth
Mt 11:19 "The Son of Man came eating and drinking, and they say, 'Here is a glutton and a drunkard, a friend of tax collectors and "sinners".' . . ."   pp **Lk** 7:34   *See also* **Lk** 7:39; 19:7
In his death on the cross
Jn 15:13 "Greater love has no-one than this, to lay down one's life for one's friends."
Ro 5:7–8 Very rarely will anyone die for a righteous person, though for a good person someone might possibly dare to die. But God

demonstrates his own love for us in this: While we were still sinners, Christ died for us. *See also* **Lk** 12:4; **Jn** 3:16; **1Pe** 3:18

God's delight in friendship with those who he loves
Isa 5:7 The vineyard of the LORD Almighty is the house of Israel, and the people of Judah are the garden of his delight . . .
Hos 11:1–4 "When Israel was a child, I loved him, and out of Egypt I called my son. But the more I called Israel, the further they went from me. They sacrificed to the Baals and they burned incense to images. It was I who taught Ephraim to walk, taking them by the arms; but they did not realise it was I who healed them. I led them with cords of human kindness, with ties of love; I lifted the yoke from their neck and bent down to feed them." *See also* **1Jn** 1:3

The reliability of God as a friend
Isa 54:10 "Though the mountains be shaken and the hills be removed, yet my unfailing love for you will not be shaken nor my covenant of peace be removed," says the LORD, who has compassion on you. *See also* **Dt** 7:9; **Jos** 1:5; **Pr** 18:24; **Jn** 13:1; **Heb** 13:5

God's invitation for people to know his friendship
Ps 145:18 The LORD is near to all who call on him, to all who call on him in truth.
Jas 4:8 Come near to God and he will come near to you. Wash your hands, you sinners, and purify your hearts, you double-minded.
Rev 3:20 "Here I [Jesus] am! I stand at the door and knock. If anyone hears my voice and opens the door, I will come in and eat with them, and they with me." *See also* **Zec** 1:3; **Mal** 3:7; **Ac** 17:27; **Jas** 4:4 *See also fellowship, with God.*

---

fruit, spiritual
The spiritual life and growth of believers is likened to a fruit-bearing tree. As the fruit is evidence of the health and vigour of the tree, so the believer's life, attitudes and behaviour should reflect the presence of the Holy Spirit.

Believers should exhibit evidence of their conversion
Jas 3:13 Who are wise and understanding among you? Let them show it by their good life, by deeds done in the humility that comes from wisdom. *See also* **Mt** 3:8 pp Lk 3:8–9; **Mt** 7:15–20; 12:33; **Jn** 15:16; **Ro** 7:4–5; **Tit** 3:14; **Jas** 2:14–26

The nature of spiritual fruit
Gal 5:22–23 But the fruit of the Spirit is love, joy, peace, patience, kindness, goodness, faithfulness, gentleness and self-control . . .
See also **Ro** 8:5–6; **Php** 1:9–11; **Jas** 3:17

The sources of spiritual fruit
Acceptance of the gospel
Lk 8:15 "But the seed on good soil stands for those with a noble and good heart, who hear the word, retain it, and by persevering produce a crop." pp Mt 13:23 pp Mk 4:20
The old way of life put to death
Jn 12:24 "I [Jesus] tell you the truth, unless a grain of wheat falls to the ground and dies, it remains only a single seed. But if it dies, it produces many seeds." *See also* **Ro** 6:6,11–14; 8:13–14; **Gal** 5:24; **Eph** 4:22–24; **Col** 3:5–10
Actively living a new life in Jesus Christ
Gal 6:7–9 Do not be deceived: God cannot be mocked. People reap what they sow. Those who sow to please their sinful nature, from that nature will reap destruction; those who sow to please the Spirit, from the Spirit will reap eternal life. Let us not become weary in doing good, for at the proper time we will reap a harvest if we do not give up. *See also* **Ro** 6:11–14; **Gal** 5:25; **Eph** 5:8–9; **Col** 1:10; 3:12–15; **2Ti** 2:22; **2Pe** 1:5–8; **Tit** 3:14; **1Jn** 3:18
Remaining close to Jesus Christ
Jn 15:4–5 "Remain in me [Jesus], and I will remain in you. No branch can bear fruit by itself; it must remain in the vine. Neither can you bear fruit unless you remain in me. I am the vine; you are the branches. If you remain in me and I in

you, you will bear much fruit; apart from me you can do nothing."

Submission to God's discipline

Heb 12:10–11 Our parents disciplined us for a little while as they thought best; but God disciplines us for our good, that we may share in his holiness. No discipline seems pleasant at the time, but painful. Later on, however, it produces a harvest of righteousness and peace for those who have been trained by it.   *See also* **Jn** 15:1–2
See also abiding in Christ; spiritual growth, nature of; spirituality.

---

gentleness

An expression of compassion, seen in God's dealings with the frail and weak, and expected of believers in their dealings with others.

The gentleness of God
In dealing with the wayward

Isa 40:1–2 Comfort, comfort my people, says your God. Speak tenderly to Jerusalem, and proclaim to her that her hard service has been completed, that her sin has been paid for, that she has received from the LORD's hand double for all her sins.

Lk 1:76–79 "And you, my child, will be called a prophet of the Most High; for you will go on before the Lord to prepare the way for him, to give his people the knowledge of salvation through the forgiveness of their sins, because of the tender mercy of our God, by which the rising sun will come to us from heaven to shine on those living in darkness and in the shadow of death, to guide our feet into the path of peace."   *See also* **Isa** 30:18–19; 54:8; 63:15; **Hos** 2:13–15; **Ro** 2:4

In caring for the weak

Isa 40:11 He [the LORD] tends his flock like a shepherd: He gathers the lambs in his arms and carries them close to his heart; he gently leads those that have young.   *See also* **1Ki** 19:12

The gentleness of Jesus Christ
Mt 11:29 "Take my yoke upon you and learn from me [Jesus], for I am gentle and humble in

heart, and you will find rest for your souls."
See also **Zec** 9:9; **Mt** 21:4–5; 12:18–21; **Isa** 42:1–3; **2Co** 10:1; **Php** 2:1; **Heb** 5:2

Examples of Jesus Christ's gentleness
Mk 1:40–42; 5:25–34; 10:13–16; **Jn** 8:3–11

Gentleness as strength esteemed by God

Pr 15:1 A gentle answer turns away wrath, but a harsh word stirs up anger.

Jas 3:17 . . . the wisdom that comes from heaven is first of all pure; then peace-loving, considerate, submissive, full of mercy and good fruit, impartial and sincere.   *See also* **Pr** 25:15; **Mt** 5:5; **1Pe** 3:1–4

Gentleness as a mark of Christian character

Col 3:12 . . . as God's chosen people, holy and dearly loved, clothe yourselves with compassion, kindness, humility, gentleness and patience.
See also **Gal** 5:22–23; **Eph** 4:1–2; **1Ti** 6:11

Believers are to reflect God's gentleness in their dealings with people
In correcting the wayward

Gal 6:1 Brothers and sisters, if someone is caught in a sin, you who are spiritual should restore that person gently. But watch yourself, or you also may be tempted.   *See also* **2Ti** 2:24–25

In reasoning with unbelievers

1Pe 3:15–16 . . . Always be prepared to give an answer to everyone who asks you to give the reason for the hope that you have. But do this with gentleness and respect, keeping a clear conscience, so that those who speak maliciously against your good behaviour in Christ may be ashamed of their slander.

In nurturing new believers 1Th 2:7

In showing consideration to all

Tit 3:1–2 Remind the people to be subject to rulers and authorities, to be obedient, to be ready to do whatever is good, to slander no-one, to be peaceable and considerate, and to show true humility towards everyone.   *See also* **Eph** 4:32;

Php 4:5 *See also fruit, spiritual; humility; mercifulness; patience.*

---

giving

Dedicating or offering something or oneself to others or to God. Scripture stresses the importance of giving. The generosity and love of God in giving his only Son to die for his people is understood to lead to an obligation, on their part, to love God and others in return.

---

giving possessions

Making one's possessions available for God's service in the way in which he directs, as a practical recognition that all possessions come from him.

Ministries that require the giving of material possessions
The relief of the poor
Pr 28:27 Those who give to the poor will lack nothing, but those who close their eyes to them receive many curses. *See also Lev 25:25; Dt 15:7–8; Isa 58:7; Mt 19:21 pp Mk 10:21 pp Lk 18:22; Lk 12:33; Ro 12:13; Gal 2:10*
The support of God's servants
1Ti 5:17–18 The elders who direct the affairs of the church well are worthy of double honour, especially those whose work is preaching and teaching. For the Scripture says, "Do not muzzle the ox while it is treading out the grain," and "Workers deserve their wages." *See also Nu 3:48; 5:9; 2Ki 4:8–10; Mt 10:10; Gal 6:6; Php 4:15–18*
The care of widows and orphans
Jas 1:27 Religion that God our Father accepts as pure and faultless is this: to look after orphans and widows in their distress and to keep oneself from being polluted by the world. *See also Dt 26:12; Ru 2:5–12; 1Ti 5:3–4*

Motives for the giving of material possessions
Obedience to God
2Co 9:7 Each of you should give what you have decided in your heart to give, not reluctantly or under compulsion, for God loves a cheerful giver. *See also Ex 30:11–16; Lev 12:6–8; Dt 14:28; Mal 3:8–10; Mt 22:21 pp Mk 12:17 pp Lk 20:25; Ro 13:6–7*
Gratitude for God's generosity
1Ch 29:14 ". . . Everything comes from you, and we have given you only what comes from your hand." *See also Ge 28:20–22; Dt 26:9–10; 1Sa 1:27–28*
Love for others
1Jn 3:17 If anyone of you has material possessions and sees a brother or sister in need but has no pity on them, how can the love of God be in you? *See also 2Ch 28:15; Mt 7:9–11; Lk 10:33–35*

The manner of giving material possessions
Willingly and cheerfully
Mt 10:8 ". . . Freely you have received, freely give." *See also Ex 25:2; 35:5,22; 2Ki 12:4; 1Ch 29:6,9,17; 2Ch 24:10; 35:7–9; Ezr 8:28; 2Co 8:11–12*
Unostentatiously Mt 6:1–4
Regularly 1Co 16:2
Generously Ex 36:5; Nu 7:13; 1Ch 29:3–4; Lk 6:38; 2Co 8:2–3; 1Ti 6:18

God measures his people's giving
With a reckoning different from the world's
2Ch 6:8; Mk 12:41–44 pp Lk 21:1–4
With regard for people's capacity to give Lev
14:30; 27:8; Dt 16:17; Ezr 2:69; Ac 11:29; 2Co 8:12

God rewards the giver appropriately
Php 4:18–19 . . . And my God will meet all your needs according to his glorious riches in Christ Jesus. *See also 2Ch 31:10; Pr 11:25; 22:9; 28:27; Ecc 11:1; Isa 58:10; Mt 10:42; 25:34–36; Lk 16:9; Ac 20:35; 2Co 9:6*
God's reward overwhelming the giver
Pr 3:9–10 Honour the LORD with your wealth, with the firstfruits of all your crops; then your barns will be filled to overflowing, and your vats will brim over with new wine. *See also Mal 3:10; Lk 6:38*

God's giving: the model for his people's giving
Mt 10:8 ". . . Freely you have received, freely give."   *See also* **2Co** 8:8–9; 9:15   *See also Christlikeness; tithing.*

giving talents
All human abilities and skills derive from God and are to be dedicated to his glory and the good of others.

Talents are given and sustained by God
1Co 4:7 For who makes you different from anyone else? What do you have that you did not receive? And if you did receive it, why do you boast as though you did not?
Skill, ability and knowledge given by God for the making of the Tent of Meeting: **Ex** 28:3; 31:3–6; 35:31–35; 36:1–2
Dt 8:18; **2Sa** 22:34–35; **Ps** 18:33–34; **Mt** 25:15 pp Lk 19:13; **Ac** 7:10; **Ro** 12:6; **1Co** 12:7–8; **2Co** 3:5; **Eph** 3:7; 4:7

Talents differ
Mt 25:15 "To one he [the master] gave five talents of money, to another two talents, and to another one talent, each according to his [the servants'] ability. Then he went on his journey."   *See also* **2Ch** 2:13–14; **Ro** 12:6; **1Co** 7:7; 12:4–6; **Eph** 4:11

Talents need to be developed
2Ti 1:6 . . . fan into flame the gift of God, which is in you [Timothy] . . .   *See also* **Mt** 25:16–30 pp Lk 19:12–26; **1Ti** 4:14

Talents are to be devoted to God
For his own glory
1Pe 4:11 . . . If you serve, you should do it with the strength God provides, so that in all things God may be praised through Jesus Christ. To him be the glory and the power for ever and ever. Amen.   *See also* **Ex** 35:10,25; **1Ki** 7:40; **1Ch** 9:13; **Ps** 33:2–3; 137:4–5; **1Co** 10:31
For the good of others
1Pe 4:10 Each of you should use whatever gift you have received to serve others, faithfully administering God's grace in its various forms.   *See also* **1Co** 12:7; 14:12; **Eph** 4:12

Talents are to be accounted for
Mt 25:19 "After a long time the master of those servants returned and settled accounts with them." pp Lk 19:15   *See also* **Mt** 21:34 pp Mk 12:2 pp Lk 20:10; **Lk** 12:48

Rewards according to use or misuse of talents
Mt 25:21 "His [the man with five talents] master replied, 'Well done, good and faithful servant! You have been faithful with a few things; I will put you in charge of many things. Come and share your master's happiness!' "
See also **Mt** 25:23–30 pp Lk 19:17–26   *See also faithfulness; spiritual gifts.*

giving time
People are stewards of a deposit of time given by God, and will be held responsible for the way in which they use it.

Time is governed by God
God determines every lifespan
Job 14:5 "The days of mortals are determined; you [God] have decreed the number of their months and have set limits they cannot exceed.   *See also* **Ps** 31:15; 74:16–17; 139:16; **Ac** 17:26
God will demand an account of how time has been spent
Ecc 3:17 . . . "God will bring to judgment both the righteous and the wicked, for there will be a time for every activity, a time for every deed."
See also **Mt** 12:36; **1Pe** 4:3–5

Time may be squandered
In ungodly living
1Pe 4:3 For you [God's elect] have spent enough time in the past doing what pagans choose to do—living in debauchery, lust, drunkenness, orgies, carousing and detestable idolatry.   *See also* **Joel** 2:25; **Eph** 2:2–3; **Col** 3:5–7

By neglecting God-given opportunities
Jer 8:20 "The harvest is past, the summer has ended, and we [the people of Judah] are not saved."   *See also* **Pr** 20:4; **Mt** 25:11–12; **Lk** 13:25; 19:44; **Ac** 24:25; **Rev** 2:21

Time may be saved
By understanding its brevity
Ps 90:12 Teach us [God's servants] to number our days aright, that we may gain a heart of wisdom.   *See also* **Jn** 12:35; **1Co** 7:29–31
By remembering its uncertainty
Jn 9:4 "As long as it is day, we [Jesus and his disciples] must do the work of him who sent me [Jesus]. Night is coming, when no-one can work."   *See also* **Ecc** 8:5–7; **Jas** 4:13–15
By making the most of present opportunities
Eph 5:16 making the most of every opportunity, because the days are evil.   *See also* **Ps** 32:6; **Ecc** 12:1; **Est** 4:14; **Mt** 4:17; **Mk** 1:15; **2Co** 6:1–2; **Gal** 6:10; **Col** 4:5; **Heb** 3:7–13
By allocating it wisely
1Ch 12:32 . . . [people] from Issachar, who understood the times and knew what Israel should do . . .   *See also* **Ex** 18:13–26; **Ac** 6:1–4

Time is to be spent wisely
In worship and meditation
Ps 119:164 Seven times a day I [David] praise you for your righteous laws.   *See also* **Ps** 4:4; 55:17; **La** 3:40; **Da** 6:10,13; **Mk** 1:35; **1Co** 11:28
In work
Ps 104:23 Then people go out to their work, to their labour until evening.   *See also* **Ex** 20:9 pp Dt 5:13; **Ro** 13:6
In rest
Ex 20:8–10 ". . . but the seventh day is a Sabbath to the LORD your God. On it you shall not do any work, neither you, nor your son or daughter, nor your male or female servant, nor your animals, nor the alien within your gates. *See also* **Lev** 16:29; **Mk** 6:31
With one's family
Dt 24:5 If a man has recently married, he must not be sent to war or have any other duty laid on him. For one year he is to be free to stay at

home and bring happiness to the wife he has married.   *See also* **Dt** 6:7; **Ecc** 9:9; **1Ti** 3:4
In fellowship
1Co 16:7 I [Paul] do not want to see you now and make only a passing visit; I hope to spend some time with you, if the Lord permits. *See also* **Ac** 2:42; 20:7; **Heb** 10:25

Time is to be allocated according to priorities
Lk 10:41–42 "Martha, Martha," the Lord answered, "you are worried and upset about many things, but only one thing is needed. Mary has chosen what is better, and it will not be taken away from her."   *See also* **Ps** 1:1–3; **Hag** 1:2–4; **Mt** 6:33; **Ac** 13:46–47; 17:16–17
See also fellowship, among believers; work; worship.

godliness
Reverence for or devotion to God, producing a practical awareness of God in every aspect of life.

Examples of godliness in the OT
Ge 5:24; 6:9; **1Ki** 18:3–4; **2Ch** 31:20–21; **Job** 1:1

Examples of godliness in the NT
Lk 2:25,37; **Jn** 1:47
Jesus Christ: **Jn** 8:29; **Heb** 5:7
Ac 2:5; 8:2
Cornelius and his family: **Ac** 10:2,7
Ac 11:24; 22:12

God has a special concern for the godly
Ps 4:3 Know that the LORD has set apart the godly for himself; the LORD will hear when I call to him.   *See also* **Ps** 32:6; **Jn** 9:31

Godly living
Godliness should be seen in the lives of believers
2Pe 3:11 . . . You ought to live holy and godly lives   *See also* **1Ti** 2:2; 6:11; **Tit** 2:12

Jesus Christ is the beginning and end of godliness
1Ti 3:16 Beyond all question, the mystery of godliness is great: He [Christ] appeared in a body, was vindicated by the Spirit, was seen by angels, was preached among the nations, was believed on in the world, was taken up in glory. *See also* **Heb** 5:7; **2Pe** 1:3

The basis for godly living is true teaching about Jesus Christ
1Ti 6:3–4 Anyone who teaches false doctrines and does not agree to the sound instruction of our Lord Jesus Christ and to godly teaching, is conceited and understands nothing . . . *See also* **Tit** 1:1

Godly living demands self-discipline 1Co 9:24–27; **2Co** 10:5; **1Ti** 4:7–8

Sorrow for sin is a sign of godliness 2Co 7:10–11

The benefits of godliness
Its value in both this world and the next
1Ti 4:8 . . . godliness has value for all things, holding promise for both the present life and the life to come.

Its present blessings
Dt 4:40 Keep his [the LORD's] decrees and commands, which I am giving you today, so that it may go well with you and your children after you and that you may live long in the land the LORD your God gives you for all time.

1Ti 6:6 But godliness with contentment is great gain. *See also* **Isa** 3:10; **Tit** 3:8

The promise of future blessing
Tit 2:11–13 For the grace of God . . . teaches us to say "No" to ungodliness and worldly passions, and to live self-controlled, upright and godly lives in this present age, while we wait for the blessed hope—the glorious appearing of our great God and Saviour, Jesus Christ, *See also* **2Pe** 3:11–12

Godliness does not guarantee escape from suffering
Ps 12:1 Help, LORD, for the godly are no more; the faithful have vanished from the human race. *See also* **Mic** 7:2; **2Ti** 3:12; **2Pe** 2:9

Apparent godliness may not be genuine
1Ti 6:5; **2Ti** 3:4–5 *See also Christlikeness; holiness; sanctification.*

---

good works
Acts designed specifically to benefit others, which are characteristic of God. He requires and enables his people to do good, although such is contrary to their sinful human nature. Salvation does not depend on good works, but leads to them.

Good works are characteristic of God
Jer 32:36–40 ". . . I [the LORD] will make an everlasting covenant with them [my people]: I will never stop doing good to them, and I will inspire them to fear me, so that they will never turn away from me." *See also* **Ps** 119:17,65; 125:1–4; **Jer** 32:41; **Mic** 2:7; **Zec** 8:14–15; **Ac** 10:37–38

Good works are unnatural for sinful human beings
Jer 13:23 Can Ethiopians change their skin or leopards their spots? Neither can you do good who are accustomed to doing evil. *See also* **Ps** 5:9; 10:7; 14:1–3 pp Ps 53:1–3; **Ps** 36:1–4; 140:3; **Ecc** 7:20; **Isa** 59:7–8; **Jer** 4:22; **Ro** 3:9–18; 7:13–23

God's people are encouraged to do good works
Gal 6:9–10 Let us [believers] not become weary in doing good, for at the proper time we will reap a harvest if we do not give up. Therefore, as we have opportunity, let us do good to all people, especially to those who belong to the family of believers. *See also* **Ps** 37:3; **Ecc** 3:12; **Mt** 5:38–48 pp Lk 6:27–36; **1Pe** 3:8–13; **Ps** 34:12–16; **1Pe** 4:19

God is pleased with the good works of his people
Heb 13:16 . . . do not forget to do good and to share with others, for with such sacrifices God is pleased. *See also* **1Pe** 2:20,15; 3:17

Good works will be rewarded

Jn 5:28–29 ". . . a time is coming when all who are in their graves will hear his [the Son of God's] voice and come out—those who have done good will rise to live, and those who have done evil will rise to be condemned."   *See also* **Lk** 6:35; **Ro** 2:5–11; **Gal** 6:9–10; **1Ti** 6:17–19

Good works as evidence of repentance

Ps 34:14 Turn from evil and do good; seek peace and pursue it.   *See also* **Ps** 37:27; **2Ti** 2:20–21; **Jas** 2:14–21,26; 3:13; **1Pe** 3:10–12

Good works as evidence of God's grace in the lives of believers

2Co 9:8 . . . God is able to make all grace abound to you [believers], so that in all things at all times, having all that you need, you will abound in every good work.   *See also* **Ac** 9:36; **Php** 2:12–13; **Col** 1:10–12

Good works are the purpose of the new creation

Eph 2:10 For we [believers] are God's handiwork, created in Christ Jesus to do good works, which God prepared in advance for us to do.   *See also* **2Ti** 2:21; 3:16–17; **1Pe** 2:13–15

Jesus Christ criticised for doing good works on the Sabbath

Mt 12:9–14 Going on from that place, he [Jesus] went into their synagogue, and a man with a shrivelled hand was there. Looking for a reason to accuse Jesus, they [the Pharisees] asked him, "Is it lawful to heal on the Sabbath?" He said to them, "If any of you has a sheep and it falls into a pit on the Sabbath, will you not take hold of it and lift it out? How much more valuable is a human being than a sheep! Therefore it is lawful to do good on the Sabbath." . . . pp Mk 3:1–6 pp Lk 6:6–11   *See also* **Lk** 13:10–17; **Jn** 9:1–41   *See also faith, nature of; repentance; sin.*

grace

The unmerited favour of God, made known through Jesus Christ, and expressed supremely in the redemption and full forgiveness of sinners through faith in Jesus Christ. The Christian life, from its beginning to its end, is totally dependent upon the grace of God.

God's grace compensates for human weaknesses

2Co 12:8–9 Three times I pleaded with the Lord to take it [thorn in the flesh] away from me. But he said to me, "My grace is sufficient for you, for my power is made perfect in weakness." Therefore I will boast all the more gladly about my weaknesses, so that Christ's power may rest on me.

1Pe 5:10 And the God of all grace, who called you to his eternal glory in Christ, after you have suffered a little while, will himself restore you and make you strong, firm and steadfast.   *See also* **1Co** 2:1–5; **2Co** 9:8; **Heb** 2:14; 4:15; 5:2; **Jas** 4:6; **2Pe** 3:17–18

Believers are to pray for grace

Heb 4:16 Let us then approach the throne of grace with confidence, so that we may receive mercy and find grace to help us in our time of need.   *See also* **Ps** 25:16; **Hos** 14:1–2; **Col** 1:9; 4:12

Christian experience may be summed up in terms of grace

1Co 15:10 . . . by the grace of God I [Paul] am what I am, and his grace to me was not without effect. No, I worked harder than all of them [the other apostles]—yet not I, but the grace of God that was with me.   *See also* **Ac** 18:27; **Ro** 5:2; **Gal** 1:15; **Php** 1:7

Believers should go on to experience more of God's grace

Ac 20:32 "Now I [Paul] commit you [the Ephesian elders] to God and to the word of his grace, which can build you up and give you an inheritance among all those who are sanctified."   *See also* **Ac** 13:43; **Col** 1:3–6; **Heb** 13:9; **1Pe** 5:12; **2Pe** 3:18

Believers are enabled to serve Jesus Christ by his grace

1Pe 4:10 Each of you should use whatever gift you have received to serve others, faithfully administering God's grace in its various forms. *See also* **Ac** 15:39–40; **Ro** 5:17; 12:6; 15:15; **1Co** 3:10; **2Co** 12:9; **Gal** 2:9; **Eph** 3:7–9

God's grace is seen in Christian character, especially in generosity

2Co 8:6–7 . . . we [Paul and Timothy] urged Titus, since he had earlier made a beginning, to bring also to completion this act of grace on your part. But just as you excel in everything—in faith, in speech, in knowledge, in complete earnestness and in your love for us—see that you also excel in this grace of giving. *See also* **Ac** 4:33; 11:22–23; **2Co** 9:13–14; **Col** 4:6

An ongoing experience of God's grace requires the believer's co-operation

2Co 6:1 As God's co-workers we [Paul and Timothy] urge you not to receive God's grace in vain. *See also* **Php** 2:12–13; **Heb** 12:15; **1Pe** 5:5; **Jas** 4:6 *See also giving; maturity; spiritual growth.*

---

guidance

God has purposes and plans for his people, as individuals and communities. Believers and churches should seek his direction and counsel in discerning these purposes and plans in their lives.

---

guidance, examples

Scripture provides numerous examples of individuals who have realised their need of God's guidance and who have been given direction by him.

Examples of God taking the initiative to lead his people

God's guidance of Israel and her leaders at the exodus Ex 13:17–18; **Dt** 8:2,15; 32:12; **Jos** 24:2–3; **Ps** 77:19–20; 106:9; **Ac** 7:36; 13:17
God's guidance likened to that of a shepherd Ps 23:1–3 The LORD is my shepherd, I shall not be in want. He makes me lie down in green

pastures, he leads me beside quiet waters, he restores my soul. He guides me in paths of righteousness for his name's sake. *See also* **Ps** 78:52–54; **Isa** 40:11; 63:11–14; **Jer** 23:3; **Eze** 34:12–13; **Hos** 11:3–4; **Jn** 10:3
God's guidance of Paul during his missionary journeys Ac 16:6–10

Examples of God responding to requests for guidance

Abraham's servant Ge 24:12–27
Balaam Nu 23:3–8
Gideon Jdg 6:36–40
Israel Jdg 20:23–28; **Ps** 107:4–7,23–30
Saul and Samuel 1Sa 9:6–10,15–20; 10:20–24
David 1Sa 23:1–5; 30:7–8; **2Sa** 2:1; 5:18–19,22–25
Ahab and Micaiah 1Ki 22:12–23
Josiah and Huldah the prophetess 2Ki 22:13–20
Jehoshaphat and Jahaziel the son of Zechariah 2Ch 20:15–17
Zedekiah and Jeremiah Jer 21:1–7

Examples of God's guidance being refused or disobeyed

Saul 1Sa 28:4–7
The people of Jerusalem Jer 2:13–17; 43:1–4

---

guidance, need for

God's guidance is needed because people are naturally ignorant and rebellious and there are many who lead others astray.

The need to know and do the will of God

Jer 10:23 I [Jeremiah] know, O LORD, that people's lives are not their own; it is not for them to direct their steps. *See also* **Ezr** 7:18; **1Th** 4:3; **Heb** 13:20–21; **1Pe** 2:15; **Mt** 6:10; 7:21; 12:50 pp **Mk** 3:35 pp **Lk** 8:21; **Jn** 7:17
The concern of Jesus Christ to do the will of God
Jn 6:38 "For I [Jesus] have come down from heaven not to do my will but to do the will of him who sent me." *See also* **Jn** 4:34

By themselves people are ignorant of the right way in life

Pr 14:12 There is a way that seems right to a person, but in the end it leads to death. *See also* **Ecc** 6:12; 8:7; **Isa** 53:6; 59:10; **Mt** 9:36; **1Pe** 2:25

Warnings against false guidance

False prophets and teachers

Jer 23:25–27 "I [the Lord] have heard what the prophets say who prophesy lies in my name. They say, 'I had a dream! I had a dream!' How long will this continue in the hearts of these lying prophets, who prophesy the delusions of their own minds? They think the dreams they tell one another will make my people forget my name, just as their fathers forgot my name through Baal worship."

Lk 11:52 "Woe to you experts in the law, because you have taken away the key to knowledge. You yourselves have not entered, and you have hindered those who were entering." pp **Mt** 23:13   *See also* **Isa** 9:16; **Jer** 23:13; 27:9–10; **Mic** 3:5; **2Pe** 2:1–3; **Jude** 17–19

False shepherds and guides

Jer 50:6 "My [the Lord's] people have been lost sheep; their shepherds have led them astray and caused them to roam on the mountains. They wandered over mountain and hill and forgot their own resting place."

Mt 24:24 "For false Christs and false prophets will appear and perform great signs and miracles to deceive even the elect—if that were possible." *See also* **Isa** 3:12; **Jer** 10:21; 23:1–2; **Eze** 34:4–6; **Mt** 15:14; **Ac** 20:30

Idols and mediums

Zec 10:2 The idols speak deceit, diviners see visions that lie; they tell dreams that are false, they give comfort in vain. Therefore the people wander like sheep oppressed for lack of a shepherd.   *See also* **Lev** 19:31; **Isa** 41:22–24; **Am** 2:4; **Hab** 2:19

Other agencies **1Ki** 11:3; **2Ki** 21:9; **2Ch** 21:11; **Pr** 16:29; **1Co** 15:33; **Rev** 12:9; 18:23

Despite knowing God's will, sinners still rebel against him

Jer 18:11–12 "Now therefore say to the people of Judah and those living in Jerusalem, 'This is what the Lord says: Look! I am preparing a disaster for you and devising a plan against you. So turn from your evil ways, each one of you, and reform your ways and your actions.' But they will reply, 'It's no use. We will continue with our own plans; we will all follow the stubbornness of our evil hearts.'" *See also* **Isa** 30:9–11; **Jer** 6:16; 42:5–6,19–21; **2Ti** 4:3

The adverse consequences of false guidance and disobedience

1Ch 10:13–14 Saul died because he was unfaithful to the Lord; he did not keep the word of the Lord, and even consulted a medium for guidance, and did not enquire of the Lord. So the Lord put him to death and turned the kingdom over to David son of Jesse. *See also* **Job** 5:12; **Ps** 33:10–11; 146:3–4; **Isa** 19:3; 30:1; **Jer** 19:7; **Hos** 11:5–7; **Heb** 3:7–11; **Ps** 95:7–11

guidance, promises

Scripture bears witness to God's promises of guidance for his people.

All God's intentions will be realised

God has purposes

Isa 14:27 For the Lord Almighty has purposed, and who can thwart him? His hand is stretched out, and who can turn it back? *See also* **Job** 36:5; **Isa** 55:10–11; **Jer** 23:20; **Ro** 8:28; **Eph** 3:10–11; **2Ti** 1:9; **Heb** 6:17

God has plans

La 2:17 The Lord has done what he planned; he has fulfilled his word, which he decreed long ago . . .   *See also* **Ps** 33:11; 40:5; **Pr** 16:9; **Isa** 14.24, 25.1; 37:26

God desires his purposes and plans to be fulfilled

Lk 22:42 "Father [God], if you are willing, take this cup from me [Jesus]; yet not my will, but yours be done." pp **Mt** 26:39 pp **Mk** 14:36

Ac 21:14 When he [Paul] would not be dissuaded, we [Paul's companions] gave up and said, "The Lord's will be done."   *See also* **1 Ch** 13:2; **Ps** 57:2; 138:8; **Ac** 18:21; **Ro** 1:10; 15:32; **Jas** 4:13–15

Examples of God working out his purposes
Ac 2:23 "This man [Jesus] was handed over to you by God's set purpose and foreknowledge; and you, with the help of wicked people, put him to death by nailing him to the cross."
Babylon and Israel: **Isa** 46:10–11; 48:14
Jer 29:10–11; **Ac** 13:36; **Ro** 9:11–12,17

God promises to guide Israel and Judah
Ex 15:13 "In your unfailing love you will lead the people you have redeemed. In your strength you will guide them to your holy dwelling."
See also **Ex** 32:34; **Ps** 23:2–3; 48:14; **Isa** 30:21; 49:10; 58:11; **Jer** 31:8–9; **Eze** 34:11–16; **Lk** 1:76–79

Other promises of God's guidance
Ge 12:1; 26:2–3; **1Sa** 16:3; **Ps** 32:8; 67:4; **Isa** 42:16; **Rev** 7:17   *See also life, of faith.*

---

guidance, receiving
God's guidance is promised to those who genuinely desire it and seek it.

God's readiness to guide his people
Ps 25:4–5 Show me [David] your ways, O LORD, teach me your paths; guide me in your truth and teach me, for you are God my Saviour, and my hope is in you all day long.
Jas 1:5 If any of you lacks wisdom, you should ask God, who gives generously to all without finding fault, and it will be given to you.
See also **Ex** 33:12–16; **Job** 6:24; **Ps** 5:8; 27:11; 31:3; 61:1–2; 86:11; 143:8

Guidance is given through the truth and counsel of God
Ps 43:3 Send forth your light and your truth, let them guide me . . .   *See also* **Ps** 16:7–8; 73:23–24; 119:35,105,133; **Jn** 10:3–4,27

Guidance is given to the humble and penitent
Pr 3:5–6 Trust in the LORD with all your heart and lean not on your own understanding; in all your ways acknowledge him, and he will make your paths straight.   *See also* **2Ch** 6:26–27; **Ps** 25:9; 139:23–24; **Isa** 57:15,18–19; **Jer** 50:4–5; **Eze** 20:1–3,30–31

Guidance is given to those willing to obey God's will
Mt 26:39 Going a little farther, he [Jesus] fell with his face to the ground and prayed, "My Father, if it is possible, may this cup be taken from me. Yet not as I will, but as you will."
pp Mk 14:35–36 pp Lk 22:42   *See also* **Nu** 14:8–9; **Ps** 32:8–9; **Isa** 48:17–18; **Ro** 12:1–2

The role of the Holy Spirit in guidance
Lk 12:11–12 "When you [disciples of Jesus Christ] are brought before synagogues, rulers and authorities, do not worry about how you will defend yourselves or what you will say, for the Holy Spirit will teach you at that time what you should say."   *See also* **Ps** 143:10; **Jn** 16:13; **Ac** 10:19–20; 13:2; 16:6–7; **Gal** 5:18; **1Jn** 2:26–27

Receiving guidance from Scripture
Ps 119:105 Your word is a lamp to my feet and a light for my path.
Ps 119:133 Direct my footsteps according to your word; let no sin rule over me.   *See also* **Ps** 19:8; **Isa** 8:19–20; **Ac** 17:11; **2Pe** 1:19

Means of being guided by God
The pillar of cloud and the pillar of fire
Ex 13:21–22 By day the LORD went ahead of them in a pillar of cloud to guide them on their way and by night in a pillar of fire to give them light, so that they could travel by day or night. Neither the pillar of cloud by day nor the pillar of fire by night left its place in front of the people.   *See also* **Ex** 14:19–20; **Ne** 9:19
The Urim and the Thummim Ex 28:29–30; **Nu** 27:21
The casting of lots 1Sa 14:36–42; **Pr** 16:33; **Jnh** 1:7; **Ac** 1:26

Dreams and visions
Mt 2:19–20 After Herod died, an angel of the Lord appeared in a dream to Joseph in Egypt and said, "Get up, take the child and his mother and go to the land of Israel, for those who were trying to take the child's life are dead."
Ac 9:10–11 In Damascus there was a disciple named Ananias. The Lord called to him in a vision, "Ananias!" "Yes, Lord," he answered. The Lord told him, "Go to the house of Judas on Straight Street and ask for a man from Tarsus named Saul, for he is praying."   *See also* **Ge** 40:5–8; **Joel** 2:28; **Ac** 10:3–6; 11:5–9
Angels
Ac 8:26 Now an angel of the Lord said to Philip, "Go south to the road—the desert road—that goes down from Jerusalem to Gaza."   *See also* **Ac** 5:19   *See also discernment; humility; prayer; repentance; waiting on God.*

---

holiness
The quality of God that sets him utterly apart from his world, especially in terms of his purity and sanctity. The holiness of God is also manifested in the persons and work of Jesus Christ and the Holy Spirit. Believers are called upon to become like God in his holiness.

---

holiness, believers' growth in
Believers are enabled to grow in holiness on account of the sacrificial death of Jesus Christ, foreshadowed by the OT sacrificial system, and through the sanctifying work of the Holy Spirit.

Holiness begins with God's initiative
God chooses who and what is to be holy
2Ch 7:16 "I [the LORD] have chosen and consecrated this temple so that my Name may be there for ever. My eyes and my heart will always be there." pp 1Ki 9:3   *See also* **Ex** 20:11; **Nu** 16:7; **2Ch** 29:11; **Zec** 2:12
God chooses and calls his people to holiness
Dt 7:6 For you [Israel] are a people holy to the LORD your God. The LORD your God has chosen you out of all the peoples on the face of the earth to be his people, his treasured possession.

Eph 1:4 For he [God] chose us [Christians] in him [Christ] before the creation of the world to be holy and blameless in his sight . . .   *See also* **Dt** 14:2; **Ro** 1:7; **Col** 3:12; **1Pe** 1:2,15

Holiness is conferred by the holy God
Holiness is conferred by the presence of God
Ex 29:42–43 "For the generations to come this burnt offering is to be made regularly at the entrance to the Tent of Meeting before the LORD. There I [the LORD] will meet you and speak to you; there also I will meet with the Israelites, and the place will be consecrated by my glory."
See also **Ex** 3:4–5; 19:23; **2Ch** 7:1–2
Holiness is conferred through covenant relationship with God
Ex 19:5–6 " 'Now if you obey me [the LORD] fully and keep my covenant, then out of all nations you will be my treasured possession. Although the whole earth is mine, you will be for me a kingdom of priests and a holy nation.' . . ."   *See also* **Dt** 28:9; **Eze** 37:26–28; **1Pe** 2:9
Holiness is conferred by the sovereign action of God
1Th 5:23 May God himself, the God of peace, sanctify you through and through. May your whole spirit, soul and body be kept blameless at the coming of our Lord Jesus Christ.   *See also* **Lev** 20:8; **Isa** 4:3–4; **Eze** 36:25; **Zep** 1:7; **Ac** 15:9; **Heb** 2:11

Holiness through the OT rituals
Cleansing from what is unclean
Nu 8:6–7 "Take the Levites from among the other Israelites and make them ceremonially clean To purify them, do this: Sprinkle the water of cleansing on them; then make them shave their whole bodies and wash their clothes, and so purify themselves."   *See also* **Ex** 19:14; **Nu** 19:9; **Ne** 12:30
Purification and atonement through sacrifice
Nu 8:12–14 "After the Levites lay their hands on the heads of the bulls, use the one for a sin offering to the LORD and the other for a burnt offering, to make atonement for the Levites. Make the Levites stand in front of Aaron and his sons

and then present them as a wave offering to the LORD. In this way you are to set the Levites apart from the other Israelites, and the Levites will be mine."   *See also* **Ex** 29:35–37; **Lev** 8:14–15; 16:5–10,15–22,29–30

Consecration by anointing
Lev 8:10–12 Then Moses took the anointing oil and anointed the tabernacle and everything in it, and so consecrated them. He sprinkled some of the oil on the altar seven times, anointing the altar and all its utensils and the basin with its stand, to consecrate them. He poured some of the anointing oil on Aaron's head and anointed him to consecrate him.   *See also* **Ex** 29:21; 40:9

Holiness through Jesus Christ
Through the sacrifice of Jesus Christ
Heb 10:10 . . . we have been made holy through the sacrifice of the body of Jesus Christ once for all.   *See also* **Eph** 5:25–27; **Col** 1:22; **Heb** 1:3; 9:13–14,23–28; 10:14,19–22; 13:12; **1Jn** 1:7; 2:2; 4:10

Through relationship with Jesus Christ
1Co 1:2 To the church of God in Corinth, to those sanctified in Christ Jesus and called to be holy, together with all those everywhere who call on the name of our Lord Jesus Christ—their Lord and ours: *See also* **1Co** 1:30

Holiness through the sanctifying work of the Holy Spirit
2Th 2:13 But we ought always to thank God for you, brothers and sisters loved by the Lord, because from the beginning God chose you to be saved through the sanctifying work of the Spirit and through belief in the truth.   *See also* **Jn** 3:5–8; **Ro** 15:16; **1Co** 6:11; **1Th** 4:7–8; **Tit** 3:5; **1Pe** 1:2

The human response to holiness
Repentance
1Jn 1:9 If we confess our sins, he is faithful and just and will forgive us our sins and purify us from all unrighteousness.   *See also* **Ezr** 9:1–7; 10:1–4; **Ps** 51:1–10; **Ac** 2:38; **Ro** 6:11–13; **Jas** 4:8

Faith
Gal 5:5 But by faith we eagerly await through the Spirit the righteousness for which we hope.   *See also* **Ro** 1:17–18; **2Th** 2:13
Obedience
1Pe 1:22 Now that you have purified yourselves by obeying the truth so that you have sincere mutual affection, love one another deeply, from the heart.   *See also* **Ps** 119:9; **Jn** 17:17; **Ro** 6:16–19   *See also faith; obedience; repentance; sanctification; spiritual growth.*

---

holiness, in behaviour
Behaviour that reflects the holy character of God himself is to be expressed in both social and personal dimensions of life.

Holiness in practice is a reflection of God's own character
1Pe 1:15–16 . . . just as he who called you is holy, so be holy in all you do; for it is written: "Be holy, because I am holy."   *See also* **Lev** 11:44–45; 19:2; 20:7; **Eph** 4:24; **1Jn** 3:3

Holiness demands a different way of life
Shunning practices that defile
Lev 18:1–3 The LORD said to Moses, "Speak to the Israelites and say to them: 'I am the LORD your God. You must not do as they do in Egypt, where you used to live, and you must not do as they do in the land of Canaan, where I am bringing you. Do not follow their practices.'"
Eph 5:11–12 Have nothing to do with the fruitless deeds of darkness, but rather expose them . . .
1Ti 5:22 Do not be hasty in the laying on of hands, and do not share in the sins of others. Keep yourself pure.   *See also* **Lev** 18:21–24, 29–30; 20:1–3,6–7,23–26; 21:7; **2Co** 6:17–7:1; **Gal** 5:19–21,24; **Eph** 5:3–7; **Col** 3:5–10
Obedience to God's law
Lev 20:7–8 "'Consecrate yourselves and be holy, because I am the LORD your God. Keep my decrees and follow them. I am the LORD, who makes you holy.'"   *See also* **Lev** 18:4–5;

19:37; **Dt** 6:25; 28:9; **Ps** 119:9; **Ro** 7:12; **1Pe** 1:22

Holiness is expressed in social behaviour

Care for the disadvantaged

Lev 19:9–10 " 'When you reap the harvest of your land, do not reap to the very edges of your field or gather the gleanings of your harvest. Do not go over your vineyard a second time or pick up the grapes that have fallen. Leave them for the poor and the alien. I am the LORD your God.' "   *See also* **Lev** 19:14,33–34; **1Ti** 5:3–4,8; **Jas** 1:27

A concern for truth and justice

Lev 19:15–16 " 'Do not pervert justice; do not show partiality to the poor or favouritism to the great, but judge your neighbour fairly. Do not go about spreading slander among your people. Do not do anything that endangers your neighbour's life. I am the LORD.' "   *See also* **Lev** 19:11–13,35–37

Loving one's neighbour

Lev 19:18 " 'Do not seek revenge or bear a grudge against one of your people, but love your neighbour as yourself. I am the LORD.' "
See also **Lev** 19:16–17

Holiness is expressed in family and sexual relations

1Th 4:3–7 It is God's will that you should be sanctified: that you should avoid sexual immorality; that each of you should learn to control your own body in a way that is holy and honourable, not in passionate lust like the heathen, who do not know God; and that in this matter no-one should wrong or take advantage of a brother or sister. The Lord will punish those who commit all such sins, as we have already told you and warned you. For God did not call us to be impure, but to live a holy life.   *See also* **Lev** 18:5–20,22–23; 19:3; 20:9; **Eph** 5:3; **1Co** 6:13–15,18–19

Holiness is seen in personal character

Col 3:12 . . . as God's chosen people, holy and dearly loved, clothe yourselves with compassion, kindness, humility, gentleness and patience.
See also **Eph** 4:23–24,32–5: ; **2Ti** 2:22

hope

In Scripture, a confident expectation for the future, describing both the act of hoping and the object hoped for. When grounded in God, hope provides the motivation to live the Christian life even in the face of trouble.

hope, as confidence

Hope means more than a vague wish that something will happen. It is a sure and confident expectation of God's future faithfulness and presence. The horizon of Christian hope extends beyond death into an eternity prepared by God himself, the reality of which is guaranteed by Jesus Christ.

God and Jesus Christ are the hope of believers

Ps 71:5 For you have been my hope, O Sovereign LORD, my confidence since my youth.
1Ti 1:1 Paul, an apostle of Christ Jesus by the command of God our Saviour and of Christ Jesus our hope   *See also* **Jer** 14:8; 17:13; **Mt** 12:21; **Isa** 42:4; **Ac** 28:20; **Ro** 15:12–13; **Isa** 11:10; **1Ti** 4:10; **1Pe** 1:21

The hope of resurrection and eternal life

Ac 23:6 Then Paul, knowing that some of them were Sadducees and the others Pharisees, called out in the Sanhedrin, "My brothers, I am a Pharisee, the son of a Pharisee. I stand on trial because of my hope in the resurrection of the dead."
Tit 1:2 . . . the hope of eternal life, which God, who does not lie, promised before the beginning of time,   *See also* **Ac** 2:26–27; **Ps** 16:9; **Ac** 24:15; **Ro** 8:24; **1Co** 15:19; **Tit** 3:7; **Heb** 6:11; 7:19; **1Pe** 1:3

The hope of future glory

Ro 5:2 through whom [Christ] we have gained access by faith into this grace in which we now stand. And we rejoice in the hope of the glory of God.
Col 1:27 To them [the saints] God has chosen

to make known among the Gentiles the glorious riches of this mystery, which is Christ in you, the hope of glory.
Tit 2:13 . . . we wait for the blessed hope—the glorious appearing of our great God and Saviour, Jesus Christ,   *See also* **Ro** 8:18–21; **2Co** 3:10–12; **Gal** 5:5; **Eph** 1:12,18; **1Th** 2:19; 5:8; **2Ti** 4:8

Hope is a Christian virtue
Ro 5:3–4 Not only so, but we also rejoice in our sufferings, because we know that suffering produces perseverance; perseverance, character; and character, hope.
1Co 13:13 And now these three remain: faith, hope and love. But the greatest of these is love.   *See also* **Ro** 12:12; 15:13; **1Co** 13:7; **Eph** 4:4; **Col** 1:23; **Heb** 3:6; **1Pe** 3:15

The effect of future hope on living now
Col 1:4–5 . . . we [Paul and Timothy] have heard of your faith in Christ Jesus and of the love you have for all the saints—the faith and love that spring from the hope that is stored up for you in heaven and that you have already heard about in the word of truth, the gospel   *See also* **Ro** 8:22–23; **1Th** 1:3; 5:8; **Heb** 6:19; **1Pe** 1:13; **1Jn** 3:1–3   *See also eternal life.*

---

hope, in God
A total grounding of one's confidence and expectation in God's goodness and providential care even in the face of trouble.

Hope in God is commanded
Ps 131:3 O Israel, put your hope in the LORD both now and for evermore.
1Ti 6:17 Command those who are rich in this present world not to be arrogant nor to put their hope in wealth, which is so uncertain, but to put their hope in God, who richly provides us with everything for our enjoyment.   *See also* **Ps** 31:24; 130:7; **Ro** 12:12; **Heb** 10:23

Hope can be placed in Scripture as the word of God
Ps 119:74 May those who fear you rejoice when they see me, for I have put my hope in your word.   *See also* **Ps** 119:43,49,81,114,147; 130:5; **Isa** 42:4; **Ac** 26:6; **Ro** 15:4; **Col** 1:5

Hope can be placed in God in the face of difficulty or trial
Ps 42:5 Why are you downcast, O my soul? Why so disturbed within me? Put your hope in God, for I will yet praise him, my Saviour . . .
2Co 1:10 He [God] has delivered us from such a deadly peril, and he will deliver us. On him we have set our hope that he will continue to deliver us,   *See also* **Ezr** 10:2; **Job** 5:16; 13:15; **Ps** 9:18; 25:19–21; 119:116; **Jer** 14:19; **1Ti** 5:5

The outcome of hoping in God
It brings security and confidence
Ps 146:5 Blessed are those whose help is the God of Jacob, whose hope is in the LORD their God,   *See also* **Job** 11:18; **Ps** 25:3; 33:17–18,20–22; 39:7; 52:9; 71:5; 147:11; **Jer** 14:22; **La** 3:21–22; **Ac** 24:15; **Ro** 15:12; **1Ti** 4:10
It leads to specific results
Ps 37:9 For those who are evil will be cut off, but those who hope in the LORD will inherit the land.
Isa 40:31 but those who hope in the LORD will renew their strength. They will soar on wings like eagles; they will run and not grow weary, they will walk and not be faint.
Ro 15:13 May the God of hope fill you with all joy and peace as you trust in him, so that you may overflow with hope by the power of the Holy Spirit.   *See also* **Ps** 33:22; 62:5; 71:14; **Pr** 24:14–16; **Isa** 51:5; **Jer** 29:11; **La** 3:25; **Mic** 7:7; **Zec** 9:12; **Ro** 4:18; 5:2,5; **2Co** 1:7; 10:15; **1Th** 1:3; **2Ti** 2:25; **Tit** 1:2; **1Pe** 3:5; **1Jn** 3:3
See also faith.

---

hope, results of
Hope gives believers confidence and reassurance in this present life, allowing them to lead effective lives for God. It also reassures them of the reality of eternal life, allowing them to face death with confidence.

Hope reassures believers in this present life

Hope reassures believers in their faith
Heb 3:6 But Christ is faithful as a son over God's house. And we are his house, if we hold on to our courage and the hope of which we boast. *See also* **Eph** 1:18–19; **Heb** 7:18–22; 10:23

Hope encourages believers
Ps 31:2 Turn your ear to me, come quickly to my rescue; be my rock of refuge, a strong fortress to save me. *See also* **Isa** 40:31; 49:23; **Ro** 5:3–5

Hope encourages believers to rejoice
Ro 12:12 Be joyful in hope, patient in affliction, faithful in prayer. *See also* **Ro** 5:1–2
Hope encourages believers to look for restoration Ps 37:9; **Jer** 14:8; 31:17; **La** 3:29–31; **Hos** 2:15; **Zec** 9:12

Hope leads to more effective Christian living and witness

Hope encourages believers to be bold
2Co 3:12 Therefore, since we have such a hope, we are very bold.
Hope encourages believers to evangelise 1Pe 3:15
Hope leads to godly living Ps 25:21; **Heb** 6:10–12; **1Jn** 3:2
Hope equips believers for spiritual warfare 1Th 5:8
Hope enables believers to face suffering with confidence
Ro 5:3–5 Not only so, but we also rejoice in our sufferings, because we know that suffering produces perseverance; perseverance, character; and character, hope. And hope does not disappoint us, because God has poured out his love into our hearts by the Holy Spirit, whom he has given us. *See also* **Ps** 22:24; 147:11; **Php** 1:20

Hope enables believers to face the future with confidence
Hope assures believers of an eternal dimension to life
1Co 15:19 If only for this life we have hope in Christ, we are to be pitied more than all people.

Hope enables believers to face death with confidence
Ps 16:9–10 Therefore my heart is glad and my tongue rejoices; my body also will rest secure, because you will not abandon me to the grave, nor will you let your Holy One see decay. *See also* **Job** 19:25–27; **Ps** 33:18; **1Co** 6:14; **2Co** 4:10–14; **Php** 1:3–6; **Rev** 1:17–18
Hope assures believers of their eternal life Ac 2:26–27; **Ro** 8:23–25; **Tit** 1:1–2; 3:7; **1Pe** 1:3
Hope enables believers to face the coming wrath with confidence 1Th 1:10
Hope assures believers of their heavenly inheritance
1Pe 1:3–5 Praise be to the God and Father of our Lord Jesus Christ! In his great mercy he has given us new birth into a living hope through the resurrection of Jesus Christ from the dead, and into an inheritance that can never perish, spoil or fade—kept in heaven for you, who through faith are shielded by God's power until the coming of the salvation that is ready to be revealed in the last time. *See also* **Eph** 1:18 *See also discipleship, benefits; patience; peace, experience; perseverance.*

hospitality

Acts of generosity and friendship towards strangers. God's people are called to be hospitable as part of their duty to others and in gratitude for the salvation they have received from God. Showing hospitality includes the responsibility to protect those received as guests.

Hospitality is commanded by God
Heb 13:2 Do not forget to entertain strangers, for by so doing some people have entertained angels without knowing it. *See also* **Isa** 58:6–7; **Jn** 13:12–15; **Ro** 12:13; **1Pe** 4:9

Hospitality is a responsibility of leaders
1Ti 3:2 Now the overseer must be above reproach, the husband of but one wife, temperate, self-controlled, respectable, hospitable, able to teach, *See also* **1Ti** 5:9–10; **Tit** 1:8

Hospitality indicates true discipleship
Job 31:32 "but no stranger had to spend the night in the street, for my [Job's] door was always open to the traveller—" *See also* **Mt** 25:35

Hospitality crosses social barriers
Of race
Lev 19:33–34 " 'When aliens live with you in your land, do not ill-treat them. The aliens living with you must be treated as one of your native-born. Love them as yourself, for you were aliens in Egypt. I am the LORD your God.' " *See also* **Ex** 22:21; 23:9
Of class and status
Lk 14:12–14 Then Jesus said to his host, "When you give a luncheon or dinner, do not invite your friends, your brothers, sisters, relatives, or your rich neighbours; if you do, they may invite you back and so you will be repaid. But when you give a banquet, invite the poor, the crippled, the lame, the blind, and you will be blessed. Although they cannot repay you, you will be repaid at the resurrection of the righteous." *See also* **Jas** 2:2–4

Hospitality is to be offered to Christian ministers
Ro 16:1–2 I commend to you our sister Phoebe, a servant of the church in Cenchrea. I ask you to receive her in the Lord in a way worthy of the saints and to give her any help she may need from you, for she has been a great help to many people, including me. *See also* **Col** 4:10; **3Jn** 5–10

Hospitality is to be refused to false teachers
2Jn 10–11

Hospitality as a picture of salvation
Ps 23:5–6 You [the LORD] prepare a table before me in the presence of my enemies. You anoint my head with oil; my cup overflows. Surely goodness and love will follow me all the days of my life, and I will dwell in the house of the LORD for ever.

Rev 3:20 "Here I [Jesus] am! I stand at the door and knock. If anyone hears my voice and opens the door, I will come in and eat with them, and they with me." *See also* **Isa** 25:6; **Mt** 22:1–14; **Lk** 14:15–24; 19:1–10; **Jn** 14:2–3

Warnings against inhospitable behaviour
Dt 23:3–4 No Ammonite or Moabite or any of their descendants may enter the assembly of the LORD, even down to the tenth generation. For they did not come to meet you with bread and water on your way when you came out of Egypt . . . *See also* **Mt** 10:14 pp **Mk** 6:11 pp **Lk** 9:5; **Mt** 25:41–45 *See also giving.*

humility
An attitude of lowliness and obedience, grounded in the recognition of our status before God as his creatures.

God commands humility
Mic 6:8 He has showed you, O people, what is good. And what does the LORD require of you? To act justly and to love mercy and to walk humbly with your God.
Jas 4:10 Humble yourselves before the Lord, and he will lift you up.
1Pe 3:8 Finally, all of you, live in harmony with one another; be sympathetic, love one another, be compassionate and humble. *See also* **Ex** 10:3; **Pr** 16:19; **Isa** 57:15; 58:5; **Zep** 2:3; **Lk** 14:9–11; **Ro** 12:3; **1Co** 1:28; **Eph** 4:2; **Col** 3:12; **Tit** 3:2; **Jas** 3:13; **1Pe** 5:5

God exalts the humble
Lk 1:52 He has brought down rulers from their thrones but has lifted up the humble. *See also* **2Sa** 7:8; **1Ki** 14:7

Believers should humble themselves before God
2Ch 7:14 "if my people, who are called by my [the LORD's] name, will humble themselves and pray and seek my face and turn from their wicked ways, then will I hear from heaven and will

forgive their sin and will heal their land."
1Pe 5:6 Humble yourselves, therefore, under God's mighty hand, that he may lift you up in due time.   *See also* **2Sa** 22:28
Humility linked with repentance: **1Ki** 21:29; **2Ki** 22:19; **2Ch** 12:6–7,12; 30:11; 33:12,19; 34:27
Humility linked with God's favour: **Ps** 18:27; 25:9; 138:6; 147:6; 149:4; **Pr** 3:34; 18:12; **Jas** 4:6; **Isa** 29:19; 38:15; 57:15; **Pr** 15:33; 22:4
Ps 35:13; **Jer** 44:10

God humbles his people to renew and restore them

Ps 44:9 But now you [Lord] have rejected and humbled us; you no longer go out with our armies.   *See also* **Lev** 26:41; **Dt** 8:2,16; **1Ki** 11:39; **2Ch** 28:19; **Ps** 107:39; **Isa** 9:1; **2Co** 12:21

God humbles the proud

Lk 18:14 [Jesus said] ". . . all those who exalt themselves will be humbled, and those who humble themselves will be exalted."   *See also* **1Sa** 2:7; **Isa** 2:11,17; 5:15; 13:11; 23:9; 25:11; 26:5; **Da** 4:37

Examples of humble people

Outstanding individuals **Ge** 32:10; 41:16; **Nu** 12:3; **1Sa** 9:21
David: **1Sa** 18:18; **2Sa** 7:18
1Ki 3:7; **Da** 2:30; **Mt** 3:14; **Lk** 1:43,48
Paul: **1Ti** 1:15; **Ac** 20:19
Other examples **2Sa** 16:4; **Pr** 6:3; 11:2; 16:19; 29:23; **Da** 5:22; **Mt** 8:8; 15:27; 18:4

The example of Jesus Christ

Php 2:5–8 Your attitude should be the same as that of Christ Jesus: Who, being in very nature God, did not consider equality with God something to be grasped, but made himself nothing, taking the very nature of a servant, being made in human likeness. And being found in appearance as a human being, he humbled himself and became obedient to death—even death on a cross!
The humility of Jesus Christ foretold: **Isa** 53:3–5,7–8; **Zec** 9:9 pp **Mt** 21:5 pp **Jn** 12:15
Mt 11:29; 20:28; **Lk** 22:26–27; **Jn** 13:4; **2Co** 8:9   *See also* pride.

immaturity

The result of insufficient growth, or a failure to develop to one's full potential.

Marks of physical immaturity

Pride **2Sa** 15:1–4
Rejection of wise counsel **Dt** 21:18; **1Ki** 12:8
Tactlessness **1Ki** 12:13–14
Lack of respect **2Ki** 2:23; **Job** 19:18
Weakness of character **2Ch** 13:7
Foolishness **Pr** 22:15
Lack of understanding **Dt** 1:39; **Pr** 1:4; **Jnh** 4:11; **1Co** 13:11
Lack of self-control **Tit** 2:6
Disgrace **Pr** 29:15
Waste **Lk** 15:13

Spiritual immaturity is to be avoided

1Co 14:20 Brothers and sisters, stop thinking like children. In regard to evil be infants, but in your thinking be adults.
Heb 6:1 Therefore let us leave the elementary teachings about Christ and go on to maturity . . .   *See also* **2Co** 13:9,11; **Eph** 4:13,15; **Col** 1:28; 4:12; **Jas** 1:4; **2Pe** 3:18

Marks of spiritual immaturity
Backsliding

Mt 13:20–21 "Those who received the seed that fell on rocky places are people who hear the word and at once receive it with joy. But since they have no root, they last only a short time. When trouble or persecution comes because of the word, they quickly fall away." pp **Mk** 4:16–17 pp **Lk** 8:13   *See also* **Gal** 4:8–9
An over-sensitive conscience

Ro 14:2 One person's faith allows the eating of everything, but another person, whose faith is weak, eats only vegetables.
Lack of spiritual understanding

1Co 3:1–2 Brothers and sisters, I could not address you as spiritual but as worldly—mere infants in Christ. I gave you milk, not solid food, for you were not yet ready for it. Indeed, you are still not ready.   *See also* **Mt** 11:16–19 pp **Lk** 7:31–35; **Heb** 5:11–14

Divisiveness

1Co 3:3 You are still worldly. For since there is jealousy and quarrelling among you, are you not worldly? Are you not acting like mere human beings?

Instability

Eph 4:14 Then we will no longer be infants, tossed back and forth by the waves, and blown here and there by every wind of teaching and by the cunning and craftiness of people in their deceitful scheming.   *See also* **Jas** 1:6–7

Pride

1Ti 3:6 He must not be a recent convert, or he may become conceited and fall under the same judgment as the devil.   *See also* **1Pe** 5:5

Remedies for immaturity

Confession of sin

Pr 28:13 Those who conceal their sins do not prosper, but those who confess and renounce them find mercy.   *See also* **Jer** 3:13–22; **Jas** 5:16; **1Jn** 1:9

Discipline

Pr 3:11–12 My son, do not despise the LORD's discipline and do not resent his rebuke, because the LORD disciplines those he loves, as parents the children they delight in.   *See also* **Ps** 119:67–71; **1Pe** 4:1–2; **Rev** 3:19

Prayer and meditation

Ps 119:97–99 Oh, how I love your law! I meditate on it all day long. Your commands make me wiser than my enemies, for they are ever with me. I have more insight than all my teachers, for I meditate on your statutes.   *See also* **Ps** 119:27; **Jn** 17:17–19; **Ro** 8:26; **Heb** 4:16; **Jas** 1:25   *See also discipline; maturity; self-control; spiritual growth.*

immorality

Behaviour which is contrary to the will of God for his people. Although the term may be used to refer to a wide range of immoral actions, it is used especially in relation to unacceptable sexual behaviour.

immorality, examples

Prohibited sexual relationships

Incest

Lev 18:6 " 'No-one is to approach any close relative to have sexual relations. I am the LORD.' "   *See also* **Ge** 19:33–36; 35:22; 38:13–18; **Lev** 18:7–20; **2Sa** 16:22; **1Co** 5:1

Adultery 2Sa 11:4; **Jer** 23:14; 29:23; **Hos** 1:2; **Jn** 4:17–18

Prostitution

1Co 6:15–16 Do you not know that your bodies are members of Christ himself? Shall I then take the members of Christ and unite them with a prostitute? Never! Do you not know that he who unites himself with a prostitute is one with her in body? For it is said, "The two will become one flesh."   *See also* **Jdg** 16:1; **1Ki** 3:16; **Hos** 4:13–15

Fornication Nu 25:1,6; **1Sa** 2:22

Rape Ge 34:1–2; **2Sa** 13:10–14

Homosexuality Ge 19:5; **Jdg** 19:22

Sexual immorality among Christians
1Co 5:1; **2Pe** 2:13–14; **Jude** 4; **Rev** 2:14,20

Sexual immorality as a picture of spiritual unfaithfulness

Among God's people

Jer 3:20 ". . . like a woman unfaithful to her husband, so you have been unfaithful to me, O house of Israel," declares the LORD.   *See also* **Jer** 13:26–27; **Eze** 6:9; 16:15–17; **Hos** 2:1–10; 3:1; 4:10–12; 5:4; **Mt** 12:39; 16:4

In the world Rev 14:8; 17:1–2,4; 18:2; 19:2
See also holiness, in behaviour.

immorality, sexual

Sexual behaviour which is contrary to God's law.

Sexual immorality is widespread in the world

1Co 5:9–10 I [Paul] have written to you in my letter not to associate with sexually immoral people—not at all meaning the people of this world who are immoral, or the greedy and swindlers, or idolaters. In that case you would have to leave this world.   *See also* **1Co** 7:1–2; **Rev** 9:21

The cause of sexual immorality
Gal 5:19 The acts of the sinful nature are obvious: sexual immorality, impurity and debauchery;   *See also* **Mt** 15:19–20 pp **Mk** 7:21–23; **Eph** 4:17–19

The folly of sexual immorality
Pr 6:32 . . . a man who commits adultery lacks judgment; whoever does so destroys himself. *See also* **Pr** 5:3–5,20; 6:26

Sexual immorality brings punishment
Heb 13:4 Marriage should be honoured by all, and the marriage bed kept pure, for God will judge the adulterer and all the sexually immoral.   *See also* **Lev** 20:10–21; **Pr** 2:16–19; 22:14; **Eze** 16:38; **Ro** 1:24–27; **Eph** 5:5; **Col** 3:5–6; **1Th** 4:3–6; **Jude** 7; **Rev** 21:8; 22:15

Sexual immorality has no place in the Christian life
1Th 4:3 It is God's will that you should be sanctified: that you should avoid sexual immorality; **1Th 4:7** . . . God did not call us to be impure, but to live a holy life.   *See also* **Ac** 15:20,29; 21:25; **Ro** 13:13; **1Co** 6:9–11,13–20; 10:8; **Eph** 5:3; **Col** 3:5; **Heb** 12:16

Forgiveness for sexual immorality
1Co 6:11 And that [immoral] is what some of you were. But you were washed, you were sanctified, you were justified in the name of the Lord Jesus Christ and by the Spirit of our God. *See also* **Lk** 7:36–39; **Jn** 8:3–11   *See also flesh, sinful nature; forgiveness; purity; self-control; temptation.*

---

jealousy
A strong feeling of possessiveness, often caused by the possibility that something which belongs, or ought to belong, to one is about to be taken away. The word can be used in a positive sense (e.g., the jealousy of God), meaning a passionate

commitment to something which rightly belongs to one. It can also be used in a negative sense (e.g., human jealousy), to mean a self-destructive human emotion similar to envy.

God's jealousy for his people
God's jealousy demands an exclusive response from his people
Ex 20:4–6 "You shall not make for yourself an idol in the form of anything in heaven above or on the earth beneath or in the waters below. You shall not bow down to them or worship them; for I, the Lord your God, am a jealous God, punishing the children for the sin of the parents to the third and fourth generation of those who hate me, but showing love to a thousand ¸generations¸ of those who love me and keep my commandments."   *See also* **Ex** 34:14; **Dt** 32:16,21
God pictured as a jealous husband with an unfaithful wife Eze 16:1–63
God is jealously protective of his people
Joel 2:18 Then the Lord will be jealous for his land and take pity on his people.   *See also* **Isa** 26:11; **Zec** 1:14–15; 8:2
God's possessiveness expresses itself in judgment on his people's unfaithfulness
Dt 4:24 For the Lord your God is a consuming fire, a jealous God.   *See also* **Dt** 6:15; 29:20; **Jos** 24:19; **1Ki** 14:22; **Eze** 23:25; 36:6; **Na** 1:2; **Zep** 1:18; 3:8

Human jealousy is potentially destructive
Human jealousy arises from sin
Mk 7:21–23 [Jesus said] "For from within, out of your hearts, come evil thoughts, sexual immorality, theft, murder, adultery, greed, malice, deceit, lewdness, envy, slander, arrogance and folly. All these evils come from inside and make you 'unclean'." pp **Mt** 15:19–20
Human jealousy can be destructive
Pr 14:30 A heart at peace gives life to the body, but envy rots the bones.   *See also* **Job** 5:2; **Pr** 27:4; **Ecc** 9:5–6
Human jealousy is criticised by Scripture
Gal 5:19–21 The acts of the sinful nature are

obvious: sexual immorality, impurity and debauchery; idolatry and witchcraft; hatred, discord, jealousy, fits of rage, selfish ambition, dissensions, factions and envy; drunkenness, orgies, and the like. I warn you, as I did before, that those who live like this will not inherit the kingdom of God. *See also* **Ps** 37:1–2; **Pr** 23:17; **Ro** 13:13; **1Co** 13:4–7; **Tit** 3:3–5; **Jas** 3:14–16

Examples of jealousy
In the OT Ge 4:3–5; 27:41; 30:1
Joseph's brothers: **Ge** 37:4; **Ac** 7:9
1Sa 18:6–9; **Isa** 11:13
In the early church Ac 5:17; 13:45; 17:5; **1Co** 3:3; **2Co** 12:20 *See also coveting.*

---

joy, experience
Joy, a quality of delight and happiness, is experienced naturally in many circumstances of life and in human relationships. It is especially important in the life of God's people, who experience joy in response to all that God has done for them. Ultimately, joy is grounded in the work of God as Father, Son and Holy Spirit.

Poetic images of joy in creation
Ps 96:11–13 Let the heavens rejoice, let the earth be glad; let the sea resound, and all that is in it; let the fields be jubilant, and everything in them. Then all the trees of the forest will sing for joy; they will sing before the LORD, for he comes, he comes to judge the earth. He will judge the world in righteousness and the peoples in his truth. pp 1Ch 16:31–33 *See also* **Job** 39:13; **Ps** 65:12–13; 89:12; 97:1; 100:1; **Isa** 35:1–2; 49:13

Joy arising from specific circumstances
Joy because of the birth of children
Lk 1:13–15 . . . ". . . you are to give him the name John. He will be a joy and delight to you, and many will rejoice because of his birth, for he will be great in the sight of the Lord . . ." *See also* **Ge** 30:12–13; **Lk** 1:58
Joy because of victory and deliverance Ex 18:9; **1Sa** 18:6; **Jer** 41:13; **Zec** 10:7

Joy because of the behaviour of others
Pr 15:30 A cheerful look brings joy to the heart . . . *See also* **Pr** 23:24–25; **Mt** 14:6–7; **Heb** 13:17
Joy because of God's blessings in everyday life
Ecc 5:19–20 . . . when God gives people wealth and possessions, and the ability to enjoy them, to accept their lot and be happy in their work—this is a gift of God . . .

Joy arising from relationships
Php 4:1 Therefore, my brothers and sisters, you whom I [Paul] love and long for, my joy and crown, that is how you should stand firm in the Lord, dear friends! *See also* **Pr** 5:18; **SS** 1:4; 3:11; **Ro** 12:15; 15:26–27; **1Co** 12:26; **Php** 1:4–6; **Phm** 7

God's people find their joy in him
Ps 4:7 You [LORD] have filled my heart with greater joy than when their grain and new wine abound.
Ps 16:11 You [LORD] have made known to me the path of life; you will fill me with joy in your presence, with eternal pleasures at your right hand.
Hab 3:17–18 Though the fig-tree does not bud and there are no grapes on the vines, though the olive crop fails and the fields produce no food, though there are no sheep in the pen and no cattle in the stalls, yet I will rejoice in the LORD, I will be joyful in God my Saviour.
Php 3:1 Finally, my brothers and sisters, rejoice in the Lord! *See also* **1Ch** 16:10; **Ps** 43:4; **Php** 1:23–26; 4:4
God himself gives joy to his people Ne 12:43; **Job** 8:21; **Ecc** 2:26; **Isa** 9:3; **Ac** 13:52; 14:15–17
Reasons for God's people to know joy 1Sa 2:1; **2Ch** 6:41; **Job** 22:22–26; **Ps** 19:8; 94:19; 122:1; **Isa** 25:9; 58:13–14; **Jer** 15:16; 31:12; **Lk** 1:46–49; **Ro** 15:13 *See also fellowship; love.*

---

justice, believers' lives
God requires justice to be evident in the lives of his people. Through justification, believers are

granted the status of being righteous in his sight, and are called upon to live out that righteousness in their lives.

God's law demands justice
The law is written on the conscience
Ro 2:14–15 . . . Indeed, when Gentiles, who do not have the law, do by nature things required by the law, they are a law for themselves, even though they do not have the law, since they show that the requirements of the law are written on their hearts . . .   *See also* **Ge** 20:5–6; **Pr** 20:27

Isa 51:7 "Hear me, you who know what is right, you people who have my law in your hearts . . ."   *See also* **Ecc** 8:5
The law in the OT
Ex 20:1–3 And God spoke all these words: "I am the LORD your God, who brought you out of Egypt, out of the land of slavery. You shall have no other gods before me."

Dt 6:4–5 Hear, O Israel: The LORD our God, the LORD is one. Love the LORD your God with all your heart and with all your soul and with all your strength.   *See also* **Ex** 20:4–17 pp Dt 5:6–21; **Ps** 119:1,165 pp Mt 22:37–40
The law in the NT
Mt 5:17 "Do not think that I have come to abolish the Law or the Prophets; I have not come to abolish them but to fulfil them."   *See also* **Ro** 7:7,12,22; 13:10; **1Ti** 1:8–11

Justification is by faith
Ro 1:17 For in the gospel a righteousness from God is revealed, a righteousness that is by faith from first to last, just as it is written: "The righteous will live by faith."   *See also* **Hab** 2:4; **Ge** 15:6; **Ro** 3:21–24; 4:24–25; 5:1; 9:30; **Gal** 3:6,24; **Php** 3:9

The marks of the just person
Jas 2:17 In the same way, faith by itself, if it is not accompanied by action, is dead.   *See also* **Mt** 25:34–36; **Eph** 2:10; **1Jn** 3:7,9
Thinking justly
Ps 1:2 But their delight is in the law of the LORD, and on his law they meditate day and

night.   *See also* **Ps** 24:4; 40:8; 119:111–112; **Mt** 5:8; **Php** 4:8
Speaking justly
Ps 141:3 Set a guard over my mouth, O LORD; keep watch over the door of my lips.   *See also* **Pr** 4:24; 8:6–8; **Eph** 4:25; **1Pe** 3:10
Behaving justly
Mic 6:8 He has showed you, O people, what is good. And what does the LORD require of you? To act justly and to love mercy and to walk humbly with your God.   *See also* **Dt** 6:25; **Ps** 106:3; **Pr** 21:3; **Isa** 33:15–16; **Ac** 24:16

Examples of just people
Job 1:8 Then the LORD said to Satan, "Have you considered my servant Job? There is no-one on earth like him; he is blameless and upright, a man who fears God and shuns evil."   *See also* **2Sa** 8:15; **1Ki** 3:11–12,28; **Lk** 23:50–51; **Ac** 25:8,11

The vindication of the just
2Ti 4:8 Now there is in store for me the crown of righteousness, which the Lord, the righteous Judge, will award to me on that day—and not only to me, but also to all who have longed for his appearing.   *See also* **Ps** 86:17; **Da** 12:3; **Rev** 7:9–17

---

knowing God
A faith-relationship and love-relationship with God involving mind, heart and will, and bringing experience of his presence and power. To know God is to worship him and be transformed by him. Human knowledge of God, which begins with knowledge about him, comes through God's self-revelation.

---

knowing God, effects
Knowing God has a transforming effect on a person spiritually and morally and makes that person bold in actions for God. Not knowing God in the present will result in dissatisfaction and degeneration into wickedness and in the future will bring eternal alienation from him.

The effects of knowing God
Spiritual transformation: from death to life
Col 1:9 For this reason, since the day we heard about you [Colossian believers], we [Paul and Timothy] have not stopped praying for you and asking God to fill you with the knowledge of his will through all spiritual wisdom and understanding.   *See also* **Jn** 17:3; **Gal** 4:8–9; **Eph** 1:17; 3:19; **Col** 2:2

Moral transformation: from evil to good
Pr 2:1–6 My son, if you accept my words and store up my commands within you . . . then you will understand the fear of the LORD and find the knowledge of God. For the LORD gives wisdom, and from his mouth come knowledge and understanding.

2Co 10:5 We [believers] demolish arguments and every pretension that sets itself up against the knowledge of God, and we take captive every thought to make it obedient to Christ.

1Th 4:3–5 It is God's will that you should be sanctified: that you should avoid sexual immorality; that each of you should learn to control your own body in a way that is holy and honourable, not in passionate lust like the heathen, who do not know God;   *See also* **Ro** 16:26; **Eph** 4:17–24; **Php** 1:9–11; **Col** 1:10; **1Jn** 3:10; 4:8

Boldness of action for God
Jer 32:38–39 "They [the people of Israel] will be my people, and I will be their God. I will give them singleness of heart and action, so that they will always fear me for their own good and the good of their children after them."

Da 11:32 "With flattery he [the king of the North] will corrupt those who have violated the covenant, but the people who know their God will firmly resist him."   *See also* **Ps** 138:3; **Pr** 28:1; **Ac** 6:8–10; **2Co** 3:12; **1Pe** 1:13

Biblical images of knowing God
Like parent and child
2Sa 7:14 "'I [the LORD] will be his [David's offspring's] father, and he shall be my son. When he does wrong, I will punish him with a rod wielded by human beings, with floggings inflicted by human hands.'"   pp 1Ch 17:13

1Jn 3:1 How great is the love the Father has lavished on us [believers], that we should be called children of God! And that is what we are! The reason the world does not know us is that it did not know him.

God disciplines like a parent: **Heb** 12:6; **Pr** 3:12; **Dt** 8:5

Ps 2:7; 27:10; 68:5; 89:26; 103:13; **Isa** 49:15; 66:12–13; **Hos** 11:1; **Mt** 5:45,48; 6:6–9,18,32; **Lk** 15:11–32; **Jn** 14:21; **1Co** 1:3

Like husband and wife
Isa 62:5 As a young man marries a young woman, so will your [Israel's] people marry you; as a bridegroom rejoices over his bride, so will your God rejoice over you.

Jer 3:14 "Return, faithless people," declares the LORD, "for I am your husband . . ."   *See also* **Isa** 54:5; **Jer** 2:2; 3:20; 31:32; **Hos** 2:16; **Eph** 5:25; **Rev** 19:7; 21:2

Like king and subject
Ps 97:1 The LORD reigns, let the earth be glad; let the distant shores rejoice.   *See also* **1Sa** 8:7; **Ps** 5:2; 10:16; 29:10; 44:4; 84:3; 95:3; 99:1; 145:1; **Mt** 6:33 pp Lk 12:31; **1Ti** 1:17; 6:15

Like shepherd and sheep
Ge 48:15 Then he [Jacob] blessed Joseph and said, "May the God before whom my fathers Abraham and Isaac walked, the God who has been my shepherd all my life to this day,"

Ps 23:1–2 The LORD is my [David's] shepherd, I shall not be in want. He makes me lie down in green pastures, he leads me beside quiet waters,

Isa 40:11 He [the LORD] tends his flock like a shepherd: He gathers the lambs in his arms and carries them close to his heart; he gently leads those that have young.   *See also* **Ps** 28:9; 80:1; **Eze** 34:16; **Mic** 7:14; **Jn** 10:11; **Rev** 7:17

The peril of not knowing God
Lack of satisfaction and degeneration in the present
Ro 1:21–32 . . . Furthermore, since they did not think it worth while to retain the knowledge of God, he gave them over to a depraved mind, to do what ought not to be done . . .

Tit 1:15–16 To the pure, all things are pure, but to those who are corrupted and do not believe, nothing is pure. In fact, both their minds and consciences are corrupted. They claim to know God, but by their actions they deny him. They are detestable, disobedient and unfit for doing anything good.   *See also* **Ex** 5:2; **Jer** 4:22; **Ro** 10:2–3; **1Th** 4:3–5

Eternal punishment in the future
Mt 7:22–23 "Many will say to me [Jesus] on that day, 'Lord, Lord, did we not prophesy in your name, and in your name drive out demons and perform many miracles?' Then I will tell them plainly, 'I never knew you. Away from me, you evildoers!' "

Ro 1:18–19 The wrath of God is being revealed from heaven against all the godlessness and wickedness of those who suppress the truth by their wickedness, since what may be known about God is plain to them, because God has made it plain to them.   *See also* **Ro** 2:5; **2Th** 1:8   *See also sin; spiritual growth.*

---

knowing God, nature of

To know God is not merely to know things about him, such as his character, but also to experience his presence and power. To know God is to be transformed by him. Human knowledge of God is as a result of God's revelation of himself.

The origin of knowing God
Knowing God depends on revelation
Ro 11:33–36 Oh, the depth of the riches of the wisdom and knowledge of God! How unsearchable his judgments, and his paths beyond tracing out! "Who has known the mind of the Lord? Or who has been his counsellor?" "Who has ever given to God, that God should repay the gift?" For from him and through him and to him are all things. To him be the glory for ever! Amen.   *See also* **Isa** 40:13; **Dt** 29:29; **Nu** 12:6; 23:3; **Job** 12:22; **Isa** 40:5; 65:1; **Eze** 20:5; **Da** 2:20–23,28
Am 4:13; **Mt** 11:25–27 pp **Lk** 10:21–22; **Ro** 16:25–26; **Gal** 1:12; **Eph** 3:4–5

God gives knowledge of his reality through creation
Ro 1:20 For since the creation of the world God's invisible qualities—his eternal power and divine nature—have been clearly seen, being

understood from what has been made, so that they are without excuse.   *See also* **Ps** 8:1; 19:1–4; 97:6; **Ac** 14:17; 17:24–27

God gives knowledge of his mercy and his will through Scripture, both law and gospel
Ro 1:17 For in the gospel a righteousness from God is revealed, a righteousness that is by faith from first to last, just as it is written: "The righteous will live by faith."   *See also* **Dt** 31:13; **Ac** 10:36; **1Co** 1:20–21; **Heb** 8:10–11; **Jer** 31:33–34

God gives knowledge of himself through Jesus Christ
Mt 11:27 "All things have been committed to me [Jesus] by my Father. No-one knows the Son except the Father, and no-one knows the Father except the Son and those to whom the Son chooses to reveal him." pp **Lk** 10:22   *See also* **Jn** 3:2; 8:19; 10:32; 14:7; 16:30; 17:3; **Col** 2:2; **2Ti** 1:9–10; **1Pe** 1:20–21

God gives knowledge of himself and his ways through the Spirit
Eph 1:17 I [Paul] keep asking that the God of our Lord Jesus Christ, the glorious Father, may give you the Spirit of wisdom and revelation, so that you may know him better.   *See also* **Isa** 11:2; **Jn** 14:16–17,26; 15:26; 16:12–15; **Ac** 4:31; **1Co** 2:9–11; 12:8; **Eph** 3:16–19; **1Pe** 1:12

God gives knowledge of his greatness and grace through experience of him, submission to him and in answer to prayer
Ps 56:9–11 Then my [David's] enemies will turn back when I call for help. By this I will know that God is for me. In God, whose word I praise, in the LORD, whose word I praise—in God I trust; I will not be afraid. What can human beings do to me?   *See also* **Ex** 9:29; **Ps** 17:6–7; 66:19–20; **Isa** 41:19–20; 45:3–6; 50:4; 60:16; **Jer** 22:16; 24:7; **Eze** 6:7

The nature of knowing God
Knowing his character
Jnh 4:2 He [Jonah] prayed to the LORD, "O LORD, is this not what I said when I was still at home? That is why I was so quick to flee to Tarshish. I knew that you are a gracious and compassionate God, slow to anger and abounding

in love, a God who relents from sending calamity." *See also* **Dt** 7:9; **Ps** 9:10; 36:10; 135:5; **1Th** 4:3–5; **1Jn** 4:8,16

Knowing his words and works

Am 3:7 Surely the Sovereign LORD does nothing without revealing his plan to his servants the prophets. *See also* **Ge** 41:25; **Ex** 6:6–7; 7:5,17; 18:11; **Dt** 29:29

Samuel: **1Sa** 3:7,21

David: **1Sa** 17:46; **2Sa** 7:21 pp **1Ch** 17:19; **2Sa** 7:27 pp **1Ch** 17:25

2Ki 8:10; 19:19; **Ps** 147:19; **Eze** 20:9; **Lk** 2:26; **Jn** 17:8; **Ac** 2:22; 22:14

To know Jesus Christ is to know God

Jn 14:6 Jesus answered, "I am the way and the truth and the life. No-one comes to the Father except through me."

Col 1:15 He [Christ] is the image of the invisible God . . . *See also* **Mt** 16:16–17; **Jn** 8:19; 15:15; 16:15; 17:26; **Col** 2:2–3; **1Jn** 5:20

To know God is to experience his salvation

Jn 17:3 "Now this is eternal life: that they may know you, the only true God, and Jesus Christ, whom you have sent." *See also* **Ps** 17:6–7; **Isa** 25:9; 43:12; 52:10; 56:1; **1Jn** 5:13,20

See also life, spiritual.

---

last things

The doctrine of the last things ("eschatology") includes the subjects of death, the second coming of Jesus Christ, the resurrection of the dead, the last judgment, heaven and hell.

Death

Physical death is universal

Job 30:23 "I know you [God] will bring me down to death, to the place appointed for all the living." *See also* **2Sa** 14:14; **Ro** 5:12

The timing of natural death is beyond human control

Ecc 8:8 No-one has power over the wind to contain it; so no-one has power over when death comes . . . *See also* **Ps** 90:10; **Mt** 6:27; **Jas** 4:14

Death is not to be feared by the believer

Ps 23:4 Even though I walk through the valley of the shadow of death, I will fear no evil, for you are with me; your rod and your staff, they comfort me. *See also* **Ps** 116:15; **Pr** 14:32; **Ro** 14:8; **Php** 1:21; **Rev** 14:13

For believers, death is likened to falling asleep

Jn 11:11–13 . . . "Our friend Lazarus has fallen asleep; but I am going there to wake him up." . . . Jesus had been speaking of his death, but his disciples thought he meant natural sleep. *See also* **Mk** 5:39; **Ac** 13:36; **1Co** 15:6

At the second coming, believers still living on earth will not experience death

1Th 4:15–17 . . . we who are still alive, who are left till the coming of the Lord, will certainly not precede those who have fallen asleep . . . the dead in Christ will rise first. After that, we who are still alive and are left will be caught up together with them in the clouds to meet the Lord in the air. And so we will be with the Lord for ever. *See also* **1Co** 15:51–52

Death is the penalty for unforgiven sin

Ro 6:23 . . . the wages of sin is death, but the gift of God is eternal life in Christ Jesus our Lord. *See also* **1Ch** 10:13; **Pr** 11:19; **Ro** 5:12

The second coming of Jesus Christ

The second coming is foretold

Mt 26:64 ". . . In the future you will see the Son of Man sitting at the right hand of the Mighty One and coming on the clouds of heaven." pp **Mk** 14:62 *See also* **Lk** 21:27; **Ac** 1:11; **Heb** 9:28

The timing of the second coming is known only to God the Father

Mt 24:36 "No-one knows about that day or hour, not even the angels in heaven, nor the Son, but only the Father." pp **Mk** 13:32 *See also* **Mal** 3:1; **Mt** 24:44 pp **Lk** 12:40; **Rev** 16:15

God's purpose at the second coming is to gather his people together, to reward the faithful and judge the wicked

Mt 16:27 "For the Son of Man is going to come in his Father's glory with his angels, and then he will reward everyone according to what they have done." *See also* **Da** 7:13–14;

Mt 25:31–32; **Jn** 14:3; **1Co** 4:5; **1Th** 4:16–17; **1Pe** 5:4; **1Jn** 3:2; **Jude** 14–15

The right attitude towards the second coming
1Jn 2:28 And now, dear children, continue in him, so that when he appears we may be confident and unashamed before him at his coming.   *See also* **Mk** 13:35; **Ac** 3:19–20; **1Ti** 6:13–14; **2Pe** 3:11

The resurrection of the dead
All will be raised
Jn 5:28–29 ". . . all who are in their graves will hear his voice and come out—those who have done good will rise to live, and those who have done evil will rise to be condemned."
See also **Da** 12:2; **Ac** 24:15

Believers in Jesus Christ will be raised to eternal life
Jn 6:40 "For my Father's will is that all those who look to the Son and believe in him shall have eternal life, and I will raise them up at the last day."   *See also* **Jn** 11:25; **2Co** 4:14; **1Th** 4:16

Unbelievers will be condemned
Jn 5:29 ". . . those who have done evil will rise to be condemned."   *See also* **Mt** 25:46

Believers will be given resurrection bodies
1Co 15:42–44 So will it be with the resurrection of the dead. The body that is sown is perishable, it is raised imperishable . . . it is sown a natural body, it is raised a spiritual body. If there is a natural body, there is also a spiritual body.   *See also* **1Co** 15:50–53

The last judgment
All face judgment after death
Heb 9:27 Just as people are destined to die once, and after that to face judgment,   *See also* **Ro** 14:12; **1Pe** 4:5; **Rev** 20:11–12

Judgment is entrusted to Jesus Christ
Jn 5:22 "Moreover, the Father judges no-one, but has entrusted all judgment to the Son,"
See also **Ac** 10:42; 17:31; **Rev** 1:18

Those who have not responded to Christ will be condemned
Jn 12:48 "There is a judge for those who reject me and do not accept my words; that very word

which I spoke will condemn them at the last day."   *See also* **2Th** 1:7–8; **2Pe** 3:7; **Jude** 15; **Rev** 20:15

Believers will not be judged for sin
Jn 5:24 "I tell you the truth, those who hear my word and believe him who sent me have eternal life and will not be condemned; they have crossed over from death to life."   *See also* **Jn** 3:18; **Ro** 8:1–2,33–34

Believers will be judged on how they have lived their Christian lives
2Co 5:10 For we [Christians] must all appear before the judgment seat of Christ, that everyone may receive what is due to them for the things done while in the body, whether good or bad.
See also **1Co** 4:5; **Heb** 9:28; **1Jn** 4:17

Heaven
God's throne is in heaven where he is continuously worshipped
Rev 4:9–10 Whenever the living creatures give glory, honour and thanks to him who sits on the throne and who lives for ever and ever, the twenty-four elders fall down before him who sits on the throne, and worship him who lives for ever and ever . . .   *See also* **Isa** 6:1–3

God's will is perfectly served in heaven
Mt 6:10 " 'your kingdom come, your will be done on earth as it is in heaven.' "   pp Lk 11:2   *See also* **1Ki** 22:19

At Jesus Christ's second coming, a new heaven and earth will replace the old
Rev 21:1 Then I saw a new heaven and a new earth, for the first heaven and the first earth had passed away . . .

The redeemed will enjoy life in the presence of God in the new heaven
1Th 4:17 . . . And so we will be with the Lord for ever.   *See also* **Mt** 5:8; **Php** 3:20; **Jude** 24; **Rev** 21:1–4

All life in heaven is sustained by God
Rev 22:1–2 Then the angel showed me the river of the water of life, as clear as crystal, flowing from the throne of God and of the Lamb down the middle of the great street of the city . . .   *See also* **Jn** 6:58; **Rev** 2:7; 21:23

Hell
Hell is the destiny of human beings who reject God
Mt 25:41 "Then he [the King, Jesus] will say to those on his left, 'Depart from me, you who are cursed, into the eternal fire prepared for the devil and his angels.''   *See also* **Mt** 13:41–42; **Ro** 2:8; **Heb** 10:26–27; **Jude** 6; **Rev** 17:8
Those in hell are finally separated from God
2Th 1:9 They will be punished with everlasting destruction and shut out from the presence of the Lord . . .   *See also* **Mt** 25:46
Hell is a place of fire, darkness and weeping
Rev 20:15 All whose names were not found written in the book of life were thrown into the lake of fire.   *See also* **Mt** 8:12; **2Pe** 3:7; **Jude** 7
Jesus Christ himself frequently warned about the dangers of hell
Lk 12:5 "But I will show you whom you should fear: Fear him who, after the killing of the body, has power to throw you into hell . . ."   *See also* **Mt** 5:29–30; 13:40   *See also eternal life.*

life
The state of being alive, characterised by vitality, growth and development.

life, believers' experience
God is at work in all that happens to believers, whether to warn them, to draw them to himself or to do them good.

God has a purpose in all the experiences that believers have in life
Ro 8:28 And we know that in all things God works for the good of those who love him, who have been called according to his purpose.
Eph 1:11 In him [Christ] we were also chosen, having been predestined according to the plan of him [God] who works out everything in conformity with the purpose of his will,   *See also* **Ge** 21:22; 28:16; 39:20–21; 45:5–8; **1Sa** 2:6–9; **1Ch** 29:11–12; **Job** 42:10–13; **Ps** 75:6–7; **Ac** 17:28; **1Pe** 4:12
Rejection of this conviction leads to despair
Ecc 1:1–2,16–17

God uses every experience in the lives of believers for good
To warn and correct
Ps 119:67 Before I was afflicted I went astray, but now I obey your word.   *See also* **Ge** 12:17; **2Ch** 7:13–14; **Job** 5:17; **Isa** 38:17; 48:9–10; **Am** 4:10–11; **Ro** 2:4; **Heb** 12:5–11; **Rev** 9:20–21
To test and exercise believers' trust in God
Dt 8:15–16 He [the Lord] led you [Israelites] through the vast and dreadful desert, that thirsty and waterless land, with its venomous snakes and scorpions. He brought you water out of hard rock. He gave you manna to eat in the desert, something your ancestors had never known, to humble and to test you so that in the end it might go well with you.   *See also* **Ex** 15:22–25; **Jdg** 2:21–22; **Ps** 23:1–6; 81:7; **Isa** 43:1–2; **Na** 1:7; **Ro** 8:35–39; **Php** 4:12; **Heb** 11:17–19; 13:6
To purify and prepare believers for glory
2Co 4:16–17 Therefore we do not lose heart. Though outwardly we are wasting away, yet inwardly we are being renewed day by day. For our light and momentary troubles are achieving for us an eternal glory that far outweighs them all.   *See also* **Job** 23:10; **Ps** 66:10; **Isa** 48:10; **Jer** 9:7; **Zec** 13:8–9; **Ro** 5:3–5; 8:28–30; **1Pe** 1:6–7
To benefit others **Est** 4:14; **2Co** 1:3–6; 4:15; **Php** 1:12–14; **2Ti** 2:10

In all of life's experiences believers should be thankful and trusting
Php 4:6 Do not be anxious about anything, but in everything, by prayer and petition, with thanksgiving, present your requests to God.   *See also* **Ge** 8:20; **Dt** 8:18; **Job** 1:20–21; **Ps** 103:1–2; **Pr** 3:5–6; **Ac** 16:25; **Eph** 5:20; **1Ti** 4:4–5

Believers do not merit the blessings they receive
Ps 103:10 he [the Lord] does not treat us as our sins deserve or repay us according to our iniquities.   *See also* **Ge** 32:10; 50:19–21; **Ezr** 9:13; **La** 3:22; **Lk** 7:6; **Ro** 6:23   *See also Christlikeness; discipline; peace, experience; perseverance; spiritual growth; temptation; thankfulness.*

life, of faith

The way by which believers journey through this world and into the life to come. Jesus Christ himself is the way to life.

Life seen as travelling with God
Walking with God

Ge 17:1 When Abram was ninety-nine years old, the LORD appeared to him and said, "I am God Almighty; walk before me and be blameless." *See also* **Ge** 5:22,24; 6:9; 48:15; **Ps** 56:13; 89:15; **Mic** 4:5; **Zec** 10:12

Journeying from the old to the new

Isa 43:19 "See, I am doing a new thing! Now it springs up; do you not perceive it? I am making a way in the desert and streams in the wasteland." *See also* **Ex** 18:8; **Isa** 40:3–5; **Mic** 2:13

God's guidance along the way

Ex 13:21 By day the LORD went ahead of them in a pillar of cloud to guide them on their way and by night in a pillar of fire to give them light, so that they could travel by day or night. *See also* **Ex** 23:20; **Dt** 1:32–33; 8:2; **Ne** 9:12,19; **Ps** 25:9; **Jer** 2:17; **Gal** 5:25

God's ways
Walking in God's way

Isa 35:8 And a highway will be there; it will be called the Way of Holiness. The unclean will not journey on it; it will be for those who walk in that Way; wicked fools will not go about on it. **1Jn 2:6** Whoever claims to live in him [Jesus] must walk as Jesus did. *See also* **Ge** 18:19; **Ex** 18:20; **Dt** 10:12–13; 13:5; 28:9; **Jos** 22:5; **Job** 23:10–12; **Ps** 1:1 2; 18:30; **2Ti** 3:10

God teaches believers his way

Isa 48:17 This is what the LORD says—your Redeemer, the Holy One of Israel: "I am the LORD your God, who teaches you what is best for you, who directs you in the way you should go." *See also* **1Sa** 12:23; **1Ki** 8:35–36 pp 2Ch 6:26–27; **Ps** 25:8–9,12; 86:11; 119:30; **Pr** 6:23; **Isa** 2:3; 30:20–21

Characteristics of the way of life include holiness, obedience, trust, humility, joy and peace: **Ps** 16:11; 23:2; **Pr** 8:20; **Jer** 6:16; **Mic** 6:8; **Gal** 5:22–23

Sinners refuse to follow God's way

Isa 53:6 We all, like sheep, have gone astray, each of us has turned to our own way . . . *See also* **Isa** 56:11; **Ac** 14:16; **2Pe** 2:15

All other routes end in death

Pr 14:12 There is a way that seems right to a person, but in the end it leads to death. *See also* **Dt** 11:28; 31:29; **Jdg** 2:17; **2Ki** 21:22; **Ps** 1:6; **Pr** 15:10; 16:25

Those who travel God's way are blessed

Pr 4:18 The path of the righteous is like the first gleam of dawn, shining ever brighter till the full light of day. *See also* **Dt** 5:33; **1Ki** 8:23; **Pr** 11:5; **Isa** 26:7–8; **Mt** 5:3–12

Jesus Christ is the way to life

Jn 14:6 . . . "I am the way and the truth and the life. No-one comes to the Father except through me."

Col 2:3 in whom [Christ] are hidden all the treasures of wisdom and knowledge. *See also* **Jn** 8:12; **Heb** 12:2

"the Way" was an early designation of Christianity, suggestive of the content of the church's message that Jesus Christ is the way to life: **Ac** 9:2; 19:9,23; 22:4; 24:14,22

Entrance to the way to life
Entrance is restricted

Mt 7:13–14 "Enter through the narrow gate. For wide is the gate and broad is the road that leads to destruction, and many enter through it. But small is the gate and narrow the road that leads to life, and only a few find it." *See also* **Jn** 10:9; 14:6

Entrance is by faith

Heb 11:8–10 By faith Abraham, when called to go to a place he would later receive as his inheritance, obeyed and went, even though he did not know where he was going . . . *See also* **Jn** 3:15–16; **2Co** 5:7; **Heb** 11:6,13–16 *See also* assurance, and life of faith; faith; unbelief, and life of faith.

life, spiritual

Life embraces more than physical existence; it includes humanity's relationship with God. Human beings come to life spiritually only through faith in the redeeming work of God in Jesus Christ. This spiritual life is a foretaste of the life which believers will finally enjoy to the full in the new heaven and earth. Life in the Spirit means keeping in step with the promptings and guidance of the Holy Spirit, and always being open to his gifts and empowerment.

The nature of spiritual life
It is new life
Ac 5:20 "Go, stand in the temple courts," he said, "and tell the people the full message of this new life." *See also* **Ac** 11:18; **2Pe** 1:3; **1Jn** 3:14

It is true life
1Ti 6:19 In this way they will lay up treasure for themselves as a firm foundation for the coming age, so that they may take hold of the life that is truly life.

It is eternal life
Ro 5:21 so that, just as sin reigned in death, so also grace might reign through righteousness to bring eternal life through Jesus Christ our Lord. *See also* **Da** 12:2; **Mt** 19:29; **Jn** 6:27; **1Jn** 5:11,20

It is abundant life
Ps 16:11 You have made known to me the path of life; you will fill me with joy in your presence, with eternal pleasures at your right hand.

Jer 17:8 "They will be like a tree planted by the water that sends out its roots by the stream. It does not fear when heat comes; its leaves are always green. It has no worries in a year of drought and never fails to bear fruit." *See also* **Ps** 1:3; **Jn** 10:10

The origins and nature of spiritual life
Spiritual life is the work of the Holy Spirit
Jn 3:6 "Flesh gives birth to flesh, but the Spirit gives birth to spirit."

Jn 3:8 "The wind blows wherever it pleases. You hear its sound, but you cannot tell where it comes from or where it is going. So it is with everyone born of the Spirit." *See also* **Eze** 36:26; **Jn** 3:3,5–7; **Ro** 8:11; **Tit** 3:5–7

Spiritual life unites believers to Jesus Christ
Eph 2:4–5 . . . God, who is rich in mercy, made us alive with Christ . . . *See also* **Ro** 6:3–5; 8:10; **1Co** 12:13; **Col** 2:13; **1Jn** 5:12

Spiritual life makes believers the children of God
Jn 1:12–13 Yet to all who received him, to those who believed in his name, he [God] gave the right to become children of God . . . *See also* **Dt** 30:20; **Mt** 6:9; **Ro** 8:15; **Jas** 1:18; **1Jn** 4:7; 5:1

Spiritual life brings people to know God
Jn 17:3 "Now this is eternal life: that they may know you, the only true God, and Jesus Christ, whom you have sent." *See also* **Mt** 11:27

Spiritual life brings about faith
Jn 3:15 ". . . everyone who believes in him may have eternal life."

Jn 20:31 But these are written that you may believe that Jesus is the Christ, the Son of God, and that by believing you may have life in his name. *See also* **Jn** 3:16,36; 5:24; 6:40; 11:25

Keeping in step with the Spirit
A new way of life is made possible
Gal 5:25 Since we live by the Spirit, let us keep in step with the Spirit. *See also* **Ro** 8:5–6,9–16; **Gal** 5:16–18,22–24

Bondage to the written law is ended
Ro 2:29 . . . circumcision is circumcision of the heart, by the Spirit, not by the written code . . . *See also* **Ro** 7:6; 8:2; **2Co** 3:6; **Gal** 5:17–18

Obedience to God is made possible
Ro 8:4 in order that the righteous requirements of the law might be fully met in us, who do not live according to the sinful nature but according to the Spirit. *See also* **Eze** 36:27; **Ro** 8:13; **Gal** 5:16; **1Th** 4:7–8

Deepening unity is encouraged
Eph 4:3 Make every effort to keep the unity of the Spirit through the bond of peace. *See also* **Col** 2:13; **Php** 2:1–4

Strength and encouragement are received **Ac** 9:31

Gifts for those living in the Spirit
Gifts are given for building up the church
1Co 12:4–11 . . . Now to each one the manifestation of the Spirit is given for the common good . . . *See also* **Ro** 12:6–8; **1Co** 12:27–30
Visions are given Ac 2:17; **Joel** 2:28; **Rev** 1:10,12–13; 4:2; 17:3; 21:10
Miracles are worked
Mt 12:28 "But if I [Jesus] drive out demons by the Spirit of God, then the kingdom of God has come upon you." *See also* **Ac** 10:38; **Ro** 15:19; **Gal** 3:5
Ministry is enhanced
2Co 3:6 He has made us competent as ministers of a new covenant—not of the letter but of the Spirit; for the letter kills, but the Spirit gives life. *See also* **2Co** 3:7–9

Those living in the Spirit receive revelation and guidance
God is revealed as Father
Gal 4:6 Because you are his children, he sent the Spirit of his Son into our hearts, the Spirit who calls out, "*Abba*, Father." *See also* **Ro** 8:14–16
God's purposes are revealed
1Co 2:9–10 . . . "No eye has seen, no ear has heard, no mind has conceived what God has prepared for those who love him"—but God has revealed it to us by his Spirit . . . *See also* **Ro** 15:13; **2Co** 5:2–5; **Gal** 5:5; **Eph** 1:17–18
Guidance is given to believers
Ac 8:29 The Spirit told Philip, "Go to that chariot and stay near it." *See also* **Ac** 10:19; 11:12; 13:2; 16:6–7; 20:22–23
Help is given to pray Ro 8:26–27; **Eph** 6:18; **Jude** 20

The Holy Spirit sanctifies those in whom he lives
Through the Spirit, Jesus Christ lives in believers Eph 3:16–17
The Spirit transforms believers
2Co 3:18 And we, who with unveiled faces all reflect the Lord's glory, are being transformed into his likeness with ever-increasing glory, which comes

from the Lord, who is the Spirit. *See also* **Ro** 15:16; **2Th** 2:13; **1Pe** 1:2
The fruit of the Spirit is seen in believers' lives Ac 13:52; **Ro** 5:5; 8:6; 14:17; 15:30; **Gal** 5:22–23; **Col** 1:8; **1Th** 1:6

Examples of life in the Holy Spirit
Jesus Christ Mt 4:1 pp **Mk** 1:12 pp **Lk** 4:1; **Mt** 12:18,28; **Lk** 4:14,18; 10:21; **Ac** 10:38
Simeon Lk 2:25–27
Peter Ac 4:8; 10:19,44
Stephen Ac 6:5,10; 7:55
The first Christians Ac 4:31; 6:3–5; 11:24,27–29; 13:1–3; 15:28 *See also eternal life; knowing God; obedience; spiritual gifts; spirituality.*

Lord's Supper
The commemoration and remembrance of Jesus Christ's last supper, and all the benefits that result to believers. Other terms have been used subsequently by Christians, including "Communion" and "Eucharist".

Terms for the Lord's Supper in the NT
Ac 2:42; **1Co** 10:16; 11:20,24

Jesus Christ's institution of the Lord's Supper
1Co 11:23–25 For I [Paul] received from the Lord [as being something Jesus himself ordained] what I also passed on to you: The Lord Jesus, on the night he was betrayed, took bread, and when he had given thanks, he broke it and said, "This is my body, which is for you; do this in remembrance of me." In the same way, after supper he took the cup, saying, "This cup is the new covenant in my blood; do this, whenever you drink it, in remembrance of me." pp **Mt** 26:26–28 pp **Mk** 14:22–24 pp **Lk** 22:17–20

Celebrating the Lord's Supper in the NT
As part of an ordinary meal
1Co 11:21 for as you eat, each of you goes ahead without waiting for anybody else. One remains hungry, another gets drunk.

On the Lord's day
Ac 20:7 On the first day of the week we came together to break bread . . .   *See also* **Jn** 20:26
The fourfold formula for breaking bread: taking, giving thanks, breaking, giving
Mt 26:26 . . . Jesus took bread, gave thanks and broke it, and gave it to his disciples . . . pp Mk 14:22 pp Lk 22:19   *See also* **Lk** 24:30; **Jn** 6:11; **1Co** 11:24
The sharing of the cup
1Co 11:25 In the same way, after supper he [Jesus] took the cup, saying, "This cup is the new covenant in my blood; do this, whenever you drink it, in remembrance of me." pp Mt 26:27–28 pp Mk 14:23–24 pp Lk 22:20

Themes connected with the Lord's Supper
The Passover
1Co 5:7–8 . . . For Christ, our Passover lamb, has been sacrificed. Therefore let us keep the Festival, not with the old yeast, the yeast of malice and wickedness, but with bread without yeast, the bread of sincerity and truth.   *See also* **Jn** 11:50; 13:1; 19:14,33,36; **Ex** 12:46; **Nu** 9:12
The new covenant
1Co 11:25 In the same way, after supper he [Jesus] took the cup, saying, "This cup is the new covenant in my blood . . ." pp Mt 26:27–28 pp Mk 14:23–24 pp Lk 22:20
Remembrance
1Co 11:24 and when he [Jesus] had given thanks, he broke it and said, "This is my body, which is for you; do this in remembrance of me." pp Lk 22:19
Thanksgiving, fellowship and unity
1Co 10:16 Is not the cup of thanksgiving for which we give thanks a participation in the blood of Christ? And is not the bread that we break a participation in the body of Christ?   *See also* **Mt** 26:26–27 pp Mk 14:22–23 pp Lk 22:19; **1Co** 11:20–21
The Lord's return
1Co 11:26 For whenever you eat this bread and drink this cup, you proclaim the Lord's death until he comes.   *See also* **Mt** 26:29 pp Mk 14:25 pp Lk 22:16; **1Co** 16:22; **Rev** 22:20

Separation from sin
1Co 10:21 You cannot drink the cup of the Lord and the cup of demons too; you cannot have a part in both the Lord's table and the table of demons.   *See also* **1Co** 11:27–32
A foretaste of heaven
Mt 26:29 "I tell you, I will not drink of this fruit of the vine from now on until that day when I drink it anew with you in my Father's kingdom." pp Mk 14:25   *See also fellowship; forgiveness; self-examination; thankfulness.*

---

love
A caring commitment, in which affection and delight are shown to others, which is grounded in the nature of God himself. In his words and actions, and supremely in the death of Jesus Christ on the cross, God demonstrates the nature of love and defines the direction in which human love in all its forms should develop.

love, abuse of
Scripture warns that love can be misdirected and shows a number of examples.

Exaggerated love of self
Self-interest is condemned
Php 2:3–4 Do nothing out of selfish ambition or vain conceit, but in humility consider others better than yourselves. Each of you should look not only to your own interests, but also to the interests of others.   *See also* **Mt** 16:25 pp Mk 8:35 pp Lk 9:24; **Ro** 14:15; 15:1; **1Co** 8:9; 10:24; **Gal** 5:26; **Jas** 3:14–15
Examples of self-love Est 6:6; Isa 5:8; Da 4:30; 2Ti 3:2; Jas 5:5

Love of prestige
Pride in one's position or reputation is condemned
Pr 25:27 It is not good to eat too much honey, nor is it honourable to seek one's own honour.
1Co 13:4 Love is patient, love is kind. It does not envy, it does not boast, it is not proud.

See also **Pr** 21:4; 25:6–7; **Mt** 23:12 pp **Lk** 14:11; **Ro** 12:10; **Jas** 3:1

Examples of the love of prestige **2Sa** 15:1; **1Ki** 1:5; **Isa** 14:13; **Jer** 46:5; **Eze** 28:2; **Mt** 20:21; 23:6–7 pp **Lk** 20:46; **Lk** 14:7; 22:24; **Jn** 12:43; **2Th** 2:4; **3Jn** 9

Love of the world
Love of the world is condemned
1Jn 2:15 Do not love the world or anything in the world. If you love the world, the love of the Father is not in you.   *See also* **Ex** 23:2; **Mt** 16:26 pp **Mk** 8:36–37 pp **Lk** 9:25; **Ro** 12:2; **Col** 3:2; **2Ti** 2:4; **Tit** 2:12; **Jas** 4:4

Examples of the love of the world **Mt** 24:38; **Lk** 14:18; **2Ti** 4:10

Love of money
Love of money is condemned
1Ti 6:9–10 Those who want to get rich fall into temptation and a trap and into many foolish and harmful desires that plunge people into ruin and destruction. For the love of money is a root of all kinds of evil. Some people, eager for money, have wandered from the faith and pierced themselves with many griefs.   *See also* **Ps** 62:10; **Pr** 28:20; **Ecc** 5:10; **Lk** 12:15

Examples of the love of riches **Jos** 7:21; **2Ki** 5:20; **Mic** 3:11; **Mt** 19:22 pp **Mk** 10:22 pp **Lk** 18:23; **Mt** 26:15; **Lk** 16:14; **Jn** 12:6; **Ac** 16:19; 24:26; **2Pe** 2:15

Love of sin
The love of sin is condemned
2Th 2:12 . . . all will be condemned who have not believed the truth but have delighted in wickedness.   *See also* **Job** 15:16; **Pr** 2:14; 17:19; **Ro** 1:32; **2Pe** 2:10

Examples of the love of sinning **1Ki** 21:25; **Jer** 14:10; **Mic** 3:2; **2Pe** 2:13–14

Love of other gods
Idolatry is condemned
Dt 6:13–14 Fear the LORD your God, serve him only and take your oaths in his name. Do not follow other gods, the gods of the peoples around you;   *See also* **Ex** 20:3; **Lev** 26:1; **Dt** 12:30; **Ac** 17:29; **1Jn** 5:21

Examples of the love of idols **Ex** 32:4; **Jdg** 2:11–12; **2Ki** 17:15; **Da** 5:4; **Ac** 17:16; **Ro** 1:23   *See also money, attitudes; pride; sin.*

love, and enemies
God loves even those who oppose him and believers must follow his example in loving their enemies.

God's love for sinners
Isa 53:6 We all, like sheep, have gone astray, each of us has turned to our own way; and the LORD has laid on him the iniquity of us all.

Jn 3:16 "For God so loved the world that he gave his one and only Son, that whoever believes in him shall not perish but have eternal life."

2Pe 3:9 The Lord is not slow in keeping his promise, as some understand slowness. He is patient with you, not wanting anyone to perish, but everyone to come to repentance.   *See also* **Ge** 18:32; **La** 3:33; **Eze** 18:23; **Mt** 5:45; **Ro** 5:8; 8:32; **2Co** 5:19; **1Jn** 4:9–10

The example of Jesus Christ
Mt 23:37 "O Jerusalem, Jerusalem, you who kill the prophets and stone those sent to you, how often I have longed to gather your children together, as a hen gathers her chicks under her wings, but you were not willing." pp **Lk** 13:34

1Pe 3:18 For Christ died for sins once for all, the righteous for the unrighteous, to bring you to God. He was put to death in the body but made alive by the Spirit,   *See also* **Isa** 53:5; **Mt** 20:28 pp **Mk** 10:45; **Lk** 23:34; **Ro** 5:6; **2Co** 5:14; 8:9; **Heb** 13:12; **1Pe** 2:21,24; **1Jn** 2:2

God's people must love their enemies
Lev 19:18 " 'Do not seek revenge or bear a grudge against one of your people, but love your neighbour as yourself. I am the LORD.' "

Lk 6:35–36 "But love your enemies, do good to them, and lend to them without expecting to get anything back. Then your reward will be great, and you will be children of the Most High, because he is kind to the ungrateful and wicked. Be merciful, just as your Father is merciful."
See also **Ex** 23:4; **Pr** 24:17; 25:21; **Mt** 5:44; **Lk** 6:27; **Col** 3:13; **1Th** 5:15; **2Ti** 2:25; **1Pe** 3:9

Examples of love for enemies
Ge 50:20–21; Nu 12:13; 1Sa 24:17; 26:21;
2Sa 19:23; 2Ki 6:22; Ac 7:60; 9:17; 1Co
4:12   *See also forgiveness.*

love, and the world
Scripture promotes the love of family, home and
country and contains many examples of such love.

Parental love
Aspects of parental love
Pr 13:24 Those who spare the rod hate their
children, but those who love them are careful to
discipline them.
Eph 6:4 Fathers, do not exasperate your
children; instead, bring them up in the training
and instruction of the Lord.   *See also Dt 6:7;*
2Co 12:14; Col 3:21; 1Ti 3:4; 2Ti 3:15
Examples of maternal love Ge 21:16; Ex 2:3;
Jdg 5:28; 1Sa 2:19; 2Sa 21:10; 1Ki 3:26; 17:18
The Shunammite: 2Ki 4:20,27
Mt 15:22 pp Mk 7:26; Lk 2:48; 7:12–13; Jn 19:25
Examples of paternal love Ge 22:2; 31:28;
37:35; 42:38
David: 2Sa 12:16; 13:39
Mk 5:23 pp Lk 8:41–42

Love for parents
Ex 20:12 "Honour your father and your mother,
so that you may live long in the land the Lord
your God is giving you."
1Ti 5:4 But if a widow has children or
grandchildren, these should learn first of all to put
their religion into practice by caring for their own
family and so repaying their parents and
grandparents, for this is pleasing to God.   *See
also* Ge 46:29; Lev 19:3; Jdg 11:36; 1Sa 22:3;
1Ki 19:20; Jer 35:8; Mt 15:4 pp Mk 7:10; Lk
2:51; Jn 19:26–27; Eph 6:1; Col 3:20

Other instances of family love
Ge 34:7; 45:14–15; Ru 1:16–17; 2Sa 13:22
Mordecai and Esther: Est 2:7,11

Love of home and country
Examples of love of home Ge 31:30; 49:29;
50:25; Nu 10:30; Ru 1:6; 2Sa 10:12; 19:37;
23:15; Ne 4:14

Exhortations to patriotism
Ps 122:6 Pray for the peace of Jerusalem:
"May those who love you be secure."
Ps 137:5–6 If I forget you, O Jerusalem, may
my right hand forget its skill. May my tongue
cling to the roof of my mouth if I do not
remember you, if I do not consider Jerusalem my
highest joy.   *See also* 2Sa 1:20; Est 4:8; Jer
51:50
Examples of patriotism 1Sa 17:26; 27:8–10; Ne
1:3–4; 2:5; Est 8:6; Ps 137:1; Jer 51:51; Ro
9:3   *See also discipline, family; world, behaviour in.*

love, for God
Scripture teaches believers to love God and shows
how such love should be expressed in worship
and practical service.

Believers' response to God's love
1Jn 4:19 We love because he first loved us.
See also Dt 7:7–8; Ps 116:1; Jn 15:16; Eph 2:4–5;
1Jn 4:10

Love for God is commanded
Mt 22:37–38 Jesus replied [to the expert in
the law]: " 'Love the Lord your God with all your
heart and with all your soul and with all your
mind.' This is the first and greatest
commandment." pp Mk 12:29–30   *See also* Dt
6:5; 10:12; 11:1; Jos 22:5; 23:11; Ps 31:23

Loving God involves loving Jesus Christ
Jn 8:42 Jesus said to them [the Jews], "If God
were your Father, you would love me, for I came
from God and now am here. I have not come on
my own; but he sent me."   *See also* Jn 5:42;
15:23

Expressing love for God
Delight in worship and in God's house
Ps 27:4 One thing I ask of the Lord, this is
what I seek: that I may dwell in the house of
the Lord all the days of my life, to gaze upon
the beauty of the Lord and to seek him in his
temple.   *See also* Ps 26:8; 43:4; 65:4; 84:2;
122:1,6; Ac 2:46–47

Love for God's word

Ps 119:97 Oh, how I love your law! I meditate on it all day long.   *See also* **Ps** 1:2; 19:7–8,10; 119:16,35,72,163; **Jer** 15:16; **Eze** 3:3

Self-sacrifice

Lk 14:33 "In the same way, those of you who do not give up everything you have cannot be my [Jesus'] disciples."   *See also* **Jn** 21:15–17; **Ro** 12:1; **Php** 3:8

Giving

1Ch 29:3 ". . . in my devotion to the temple of my God I now give my personal treasures of gold and silver for the temple of my God, over and above everything I have provided for this holy temple"   *See also* **Ex** 25:2; 35:5; **1Ch** 29:6,9; **2Co** 8:4–5,8; 9:7

Obeying God

1Jn 5:3 This is love for God: to obey his commands. And his commands are not burdensome,   *See also* **Ps** 40:8; **Jn** 14:15,23; 15:14; **2Jn** 6

Loving others

1Jn 4:21 And he [God] has given us this command: Those who love God must also love one another.   *See also* **Jn** 13:35; 15:12; **1Jn** 4:11

The blessings of loving God

Jn 14:15–16 "If you love me [Jesus], you will obey what I command. And I will ask the Father, and he will give you another Counsellor to be with you for ever—"   *See also* **Jn** 14:23; 16:27; **1Pe** 1:8

Examples of love for God and Jesus Christ

Ps 18:1 I love you, O LORD, my strength.   *See also* **Ps** 73:25; **Mt** 26:7 pp **Mk** 14:3; **Jn** 12:3; **Lk** 2:37; 7:47; 24:53; **Jn** 11:16; 21:16; **Ac** 21:13; **Heb** 6:10   *See also commitment, to God; giving; knowing God; obedience; worship, reasons.*

love, for one another

Scripture instructs God's people to love one another and illustrates what this means in practice.

Reasons for loving one another

God commands it

Gal 5:14 The entire law is summed up in a single command: "Love your neighbour as yourself."   *See also* **Lev** 19:18

Love for foreigners commanded: **Lev** 19:34; **Dt** 10:19 **Mt** 22:39 pp **Mk** 12:31; **Jn** 15:12; **Ro** 13:10; **1Th** 4:9; **Heb** 13:1; **Jas** 2:8; **1Pe** 1:22; 2:17; **1Jn** 3:23; 4:21; **2Jn** 5

God has taken the initiative in showing love

1Jn 4:11 Dear friends, since God so loved us, we also ought to love one another.   *See also* **Mal** 2:10; **1Co** 8:11–13; **1Jn** 3:16

God's people are known by their love

Jn 13:35 "By this everyone will know that you are my [Jesus'] disciples, if you love one another."   *See also* **1Jn** 2:10; 3:14; 4:7,16,20

Love maintains fellowship

1Pe 4:8 Above all, love each other deeply, because love covers over a multitude of sins. *See also* **Pr** 10:12; 17:9; **Eph** 4:2

Love promotes sacrificial service

1Th 2:8 We loved you so much that we were delighted to share with you not only the gospel of God but our lives as well, because you had become so dear to us.   *See also* **Pr** 17:17; **2Co** 12:15; **Gal** 5:13; **Php** 2:30; 4:10; **1Th** 1:3

Expressing love for one another

In caring for the sick

Mt 25:36 " 'I needed clothes and you clothed me, I was sick and you looked after me, I was in prison and you came to visit me.' "   *See also* **Job** 2:11; **Gal** 4:14

In meeting material needs

Mt 25:35 " 'For I was hungry and you gave me something to eat, I was thirsty and you gave me something to drink, I was a stranger and you invited me in,' "   *See also* **Dt** 15:7–8; **1Jn** 3:17

In affectionate greetings

2Co 13:12 Greet one another with a holy kiss.   *See also* **Ge** 33:4; 45:14–15; **Ac** 20:37; **Ro** 16:16; **1Co** 16:20; **1Pe** 5:14

Examples of the demonstration of love for one another

Ge 14:14–16; **Ex** 32:31–32; **1Sa** 18:3; **Lk**

7:2–6; 10:29–37; **Ac** 4:32; 16:33; 20:38; **Ro** 16:4; **2Co** 2:4; **Eph** 1:15; **Php** 1:8; 4:1; **2Ti** 1:16–17; **Phm** 12; **3Jn** 6

Paul's love for his churches
Corinth: **2Co** 1:3–6; 2:4
Gal 4:19
Philippi: **Php** 1:3,7; 4:1
Thessalonica: **1Th** 2:7–8; 3:7–10,12   *See also church, life of; church, unity; discipline; fellowship, among believers; neighbours, duty to; patience; reconciliation, between believers.*

love, in relationships

Human love is ennobled by being patterned on God's love for his people. It is also safeguarded by God's commands.

The love between husband and wife
Conjugal love is commanded
Col 3:18–19 Wives, submit to your husbands, as is fitting in the Lord. Husbands, love your wives and do not be harsh with them.   *See also* **Ge** 2:24; **Dt** 24:5; **Pr** 5:18–20; **Ecc** 9:9; **Eph** 5:22,28,33; **1Pe** 3:7

It is patterned on God's love for his people
Isa 54:5 For your Maker is your husband—the LORD Almighty is his name—the Holy One of Israel is your Redeemer; he is called the God of all the earth.

Eph 5:25–27 Husbands, love your wives, just as Christ loved the church and gave himself up for her to make her holy, cleansing her by the washing with water through the word, and to present her to himself as a radiant church, without stain or wrinkle or any other blemish, but holy and blameless.   *See also* **Isa** 62:5; **Jer** 3:14; **Eze** 16:8; **Hos** 2:19; **2Co** 11:2; **Rev** 19:7

The power of human love
SS 8:6–7 Place me like a seal over your heart, like a seal on your arm; for love is as strong as death, its jealousy unyielding as the grave. It burns like blazing fire, like a mighty flame. Many waters cannot quench love; rivers cannot wash it away. If one were to give all the wealth of one's house for love, it would be utterly scorned.   *See also* **Ge** 29:20,30; **Pr** 6:34–35

Examples of love in courtship and marriage
Ge 24:67; 29:18; **Jdg** 16:4; **1Sa** 1:5; **Est** 2:17; **SS** 1:2; 4:10; **Hos** 3:1; **Mt** 1:19

Safeguards on human love
Sexual immorality is condemned
1Co 7:2 . . . since there is so much immorality, each man should have his own wife, and each woman her own husband.   *See also* **Lev** 18:22; 19:29; **Dt** 23:17–18; **Mt** 5:32; **Ac** 15:29; **Ro** 1:26–27; **1Co** 5:1; 6:18; 10:8; **Eph** 5:3; **Col** 3:5; **1Th** 4:3

Adultery is condemned
Ex 20:14 "You shall not commit adultery."
See also **Lev** 20:10; **Dt** 5:18; **Pr** 6:24; **1Co** 6:9; **Heb** 13:4

Restrictions on divorce
Mt 19:9 "I [Jesus] tell you that anyone who divorces his wife, except for marital unfaithfulness, and marries another woman commits adultery."
See also **Mal** 2:16; **Mt** 5:32; **Mk** 10:11–12; **Lk** 16:18; **1Co** 7:10–11

Lust is condemned
Mt 5:28 "But I [Jesus] tell you that anyone who looks at a woman lustfully has already committed adultery with her in his heart."   *See also* **Job** 31:1; **Pr** 6:25; **1Co** 7:9; **Eph** 4:19; **1Th** 4:5

Polygamy is forbidden
1Ti 3:2 Now the overseer must be above reproach, the husband of but one wife . . .
See also **Dt** 17:17; **Mal** 2:15; **1Ti** 3:12; **Tit** 1:6
See also faithfulness, relationships.

love, nature of
Scripture offers an understanding of the source, character and value of love, based on the nature and actions of God.

God is the source of love
His very character is love
1Jn 4:7–8 Dear friends, let us love one another, for love comes from God. Everyone who loves has been born of God and knows God. Whoever does not love does not know God, because God is love.   *See also* **1Th** 3:12; **2Ti** 1:7; **1Jn** 4:16,19

The love of God is revealed in the cross of Jesus Christ

1Jn 3:16 This is how we know what love is: Jesus Christ laid down his life for us. And we ought to lay down our lives for one another.
1Jn 4:10 This is love: not that we loved God, but that he loved us and sent his Son as an atoning sacrifice for our sins.   *See also* **Jn** 15:13; **Eph** 5:2,25

Love is part of the Holy Spirit's fruit
Gal 5:22 But the fruit of the Spirit is love . . .   *See also* **Ro** 5:5; 15:30; **Col** 1:8

The loving-kindness of God referred to in the OT
Jer 31:3 The LORD appeared to us in the past, saying: "I have loved you with an everlasting love; I have drawn you with loving-kindness."
See also **Ex** 15:13; 34:6; **2Ch** 6:42; **Ps** 6:4; 32:10; 51:1; 107:43; **Isa** 54:10; 63:7; **La** 3:22; **Hos** 2:19

The love of God in the NT
To describe God's love for humanity
Jn 3:16 "For God so loved the world that he gave his one and only Son, that whoever believes in him shall not perish but have eternal life."
See also **Jn** 5:42; 15:10; **Ro** 8:39; **2Co** 13:14; **Eph** 2:4; **Heb** 12:6; **1Jn** 3:1
To describe love for God Lk 10:27; Jn 14:21; 21:15; **Ro** 8:28; **1Th** 1:3; **Jas** 1:12; **1Pe** 1:8; **1Jn** 5:3
To describe love between believers Jn 13:35; **Ro** 13:8; **1Co** 16:24; **2Co** 8:8; **Gal** 5:13; **Eph** 4:2; **Php** 1:9; **Col** 2:2; **Phm** 5
To describe love expressed by eating together 2Pe 2:13 fn; Jude 12
To describe love in a negative sense Lk 11:43; Jn 3:19; 12:43; **2Ti** 4:10; **2Pe** 2:15; **1Jn** 2:15

Characteristics of love
1Co 13:4–8 Love is patient, love is kind. It does not envy, it does not boast, it is not proud. It is not rude, it is not self-seeking, it is not easily angered, it keeps no record of wrongs. Love does not delight in evil but rejoices with the truth. It always protects, always trusts, always hopes, always perseveres. Love never fails . . .   *See also* **Ro** 12:9; **1Ti** 1:5; **1Pe** 1:22; **1Jn** 4:18

Love is shown by deeds
1Jn 3:17–18 If anyone of you has material possessions and sees a brother or sister in need but has no pity on them, how can the love of God be in you? Dear children, let us not love with words or tongue but with actions and in truth.   *See also* **Jn** 14:15,23; **Ro** 5:8; 14:15; **Gal** 2:20; **1Jn** 4:9; 5:2–3; **2Jn** 6; **3Jn** 5–6

The pre-eminence of love
1Co 13:13 And now these three remain: faith, hope and love. But the greatest of these is love.   *See also* **Mt** 22:37–39 pp **Mk** 12:29–31; **Ro** 13:9–10; **1Co** 12:31–13:3; **Gal** 5:6; **Eph** 3:17–19; **Col** 3:14; **2Pe** 1:7; **1Jn** 2:10   *See also friendship with God.*

---

maturity
The full development at the end of a process of growth, by means of which a human being reaches adulthood.

---

maturity, spiritual
The development of Christlike character and behaviour in the Christian through a renewed mind and tested faith.

Christlikeness as the goal and model for spiritual maturity
Eph 4:13–15 until we all reach unity in the faith and in the knowledge of the Son of God and become mature, attaining to the whole measure of the fulness of Christ. Then we will no longer be infants . . . Instead, speaking the truth in love, we will in all things grow up into him who is the Head, that is, Christ.   *See also* **Col** 2:6–7; **Heb** 12:2

Marks of spiritual maturity
Spiritual understanding
Col 2:2 My [Paul's] purpose is that they may be encouraged in heart and united in love, so that they [Christians he had not met] may have the full riches of complete understanding, in order that they may know the mystery of God, namely, Christ,   *See also* **Ro** 15:14; **1Co** 2:6; 14:20; **Eph** 1:17–18; **Heb** 5:12–6:1

Discernment of God's will and changed behaviour
Col 1:9-10 . . . we [Paul and Timothy] have not stopped praying for you and asking God to fill you with the knowledge of his will through all spiritual wisdom and understanding. And we pray this in order that you may live a life worthy of the Lord and may please him in every way: bearing fruit in every good work, growing in the knowledge of God, *See also* **Ro** 12:2; **1Co** 3:1-3; **Gal** 5:22-23; **Eph** 4:22-23; **Php** 1:9-11; **2Th** 1:3

Stability
Col 4:12 Epaphras . . . is always wrestling in prayer for you, that you may stand firm in all the will of God, mature and fully assured. *See also* **Eph** 4:14; **2Pe** 3:17-18

Care for the weaker believer
Ro 15:1 We who are strong ought to bear with the failings of the weak and not to please ourselves. *See also* **Gal** 6:1-2

Maturity is to be the aim of the Christian
Php 3:13-15 . . . one thing I do: Forgetting what is behind and straining towards what is ahead, I press on towards the goal to win the prize for which God has called me heavenwards in Christ Jesus. All of us who are mature should take such a view of things. And if on some point you think differently, that too God will make clear to you. *See also* **Lk** 8:14; **2Co** 7:1; 13:11; **1Ti** 6:11

The process of maturity
God causes spiritual growth
Php 1:6 . . . he [God] who began a good work in you will carry it on to completion until the day of Christ Jesus. *See also* **Gal** 3:3; **Heb** 10:14

Possessing gifts of ministry
Eph 4:11-13 It was he [Christ] who gave some to be apostles, some to be prophets, some to be evangelists, and some to be pastors and teachers, to prepare God's people for works of service, so that the body of Christ may be built up until we all reach unity in the faith and in the

knowledge of the Son of God and become mature . . . *See also* **Ro** 1:11

Being equipped by the word of God
2Ti 3:16-17 All Scripture is God-breathed and is useful for teaching, rebuking, correcting and training in righteousness, so that God's servant may be thoroughly equipped for every good work. *See also* **Ro** 15:4; **1Pe** 2:2; **1Jn** 2:5

Persevering through trials
Ro 5:3-5 . . . we also rejoice in our sufferings, because we know that suffering produces perseverance; perseverance, character; and character, hope. And hope does not disappoint us, because God has poured out his love into our hearts by the Holy Spirit, whom he has given us. *See also* **Heb** 2:10; **Jas** 1:3-4; **1Pe** 5:10

The concern of the pastor is to help others to maturity
Col 1:28-29 We proclaim him, admonishing and teaching everyone with all wisdom, so that we may present everyone perfect in Christ. To this end I labour, struggling with all his energy, which so powerfully works in me. *See also* **2Co** 13:9-10; **Gal** 4:19 *See also church, leadership; discernment; discipline; immaturity; sanctification; spiritual growth.*

---

meditation

Spending time in quietness and usually alone, drawing close to God and listening to him, pondering on his word, his creation, his mighty works or other aspects of his self-revelation.

The importance of meditation
Ps 1:1-3 Blessed are those who do not walk in the counsel of the wicked or stand in the way of sinners or sit in the seat of mockers. But their delight is in the law of the LORD, and on his law they meditate day and night. They are like trees planted by streams of water, which yield their fruit in season and whose leaves do not wither. Whatever they do prospers. *See also* **1Sa** 12:24; **Job** 37:14; **Ps** 19:14; 48:9; 77:11-12; 104:34; 107:43; **Php** 4:8; **2Ti** 2:7

Meditation on the person of God
Ps 16:8 I have set the LORD always before me. Because he is at my right hand, I shall not be shaken.
Ps 63:6 On my bed I remember you; I think of you through the watches of the night. *See also* **Ps** 104:34

Meditation on God's word
Ps 119:15–16 I meditate on your precepts and consider your ways. I delight in your decrees; I will not neglect your word. *See also* **Jos** 1:8; **Ps** 1:1–3; 119:23,48,78,95,97,99

Meditation on the works of God
Ps 77:12 I will meditate on all your works and consider all your mighty deeds. *See also* **Ps** 111:2; 143:5; 145:5

Meditation on the creation
Ps 8:1–9 . . . When I consider your heavens, the work of your fingers, the moon and the stars, which you have set in place, what are mere mortals that you are mindful of them, human beings that you care for them? . . . *See also* **Ps** 104:1–34; **Pr** 6:6; **Mt** 6:26–30 pp **Lk** 12:24–27

Meditation at night
Ps 119:148 My eyes stay open through the watches of the night, that I may meditate on your promises. *See also* **Ps** 16:7; 42:8; 63:6

Examples of people meditating
Jos 1:8 [The LORD to Joshua] "Do not let this Book of the Law depart from your mouth; meditate on it day and night, so that you may be careful to do everything written in it. Then you will be prosperous and successful."
Ps 19:14 May the words of my [David's] mouth and the meditation of my heart be pleasing in your sight, O LORD, my Rock and my Redeemer. *See also* **Job** 22:22; **Ps** 39:3; 119:78,148; **Lk** 2:19; **Ac** 8:27–35

The results of meditation
Obedience
Ps 119:11 I have hidden your word in my heart that I might not sin against you. *See also* **Jos** 1:8; **Ps** 119:55

Understanding and wisdom
Ps 119:97–98 Oh, how I love your law! I meditate on it all day long. Your commands make me wiser than my enemies, for they are ever with me. *See also* **Ps** 119:27
Praise and worship Ps 48:9–10; 63:5–6; 104:33–35; 119:97
Prosperity and success
Jos 1:8 "Do not let this Book of the Law depart from your mouth; meditate on it day and night, so that you may be careful to do everything written in it. Then you will be prosperous and successful."
Delight in the LORD
Ps 1:2 But their delight is in the law of the LORD, and on his law they meditate day and night. *See also* **Ps** 119:15–16,23–24,77–78
Confidence and faith
Ps 16:8 I have set the LORD always before me. Because he is at my right hand, I shall not be shaken.

mercifulness

An attitude of compassion and care, grounded in the nature of God himself, made manifest in the life and ministry of Jesus Christ, and expected of believers.

The mercifulness of God
Dt 4:31 For the LORD your God is a merciful God; he will not abandon or destroy you or forget the covenant with your ancestors, which he confirmed to them by oath.
Ps 78:38 Yet he was merciful; he forgave their iniquities and did not destroy them. Time after time he restrained his anger and did not stir up his full wrath.
Jer 3:12 "Go, proclaim this message towards the north: 'Return, faithless Israel,' declares the LORD, 'I will frown on you no longer, for I am merciful,' declares the LORD, 'I will not be angry for ever.'" *See also* **Dt** 7:7–8; **Ne** 9:31; **Zec** 1:16; **Lk** 1:50–54; **Jas** 5:11

The expression of God's mercifulness
In the forgiveness of sins
Ps 78:38 Yet he was merciful; he forgave their iniquities and did not destroy them. Time after time he restrained his anger and did not stir up his full wrath.   *See also* **2Sa** 24:14; **1Ki** 8:50; **Ps** 26:11; 51:1; **Da** 9:9
In response to prayer
Ps 6:2 Be merciful to me, LORD, for I am faint; O LORD, heal me, for my bones are in agony.
Ps 27:7 Hear my voice when I call, O LORD; be merciful to me and answer me.   *See also* **1Ki** 8:28; **Ps** 9:13

The mercifulness of Jesus Christ
Mt 9:36 When he saw the crowds, he had compassion on them, because they were harassed and helpless, like sheep without a shepherd.
Heb 2:17 For this reason he had to be made like his brothers and sisters in every way, in order that he might become a merciful and faithful high priest in service to God, and that he might make atonement for the sins of the people.   *See also* **Mt** 8:16; **Heb** 4:16

The mercifulness expected of believers
Lk 6:36 "Be merciful, just as your Father is merciful."   *See also* **Mic** 6:8; **Zec** 7:9; **Mt** 9:13; 18:21–35; 23:23; **Lk** 10:29–37; **Ro** 12:8; **Eph** 4:32–5:2; **Jas** 2:12–13; 3:17; **Jude** 22–23

The blessing promised to the merciful
Mt 5:7 "Blessed are the merciful, for they will be shown mercy."   *See also* forgiveness.

---

ministry
Service of a general, as well as a religious, nature. In its broadest sense ministry refers to service rendered to God or to people. Its more restricted sense refers to the official service of individuals, specially set aside by the church.

ministry, in church
The regular ministry of officially appointed or recognised ministers is a particular instance of the duty and call of all God's people.

The responsibilities of those in recognised ministry
As shepherds
Ac 20:28 "Keep watch over yourselves and all the flock of which the Holy Spirit has made you overseers. Be shepherds of the church of God . . ."   *See also* **1Pe** 5:2
As those who keep watch
Heb 13:17 . . . your leaders . . . keep watch over you as those who must give an account . . .   *See also* **Ro** 16:17; **Php** 3:2
As teachers
1Ti 3:2 Now the overseer must be . . . able to teach,   *See also* **2Ti** 2:2,24
As examples
1Ti 4:16 Watch your life and doctrine closely. Persevere in them, because if you do, you will save both yourself and your hearers.   *See also* **Ac** 20:28; **1Pe** 5:3

What believers owe to those with recognised ministries
Respect
1Th 5:12–13 . . . respect those who work hard among you, who are over you in the Lord and who admonish you. Hold them in the highest regard in love because of their work . . .
See also **Php** 2:29; **1Ti** 5:17
Obedience
Heb 13:17 Obey your leaders and submit to their authority . . . Obey them so that their work will be a joy, not a burden, for that would be of no advantage to you.   *See also* **1Co** 16:15–16
Support
1Co 9:14 . . . the Lord has commanded that those who preach the gospel should receive their living from the gospel.   *See also* **Lk** 10:7; **Gal** 6:6; **1Ti** 5:18; **Dt** 25:4
Prayer
Ro 15:30 I [Paul] urge you, brothers and sisters . . . to join me in my struggle by praying to God for me.   *See also* **Eph** 6:19; **Php** 1:19; **1Th** 5:25; **Heb** 13:18
Hospitality
Php 2:29–30 Welcome him [Epaphroditus] in the Lord with great joy, and honour people like him, because he almost died for the work of

Christ, risking his life to make up for the help you could not give me.   *See also* **Gal** 4:14
Imitation
Heb 13:7 Remember your leaders, who spoke the word of God to you. Consider the outcome of their way of life and imitate their faith.

Recognised ministers should encourage the ministries of other believers
Col 4:17 Tell Archippus: "See to it that you complete the work you have received in the Lord."   *See also* **Ro** 12:6–8; **1Co** 12:4–11; **Eph** 4:7,11–13

The motivation of ministry is mutual love
Gal 5:13 . . . serve one another in love.
See also **Ro** 12:10; 13:8; **Col** 3:12–14; **1Th** 3:12; **Heb** 13:1; **1Pe** 1:22; **1Jn** 3:23

How love is expressed in mutual ministry
In humility
Eph 4:2 Be completely humble and gentle; be patient, bearing with one another in love.
See also **Ro** 12:10,16; **Gal** 5:26; **1Pe** 5:5
In patience
1Th 5:14 And we urge you, brothers and sisters, warn those who are idle, encourage the timid, help the weak, be patient with everyone.   *See also* **Jas** 5:9
In acceptance and forbearance
Ro 15:7 Accept one another, then, just as Christ accepted you, in order to bring praise to God.
See also **Col** 3:13
In kindness, compassion and forgiveness
Eph 4:32 Be kind and compassionate to one another, forgiving each other, just as in Christ God forgave you.   *See also* **Col** 3:13; **1Th** 5:15
In burden-bearing
Gal 6:2 Carry each other's burdens, and in this way you will fulfil the law of Christ.
In encouragement
1Th 5:11 Therefore encourage one another and build each other up, just as in fact you are doing.   *See also* **Heb** 3:13; 10:24–25

In teaching and admonition
Col 3:16 Let the word of Christ dwell in you richly as you teach and admonish one another with all wisdom . . .   *See also* **Ro** 15:14; **Eph** 5:19; **1Th** 5:14
In prayer and confession of sin
Jas 5:16 Therefore confess your sins to each other and pray for each other so that you may be healed . . .
In hospitality
1Pe 4:9 Offer hospitality to one another without grumbling.   *See also* church; fellowship, in service; forgiveness; hospitality; love; spiritual gifts.

ministry, nature of
All creatures owe their Creator a ministry of service to him and to humanity. The example and teaching of Jesus Christ illustrate this.

All human beings owe a ministry of service to God
The debt owed by the creature to the Creator
Ro 1:25 They [men and women] . . . worshipped and served created things rather than the Creator . . .
The service of the nations and their rulers
Ps 148:7–11 Praise the Lord . . . kings of the earth and all nations, you princes and all rulers on earth,   *See also* **Jer** 3:17; **Joel** 3:1–2; **Rev** 15:4
Examples of the service of rulers Ezr 1:1–2
Nebuchadnezzar: **Jer** 25:9; 27:6; 43:10
The Roman emperor and other authorities: **Ro** 13:4,6; **1Pe** 2:13–14

The ministry of the people of God
In the OT
Ex 19:6 " 'you will be for me a kingdom of priests and a holy nation.' . . ."   *See also* **Isa** 61:6
In the NT
1Pe 2:5 you also, like living stones, are being built into a spiritual house to be a holy priesthood, offering spiritual sacrifices acceptable to God through Jesus Christ.
1Pe 2:9 But you are a chosen people, a royal priesthood, a holy nation, a people belonging to

God, that you may declare the praises of him who called you out of darkness into his wonderful light.   *See also* **Rev** 1:6; 20:6

The ministry of priests, kings and prophets in the OT
The priests
Aaron: **Ex** 28:35; **Nu** 18:2
Dt 17:12
The Levites: **1Ch** 15:2; **Jer** 33:22
Ezr 2:63; **Heb** 9:6; 13:10
The rulers
David: **2Sa** 3:18; **Ps** 78:70; **Lk** 1:69; **Ac** 4:25
Hag 2:23
The prophets
Moses: **Nu** 12:7–8; **Jos** 12:6; **2Co** 3:7; **Heb** 3:5
1Sa 2:18
Elijah: **2Ki** 9:36; 10:10
1Ch 25:1; **Isa** 20:3; 42:1–4; **Jer** 7:25; 25:4; **1Pe** 1:12; **Rev** 10:7; 11:18

The ministry of those specially set aside by the church
1Co 12:28; **1Ti** 3:10; **Tit** 1:5; **1Pe** 5:2; **Eph** 4:11

Jesus Christ fulfils the OT understanding of ministry
His ministry as servant
Mt 12:18 "Here is my servant whom I have chosen, the one I love, in whom I delight; I will put my Spirit on him, and he will proclaim justice to the nations."   *See also* **Isa** 42:1; **Mt** 20:28 pp Mk 10:45; **Ac** 3:13,26; 4:27,30
His ministry as shepherd, teacher and prophet
Jn 10:11 "I am the good shepherd. The good shepherd lays down his life for the sheep."
Jn 13:13 "You call me 'Teacher' and 'Lord', and rightly so, for that is what I am."
Ac 3:22 "For Moses said, 'The Lord your God will raise up for you a prophet like me from among your own people; you must listen to everything his prophet tells you.'"
His ministry as priest
Heb 6:20 . . . Jesus . . . has become a high priest for ever, in the order of Melchizedek.
See also **Heb** 8:6

His ministry as king
Jn 18:37 "You are a king, then!" said Pilate. Jesus answered, "You are right in saying I am a king. In fact, for this reason I was born, and for this I came into the world, to testify to the truth . . ."

NT ministry follows the pattern of Jesus Christ
In servanthood
Mt 20:26–28 ". . . whoever wants to become great among you must be your servant . . . just as the Son of Man did not come to be served, but to serve . . ." pp Mk 10:43–45 pp Lk 22:26–27   *See also* **Mt** 23:11 pp Mk 10:43
In teaching
Mt 28:20 "and teaching them to obey everything I have commanded you . . ."
In shepherding
Jn 21:15–17 . . . Again Jesus said, "Simon son of John, do you truly love me?" He answered, "Yes, Lord, you know that I love you." Jesus said, "Take care of my sheep." . . .
In priesthood by self-sacrifice and intercession in prayer
Php 2:17 But even if I [Paul] am being poured out like a drink offering on the sacrifice and service coming from your faith, I am glad and rejoice with all of you.
1Ti 2:1 I urge, then, first of all, that requests, prayers, intercession and thanksgiving be made for everyone—   *See also* **1Pe** 2:5
Jesus Christ's servants can expect the same response that he received
Jn 15:20 "Remember the words I spoke to you: 'Servants are not greater than their masters.' If they persecuted me, they will persecute you also. If they obeyed my teaching, they will obey yours also."

The ministry of angels
Angels are both ministers to God's people and fellow-servants with them: **Heb** 1:7,14; **Rev** 19:10; 22:9

ministry, qualifications
God, who calls his people to minister, also equips his people. The chief qualifications are a response

to God's call, faithfulness, godliness and Christlikeness.

God calls people to minister
Qualification is by call, not gifting or achievement
Dt 7:7–8 The LORD did not set his affection on you [Israel] and choose you because you were more numerous than other peoples . . . But it was because the LORD loved you . . .   *See also* **Dt 9:4–5**
God calls those who the world regards as weak or foolish 1Co 1:27–29
Feelings of inadequacy to God's call are common Ex 3:11; **Jdg** 6:15; **1Sa** 9:21; 18:18; **1Ki** 3:7; **Isa** 6:5; **Jer** 1:6

Responding to God's call to minister
Readiness and availability 1Sa 3:10; **Isa** 6:8
Faith, rather than natural talent or moral perfection, is required
Heb 11:1–2 Now faith is being sure of what we hope for and certain of what we do not see. This is what the ancients were commended for. *See also* **Ge** 27:19–24; **Nu** 27:12–14
David committed adultery and murder: **2Sa** 11:4,14–15 **1Ki** 11:9–13

NT ministers are recognised by call rather than their achievement
The Twelve Mt 10:1–4 pp **Mk** 3:14–19 pp **Lk** 6:12–16
Paul Ac 9:15; 26:6; **2Co** 4:7–12; 12:7; **1Ti** 1:16

Ministry in the NT is described as service
Serving God Ro 1:9; **Jas** 1:1
Serving Jesus Christ Ro 1:1; **Jude** 1; **Rev** 1:1
Serving the gospel Eph 3:7; **Col** 1:23
Serving the church Ro 15:31; 16:1; **1Co** 16:15; **2Co** 9:1; **Eph** 6:21; **Col** 1:7,25

Ministry is described in terms of its source, content or nature
Its source
It is of the Spirit: **2Co** 3:6,8
2Co 4:1

Its content Ac 6:2–4; **2Co** 5:18
Its nature
Apostolic: **Ac** 1:25; **Gal** 2:8
Ro 15:16

Various ministries are equally linked by qualifications of character
Ac 1:21; 6:3
Overseers: **1Ti** 3:2–7; **Tit** 1:7–9
1Ti 3:8–13; 6:11

The personal qualifications for ministry
Faithfulness 1Ti 6:11–14; **2Ti** 4:7
"faithful" is the sole description of the ministries of Epaphras and Tychicus: **Col** 1:7; 4:7
Godliness Ac 8:21
Timothy: **1Ti** 6:11,20–21
Christlikeness Ac 1:21–22   *See also Christlikeness; faith; faithfulness; godliness.*

---

mission, of church
The continuation of Jesus Christ's mission through his followers. Believers are empowered by the Holy Spirit and sent out by Christ to bear witness to him and to preach, heal, teach, baptise and make disciples of all peoples.

The power and authority of the church's mission
Believers are sent out by Jesus Christ
Jn 15:16 "You [the disciples] did not choose me [Jesus], but I chose you and appointed you to go and bear fruit—fruit that will last . . ."   *See also* **Mt** 9:37–38; **Lk** 10:1–3; **Jn** 4:36–38
Believers are given authority by Jesus Christ
Lk 9:1 When Jesus had called the Twelve together, he gave them power and authority to drive out all demons and to cure diseases, *See also* **Mt** 10:1; 28:18; **Mk** 6:7; 16:17–18; **Lk** 10:17–19
Believers continue Jesus Christ's mission
Jn 20:21 Again Jesus said, "Peace be with you [the disciples]! As the Father has sent me, I am sending you."   *See also* **Jn** 17:18

Believers are empowered by the Holy Spirit
Ac 1:8 "But you [the apostles] will receive
power when the Holy Spirit comes on you; and
you will be my [Jesus'] witnesses in Jerusalem,
and in all Judea and Samaria, and to the ends of
the earth."   *See also* **Lk** 24:49; **Jn** 20:22; **Ac**
4:31; **Heb** 2:4

The task of the church in mission
Making disciples
Mt 28:19–20 "Therefore go and make
disciples of all nations, baptising them in the
name of the Father and of the Son and of the
Holy Spirit, and teaching them to obey everything
I [Jesus] have commanded you. And surely I am
with you always, to the very end of
the age."   *See also* **Ac** 2:41–42; 14:15;
16:14–15; 18:8; **Ro** 10:14–15; **1Jn** 1:2–3
Preaching and healing
Lk 9:2 and he [Jesus] sent them [the Twelve]
out to preach the kingdom of God and to heal the
sick.   *See also* **Mt** 10:7–8; **Mk** 16:20; **Lk** 9:6
Proclaiming the gospel
Ac 20:24 "However, I [Paul] consider my life
worth nothing to me, if only I may finish the race
and complete the task the Lord Jesus has given
me—the task of testifying to the gospel of God's
grace."   *See also* **Ac** 8:40; **Ro** 1:9; 15:20; **2Ti**
1:11
Bearing witness to Jesus Christ
Ac 5:30–32 ". . . We [the apostles] are
witnesses of these things, and so is the Holy
Spirit, whom God has given to those who obey
him."   *See also* **Lk** 24:48; **Jn** 15:26–27; **Ac** 4:20
Bringing honour to God
Eph 3:10–11 His [God's] intent was that now,
through the church, the manifold wisdom of God
should be made known to the rulers and
authorities in the heavenly realms . . .   *See also*
Jn 15:8; **1Pe** 2:12

The universal scope of the church's mission
Lk 24:47 "and repentance and forgiveness of
sins will be preached in his [Christ's] name to all
nations, beginning at Jerusalem."   *See also* **Mt**
24:14 pp Mk 13:10; **Mk** 16:15

The church reaching out in mission
To the Jews
Mt 10:5–6 These twelve Jesus sent out with
the following instructions: "Do not go among the
Gentiles or enter any town of the Samaritans. Go
rather to the lost sheep of Israel."   *See also* **Mt**
10:9–15 pp Mk 6:8–11 pp Lk 9:3–5 pp Lk 10:4–12;
Ac 11:19
To the Samaritans
Ac 8:4–8 . . . Philip went down to a city in
Samaria and proclaimed the Christ there . . .
See also **Ac** 8:14–17,25
To the Gentiles
Paul as the apostle to the Gentiles: **Ac** 9:15; **Ro**
11:13; 15:16
Ac 10:34–35; 11:20–21; 13:1–3; 15:40–41;
16:9–10; 18:23; 28:31

Missions undertaken by church officials
Ac 11:22–23
Paul and Barnabas take gifts to Jerusalem: **Ac** 11:30;
12:25
Ac 15:22–23   *See also* baptism; church, purpose;
evangelism; preaching.

---

money
Scripture stresses the positive and negative aspects
of money, making it clear that the pursuit or love
of money can easily lead to spiritual decay.

money, attitudes
Money can be a blessing or a snare according to
one's attitude.

Money as a gift from God
Dt 8:18 But remember the LORD your God, for it
is he who gives you the ability to produce
wealth . . .   *See also* **1Sa** 2:7; **1Ki** 3:13; **Pr**
8:18–21; **1Ti** 6:17

The dangers of money
Being ruled by money
Mt 6:24 "No-one can be a slave to two
masters. Either you will hate the one and love the
other, or you will be devoted to the one and
despise the other. You cannot be a slave to both

God and Money." pp Lk 16:13   *See also* **Eph** 5:5

Loving money
1Ti 6:10 For the love of money is a root of all kinds of evil. Some people, eager for money, have wandered from the faith and pierced themselves with many griefs.   *See also* **Ecc** 5:10; - **Lk** 8:14; 16:14; **1Ti** 3:3,8; **2Ti** 3:2; **Tit** 1:7; **Heb** 13:5; **1Pe** 5:2

Trusting in money
1Ti 6:17 Command those who are rich in this present world not to be arrogant nor to put their hope in wealth, which is so uncertain, but to put their hope in God, who richly provides us with everything for our enjoyment.   *See also* **Dt** 8:12–14; **Job** 31:24; **Ps** 52:7; 62:10; **Pr** 11:4,28; 27:24; **Isa** 10:3; **Jer** 48:7; **Lk** 12:16–21; **Jas** 1:11; 5:1–3; **Rev** 18:14

Boasting in money
Ps 49:5–6 . . . wicked deceivers . . . those who trust in their wealth and boast of their great riches?   *See also* **Jer** 9:23–24; **Hos** 12:8; **Jas** 4:13–16

Examples of those led astray by the love of money
Balaam: **Dt** 23:4; **2Pe** 2:15
Jos 7:20–21; **2Ki** 5:19–27; **Mt** 19:22–23 pp Mk 10:22–23 pp Lk 18:23–24; **Mt** 26:14–15 pp Mk 14:10–11 pp Lk 22:4–5

Gifts and qualities that are better than money
Redemption
Ps 49:7–9 No-one can redeem the life of another or give to God a sufficient ransom . . .   *See also* **Isa** 52:3; **Mt** 16:26 pp Mk 8:37 pp Lk 9:25; **1Pe** 1:18–19

Wisdom
Pr 4:7 Wisdom is supreme; therefore get wisdom. Though it cost all you have, get understanding.   *See also* **Ps** 49:20; **Pr** 3:13–16; 8:10–11; 16:16; 17:16; 20:15

A good reputation
Pr 22:1 A good name is more desirable than great riches; to be esteemed is better than silver or gold.

A good wife
Pr 31:10 A wife of noble character who can find? She is worth far more than rubies.

Healing
Ac 3:6 . . . "Silver or gold I [Peter] do not have, but what I have I give you [the crippled beggar]. In the name of Jesus Christ of Nazareth, walk."

Spiritual power
Ac 8:19–20 . . . "May your [Simon the sorcerer's] money perish with you, because you thought you could buy the gift of God with money!"

Spiritual riches
Isa 55:1 ". . . Come, buy wine and milk without money and without cost."   *See also* **Rev** 3:18   *See also coveting; love, abuse of.*

---

money, stewardship
The righteous handling of money is an important practical test of godliness.

Money must be obtained honestly
Not by theft
Ex 20:15 "You shall not steal." pp Dt 5:19
See also **Pr** 10:2; 19:26; **Mk** 10:19
Not by fraudulent practices
Lev 19:13 " 'Do not defraud your neighbours or rob them . . .' "   *See also* **Pr** 11:1; 13:11; 20:10; **Eze** 28:18
Not by usury
Ex 22:25 "If you lend money to one of my people among you who is needy, do not be like a money-lender; charge no interest."   *See also* **Ps** 15:5; **Pr** 28:8
Not at the expense of justice
Ex 23:8 "Do not accept a bribe . . ."
See also **Pr** 15:27; 16:8; **Jer** 17:11
Not by extortion
Lk 3:13 "Don't collect any more than you [tax collectors] are required to . . ."   *See also* **Eze** 22:12
Not by oppression
Jas 5:4 Look! The wages you [rich people] failed to pay the workers who mowed your fields are crying out against you . . .   *See also* **Pr** 22:16; **Eze** 18:7–8; **Am** 5:11; **Mal** 3:5

Not at the expense of health Pr 23:4

Not at the expense of witness Ge 14:22–23;
3Jn 7

Not at the expense of spiritual well-being Mt
16:26 pp Mk 8:36 pp Lk 9:25; **Lk** 12:16–21; 1Ti
6:9

By work, trade, investment or inheritance
2Th 3:12 Such people we command and urge
in the Lord Jesus Christ to settle down and earn
the bread they eat.   *See also* **Ge** 15:2; 34:21;
Pr 13:11,22; 14:23; 19:14; Mt 25:27 pp Lk 19:23

Money must be cared for diligently
Personal money Pr 27:23–24
Money held on trust 2Ki 22:4–7; Mt 25:14–27;
Lk 16:10–12; 1Co 4:2

Money must be used in a God-honouring way
For the support of the family
1Ti 5:8 Anyone who does not provide for
relatives, and especially for immediate family
members, has denied the faith and is worse than
an unbeliever.   *See also* 1Ti 5:16
**For benefiting the poor, especially God's
people**
Gal 6:10 Therefore, as we have opportunity, let
us do good to all people, especially to those who
belong to the family of believers.   *See also* **Pr**
19:17; 28:27; **Mt** 6:3–4; **Lk** 12:33; **Jn** 13:29; **Ac**
2:45; **Ro** 15:26; **Gal** 2:10; 1Ti 6:18
For the work of God's kingdom
Gal 6:6 Those who receive instruction in the
word must share all good things with their
instructor.   *See also* Pr 3:9–10; **Mal** 3:10; Lk
8:3; 16:9; **Php** 4:14–19; 1Ti 5:17–18

Examples of godly people who have used their money well
Those who were wealthy but godly Ge 13:2;
26:14; 30:43; 2Sa 19:32; 2Ch 9:22; Job 1:3; Mt
27:57; Ac 4:34–36
Those who had little but gave much Mk
12:41–44 pp Lk 21:1–4; 2Co 8:1–4   *See also*
giving; ministry; tithing; work.

money, uses of
Monetary transactions have taken place from the
earliest biblical times. Originally precious metals
were weighed out; coins were introduced later.

The first mention of money
Ge 17:12 ". . . every male . . . must be
circumcised, including those born in your household
or bought with money from a foreigner . . ."

The use of money
For the purchase and sale of land
Ge 23:14–15 Ephron answered Abraham,
"Listen to me, my lord; the land [the burial place
at Machpelah] is worth four hundred shekels of
silver . . ."   *See also* **Jer** 32:9–10; **Mt** 27:7; **Ac**
4:34; 5:1–2; 7:16
For the purchase and sale of food Ge 41:57;
42:5,35; 2Ki 7:16; Jn 6:5,7; Rev 6:6
For other merchandise
Rev 18:11–13 ". . . cargoes of gold, silver,
precious stones and pearls; fine linen, purple, silk
and scarlet cloth; every sort of citron wood, and
articles of every kind made of ivory, costly wood,
bronze, iron and marble; cargoes of cinnamon and
spice, of incense, myrrh and frankincense, of wine
and olive oil, of fine flour and wheat; cattle and
sheep; horses and carriages; and slaves—human
beings!"   *See also* **Ge** 37:25; **Jas** 4:13
For religious offerings
Ex 30:11–16 . . . ". . . Receive the
atonement money from the Israelites and use it
for the service of the Tent of Meeting . . ."
See also **Nu** 3:44–48; **Dt** 12:4–6; 2Ki 22:4–6
pp 2Ch 34:9–11; **Ezr** 7:15–17
For gifts to the poor
Mt 26:9 "This perfume could have been sold at
a high price and the money given to the poor."
pp Mk 14:5 pp Jn 12:5   *See also* **Ac** 3:3
For wages
Mt 20:2 "He [the landowner] agreed to pay
them a denarius for the day and sent them into
his vineyard."   *See also* **Jas** 5:4
For investment and moneylending
Mt 25:27 "'. . . you should have put my
money on deposit with the bankers, so that when

I [the master] returned I would have received it
back with interest.'" pp Lk 19:23   *See also* **Ex**
22:25; **Ne** 5:10–11; **Lk** 6:34–35
For provision for the future Ecc 7:12
For the settlement of disputes Ex 21:8–11,35;
22:15
For taxes
Mt 17:24 . . . "Doesn't your teacher pay the
temple tax?"   *See also* **1Ki** 10:15; **Ne** 5:4; **Mt**
22:17–19 pp Mk 12:15 pp Lk 20:22–24
For tribute money 2Ki 15:19–20
For the purchase of slaves Lev 22:11
For bribery Est 3:9; **Mt** 28:12–13; **Ac** 24:26
Fortune-telling for money Mic 3:11; **Ac** 16:16
Blood money Mt 27:6

Money changers
Mt 21:12 Jesus entered the temple area and
drove out all who were buying and selling there.
He overturned the tables of the money changers
and the benches of those selling doves. pp Mk
11:15 pp Jn 2:14

---

neighbours, duty to
Scripture defines the identity of neighbours in
various ways, and indicates the nature and extent
of believers' obligations to them.

Neighbours defined
Those who live nearby
Pr 3:29 Do not plot harm against your neighbour,
who lives trustfully near you.   *See also* **Ex** 3:22;
12:4; **Dt** 19:14; **2Ki** 4:3; **Pr** 27:10; **Lk** 15:4–6
Those of the same race
Lev 19:18 "'Do not seek revenge or bear a
grudge against one of your people, but love your
neighbour as yourself. I am the LORD.'"   *See*
also **1Sa** 15:27–28; 28:17; **1Ch** 12:38–40
Peoples of surrounding nations
Dt 1:7 ". . . go to all the neighbouring peoples
in the Arabah, in the mountains, in the western
foothills, in the Negev and along the coast, to the
land of the Canaanites and to Lebanon, as far as
the great river, the Euphrates."   *See also* **Jos**
9:16; **1Sa** 7:14; **Ezr** 9:1; **Ne** 9:30; 10:28,31; **Ps**
76:11; **Eze** 16:26

Those who show mercy to people in need
Lk 10:29–37 . . . "And who is my
neighbour?" . . . ". . . Which of these three do
you think was a neighbour to the man who fell
into the hands of robbers?" The expert in the
law replied, "The one who had mercy on him."
Jesus told him, "Go and do likewise."
Fellow Christians
Eph 4:25 Therefore each of you must put off
falsehood and speak truthfully to your neighbour,
for we are all members of one body.   *See also*
Ro 15:1–2; **Gal** 5:13–16; **Jas** 4:11–12

Duties to neighbours
Love
Mt 22:34–39 . . . Jesus replied: "'Love the
Lord your God with all your heart and with all
your soul and with all your mind.' This is the first
and greatest commandment. And the second is
like it: 'Love your neighbour as yourself.'" pp Mk
12:28–34 pp Lk 10:25–28   *See also* **Lev**
19:18; **Dt** 6:5; **Mt** 19:19; **Ro** 13:8–10; **Gal** 5:14;
Jas 2:8–9
Assistance
Ex 23:4–5 "If you come across your enemy's
ox or donkey wandering off, be sure to return it.
If you see the donkey of someone who hates you
fallen down under its load, do not leave it there;
be sure you help your enemy with it."
See also **Dt** 22:1–4; **Pr** 14:21; **Mt** 25:34–40
Fair treatment
Ex 22:14 "If anyone borrows an animal from a
neighbour and it is injured or dies while the
owner is not present, restitution must be
made."   *See also* **Ex** 20:17; **Lev** 6:2–5; 19:15;
Dt 5:21
Honest dealings
Lev 19:13 "'Do not defraud your neighbours or
rob them . . .'"   *See also* **Zec** 8:16–17; **Eph**
4:25
Forgiveness
Eph 4:32 Be kind and compassionate to one
another, forgiving each other, just as in Christ God
forgave you.   *See also* **Mt** 18:21–35; **Lk** 17:3–4;
Ro 15:1–2; **Col** 3:13
Reproof
Lev 19:17 "'. . . Rebuke your neighbour

frankly so that you will not share in the guilt.'"   *See also* **Lk** 17:3; **Gal** 6:1–2

Prohibition of negative actions towards neighbours
False witness
Ex 20:16 "You shall not give false testimony against your neighbour."   *See also* **Lev** 19:16 pp **Dt** 5:20; **Pr** 24:28
Oppression
Jer 22:13 "Woe to him who builds his palace by unrighteousness, his upper rooms by injustice, making his countrymen work for nothing, not paying them for their labour."   *See also* **Pr** 3:28
Judgment
Jas 4:12 There is only one Lawgiver and Judge, the one who is able to save and destroy. But you—who are you to judge your neighbour? *See also* **Mt** 7:1–2; **Lk** 6:41–42; **Ro** 14:13

---

obedience
A willingness to submit to the authority of someone else and to actually do what one is asked or told to do. Scripture lays particular emphasis upon the need for believers to obey God, stressing his trustworthiness. This obedience is especially clear in the life and death of Jesus Christ.

---

obedience, to authorities
Scripture teaches that all people, Christians included, should submit not only to God himself but also to divinely instituted secular authorities.

Obedience is owed to rulers
Ro 13:1–7 Let everyone be subject to the governing authorities, for there is no authority except that which God has established. The authorities that exist have been established by God. Consequently, whoever rebels against the authority is rebelling against what God has instituted, and those who do so will bring judgment on themselves . . .   *See also* **1Ti** 2:1–3; **Tit** 3:1; **1Pe** 2:13–14,17
Jesus Christ expounds this principle
Mk 12:17 Then Jesus said to them, "Give to Caesar what is Caesar's and to God what is God's." . . . pp **Mt** 22:21 pp **Lk** 20:25

Obedience is owed to church leaders
Heb 13:17 Obey your leaders and submit to their authority . . .   *See also* **1Pe** 5:5

Obedience is owed within the household
Eph 6:1–3 Children, obey your parents in the Lord, for this is right . . .   *See also* **Pr** 15:5; **Col** 3:20
Jesus Christ sets the example
Lk 2:51 Then he [Jesus] went down to Nazareth with them [his parents] and was obedient to them . . .

Obedience to secular authority is limited by obedience to God
Ac 5:29 Peter and the other apostles replied: "We must obey God rather than human beings!"   *See also* **Ac** 4:19

---

obedience, to God
A willingness to submit oneself to the will of God and to put it into effect. Scripture emphasises the necessity for God's laws to be followed, gives examples and reasons, and describes the rewards.

Obedience is demanded of God's people
Lev 25:18 "'Follow my decrees and be careful to obey my laws, and you will live safely in the land.'"
1Sa 15:22 . . . ". . . To obey is better than sacrifice, and to heed is better than the fat of rams."   *See also* **Dt** 26:16; 32:46; **Ro** 6:16–18; **1Pe** 1:14–16
Examples of obedience in the OT
Jos 11:15 As the Lᴏʀᴅ commanded his servant Moses, so Moses commanded Joshua, and Joshua did it; he left nothing undone of all that the Lᴏʀᴅ commanded Moses.   *See also* **Ge** 6:22; 12:1–4; 22:2–3; **Ex** 40:16; **Jnh** 3:3
The example of Jesus Christ
Mt 26:39 . . . "My Father, if it is possible, may this cup be taken from me. Yet not as I

will, but as you will." pp Mk 14:36 pp Lk 22:42
Jn 14:31 "but the world must learn that I love
the Father and that I do exactly what my Father
has commanded me . . ."   *See also* **Jn** 17:4;
Ro 5:19; **Php** 2:8; **Heb** 5:8

Jesus Christ is obeyed
By the wind and the waves
Mt 8:26–27 . . . he got up and rebuked the
winds and the waves, and it was completely
calm. The disciples were amazed and asked,
"What kind of man is this? Even the winds and
the waves obey him!" pp Mk 4:39–41 pp Lk
8:24–25

By evil spirits
Mk 1:27 The people were all so amazed that they
asked each other, "What is this? A new teaching—
and with authority! He even gives orders to evil
spirits and they obey him." pp Lk 4:36

Obedience and love
Jn 14:15 "If you love me, you will obey what
I command."
1Jn 5:3 This is love for God: to obey his
commands. And his commands are not
burdensome,   *See also* **Ps** 119:167; **1Jn** 2:5;
3:10; **2Jn** 6

Obedience and faith
Heb 11:8 By faith Abraham, when called to go
to a place he would later receive as his
inheritance, obeyed and went, even though he did
not know where he was going.
Mt 7:21 " 'Not everyone who says to me,
'Lord, Lord,' will enter the kingdom of heaven,
but only those who do the will of my Father who
is in heaven."   *See also* **Ro** 1:5; **Jas** 2:14–26

God rewards those who obey him
Ex 19:5 " 'Now if you obey me fully and keep
my covenant, then out of all nations you will be
my treasured possession.' "
Jn 15:10 "If you obey my commands, you will
remain in my love . . ."   *See also* **Dt** 5:29; **1Ki**
3:14; **2Ki** 18:5–7; **Mt** 7:21,24–25 pp Lk 6:47–48;
Mt 12:50 pp Mk 3:35 pp Lk 8:21; **Jn** 12:26;
14:21,23; 21:4–6; **1Jn** 2:17

Obedience to the word of God
Mt 7:24–27 "Therefore everyone who hears
these words of mine and puts them into practice
is like a wise man who built his house on the
rock. The rain came down, the streams rose, and
the winds blew and beat against that house; yet
it did not fall, because it had its foundation on
the rock . . ."
Jas 1:22 Do not merely listen to the word, and
so deceive yourselves. Do what it says.
See also **Ps** 119:9–11; **Jnh** 3:3; **Lk** 11:28; **Jn** 17:6;
Jas 2:14–20

Examples of people who obeyed God
Ge 6:9
Abraham: **Ge** 12:1–4; 17:23
The psalmist: **Ps** 119:30,100–106
The apostles: **Ac** 4:19–20; 5:29
Php 3:7–14   *See also commitment, to God;*
disobedience; faith, nature of; faithfulness, to God;
holiness.

---

patience
The quality of forbearance and self-control which
shows itself particularly in a willingness to wait
upon God and his will. Believers are called upon
to be patient in their expectations of God's
actions, and in their relationships with one
another.

God's patience
Ex 34:6–7 . . . "The LORD, the LORD, the
compassionate and gracious God, slow to anger,
abounding in love and faithfulness, maintaining
love to thousands, and forgiving wickedness,
rebellion and sin . . ."
Ro 2:4 Or do you show contempt for the riches
of his kindness, tolerance and patience, not
realising that God's kindness leads you towards
repentance?   *See also* **Ne** 9:30; **Isa** 48:9; 65:2;
Joel 2:13; **Jnh** 4:2; **Na** 1:3; **Ac** 17:30; **Ro** 3:25;
9:22; **1Pe** 3:20; **2Pe** 3:9

The patience of Jesus Christ
1Ti 1:16 . . . I [Paul] was shown mercy so
that in me, the worst of sinners, Christ Jesus

might display his unlimited patience as an
example for those who would believe on him and
receive eternal life.   *See also* **Mt** 17:17 pp Mk
9:19 pp Lk 9:41; **Jn** 14:9; **2Pe** 3:15; **Rev** 2:21

Other examples of patience
2Th 1:4; **Jas** 5:11; **Heb** 6:15
The churches of Asia Minor: **Rev** 1:9; 2:2

Patience is part of the fruit of the Spirit
Gal 5:22 . . . the fruit of the Spirit is love, joy,
peace, patience . . .   *See also* **Col** 1:10–11

God's people should exercise patience
Pr 19:11 A person's wisdom yields patience; it
is to one's glory to overlook an offence.
Col 3:12 Therefore, as God's chosen people,
holy and dearly loved, clothe yourselves with
compassion, kindness, humility, gentleness and
patience.   *See also* **Pr** 14:29; 16:32; 25:15; **Mt**
6:14–15; 18:35

People who need particular patience
Christian leaders
2Ti 4:2 Preach the Word; be prepared in season
and out of season; correct, rebuke and
encourage—with great patience and careful
instruction.   *See also* **2Ti** 3:10
Christian masters
Eph 6:9 And masters, treat your slaves in the
same way. Do not threaten them, since you know
that he who is both their Master and yours is in
heaven, and there is no favouritism with him.

Patience is necessary in church life
Eph 4:2 Be completely humble and gentle; be
patient, bearing with one another in love.
See also **Ro** 15:1; **Col** 3:13; **1Th** 5:14

God's word is to be received with
patience
Heb 13:22 Brothers and sisters, I urge you to
bear with my word of exhortation, for I have
written you only a short letter.   *See also* **Pr**
2:1–5; **2Ti** 4:3

Patience is a characteristic of love
1Co 13:4 Love is patient, love is kind. It does
not envy, it does not boast, it is not proud.

Patience is an aspect of faith and hope
Ps 33:20 We wait in hope for the LORD; he is
our help and our shield.
Jas 5:7–8 Be patient, then, brothers and sisters,
until the Lord's coming. See how the farmer waits
for the land to yield its valuable crop, patiently
waiting for the autumn and spring rains. You too,
be patient and stand firm, because the Lord's
coming is near.
David waits for the LORD to act on his behalf: **Ps** 5:2;
27:14; 37:7,34; 38:15
Ps 119:166; 130:5–6; **Pr** 20:22; **Isa** 8:17; 30:18;
La 3:24,26; **Mic** 7:7; **Zep** 3:8; **Ac** 1:4; **Ro** 8:25;
12:12; **Tit** 2:13; **Heb** 6:12,15; **Jas** 5:10; **Rev**
6:11   *See also perseverance; self-control.*

---

peace
The state of harmony that is available to believers
through having a right relationship with God and
others and is especially associated with the
presence of the Holy Spirit.

peace, experience
Peace is the birthright of every believer in all
circumstances. It is found only in God and is
maintained through having a close relationship
with him.

Peace for believers in differing
situations
In times of sickness, pressure and hardships
Ps 41:1–3 Blessed are those who have regard
for the weak; the LORD delivers them in times of
trouble. The LORD will protect them and preserve
their lives; he will bless them in the land and not
surrender them to the desire of their foes. The
LORD will sustain them on their sick-bed and
restore them from their bed of illness.
Mt 11:28 "Come to me, all you who are
weary and burdened, and I will give you rest."
See also **Job** 1:13–22; 2:7–10; **Ac** 16:22–25; **2Co**
12:7–10; **2Ti** 4:16–18

In times of death and grief
Jn 14:1-3 "Do not let your hearts be troubled. Trust in God; trust also in me. In my Father's house are many rooms; if it were not so, I would have told you. I am going there to prepare a place for you. And if I go and prepare a place for you, I will come back and take you to be with me that you also may be where I am." *See also* **Job** 19:25-26; **2Ki** 22:18-20; **Isa** 57:1-2; **1Th** 4:13-18

The effects of peace for believers
Forgiveness
Ac 7:60 Then he [Stephen] fell on his knees and cried out, "Lord, do not hold this sin against them." When he had said this, he fell asleep. *See also* **Ro** 12:17-19
Encouragement
2Co 1:3-6 Praise be to the God and Father of our Lord Jesus Christ, the Father of compassion and the God of all comfort, who comforts us in all our troubles, so that we can comfort those in any trouble with the comfort we ourselves have received from God . . . *See also* **Php** 4:11-13
Health and healing
Pr 14:30 A heart at peace gives life to the body, but envy rots the bones. *See also* **Isa** 57:18-19
Security
Pr 1:33 "but whoever listens to me will live in safety and be at ease, without fear of harm." *See also* **Ac** 27:21-26; **Ro** 8:28,35-39
Hope
Ro 15:13 May the God of hope fill you with all joy and peace as you trust in him, so that you may overflow with hope by the power of the Holy Spirit. *See also* **Ro** 5:1-5

How believers maintain peace
Through remaining in Christ
Jn 15:4-7 "Remain in me, and I will remain in you. No branch can bear fruit by itself; it must remain in the vine. Neither can you bear fruit unless you remain in me. I am the vine; you are the branches. If you remain in me and I in you, you will bear much fruit; apart from me you can do nothing. If you do not remain in me, you are

like a branch that is thrown away and withers; such branches are picked up, thrown into the fire and burned. If you remain in me and my words remain in you, ask whatever you wish, and it will be given you." *See also* **Jn** 16:33; **Ro** 5:1-5
Through living by the Holy Spirit
Ro 8:6 . . . the mind controlled by the Spirit is life and peace; *See also* **Ro** 14:17-19; **Gal** 5:22
Through obedience to God's word
Jos 1:8-9 "Do not let this Book of the Law depart from your mouth; meditate on it day and night, so that you may be careful to do everything written in it. Then you will be prosperous and successful. Have I not commanded you? Be strong and courageous. Do not be terrified; do not be discouraged, for the LORD your God will be with you wherever you go." *See also* **Ps** 119:165-167
Through prayer and meditation
Php 4:6-9 Do not be anxious about anything, but in everything, by prayer and petition, with thanksgiving, present your requests to God. And the peace of God, which transcends all understanding, will guard your hearts and your minds in Christ Jesus . . . *See also* **Ps** 1:1-3; **Isa** 26:3; **1Ti** 2:1-2

Final peace in death for believers
Isa 57:2 Those who walk uprightly enter into peace; they find rest as they lie in death.
Rev 14:13 Then I heard a voice from heaven say, "Write: Blessed are the dead who die in the Lord from now on." "Yes," says the Spirit, "they will rest from their labour, for their deeds will follow them." *See also* **2Ki** 22:19-20; **Lk** 2:29

Hope of future peace for believers
Peace in heaven
1Pe 1:4 . . . an inheritance that can never perish, spoil or fade—kept in heaven for you, *See also* **Jn** 14:1-3; **1Th** 4:13-14; **Rev** 7:9-17
Peace in God's new creation
Rev 21:1-4 . . . And I heard a loud voice from the throne saying, "Now the dwelling of God is with human beings, and he will live with them. They will be his people, and God himself will be with them and be their God. He will wipe

every tear from their eyes. There will be no more death or mourning or crying or pain, for the old order of things has passed away." *See also* **Isa 11:6–9; Ro** 8:18–23; **Rev** 22:3–5 *See also abiding in Christ; discipleship, benefits; forgiveness; hope; life, of faith; meditation; prayer.*

---

peace, with God
God's ultimate provision of peace is discovered in the person and work of Jesus Christ. It is only through Christ that peace with God can be achieved and maintained.

Provision of peace through the Father
Peace in a believer's relationship with the Father
Ro 5:1 Therefore, since we have been justified through faith, we have peace with God through our Lord Jesus Christ, *See also* **Ro** 8:1,31–39; **1Co** 1:2–3
Peace through the Father's provision for the believer
1Ti 6:17 . . . God, who richly provides us with everything for our enjoyment. *See also* **Mt** 6:25–34 pp Lk 12:22–31; **Mt** 7:7–11 pp Lk 11:9–13

Provision of peace through Jesus Christ
Through Jesus Christ's coming
Lk 2:10–14 But the angel said to them [the shepherds], "Do not be afraid. I bring you good news of great joy that will be for all the people. Today in the town of David a Saviour has been born to you; he is Christ the Lord . . . Suddenly a great company of the heavenly host appeared with the angel, praising God and saying, "Glory to God in the highest, and on earth peace to those on whom his favour rests."
These OT prophecies are fulfilled in the coming of Jesus Christ: **Isa** 9:6–7; **Mic** 5:2–5; **Zec** 9:9–10 **Lk** 2:25–32; **Eph** 2:17
Through Jesus Christ's teaching
Jn 16:33 "I have told you these things, so that in me you may have peace . . ." *See also* **Jn** 14:23–27; 15:3
Through Jesus Christ's ministry
Ac 10:36 "You know the message God sent to

the people of Israel, telling the good news of peace through Jesus Christ, who is Lord of all." *See also* **Mk** 4:35–41 pp Mt 8:23–27 pp Lk 8:22–25; **Lk** 4:33–35 pp Mk 1:23–25; **Lk** 4:38–41 pp Mt 8:14–17 pp Mk 1:29–34

Through Jesus Christ's death
Col 1:19–20 For God was pleased to have all his fulness dwell in him [Christ], and through him to reconcile to himself all things, whether things on earth or things in heaven, by making peace through his blood, shed on the cross. *See also* **Isa** 53:5; **Mt** 26:26–28 pp Mk 14:22–24 pp Lk 22:19–20; **Gal** 6:14–16; **Eph** 2:13–17

Through Jesus Christ's resurrection
Lk 24:36 While they [the disciples] were still talking about this, Jesus himself stood among them and said to them, "Peace be with you." *See also* **Mk** 16:4–6 pp Lk 24:1–8; **Jn** 20:19–21,26–29; **2Co** 4:14; **Heb** 13:20–21

Through Jesus Christ's ascension
Ro 8:34 Who then can condemn? Christ Jesus, who died—more than that, who was raised to life—is at the right hand of God and is also interceding for us. *See also* **Lk** 24:51–53; **Ac** 2:33–39

Provision of peace through the Holy Spirit
Through the Holy Spirit's inner witness
2Co 1:21–22 Now it is God who makes both us and you stand firm in Christ. He anointed us, set his seal of ownership on us, and put his Spirit in our hearts as a deposit, guaranteeing what is to come. *See also* **Ro** 8:14–17; **Gal** 4:6–7
Through the Holy Spirit's presence
Ac 9:31 Then the church throughout Judea, Galilee and Samaria enjoyed a time of peace. It was strengthened; and encouraged by the Holy Spirit, it grew in numbers, living in the fear of the Lord. *See also* **Jn** 14:16–18; **Gal** 5:16–18; **Rev** 22:17
Peace as the Holy Spirit's fruit and gift
Gal 5:22 But the fruit of the Spirit is love, joy, peace . . . *See also* **Ro** 14:17

persecution

Scripture indicates that believers can expect to face hardship, ridicule and oppression, from individuals and state authorities, on account of their faith. It encourages believers to remain faithful in the face of such persecution and to draw strength from the example of Jesus Christ himself.

persecution, attitudes

Scripture outlines the attitudes which believers should adopt in the face of persecution, laying particular emphasis upon the faithfulness of God, the example of Jesus Christ and the need for patience and hope by believers.

The call to endure in the face of persecution
Passively
Ps 119:87 They almost wiped me from the earth, but I have not forsaken your precepts. *See also* **Mt** 10:22,28; **1Co** 4:12; **2Th** 1:4; **Jas** 5:8
Actively
Heb 12:1 Therefore, since we are surrounded by such a great cloud of witnesses, let us throw off everything that hinders and the sin that so easily entangles, and let us run with perseverance the race marked out for us. *See also* **Eph** 6:10–20; **2Ti** 2:3; **1Pe** 5:9; **Rev** 2:3

Attitudes believers are to adopt in facing persecution
Living holy and forgiving lives
1Pe 2:12 Live such good lives among the pagans that, though they accuse you of doing wrong, they may see your good deeds and glorify God on the day he visits us. *See also* **Mt** 5:44; **Ro** 12:19–20; **1Pe** 2:15,23; 3:16

Rejoicing in suffering
Ro 5:3–5 Not only so, but we also rejoice in our sufferings, because we know that suffering produces perseverance; perseverance, character; and character, hope. And hope does not disappoint us, because God has poured out his love into our hearts by the Holy Spirit, whom he has given us. *See also* **Ps** 30:5; **Mt** 5:11–12 pp Lk

6:22–23; **Ac** 5:41; 16:22–25; **Ro** 12:15; **Col** 1:24; **1Pe** 1:6,8; 4:12,16
Relying on the promise of God's grace to endure
La 3:22–23 Because of the LORD's great love we are not consumed, for his compassions never fail. They are new every morning; great is your faithfulness. *See also* **Ps** 18:17–19; **Na** 1:7–8; **Ro** 8:18,35–39; **2Ti** 3:10–11; **Heb** 13:6; **Rev** 3:10
Trusting in the promise of God's presence
Heb 13:5 . . . God has said, "Never will I leave you; never will I forsake you." *See also* **Ps** 23:4; **Isa** 43:2,5; **Mt** 28:20; **2Co** 4:9
Praying always
Eph 6:18 And pray in the Spirit on all occasions with all kinds of prayers and requests. With this in mind, be alert and always keep on praying for all the saints. *See also* **Ps** 35:24; 38:15–16; 129:5; 143:9; **Mic** 7:7–8; **Lk** 6:28; 18:7–8; **1Pe** 4:7

The certain prospect of victory over persecution
The triumph of Jesus Christ
1Co 15:25 For he must reign until he has put all his enemies under his feet. *See also* **Ob** 21; **Php** 3:20–21; **2Th** 1:6–8; **Rev** 11:15
The vindication of the saints
Jude 24 To him who is able to keep you from falling and to present you before his glorious presence without fault and with great joy— *See also* **Ezr** 6:8; **Est** 6:11–13; **Ps** 126:1; **Da** 6:26; **Hag** 2:22–23; **2Ti** 1:12; **Rev** 2:10; 7:13–17; 12:11

Believers are to take heart from the example of Jesus Christ in facing persecution
The persecution of Jesus Christ was predicted in the OT Ps 22:1–18; **Isa** 50:6; 53:7–12
The fulfilment of these predictions Mt 27:26–31 pp Mk 15:15–20
The relevance of Jesus Christ's innocent suffering to believers
1Pe 2:20–23 But how is it to your credit if you receive a beating for doing wrong and endure it? But if you suffer for doing good and you endure it, this is commendable before God. To this

you were called, because Christ suffered for you, leaving you an example, that you should follow in his steps. "He committed no sin, and no deceit was found in his mouth." When they hurled their insults at him, he did not retaliate; when he suffered, he made no threats. Instead, he entrusted himself to him who judges justly.
See also **1Pe** 3:14–17; 4:13–14   *See also forgiveness; patience; perseverance; prayer; spiritual warfare.*

persecution, forms of

Scripture identifies a number of reasons why individuals and governments may attempt to persecute believers and also the methods by which they may carry this out.

The motives for persecution
Envy
Ac 5:17–18 Then the high priest and all his associates, who were members of the party of the Sadducees, were filled with jealousy. They arrested the apostles and put them in the public jail.
See also **Ge** 26:14–15; 37:4,8; **1Sa** 18:8–9; **Ps** 106:16; **Da** 6:1–5; **Mt** 27:18; **Ac** 13:45; **Jas** 3:16
Fear
Lk 22:2 and the chief priests and the teachers of the law were looking for some way to get rid of Jesus, for they were afraid of the people.
See also **Ex** 1:10; **1Sa** 18:15,29; **Mt** 2:3; **Ac** 19:23–27
Hatred
1Jn 3:12 Do not be like Cain, who belonged to the evil one and murdered his brother. And why did he murder him? Because his own actions were evil and his brother's were righteous.
See also **Ge** 4:3–8; **1Ki** 22:8 pp 2Ch 18:7; **Jn** 7:7

The means of persecution
Deception
Ps 38:12 Those who seek my life set their traps, those who would harm me talk of my ruin; all day long they plot deception.   *See also* **1Ki** 21:10; **Ezr** 4:12–13; **Ps** 35:11; **Jer** 20:10; **Am** 7:10; **Mt** 5:11; **Jn** 7:12; **Ac** 6:11; 21:21,28; 24:5
Threats
Ps 10:7 Their mouths are full of curses and lies

and threats; trouble and evil are under their tongues.   *See also* **Ezr** 4:4; **Da** 3:15; **Jn** 9:22; **Ac** 4:17
Ridicule
Ne 4:1–3 When Sanballat heard that we were rebuilding the wall, he became angry and was greatly incensed. He ridiculed the Jews, and in the presence of his associates and the army of Samaria, he said, "What are those feeble Jews doing? Will they restore their wall? Will they offer sacrifices? Will they finish in a day? Can they bring the stones back to life from those heaps of rubble—burned as they are?" Tobiah the Ammonite, who was at his side, said, "What they are building—even a fox climbing up on it would break down their wall of stones!"   *See also* **Hos** 9:7; **1Co** 4:13; **Heb** 13:13; **Rev** 2:9
Ostracism
Mt 10:22 "Everyone will hate you because of me, but those who stand firm to the end will be saved."   *See also* **Jn** 9:29,34; 12:42; 16:2
Violence
Ro 8:35 Who shall separate us from the love of Christ? Shall trouble or hardship or persecution or famine or nakedness or danger or sword?   *See also* Jer 38:6; **Mt** 10:17 pp Mk 13:9; **Jn** 21:18–19; **Ac** 5:40; 16:37; **2Co** 11:25; **Gal** 6:17; **Heb** 11:36–39

How God deals with persecutors
1Ti 1:13 Even though I was once a blasphemer and a persecutor and a violent man, I was shown mercy because I acted in ignorance and unbelief.   *See also* **Da** 4:34–35; **Ac** 12:1,21–23; **Gal** 1:23   *See also suffering; witnessing; and Holy Spirit.*

persecution, nature of

Persecution by the world and secular powers is a likely consequence of faith. Scripture identifies a number of potential sources of such persistent harassment.

Persecution is characteristic of this world
Ps 10:2 In their arrogance the wicked hunt down the weak, who are caught in the schemes

they devise.   *See also* **Am** 1:6,9; 2:1; **Hab**
1:6–11; **Rev** 6:8; 9:7–10

Satan is the arch-persecutor of the church
Ge 3:15 "And I [the LORD God] will put enmity
between you [the serpent] and the woman [Eve],
and between your offspring and hers; he will crush
your head, and you will strike his heel."   *See*
also **Job** 2:6–7; **Zec** 3:1; **Lk** 22:3–4; **1Pe** 5:8; **Rev**
2:10,13

The agencies of persecution
The world
Jn 15:18 "If the world hates you, keep in
mind that it hated me first."
1Jn 3:13 Do not be surprised, my brothers and
sisters, if the world hates you.   *See also* **Mk**
12:7; **Jn** 5:18; 15:19; 17:14; **Ac** 14:22; **1Th**
2:14–15; **1Jn** 3:1
Earthly governments
Mk 13:9 "You must be on your guard. You will
be handed over to the local councils and flogged
in the synagogues. On account of me you will
stand before governors and kings as witnesses to
them."   *See also* **1Ki** 19:2; **Ne** 6:1,9; **Est** 3:6;
Ps 119:161; **Jer** 38:6; **Da** 3:13–17; **Mt** 10:17; **Ac**
12:1–3
Religious authorities
1Th 2:13–16 . . . You suffered from your own
people the same things those churches suffered
from the Jews, who killed the Lord Jesus and the
prophets and also drove us out. They displease
God and are hostile to everyone in their effort to
keep us from speaking to the Gentiles so that
they may be saved   *See also* **Jer** 26:8; **Am**
7:12–13; **Mt** 23:34–37; **Ac** 4:27–29; 5:17–18;
22:4
Powers that persecute the church are symbolised by
beasts and Babylon: **Rev** 13:7,15; 17:6
Family and friends
Mt 10:36 " 'Your enemies will be the members
of your own household.' "   *See also* **Mic** 7:6;
Ge 4:8; **Mt** 10:21; **Mk** 3:21; **Gal** 4:29

The experience of persecution
2Co 12:10 . . . for Christ's sake, I [Paul]
delight in weaknesses, in insults, in hardships, in
persecutions, in difficulties. For when I am weak,
then I am strong.   *See also* **1Sa** 24:14; **Ps**
59:1–4; 64:1–4; **2Co** 4:8–12; 11:23–26; **Heb**
11:32–38

Believers must expect persecution
2Ti 3:12 In fact, everyone who wants to live a
godly life in Christ Jesus will be persecuted,
See also **Mt** 13:21; **Mk** 10:29–30; **1Th** 3:4

Persecution is part of the tribulation of the church
Mt 24:7–10 ". . . Then you will be handed
over to be persecuted and put to death, and you
will be hated by all nations because of
me . . ."   *See also* **2Th** 2:3–4; **Rev** 6:11

Persecution is sometimes part of God's judgment on his people
La 4:16–19 . . . People stalked us at every
step, so we could not walk in our streets. Our
end was near, our days were numbered, for our
end had come. Our pursuers were swifter than
eagles in the sky; they chased us over the
mountains and lay in wait for us in the desert.
See also **Jer** 6:22–26; 32:26–29; 39:5–10
See also discipleship, cost; world.

---

perseverance
Enduring in a course of action or belief. In its
negative sense, it can mean being stubborn; in its
positive sense, it means continuing commitment to
the gospel of Jesus Christ.

Human perseverance in sin
2Ki 17:41 Even while these people were
worshipping the LORD, they were serving their
idols. To this day their children and grandchildren
continue to do as their fathers did.
Isa 1:5 Why should you be beaten any more?
Why do you persist in rebellion? Your whole head
is injured, your whole heart afflicted.
Ro 1:32 Although they know God's righteous
decree that those who do such things deserve
death, they not only continue to do these very

things but also approve of those who practise them.   *See also* **Ex** 9:1–3; **Dt** 29:19; **Jdg** 14:17; **2Ki** 13:11; **Da** 12:10

God's perseverance in calling Israel to obedience

Ne 9:30–31 "For many years you were patient with them. By your Spirit you admonished them through your prophets. Yet they paid no attention, so you handed them over to the neighbouring peoples. But in your great mercy you did not put an end to them or abandon them, for you are a gracious and merciful God."   *See also* **Ex** 32:14; **1Ki** 3:6; **Isa** 40:28; **Jer** 26:13; **Jnh** 3:10

Jesus Christ's perseverance with those who would not believe

Heb 12:1–3 . . . and let us run with perseverance the race marked out for us. Let us fix our eyes on Jesus, the author and perfecter of our faith, who for the joy set before him endured the cross, scorning its shame, and sat down at the right hand of the throne of God. Consider him who endured such opposition from sinners, so that you will not grow weary and lose heart.   *See also* **Mt** 17:17 pp Mk 9:19; **2Th** 3:5

Christians' perseverance in faith

Col 2:6–7 So then, just as you received Christ Jesus as Lord, continue to live in him, rooted and built up in him, strengthened in the faith as you were taught, and overflowing with thankfulness.
Col 1:10–12 And we pray this in order that you may live a life worthy of the Lord and may please him in every way: bearing fruit in every good work, growing in the knowledge of God, being strengthened with all power according to his glorious might so that you may have great endurance and patience, and joyfully giving thanks to the Father, who has qualified you to share in the inheritance of the saints in the kingdom of light.   *See also* **Mt** 24:12–13; 10:22; **Jn** 15:4–10; **Ro** 11:22; **1Co** 1:8; **2Co** 10:15; **Php** 2:12; **Col** 1:23; **2Th** 3:4; **Heb** 6:1; 10:36–38; **2Pe** 3:18

Perseverance in prayer

Lk 18:1–8 Then Jesus told his disciples a parable to show them that they should always

pray and not give up . . . " . . . there was a judge . . . and there was a widow . . ." . . .   *See also* **Lk** 11:5–13; **Ro** 12:12; **Eph** 6:18; **1Th** 5:17

Perseverance arises from suffering

Ro 5:3 . . . we also rejoice in our sufferings, because we know that suffering produces perseverance;   *See also* **Ro** 12:12; **2Co** 1:6; **2Th** 1:4; **2Ti** 3:10–11; **Jas** 1:2–3; **1Pe** 4:19; **Rev** 2:2–3,19

Perseverance builds and demonstrates Christian character

Ro 5:4 perseverance [produces] character . . .   *See also* **1Co** 13:7; **2Co** 1:21–22; 12:12; **Jas** 1:4; **2Pe** 1:5–8

Encouragements for Christians to persevere

Ac 11:23; 13:43; **1Co** 15:58; 16:13; **Php** 1:27; **2Ti** 1:13; **Heb** 2:1; 4:14; **Rev** 3:11
See also faithfulness; patience; prayer; persistence; suffering.

praise

The celebration, honouring and adoration of God, in the power of the Holy Spirit, whether by individual believers or communities of believers.

praise, examples

Scripture provides many examples of individuals who praised God. These examples illustrate the variety of ways and methods in which God can be praised, as well as the motivation for that praise.

OT examples of those who praised God

Melchizedek

Ge 14:18–20 Then Melchizedek king of Salem brought out bread and wine. He was priest of God Most High, and he blessed Abram, saying, "Blessed be Abram by God Most High, Creator of heaven and earth. And blessed be God Most High, who delivered your enemies into your hand." Then Abram gave him a tenth of everything.

Moses

Ex 15:1-2 Then Moses and the Israelites sang this song to the LORD: "I will sing to the LORD, for he is highly exalted. The horse and its rider he has hurled into the sea. The LORD is my strength and my song; he has become my salvation. He is my God, and I will praise him, my father's God, and I will exalt him."

Jethro

Ex 18:9-10 Jethro was delighted to hear about all the good things the LORD had done for Israel in rescuing them from the hand of the Egyptians. He said, "Praise be to the LORD, who rescued you [Moses] from the hand of the Egyptians and of Pharaoh, and who rescued the people from the hand of the Egyptians."

David

1Ch 29:10-13 David praised the LORD in the presence of the whole assembly, saying, "Praise be to you, O LORD, God of our father Israel, from everlasting to everlasting. Yours, O LORD, is the greatness and the power and the glory and the majesty and the splendour, for everything in heaven and earth is yours. Yours, O LORD, is the kingdom; you are exalted as head over all. Wealth and honour come from you; you are the ruler of all things. In your hands are strength and power to exalt and give strength to all. Now, our God, we give you thanks, and praise your glorious name."

Ezra

Ne 8:6 Ezra praised the LORD, the great God; and all the people lifted their hands and responded, "Amen! Amen!" Then they bowed down and worshipped the LORD with their faces to the ground.

NT examples of those who praised God

Jesus Christ

Lk 10:21 At that time Jesus, full of joy through the Holy Spirit, said, "I praise you, Father, Lord of heaven and earth, because you have hidden these things from the wise and learned, and revealed them to little children. Yes, Father, for this was your good pleasure."

Zechariah

Lk 1:67-68 His [John's] father Zechariah was filled with the Holy Spirit and prophesied: "Praise be to the Lord, the God of Israel, because he has come and has redeemed his people."

The shepherds

Lk 2:20 The shepherds returned, glorifying and praising God for all the things they had heard and seen, which were just as they had been told.

Simeon

Lk 2:28 Simeon took him [Jesus] in his arms and praised God . . .

The disciples

Lk 19:37 When he [Jesus] came near the place where the road goes down the Mount of Olives, the whole crowd of disciples began joyfully to praise God in loud voices for all the miracles they had seen:

Ac 2:46-47 Every day they [the believers] continued to meet together in the temple courts. They broke bread in their homes and ate together with glad and sincere hearts, praising God and enjoying the favour of all the people. And the Lord added to their number daily those who were being saved.   *See also* **Lk** 24:50-53; **Ac** 16:25

Those who were healed by Jesus Christ Lk 18:35-43; **Ac** 3:1-10

The citizens of heaven

Rev 15:2-3 And I saw what looked like a sea of glass mixed with fire and, standing beside the sea, those who had been victorious over the beast and his image and over the number of his name. They held harps given them by God and sang the song of Moses the servant of God and the song of the Lamb: "Great and marvellous are your deeds, Lord God Almighty. Just and true are your ways, King of the ages."   *See also prayer, as praise and thanksgiving.*

---

praise, manner and methods

Praise is the natural response of believers to God at all times and in all places, involving adoration in music and song. God himself assists believers to praise him through his Spirit.

The manner of praise

God is praised in faith

Ps 28:7 The LORD is my strength and my shield; my heart trusts in him, and I am helped. My heart leaps for joy and I will give thanks to him in song.

Ps 106:12 Then they believed his promises and sang his praise.

God is praised through Jesus Christ
Heb 13:15 Through Jesus, therefore, let us continually offer to God a sacrifice of praise—the fruit of lips that confess his name.   *See also* **Php** 2:9–11

God can be praised at any time and in any place
Ps 104:33 I will sing to the LORD all my life; I will sing praise to my God as long as I live.
Ps 145:2 Every day I will praise you and extol your name for ever and ever.   *See also* **Ps** 146:2

God helps believers to praise him
Ps 51:15 O Lord, open my lips, and my mouth will declare your praise.   *See also* **Ps** 40:3; **Isa** 61:3

The Holy Spirit moves believers to praise
Lk 1:67 His [John's] father Zechariah was filled with the Holy Spirit and prophesied:
Eph 5:18–20 Do not get drunk on wine, which leads to debauchery. Instead, be filled with the Spirit. Speak to one another with psalms, hymns and spiritual songs. Sing and make music in your heart to the Lord, always giving thanks to God the Father for everything, in the name of our Lord Jesus Christ.   *See also* **Lk** 10:21; **Ac** 2:11; 10:44–46; **Col** 3:16–17

The methods of praise
In singing
Eph 5:19 Speak to one another with psalms, hymns and spiritual songs. Sing and make music in your heart to the Lord,   *See also* **Ne** 12:46; **Ps** 149:1; **Isa** 42:10; **Lk** 1:46–47,68; **Ac** 16:25; **Col** 3:16

With musical instruments
Ps 150:3–5 Praise him with the sounding of the trumpet, praise him with the harp and lyre, praise him with tambourine and dancing, praise him with the strings and flute, praise him with the clash of cymbals, praise him with resounding cymbals.   *See also* **1Ch** 25:3; **2Ch** 7:6; **Ps** 33:2; 92:1–3; **Isa** 38:20

In dancing
Ps 149:3 Let them praise his name with dancing and make music to him with tambourine and harp.   *See also* **Ex** 15:19–20; **2Sa** 6:14; **Ps** 150:4

With thanksgiving
Ps 42:4 These things I remember as I pour out my soul: how I used to go with the multitude, leading the procession to the house of God, with shouts of joy and thanksgiving among the festive throng.
Ps 100:4 Enter his gates with thanksgiving and his courts with praise; give thanks to him and praise his name.   *See also* **2Ch** 5:13

Hallelujah as a frequent expression of praise to God
Ps 106:48 Praise be to the LORD, the God of Israel, from everlasting to everlasting. Let all the people say, "Amen!" Praise the LORD.   *See also* **Ps** 111:1; 113:1; 135:1; 149:1; 150:1; **Rev** 19:3–4

Praise for his patient love
Ps 106:1 Praise the LORD. Give thanks to the LORD, for he is good; his love endures for ever. *See also* **Ps** 117:2

Praise for his election of Israel
Ps 135:3–4 Praise the LORD, for the LORD is good; sing praise to his name, for that is pleasant. For the LORD has chosen Jacob to be his own, Israel to be his treasured possession. *See also* **1Ch** 16:36; **Ps** 148:14

Praise for his sovereign rule
Ps 146:10 The LORD reigns for ever, your God, O Zion, for all generations. Praise the LORD.
Rev 19:6 Then I heard what sounded like a great multitude, like the roar of rushing waters and like loud peals of thunder, shouting: "Hallelujah! For our Lord God Almighty reigns."   *See also* **Rev** 19:1

Hosanna as an acclamation of praise
At Jerusalem
Mt 21:9 The crowds that went ahead of him and those that followed shouted, "Hosanna to the Son of David!" "Blessed is he who comes in the name of the Lord!" "Hosanna in the highest!" pp **Mk** 11:9–10 pp **Jn** 12:13   *See also* **Mt** 21:5

The OT background

Ps 118:25-26 O Lord, save us; O Lord, grant us success. Blessed is he who comes in the name of the Lord. From the house of the Lord we bless you.   *See also* **1Ch** 16:35-36; **Ps** 79:9; 106:47

"Selah" in the context of praise
Following the assurance of answered prayer
Ps 3:4 To the Lord I cry aloud, and he answers me from his holy hill. *Selah   See also* **Ps** 21:2; 24:6; 32:5; 81:7; 84:8
Following an expression of deliverance
Ps 3:8 From the Lord comes deliverance. May your blessing be on your people. *Selah   See also* **Ps** 32:7; 49:15; 57:3; 68:19; 76:9; **Hab** 3:13
After a statement comparing God's greatness with human insignificance
Ps 9:20 Strike them with terror, O Lord; let the nations know they are only mortals. *Selah   See also* **Ps** 39:5,11; 47:4; 52:5; 55:19; 59:5; 67:4; 75:3; 89:37; **Hab** 3:3
After an affirmation of security in God
Ps 46:7 The Lord Almighty is with us; the God of Jacob is our fortress. *Selah   See also* **Ps** 46:11; 48:8; 61:4
On reflection of evil opposition
Ps 54:3 Strangers are attacking me; ruthless people seek my life—people without regard for God. *Selah   See also* **Ps** 62:4; 140:3,5

---

praise, reasons

Scripture treats praise as the natural response of believers to God's person and actions.

Praise is commanded of God's people
Ps 68:32 Sing to God, O kingdoms of the earth, sing praise to the Lord . . .
1Pe 2:9 But you are a chosen people, a royal priesthood, a holy nation, a people belonging to God, that you may declare the praises of him who called you out of darkness into his wonderful light.
Rev 19:5 Then a voice came from the throne, saying: "Praise our God, all you his servants, you who fear him, both small and great!"   *See also* **Ps** 30:4; 150:6; **Isa** 42:10; **Php** 2:9-11

Praise is due to God alone
Dt 10:21 He is your praise; he is your God, who performed for you those great and awesome wonders you saw with your own eyes.
1Ch 16:25 For great is the Lord and most worthy of praise; he is to be feared above all gods.
Isa 42:8 "I am the Lord; that is my name! I will not give my glory to another or my praise to idols."   *See also* **Ps** 66:4; 118:15-21; 148:13; **Rev** 4:11

Praise is pleasing to God
Ps 69:30-31 I will praise God's name in song and glorify him with thanksgiving. This will please the Lord more than an ox, more than a bull with its horns and hoofs.   *See also* **Ps** 135:3; 147:1; **Isa** 43:20-21; 61:10-11; **Jer** 13:11

Praise as an act of witness
Ps 9:11 Sing praises to the Lord, enthroned in Zion; proclaim among the nations what he has done.   *See also* **2Sa** 22:50; **Ps** 34:1-3; **Isa** 42:12; **2Co** 9:13

Praise in response to God's nature
For his greatness
Dt 32:3 I will proclaim the name of the Lord. Oh, praise the greatness of our God!
Ps 150:2 Praise him for his acts of power; praise him for his surpassing greatness.   *See also* **1Ch** 16:25; **Ne** 8:6; **Ps** 104:1; **Mt** 9:8
For his righteousness
Ps 98:8-9 Let the rivers clap their hands, let the mountains sing together for joy; let them sing before the Lord, for he comes to judge the earth. He will judge the world in righteousness and the peoples with equity.   *See also* **Da** 4:37
For his faithfulness
Ps 57:9-10 I will praise you, O Lord, among the nations; I will sing of you among the peoples. For great is your love, reaching to the heavens; your faithfulness reaches to the skies.
Ps 138:2 I will bow down towards your holy temple and will praise your name for your love and your faithfulness, for you have exalted above all things your name and your word.   *See also* **1Ki** 8:15-20,56; **Ps** 89:1

For his strength
Ps 59:16 But I will sing of your strength, in the morning I will sing of your love; for you are my fortress, my refuge in times of trouble. *See also* **Ps** 28:7; 81:1

Praise in response to God's deeds
For deliverance from enemies
Ex 18:10 He [Jethro] said, "Praise be to the Lord, who rescued you from the hand of the Egyptians and of Pharaoh, and who rescued the people from the hand of the Egyptians."
Ps 18:46–48 The Lord lives! Praise be to my Rock! Exalted be God my Saviour! He is the God who avenges me, who subdues nations under me, who saves me from my enemies. You exalted me above my foes; from violent people you rescued me. *See also* **Ge** 14:20; **Jdg** 16:24; **Ps** 43:1–4; 124:1–7
For answered prayer
Ps 28:6 Praise be to the Lord, for he has heard my cry for mercy. *See also* **Ps** 66:19–20
For sending his Son, Jesus Christ
Lk 1:68–69 "Praise be to the Lord, the God of Israel, because he has come and has redeemed his people. He has raised up a horn of salvation for us in the house of his servant David"
Eph 1:3 Praise be to the God and Father of our Lord Jesus Christ, who has blessed us in the heavenly realms with every spiritual blessing in Christ. *See also* **Lk** 2:10–14,25–28; 24:53; **1Pe** 1:3–6 *See also church, purpose; worship, reasons.*

prayer
Fellowship with God through Jesus Christ, expressed in adoration, thanksgiving and intercession, through which believers draw near to God and learn more of his will for their lives. Scripture stresses the vital role of the Holy Spirit in stimulating and guiding prayer.

prayer, and faith
Effective prayer depends on faith, especially on a willingness to trust in God's faithfulness to his promises to his people.

Faith is necessary in order to approach God
Heb 11:6 And without faith it is impossible to please God, because anyone who comes to him must believe that he exists and that he rewards those who earnestly seek him.

Faith is necessary to receive benefits from God
Mk 6:5–6 He [Jesus] could not do any miracles there, except lay his hands on a few sick people and heal them. And he was amazed at their lack of faith. Then Jesus went round teaching from village to village.
Jas 5:16–18 . . . The prayer of a righteous person is powerful and effective. Elijah was human just as we are. He prayed earnestly that it would not rain, and it did not rain on the land for three and a half years. Again he prayed, and the heavens gave rain, and the earth produced its crops. *See also* **Eph** 3:12; **Heb** 10:22

Faith is necessary for effective prayer
Mt 21:21–22 Jesus replied, "I tell you the truth, if you have faith and do not doubt, not only can you do what was done to the fig-tree, but also you can say to this mountain, 'Go, throw yourself into the sea,' and it will be done. If you believe, you will receive whatever you ask for in prayer." pp **Mk** 11:22–24
Jas 1:5–8 If any of you lacks wisdom, you should ask God, who gives generously to all without finding fault, and it will be given to you. But when you ask, you must believe and not doubt, because the one who doubts is like a wave of the sea, blown and tossed by the wind. Those who doubt should not think they will receive anything from the Lord; they are double-minded and unstable in all they do. *See also* **Jas** 5:14–15

Jesus Christ responded to people's need on the basis of faith
Mt 9:27–30 As Jesus went on from there, two blind men followed him, calling out, "Have mercy on us, Son of David!" When he had gone indoors, the blind men came to him, and he

asked them, "Do you believe that I am able to do this?" "Yes, Lord," they replied. Then he touched their eyes and said, "According to your faith will it be done to you"; and their sight was restored . . .   *See also* **Mt** 8:5–13 pp Lk 7:1–10; **Mt** 9:20–22 pp Mk 5:25–34 pp Lk 8:43–48; **Mt** 15:21–28 pp Mk 7:24–30

Examples of notable prayers of faith
1Ki 18:36–37; **Jas** 5:17–18; **1Ki** 17:19–22; **2Ki** 4:32–35   *See also faith; waiting on God; watchfulness.*

prayer, and God's will
Prayer is concerned not only with the well-being of the one who prays. A vital aspect of its purpose is to allow the will of God to be done, and to bring glory and honour to his name.

True motives for prayer
The desire that God's name be honoured
Mt 6:9–13 "This, then, is how you should pray: 'Our Father in heaven, hallowed be your name . . .'" pp Lk 11:2–4   *See also* **Nu** 14:13–16; **Jos** 7:7–9; **2Sa** 7:25–26; **1Ki** 18:36–37; **Ps** 115:1; **Jn** 17:1
The desire that God's will be fulfilled
Mt 6:9–13 "This, then, is how you should pray: '. . . your kingdom come, your will be done on earth as it is in heaven . . .'" pp Lk 11:2–4   *See also* **Mt** 26:39 pp Mk 14:36 pp Lk 22:42; **Mt** 26:42; **Heb** 10:7

God answers prayer that accords with his will
1Jn 5:14–15 This is the confidence we have in approaching God: that if we ask anything according to his will, he hears us. And if we know that he hears us—whatever we ask—we know that we have what we asked of him.
Petitioners may enquire of God to discover his will
Ps 143:10 Teach me to do your will, for you are my God . . .   *See also* **Ge** 25:22–23; **Jdg** 1:1–2; **2Sa** 2:1; **1Ch** 14:14–15

The Holy Spirit helps believers to pray in God's will
Ro 8:26–27 In the same way, the Spirit helps us in our weakness. We do not know what we ought to pray for, but the Spirit himself intercedes for us with groans that words cannot express. And he who searches our hearts knows the mind of the Spirit, because the Spirit intercedes for the saints in accordance with God's will.

God's response to prayers allows believers to discern his will
2Co 12:7–9 To keep me [Paul] from becoming conceited because of these surpassingly great revelations, there was given me a thorn in my flesh, a messenger of Satan, to torment me. Three times I pleaded with the Lord to take it away from me. But he said to me, "My grace is sufficient for you, for my power is made perfect in weakness." Therefore I will boast all the more gladly about my weaknesses, so that Christ's power may rest on me.   *See also* **Ex** 33:18–20; **2Sa** 12:15–18; **Job** 19:7–8; **Ps** 35:13–14

God does not respond to the prayers of the wicked
Jn 9:31 We know that God does not listen to sinners. He listens to the godly person who does his will.   *See also* **Ps** 66:18; **Pr** 15:8; **Isa** 1:15; 59:1–2; **La** 3:44; **1Pe** 3:12   *See also guidance.*

prayer, answers
God has promised to answer prayer for personal or corporate needs and for the needs of others.

God answers the prayers of individuals
God answers the psalmists' prayers
Ps 145:18–19 The LORD is near to all who call on him, to all who call on him in truth. He fulfils the desires of those who fear him; he hears their cry and saves them.   *See also* **Ps** 3:4; 6:8–9; 30:2–3; 66:19–20; 116:1–2; 118:5; 138:3
God answers Moses' prayers Ex 15:23–25; 17:4–7; **Nu** 11:10–17
God answers Hannah's prayer for a son
1Sa 1:27 "I prayed for this child, and the LORD has granted me what I asked of him."   *See also* **1Sa** 1:10–20

God answers the prayers of the prophets
Ps 99:6 Moses and Aaron were among his priests, Samuel was among those who called on his name; they called on the LORD and he answered them. *See also* **1Sa** 7:9; **La** 3:55–57; **Jnh** 2:1–2; **Jas** 5:17–18

God answers the prayers of the kings of Israel 1Ki 9:3; **2Ch** 18:31

God answers corporate petition
Answered prayer for deliverance from hardship
Dt 26:7–8 "Then we cried out to the LORD, the God of our ancestors, and the LORD heard our voice and saw our misery, toil and oppression. So the LORD brought us out of Egypt with a mighty hand and an outstretched arm, with great terror and with miraculous signs and wonders. *See also* **Ex** 2:23–25; 3:7–9; **Nu** 20:16; **1Sa** 12:8; **Ps** 81:7

Answered prayer for deliverance from enemies
1Sa 12:10–11 "They cried out to the LORD and said, 'We have sinned; we have forsaken the LORD and served the Baals and the Ashtoreths. But now deliver us from the hands of our enemies, and we will serve you.' Then the LORD sent Jerub-baal, Barak, Jephthah and Samuel, and he delivered you from the hands of your enemies on every side, so that you lived securely." *See also* **Jdg** 3:9,15; **2Ki** 19:19–20; **1Ch** 5:20

God answers the prayer of the oppressed
Jas 5:4 Look! The wages you failed to pay the workers who mowed your fields are crying out against you. The cries of the harvesters have reached the ears of the Lord Almighty. *See also* **Ex** 22:22–23; **Job** 34:28

God answers prayer for healing
Jas 5:14–16 Is any one of you sick? Call the elders of the church to pray over you and anoint you with oil in the name of the Lord. And the prayer offered in faith will make you well; the Lord will raise you up. If you have sinned, you will be forgiven. Therefore confess your sins to each other and pray for each other so that you

may be healed. The prayer of a righteous person is powerful and effective. *See also* **Nu** 12:10–15; **1Ki** 17:21–22; **2Ki** 4:32–35; 20:1–6 pp 2Ch 32:24 pp Isa 38:1–6; **Mt** 8:2–3 pp Mk 1:40–42 pp Lk 5:12–13; **Ac** 9:40

God answers prayer for others
Dt 9:18–19 Then once again I fell prostrate before the LORD for forty days and forty nights; I ate no bread and drank no water, because of all the sin you [Israel] had committed, doing what was evil in the LORD's sight and so provoking him to anger. I feared the anger and wrath of the LORD, for he was angry enough with you to destroy you. But again the LORD listened to me. *See also* **1Sa** 7:8–9; **Ac** 12:5–8

prayer, as praise and thanksgiving
Prayer embraces praising God for who he is, thanking him for what he has already done, and looking forward with joy to what he has promised to do in the future.

Scripture exhorts God's people to praise and thank him
Php 4:6 Do not be anxious about anything, but in everything, by prayer and petition, with thanksgiving, present your requests to God. *See also* **Ps** 66:1; 68:4; 95:1–2; 105:1–3; **Eph** 5:19–20; **Col** 4:2; **1Th** 5:16–18; **Heb** 13:15

Praise and thanksgiving in prayer for God's goodness towards his people
Praise and thanksgiving for deliverance and salvation
Ps 65:1–5 Praise awaits you, O God, in Zion; to you our vows will be fulfilled. O you who hear prayer, to you all people will come. When we were overwhelmed by sins, you forgave our transgressions . . . *See also* **Ps** 66:5–6; 81:1–7; 124:1–8; **Jnh** 2:1–9
Praise and thanksgiving for provision of material needs
Mk 8:6 . . . When he [Jesus] had taken the seven loaves and given thanks, he broke them and gave them to his disciples to set before the

people . . . pp Mt 15:36   *See also* **Ps** 65:9–13; **Mt** 26:26–27 pp Mk 14:22–23 pp Lk 22:19–20

Praise and thanksgiving for help in time of trouble

Ps 34:1–4 I will extol the LORD at all times; his praise will always be on my lips. My soul will boast in the LORD; let the afflicted hear and rejoice. Glorify the LORD with me: let us exalt his name together. I sought the LORD, and he answered me; he delivered me from all my fears.   *See also* **Ps** 30:1–12; 40:1–5; 103:1–5; 116:1–19

Praise and thanksgiving for the encouragement of other believers

Php 1:3–6 I thank my God every time I remember you. In all my prayers for all of you, I always pray with joy because of your partnership in the gospel from the first day until now, being confident of this, that he who began a good work in you will carry it on to completion until the day of Christ Jesus.   *See also* **Ro** 1:8; **2Co** 8:1; **Eph** 1:16; **2Th** 1:3

Notable songs of praise and thanksgiving

Ex 15:1–18

David, on his deliverance from Saul: **2Sa** 22:2–51; **Ps** 18:1–50

1Ch 16:8–36; **Lk** 1:46–55   *See also praise; thankfulness; worship.*

---

prayer, asking God

God wants his people to turn to him in prayer, individually and corporately, in times of need or crisis, and to bring requests to him as a Father.

God's people are commanded to bring their requests to him

Php 4:6 Do not be anxious about anything, but in everything, by prayer and petition, with thanksgiving, present your requests to God.   *See also* **1Ch** 16:11; **Mt** 7:7 pp Lk 11:9; **Jn** 16:24; **Eph** 6:18–20; **1Th** 5:17; **Jas** 5:13

Prayer for deliverance from difficulty

Ps 4:1 Answer me when I call to you, O my righteous God. Give me relief from my distress; be

merciful to me and hear my prayer.

Ps 107:6 Then they cried out to the LORD in their trouble, and he delivered them from their distress.   *See also* **Ps** 40:2–3; **Jnh** 2:1–3; **Ac** 12:5

Prayer for deliverance from enemies

Ps 17:8–9 Keep me as the apple of your eye; hide me in the shadow of your wings from the wicked who assail me, from my mortal enemies who surround me.

Ps 35:4 May those who seek my life be disgraced and put to shame; may those who plot my ruin be turned back in dismay.   *See also* **2Ki** 19:9–11; **2Ch** 14:11

Prayers of individuals in time of crisis

Jacob's prayer **Ge** 32:9–12

David's prayers

Ps 28:1–9 To you I call, O LORD my Rock; do not turn a deaf ear to me. For if you remain silent, I shall be like those who have gone down to the pit. Hear my cry for mercy as I call to you for help, as I lift up my hands towards your Most Holy Place . . .   *See also* **Ps** 4:1; 5:1–3; 30:8–10; 142:1–7

Elijah's prayer

1Ki 19:4 . . . He [Elijah] came to a broom tree, sat down under it and prayed that he might die. "I have had enough, LORD," he said. "Take my life; I am no better than my ancestors."

Jeremiah's prayer **Jer** 15:15–18

Jesus Christ's prayers

Mt 26:39 Going a little farther, he [Jesus] fell with his face to the ground and prayed, "My Father, if it is possible, may this cup be taken from me. Yet not as I will, but as you will." pp Mk 14:35–36 pp Lk 22:42–44

Individual petition to God in prayer

Individual prayer for guidance

Ge 24:12–14 Then he [Abraham's servant] prayed, "O LORD, God of my master Abraham, give me success today, and show kindness to my master Abraham. See, I am standing beside this spring, and the daughters of the townspeople are coming out to draw water. May it be that when I say to a girl, 'Please let down your jar that I may have a drink,' and she says, 'Drink, and I'll water your camels too'—let her be the one you have chosen for your servant Isaac. By this I will know that you have shown kindness to my master." *See also* Jdg 1:1–2; 6:36–40; **1Sa** 14:41; **2Sa** 2:1; **1Ch** 14:14–15

Individual prayer for healing
2Ki 20:1–11 . . . Hezekiah turned his face to the wall and prayed to the Lord, "Remember, O Lord, how I have walked before you faithfully and with wholehearted devotion and have done what is good in your eyes." And Hezekiah wept bitterly . . . pp Isa 38:1–10

Individual prayer for the birth of a child
1Sa 1:10–11 In bitterness of soul Hannah wept much and prayed to the Lord. And she made a vow, saying, "O Lord Almighty, if you will only look upon your servant's misery and remember me, and not forget your servant but give her a son, then I will give him to the Lord for all the days of his life, and no razor will ever be used on his head." *See also* Ge 25:21; 30:17

Corporate petition to God
Corporate prayer for deliverance
Ex 2:23 . . . The Israelites groaned in their slavery and cried out, and their cry for help because of their slavery went up to God. *See also* Nu 20:15–16; Dt 26:6–8; Jdg 3:9; 4:3; 6:7–10; **1Sa** 12:8
Corporate prayer for restoration Ps 44:23–26; 79:8–9; 80:4–7; 85:4–7
Corporate prayer for protection, especially at times of crisis
Ezr 8:21–23 There, by the Ahava Canal, I [Ezra] proclaimed a fast, so that we might humble ourselves before our God and ask him for a safe journey for us and our children, with all our possessions . . . So we fasted and petitioned our God about this, and he answered our prayer. *See also* 2Ch 20:12–13; Ezr 10:1; **Est** 4:16; Ps 74:18–23; Da 2:17–18

The first Christians prayed together when they met
Ac 1:13–14 When they arrived, they went upstairs to the room where they were staying. Those present were Peter, John, James and Andrew; Philip and Thomas, Bartholomew and Matthew; James son of Alphaeus and Simon the Zealot, and Judas son of James. They all joined together constantly in prayer, along with the women and Mary the mother of Jesus, and with his brothers. *See also* Ac 2:42,46–47; 16:13,16; 20:36; 21:5

The first Christians prayed together at times of crisis or important decisions
When threatened with punishment
Ac 4:24–31 When they [the Jerusalem believers] heard this [what the chief priests and elders had said to Peter and John], they raised their voices together in prayer to God . . .
See also Ac 12:5,12
When Barnabas and Saul were sent off by the church at Antioch Ac 13:3
When Paul and Silas experienced persecution Ac 16:25

Prayers for mercy and grace
Ps 143:1 O Lord, hear my prayer, listen to my cry for mercy; in your faithfulness and righteousness come to my relief.
Heb 4:16 Let us then approach the throne of grace with confidence, so that we may receive mercy and find grace to help us in our time of need. *See also* 2Ch 6:18–19; Ps 130:1–2; **Mt** 20:30–31

prayer, doubts

Sometimes God does not seem to answer prayer, causing his people to doubt him. Scripture affirms God's faithfulness to those who pray according to his will, and points out that the human understanding of a situation is limited.

Examples of God's servants questioning his promises
Ex 5:22–23 Moses returned to the Lord and said, "O Lord, why have you brought trouble upon this people? Is this why you sent me? Ever since I went to Pharaoh to speak in your name, he has brought trouble upon this people, and you

have not rescued your people at all."   *See also*
Ge 15:2-3; **Jos** 7:7-9

Examples of God's servants questioning the tasks he has given them

Nu 11:11-15 He asked the LORD, "Why have you brought this trouble on your servant? What have I done to displease you that you put the burden of all these people on me? . . . I cannot carry all these people by myself; the burden is too heavy for me. If this is how you are going to treat me, put me to death right now—if I have found favour in your eyes—and do not let me face my own ruin."   *See also* **1Ki** 19:4; **Jer** 15:15-18; 20:7-9,14-18; **Jnh** 4:1-3; **Mt** 27:46 pp **Mk** 15:34; **Ps** 22:1

Examples of God's servants expressing their anger and confusion in prayer

Job 10:2-22 "I [Job] will say to God: Do not condemn me, but tell me what charges you have against me. Does it please you to oppress me, to spurn the work of your hands, while you smile on the schemes of the wicked? . . ."   *See also* **Job** 13:20-27; 14:1-22; **Ps** 13:1-2; 42:9-10; 44:22-26; 77:7-9; 80:4-6; 88:6-9; **Hab** 1:2-3

God's response to prayers of questioning or complaint

God reiterates his promises to those who question him

Ge 15:2-5 But Abram said, "O Sovereign LORD, what can you give me since I remain childless and the one who will inherit my estate is Eliezer of Damascus?" And Abram said, "You have given me no children; so a servant in my household will be my heir." Then the word of the LORD came to him: "This man will not be your heir, but a son coming from your own body will be your heir." He took him outside and said, "Look up at the heavens and count the stars—if indeed you can count them." Then he said to him, "So shall your offspring be."   *See also* **Ex** 6:1-8

God provides help for those who question him
1Ki 19:1-8

God rebukes those who question him

Job 40:1-9 The LORD said to Job: "Will the one who contends with the Almighty correct him? Let him who accuses God answer him!" . . .
See also **Jer** 15:19-21

God explains events to those who question him **Hab** 1:5-11   *See also* doubt; spiritual warfare; suffering, encouragements in.

---

prayer, effective

Scripture provides guidance concerning what attitudes and actions are appropriate for effective prayer. It also identifies a number of motives which are likely to lead to prayers being unanswered.

Hindrances to prayer
Sin

Isa 59:2 But your [Israel's] iniquities have separated you from your God; your sins have hidden his face from you, so that he will not hear.   *See also* **Ps** 66:18; **Jer** 14:10-12; **La** 3:42-44; **Mic** 3:4

Disobedience

Zec 7:13 "'When I called, they did not listen; so when they called, I would not listen,' says the LORD Almighty."   *See also* **Dt** 1:43-45; **Pr** 1:28-31

Selfishness

Jas 4:3 When you ask, you do not receive, because you ask with wrong motives, that you may spend what you get on your pleasures.

Injustice

Isa 1:15-17 "When you spread out your hands in prayer, I will hide my eyes from you; even if you offer many prayers, I will not listen. Your hands are full of blood; wash and make yourselves clean. Take your evil deeds out of my sight! Stop doing wrong, learn to do right! Seek justice, encourage the oppressed. Defend the cause of the fatherless, plead the case of the widow."   *See also* **Pr** 21:13; **Isa** 58:1-7

Lack of faith

Jas 1:6-7 But when you ask, you must believe and not doubt, because the one who doubts is like a wave of the sea, blown and tossed by the wind. Those who doubt should not think they will receive anything from the Lord;

Qualities that lead to effective prayer
Humility
Lk 18:9–14 . . . ". . . I tell you that this man [the tax collector], rather than the other [the Pharisee], went home justified before God. For all those who exalt themselves will be humbled, and those who humble themselves will be exalted."
See also **2Sa** 7:18; **2Ch** 7:14; **Ps** 51:16–17; **Isa** 57:15; **Mt** 8:8 pp Lk 7:6

Obedience
1Jn 3:21–22 Dear friends, if our hearts do not condemn us, we have confidence before God and receive from him anything we ask, because we obey his commands and do what pleases him.
See also **1Sa** 15:22; **Jer** 7:22–23

Righteousness
Pr 15:29 The LORD is far from the wicked but he hears the prayer of the righteous. *See also* **1Ki** 3:11–12; **Ps** 34:15

Single-mindedness
Jer 29:13 "You will seek me and find me when you seek me with all your heart."
See also **Dt** 4:29; **1Ch** 28:9

Faith
Mt 21:21–22 Jesus replied, "I tell you the truth, if you have faith and do not doubt, not only can you do what was done to the fig-tree, but also you can say to this mountain, 'Go, throw yourself into the sea,' and it will be done. If you believe, you will receive whatever you ask for in prayer." pp Mk 11:22–24 *See also* **Mt** 7:7–11 pp Lk 11:9–13; **Mt** 8:5–13 pp Lk 7:1–10; **Mt** 15:21–28 pp Mk 7:24–30; **Jn** 14:12–14
See also humility; obedience; sin.

---

prayer, for others
Believers should pray, not only for their own needs, but for those of others. Scripture provides many examples of intercession, and commends it as pleasing to God.

Believers must value others
Php 2:3–4 Do nothing out of selfish ambition or vain conceit, but in humility consider others better than yourselves. Each of you should look not only to your own interests, but also to the interests of others.

Examples of praying for others
Moses prays for the Israelites
Dt 9:18–19 Then once again I fell prostrate before the LORD for forty days and forty nights; I ate no bread and drank no water, because of all the sin you [the Israelites] had committed, doing what was evil in the LORD's sight and so provoking him to anger. I feared the anger and wrath of the LORD, for he was angry enough with you to destroy you. But again the LORD listened to me. *See also* **Ex** 32:9–14; 34:9; **Nu** 14:11–19; **Dt** 9:25–29

Samuel prays for Israel
1Sa 7:5–9 Then Samuel said, "Assemble all Israel at Mizpah and I will intercede with the LORD for you." . . . Then Samuel took a suckling lamb and offered it up as a whole burnt offering to the LORD. He cried out to the LORD on Israel's behalf, and the LORD answered him. *See also* **1Sa** 12:19–23

Job prays for his friends
Job 42:10 After Job had prayed for his friends, the LORD made him prosperous again and gave him twice as much as he had before.

Jeremiah prays for Judah
Jer 7:16 "So do not pray for this people nor offer any plea or petition for them; do not plead with me, for I will not listen to you." *See also* **Jer** 11:14; 14:11

Jesus Christ intercedes for believers
Ro 8:34 Who then can condemn? Christ Jesus, who died—more than that, who was raised to life—is at the right hand of God and is also interceding for us. *See also* **Isa** 53:12; **Heb** 7:25; **1Jn** 2:1

The Holy Spirit intercedes for believers
Ro 8:26–27 . . . the Spirit helps us in our weakness. We do not know what we ought to pray for, but the Spirit himself intercedes for us with groans that words cannot express. And he who searches our hearts knows the mind of the Spirit, because the Spirit intercedes for the saints in accordance with God's will.

Christians are to intercede for others
Christians are to pray for their enemies
Mt 5:44 "But I tell you: Love your enemies, and pray for those who persecute you,"
See also **Lk** 6:28; 23:34; **Ac** 7:60
Christians are to pray for one another
Eph 6:18 And pray in the Spirit on all occasions with all kinds of prayers and requests. With this in mind, be alert and always keep on praying for all the saints.   *See also* **1Th** 5:25; **Phm** 22; **Heb** 13:18–19; **Jas** 5:14–16; **1Jn** 5:16
Christians are to pray for rulers
1Ti 2:1–2 I urge, then, first of all, that requests, prayers, intercession and thanksgiving be made for everyone — for kings and all those in authority, that we may live peaceful and quiet lives in all godliness and holiness.

Examples of pleas made to Jesus Christ on behalf of others
Mt 8:5–13 pp Lk 7:1–10; **Mt** 15:21–28 pp Mk 7:24–30; **Mt** 17:14–20 pp Mk 9:14–29 pp Lk 9:37–42

Examples of notable prayers of intercession
2Ki 19:14–19 pp Isa 37:14–20; **Ezr** 8:21–23; **Da** 9:1–19; **Jn** 17:6–26
Paul for the believers in Ephesus: **Eph** 1:15–21; 3:14–21
Col 1:9–13   *See also forgiveness, application.*

prayer, God's promises
God promises to hear and respond to the prayers of his people, when they pray in the name of his Son and according to his will.

God expects his people to make requests of him in prayer
Mt 7:7–11 "Ask and it will be given to you; seek and you will find; knock and the door will be opened to you. For everyone who asks receives; everyone who seeks finds; and to everyone who knocks, the door will be opened. "Which of you, if your children ask for bread, will give them a stone? Or if they ask for a fish, will give them a snake? If you, then, though you are

evil, know how to give good gifts to your children, how much more will your Father in heaven give good gifts to those who ask him!" pp Lk 11:9–13   *See also* **Mt** 21:22

God promises to answer prayer in the name of Jesus Christ
Jn 14:13–14 "And I will do whatever you ask in my name, so that the Son may bring glory to the Father. You may ask me for anything in my name, and I will do it."
Jn 15:7 "If you remain in me [Jesus] and my words remain in you, ask whatever you wish, and it will be given you."   *See also* **Jn** 15:16; 16:23–24

God promises to respond to the prayers of his people in times of need
Ps 91:14–16 "Because you love me," says the LORD, "I will rescue you; I will protect you, for you acknowledge my name. You will call upon me, and I will answer you; I will be with you in trouble, I will deliver you and honour you. With long life will I satisfy you and show you my salvation."   *See also* **Ps** 50:14–15

God promises to hear the prayers of the oppressed
Ps 10:17 You hear, O LORD, the desire of the afflicted; you encourage them, and you listen to their cry,   *See also* **Ex** 22:22–23,26–27; **Ps** 102:19–20; **Isa** 41:17

God promises to hear the prayers of the truly penitent
2Ch 7:14 ". . . if my people, who are called by my name, will humble themselves and pray and seek my face and turn from their wicked ways, then will I hear from heaven and will forgive their sin and will heal their land." *See also* **Eze** 36:37; **Zec** 10:6; 13:8–9

God promises to hear the prayers of his obedient people
1Jn 3:22 and receive from him anything we ask, because we obey his commands and do what pleases him.

The need in prayer to have confidence in God's promises
Mk 11:24 "Therefore I tell you, whatever you ask for in prayer, believe that you have received it, and it will be yours."
1Jn 5:14 This is the confidence we have in approaching God: that if we ask anything according to his will, he hears us. *See also* **Mt** 18:19 *See also faith, and blessings.*

prayer, in the church
The prayer life of the NT provides a pattern from which the modern church can learn, both in terms of the importance of prayer, and also matters for prayer.

Prayer was at the centre of the life of the early church
They prayed when they met together
Ac 1:14 They all joined together constantly in prayer, along with the women and Mary the mother of Jesus, and with his brothers.
See also **Ac** 2:42; 4:23–31; 12:12; 20:36; 21:5
They prayed about the selection and ordination of Christian leaders
Ac 13:2–3 While they [the leaders of the church at Antioch] were worshipping the Lord and fasting, the Holy Spirit said, "Set apart for me Barnabas and Saul for the work to which I have called them." So after they had fasted and prayed, they placed their hands on them and sent them off. *See also* **Ac** 1:24–25; 6:6; 14:23
They prayed during persecution
Ac 12:5 So Peter was kept in prison, but the church was earnestly praying to God for him.
See also **Ac** 7:59–60; 12:12; 16:22–25
They prayed for healing
Ac 9:40 Peter sent them all out of the room; then he got down on his knees and prayed. Turning towards the dead woman, he said, "Tabitha, get up." She opened her eyes, and seeing Peter she sat up. *See also* **Ac** 28:7–8

The apostles' teaching on prayer in church life
The importance of prayer
Col 4:2 Devote yourselves to prayer, being

watchful and thankful. *See also* **Ro** 12:12; **Eph** 6:18; **1Th** 5:17; **1Ti** 2:1; **1Pe** 4:7
Prayer for the spread of the gospel
Col 4:3–4 And pray for us, too, that God may open a door for our message, so that we may proclaim the mystery of Christ, for which I am in chains. Pray that I may proclaim it clearly, as I should. *See also* **Eph** 6:19–20; **2Th** 3:1
Prayer for the sick
Jas 5:14 Is any one of you sick? Call the elders of the church to pray over you and anoint you with oil in the name of the Lord.
Prayer for sinners
1Jn 5:16–17 If you see your brother or sister commit a sin that does not lead to death, you should pray and God will give them life. I refer to those whose sin does not lead to death. There is a sin that leads to death. I am not saying that you should pray about that. All wrongdoing is sin, and there is sin that does not lead to death.
See also **Jas** 5:16
Prayer for God's servants
Ro 15:30 I urge you, brothers and sisters, by our Lord Jesus Christ and by the love of the Spirit, to join me in my struggle by praying to God for me. *See also* **2Co** 1:11
Orderly conduct of public prayer
1Co 11:4–5 Every man who prays or prophesies with his head covered dishonours his head. And every woman who prays or prophesies with her head uncovered dishonours her head—it is just as though her head were shaved.
See also **1Co** 11:13–15

The practice of the apostles
Prayer was central to their ministry
Ac 6:3–4 ". . . We [the apostles] will turn this responsibility over to them [deacons] and will give our attention to prayer and the ministry of the word."
They prayed for the church
Col 1:9–10 For this reason, since the day we [Paul and Timothy] heard about you, we have not stopped praying for you and asking God to fill you with the knowledge of his will through all spiritual wisdom and understanding. And we pray this in order that you may live a life worthy of

the Lord and may please him in every way: bearing fruit in every good work, growing in the knowledge of God,   *See also* **Eph** 1:16–21; 3:16–19; **Php** 1:9–11; **Col** 1:3; **1Th** 1:2; **2Th** 1:11–12   *See also church, life of.*

prayer, persistence

An answer to prayer may not come immediately. Petitioners are to continue praying earnestly. This requires patience, determination and, at times, a willingness to wrestle with God for the desired outcome.

The principle of persistence in prayer
Prayer should be made with patience and perseverance
Ps 40:1 I waited patiently for the LORD; he turned to me and heard my cry.
Ps 88:1 O LORD, the God who saves me, day and night I cry out before you.   *See also* **1Ch** 16:11; **Ps** 116:2
Jesus Christ taught his disciples to persist in prayer
Lk 18:1–8 Then Jesus told his disciples a parable to show them that they should always pray and not give up. He said: "In a certain town there was a judge who neither feared God nor cared about people. And there was a widow in that town who kept coming to him with the plea, 'Grant me justice against my adversary.' For some time he refused. But finally he said to himself, 'Even though I don't fear God or care about people, yet because this widow keeps bothering me, I will see that she gets justice, so that she won't eventually wear me out with her coming!'" And the Lord said, "Listen to what the unjust judge says . . ."   *See also* **Lk** 11:5–10
Persistence in prayer was exemplified in the early church
Ac 1:14 They all joined together constantly in prayer, along with the women and Mary the mother of Jesus, and with his brothers.
See also **Ac** 2:42
Paul exhorted the churches to practise persistent prayer
Eph 6:18 And pray in the Spirit on all occasions with all kinds of prayers and requests. With this

in mind, be alert and always keep on praying for all the saints.   *See also* **Ro** 12:12; **1Th** 5:17

Examples of persistence in prayer
Abraham pleads persistently for Sodom
Ge 18:23–33 Then Abraham approached him and said: "Will you sweep away the righteous with the wicked? What if there are fifty righteous people in the city? Will you really sweep it away and not spare the place for the sake of the fifty righteous people in it? Far be it from you to do such a thing—to kill the righteous with the wicked, treating the righteous and the wicked alike. Far be it from you! Will not the Judge of all the earth do right?" . . .
Jacob persists in wrestling with God
Ge 32:24–32 . . . Then the man said, "Let me go, for it is daybreak." But Jacob replied, "I will not let you go unless you bless me." . . .
Moses persists in interceding for Israel
Dt 9:25–29 . . . "O Sovereign LORD, do not destroy your people, your own inheritance that you redeemed by your great power and brought out of Egypt with a mighty hand. Remember your servants Abraham, Isaac and Jacob. Overlook the stubbornness of this people, their wickedness and their sin . . ."   *See also* **Ex** 32:31–32
Hannah persistently asks for a son
1Sa 1:10–11 In bitterness of soul Hannah wept much and prayed to the LORD. And she made a vow, saying, "O LORD Almighty, if you will only look upon your servant's misery and remember me, and not forget your servant but give her a son, then I will give him to the LORD for all the days of his life, and no razor will ever be used on his head."
Elijah persists in prayer about the rain
Jas 5:17–18 Elijah was human just as we are. He prayed earnestly that it would not rain, and it did not rain on the land for three and a half years. Again he prayed, and the heavens gave rain, and the earth produced its crops.   *See also* **1Ki** 18:36–44
The psalmists persist in calling out to God Ps 88:1–18; 119:147–149; 130:1–6

Jesus Christ persisted in pursuing the Father's will
Lk 22:42–44 "Father, if you are willing, take this cup from me; yet not my will, but yours be done." . . . And being in anguish, he prayed more earnestly, and his sweat was like drops of blood falling to the ground. pp Mt 26:36–43 pp Mk 14:32–40

Persistence in prayer is exemplified in waiting for God
Mic 7:7 But as for me, I watch in hope for the LORD, I wait for God my Saviour; my God will hear me.   *See also* Ps 27:14; 33:20; 37:7; 38:15; 40:1; Isa 26:8   *See also perseverance.*

---

prayer, practicalities
Scripture commends a life of prayer, characterised by simplicity of expression, sincerity of heart and trust in the promises of God. It gives guidance on how, when and where to pray.

Scripture stresses the importance of prayer
1Th 5:16–18 . . . pray continually; give thanks in all circumstances, for this is God's will for you in Christ Jesus.   *See also* Ac 6:3–4; Ro 12:12

Judgment comes on those who do not pray
Ps 79:6 Pour out your wrath on the nations that do not acknowledge you, on the kingdoms that do not call on your name;   *See also* Ps 53:4; Jer 10:21; Zep 1:4–6; Jas 4:2

Prayers should be expressed simply
Mt 6:7–8 "And when you pray, do not keep on babbling like pagans, for they think they will be heard because of their many words. Do not be like them, for your Father knows what you need before you ask him."   *See also* Ecc 5:1–3; Lk 18:9–14

Prayer should not be ostentatious
Mt 6:5–6 "And when you pray, do not be like the hypocrites, for they love to pray standing in the synagogues and on the street corners to be

seen by others. I tell you the truth, they have received their reward in full. But when you pray, go into your room, close the door and pray to your Father, who is unseen. Then your Father, who sees what is done in secret, will reward you."   *See also* Mt 14:23 pp Mk 6:46; Lk 5:16

Physical positions for prayer
Sitting while praying
2Sa 7:18 Then King David went in and sat before the LORD, and he said: "Who am I, O Sovereign LORD, and what is my family, that you have brought me this far?"   *See also* Jdg 20:26; Ne 1:4
Kneeling while praying
Lk 22:41 He [Jesus] withdrew about a stone's throw beyond them, knelt down and prayed,
See also 1Ki 8:54; 2Ch 6:13; Ezr 9:5; Ac 9:40; 21:5; Eph 3:14
Standing while praying
1Ki 8:22 Then Solomon stood before the altar of the LORD in front of the whole assembly of Israel . . .   *See also* 1Sa 1:26; Mk 11:25
Lying prostrate while praying
2Ch 20:18 Jehoshaphat bowed with his face to the ground, and all the people of Judah and Jerusalem fell down in worship before the LORD.   *See also* Ge 24:52; Nu 20:6
Praying with arms outstretched
Ex 9:29 Moses replied, "When I have gone out of the city, I will spread out my hands in prayer to the LORD. The thunder will stop and there will be no more hail, so you may know that the earth is the LORD's."
Isa 1:15 "When you spread out your hands in prayer, I will hide my eyes from you; even if you offer many prayers, I will not listen. Your hands are full of blood;"   *See also* 1Ki 8:54; 2Ch 6:13
Praying with hands raised
1Ti 2:8 I want men everywhere to lift up holy hands in prayer, without anger or disputing.
See also Ex 9:29; 1Ki 8:22,54; Ps 63:4; 77:1–2

Prayer can be offered at any time
Praying several times a day
Da 6:10 Now when Daniel learned that the decree had been published, he went home to his

upstairs room where the windows opened towards Jerusalem. Three times a day he got down on his knees and prayed, giving thanks to his God, just as he had done before.   *See also* **Ps** 55:17; 88:1

Praying early in the morning
Mk 1:35 Very early in the morning, while it was still dark, Jesus got up, left the house and went off to a solitary place, where he prayed.
See also **Ps** 5:3; 119:147

Praying all night
Lk 6:12 One of those days Jesus went out to a mountainside to pray, and spent the night praying to God.   *See also* **1Sa** 15:11; **Lk** 2:37

Prayer is not confined to any single place
Jn 4:21–24 Jesus declared, "Believe me, woman, a time is coming when you will worship the Father neither on this mountain nor in Jerusalem . . . Yet a time is coming and has now come when the true worshippers will worship the Father in spirit and truth, for they are the kind of worshippers the Father seeks. God is spirit, and his worshippers must worship in spirit and in truth."

Praying inside a building
Da 6:10 Now when Daniel learned that the decree had been published, he went home to his upstairs room where the windows opened towards Jerusalem. Three times a day he got down on his knees and prayed, giving thanks to his God, just as he had done before.
Mt 6:6 "But when you pray, go into your room, close the door and pray to your Father, who is unseen. Then your Father, who sees what is done in secret, will reward you."   *See also* **1Ki** 8:28–30

Praying outside a building
Mk 1:35 Very early in the morning, while it was still dark, Jesus got up, left the house and went off to a solitary place, where he prayed.
Lk 5:16 But Jesus often withdrew to lonely places and prayed.   *See also* **Ac** 10:9; 21:5

Prayer may be accompanied by fasting
Ac 13:2–3 While they were worshipping the

Lord and fasting, the Holy Spirit said, "Set apart for me Barnabas and Saul for the work to which I have called them." So after they had fasted and prayed, they placed their hands on them and sent them off.   *See also* **Ezr** 8:23; **Ne** 1:4; **Ps** 35:13; **Da** 9:3; **Lk** 2:37; 5:33; **Ac** 14:23; **Mt** 17:21 fn pp **Mk** 9:29 fn   *See also fasting.*

---

preaching
The announcing of the good news of God by his servants through the faithful revelation of God's will, the exposition of God's word and the proclamation of Jesus Christ, the Son of God. Jesus Christ had an important preaching ministry.

---

preaching, content
Preaching is centred on the nature and will of God and his claims on all people. Expressed in prophecy, declaration or teaching, it includes the proclamation of the way of salvation to unbelievers and instruction about the faith to believers.

Preaching and the revelation of God's character, word and will
Ac 20:26–27 "Therefore, I [Paul] declare to you today that I am innocent of the blood of everyone. For I have not hesitated to proclaim to you the whole will of God."   *See also* **Ex** 8:1; **1Ki** 12:21–24; **Jer** 7:1–11; **Eze** 2:3–3:4

Preaching and the declaration of the gospel
Declaring the kingdom
Mk 1:14–15 After John was put in prison, Jesus went into Galilee, proclaiming the good news of God. "The time has come," he said. "The kingdom of God is near. Repent and believe the good news!" pp **Mt** 4:17   *See also* **Mt** 4:23 pp **Lk** 8:1; **Ac** 19:8; 20:25
Declaring the person of Jesus Christ and his life
Ac 2:22 "People of Israel, listen to this: Jesus of Nazareth was a man accredited by God to you by miracles, wonders and signs, which God did

among you through him, as you yourselves know."   *See also* **Ac** 10:36–38; 28:31; **2Co** 1:19

Declaring the facts of the cross and the resurrection

Ac 2:23–24 "This man was handed over to you by God's set purpose and foreknowledge; and you, with the help of wicked people, put him to death by nailing him to the cross. But God raised him from the dead, freeing him from the agony of death, because it was impossible for death to keep its hold on him."   *See also* **Ac** 5:30; 10:39–42; 13:28–31; **1Co** 1:22–24; 15:12–17

Declaring the victory and exaltation of Jesus Christ

Ac 2:33–35 "Exalted to the right hand of God, he has received from the Father the promised Holy Spirit and has poured out what you now see and hear . . ."   *See also* **Ac** 5:31; **1Pe** 3:18–22

Declaring that Jesus is both Messiah (Christ) and Lord

Ac 2:36 "Therefore let all Israel be assured of this: God has made this Jesus, whom you crucified, both Lord and Christ."   *See also* **Ac** 5:42; 8:5; 9:20–22; 10:36; 18:5

Declaring the call to repent

Ac 17:30 "In the past God overlooked such ignorance, but now he commands all people everywhere to repent."   *See also* **Mk** 1:15 pp Mt 4:17; **Ac** 2:38; 3:19; 26:20

Declaring the promise of forgiveness

Ac 13:38 "Therefore, my brothers and sisters, I want you to know that through Jesus the forgiveness of sins is proclaimed to you."   *See also* **Lk** 24:46–47; **Ac** 2:38; 5:31; 10:43

Preaching finds expression in the teaching of believers

The central place of teaching in the lives of the first Christians

Ac 2:42 They devoted themselves to the apostles' teaching . . .   *See also* **Ac** 6:2; 11:25–26; 15:35; 18:24–26; 20:20

Teaching from the Scriptures

Ac 18:11 So Paul stayed for a year and a half, teaching them the word of God.   *See also* **2Ch** 17:7–9; **Ne** 8:2–8

Teaching on how to live

Mt 28:19–20 "Therefore go and make disciples of all nations . . . teaching them to obey everything I have commanded you . . ."   *See also* **Eph** 4:20–24; **1Th** 4:1–2; **Tit** 2:1–15

Preaching and the edification of believers

2Ti 4:2 Preach the Word; be prepared in season and out of season; correct, rebuke and encourage—with great patience and careful instruction.   *See also* **Ac** 13:42–43; 14:21–22; 20:2; **1Co** 14:26–31

Preaching and the continuation of apostolic doctrine

Preaching should be rooted in apostolic doctrine, which is to be faithfully handed on

2Ti 2:2 And the things you have heard me say in the presence of many witnesses entrust to reliable people who will also be qualified to teach others.   *See also* **1Co** 11:2; **2Th** 2:15; **2Ti** 1:13–14

Preaching that does not conform to apostolic doctrine is to be rejected

1Ti 1:3–4 . . . command certain persons not to teach false doctrines any longer nor to devote themselves to myths and endless genealogies. These promote controversies rather than God's work—which is by faith.   *See also* **Gal** 1:6–9; **1Ti** 4:1–7; **Tit** 1:9–14

Preaching and the rejection of merely human wisdom

1Co 2:1–5 When I came to you, brothers and sisters, I did not come with eloquence or superior wisdom as I proclaimed to you the testimony about God . . . My message and my preaching were not with wise and persuasive words, but with a demonstration of the Spirit's power . . .   *See also* **1Co** 1:18–25

See also evangelism.

---

preaching, effects

Faithful preaching leads, through the grace of God, to the repentance of sinners, the birth of faith and the nourishment of believers. It can also evoke hostility from unbelievers.

The basis of effective preaching
It depends upon the grace of God
Ac 4:33 With great power the apostles continued to testify to the resurrection of the Lord Jesus, and much grace was upon them all.   *See also* **Isa** 55:10–11; **Ac** 14:26–27; **1Co** 15:10–11
It depends upon the power of the cross, not human wisdom
1Co 1:17–25 For Christ did not send me to baptise, but to preach the gospel—not with words of human wisdom, lest the cross of Christ be emptied of its power . . .   *See also* **1Co** 2:1–5
It depends upon the power of the Holy Spirit
Lk 4:18–19 "The Spirit of the Lord is on me, because he has anointed me to preach good news to the poor. He has sent me to proclaim freedom for the prisoners and recovery of sight for the blind, to release the oppressed, to proclaim the year of the Lord's favour."   *See also* **Isa** 61:1–2; **Ac** 2:1–11; 10:44–48; **1Co** 2:4–5
It requires effective, supporting prayer
Col 4:3–4 And pray for us, too, that God may open a door for our message, so that we may proclaim the mystery of Christ . . .   *See also* **Ac** 4:29–31; 6:2–4; 13:1–5; **2Th** 3:1
It needs to be received with faith
Heb 4:2 For we also have had the gospel preached to us, just as they did; but the message they heard was of no value to them, because those who heard did not combine it with faith. *See also* **1Th** 2:13

Preaching and the repentance of sinners
Mt 12:41 "The people of Nineveh will stand up at the judgment with this generation and condemn it; for they repented at the preaching of Jonah . . ." pp **Lk** 11:32   *See also* **Jnh** 3:1–10; **Mt** 3:1–6 pp **Mk** 1:3–5 pp **Lk** 3:3–6

Preaching and the birth of faith
Ac 4:4 But many who heard the message believed, and their number grew to about five thousand.   *See also* **Ac** 2:38–41; 8:9–13; 17:11–12; **1Co** 15:1–2

Preaching and the nourishment of believers
Ac 14:21–22 They preached the good news in that city and won a large number of disciples. Then they returned to Lystra, Iconium and Antioch, strengthening the disciples and encouraging them to remain true to the faith. "We must go through many hardships to enter the kingdom of God," they said.   *See also* **Ro** 16:25–27; **Eph** 4:11–16; **Col** 2:6–7

Effective preaching and its authentication by miracles
Mk 16:20 Then the disciples went out and preached everywhere, and the Lord worked with them and confirmed his word by the signs that accompanied it.   *See also* **Mt** 4:23–25; **Lk** 9:1–6 pp **Mt** 10:5–14 pp **Mk** 6:7–11; **Ac** 4:29–30; 8:5–8; 14:1–3

Inappropriate responses to preaching
Amazement
Mt 7:28–29 When Jesus had finished saying these things, the crowds were amazed at his teaching, because he taught as one who had authority, and not as their teachers of the law. *See also* **Lk** 4:31–32 pp **Mk** 1:21–22; **Ac** 2:5–12; 4:13–14
Offence
Mk 6:1–6 . . . ". . . Isn't this the carpenter? Isn't this Mary's son and the brother of James, Joseph, Judas and Simon? Aren't his sisters here with us?" And they took offence at him . . . pp **Mt** 13:54–58   *See also* **1Co** 1:22–23
Mere academic interest Ac 17:16–32; 24:22–26
Mockery
Ac 17:32 When they heard about the resurrection of the dead, some of them sneered . . .   *See also* **2Ch** 36:15–16; **Ac** 2:13
Hostility
Ac 17:13 When the Jews in Thessalonica learned that Paul was preaching the word of God at Berea, they went there too, agitating the crowds and stirring them up.   *See also* **Ac** 4:1–3; 5:27–40; 7:54–60; 13:49–51; 17:5–9
See also baptism; church; faith; repentance.

pride

Arrogance or delusions of greatness on account of one's achievements, status or possessions. Scripture frequently speaks of God humbling the proud.

pride, evil of

Pride is viewed as a great evil because it involves pretending to a greatness and glory that belong rightly to God alone.

The sinfulness of pride
It is condemned as evil

1Sa 15:23 "For rebellion is like the sin of divination, and arrogance like the evil of idolatry . . ."
Pr 21:4 Haughty eyes and a proud heart, the lamp of the wicked, are sin!
Jas 4:16 As it is, you boast and brag. All such boasting is evil.   *See also* **Mk** 7:22–23; **2Co** 12:20; **Ro** 1:29–30; **2Ti** 3:1–2; **1Jn** 2:16
It is a characteristic of Satan

Eze 28:2 ". . . '. . . In the pride of your heart you [the King of Tyre] say, "I am a god; I sit on the throne of a god in the heart of the seas." But you are a mortal and not a god, though you think you are as wise as a god.'"
1Ti 3:6 He [the church overseer] must not be a recent convert, or he may become conceited and fall under the same judgment as the devil.
See also **2Th** 2:4

Warnings against pride
In the book of Proverbs

Pr 16:5 The Lord detests all the proud of heart. Be sure of this: They will not go unpunished.
Pr 16:18 Pride goes before destruction, a haughty spirit before a fall.   *See also* **Pr** 3:7,34; 6:16–17; 11:2; 25:6–7,27; 26:12; 27:1; 29:23
Elsewhere in Scripture

Ps 119:21 You [the Lord] rebuke the arrogant, who are cursed and who stray from your commands.   *See also* **Lev** 26:19
Proud talk: **1Sa** 2:3; **Ps** 12:2–3; **Jer** 9:23–24
Ps 5:5; 40:4; 138:6; **Isa** 5:21; **Jer** 13:15–17; **Mt** 23:12 pp **Lk** 14:11; **Ro** 12:16; **1Co** 10:12
God opposes the proud: **1Pe** 5:5; **Jas** 4:6; **Pr** 3:34

The gospel excludes pride

Ro 3:27 Where, then, is boasting? It is excluded. On what principle? On that of observing the law? No, but on that of faith.   *See also* **Lk** 18:9–14; **Ro** 4:2–3; 11:17–20; **1Co** 1:26–31; **Eph** 2:8–9

Godliness involves rejecting pride

Pr 8:13 "To fear the Lord is to hate evil; I hate pride and arrogance, evil behaviour and perverse speech."   *See also* **Ps** 101:5; 131:1; **Ro** 12:3; **1Co** 13:4; **Gal** 6:14   *See also* humility.

pride, examples

Scripture illustrates the many different ways in which pride manifests itself.

Pride in status

Ex 5:2; **2Ki** 5:11
Hezekiah: **2Ki** 20:13; **2Ch** 32:25
Est 5:11–12
Moab: **Isa** 16:6; **Jer** 48:29
Isa 47:8; **Eze** 16:49–50; 28:2
Assyria: **Eze** 31:3,10
Da 5:23; **Ob** 3; **Zep** 2:15
Teachers of the law and Pharisees: **Mt** 23:6–7 pp **Mk** 12:38–39 pp **Lk** 20:46; **Lk** 11:43
Ac 8:9; **Rev** 18:7

Pride in strength

1Sa 17:42; **2Ki** 14:9–10; 18:33–35
Israel: **Isa** 9:9–10; **Hos** 10:13
Isa 10:13
Nebuchadnezzar: **Da** 3:15; 4:30
Peter: **Mt** 26:33–35 pp **Mk** 14:29–31 pp **Lk** 22:33; **Jn** 13:37

Pride in wisdom

Isa 10:13; **Ac** 17:21; **Ro** 1:22; **1Co** 1:20; 3:18

Proud ambition

Isa 14:13–14; **2Th** 2:3–4

Spiritual pride

2Ki 10:16; **Job** 32:1; 33:9; **Isa** 65:5; **Mt** 6:2,3,16

Teachers of the law and Pharisees: **Mt** 23:5,30; **Mk** 12:40 pp Lk 20:47; **Lk** 16:14–15; 18:9,11–12; **Jn** 9:40–41
Lk 10:29
Some Jews: **Jn** 8:33; 9:34; **Ro** 2:17–20
1Co 4:7,18; **Rev** 3:17

pride, results
The real nature of pride can be seen in the fact that it leads to many other evils and ends in destruction.

Pride leads to other forms of evil
Self-deception
Gal 6:3 If any of you think you are something when you are nothing, you deceive yourselves. *See also* **Dt** 8:17–18; **Isa** 16:6; 47:10; **Jer** 49:16 pp Ob 3; **1Co** 8:2; **1Ti** 6:3–4
Spiritual blindness
Jer 43:2 Azariah son of Hoshaiah and Johanan son of Kareah and all the arrogant people said to Jeremiah, "You are lying! The LORD our God has not sent you to say, 'You must not go to Egypt to settle there.'" *See also* **Dt** 8:14; **Ne** 9:16,29
A hard heart
Ps 36:2 For in their [the wicked person's] own eyes they flatter themselves too much to detect or hate their sin. *See also* **Ps** 10:3; 52:1; **Da** 5:20
A malicious spirit
Ps 119:85 The arrogant dig pitfalls for me, contrary to your law. *See also* **Ps** 73:8; 140:5
Contempt for others
Ps 123:4 We have endured much ridicule from the proud, much contempt from the arrogant. *See also* **Ps** 119:51; **Pr** 21:24
Quarrelling
Pr 13:10 Pride only breeds quarrels, but wisdom is found in those who take advice.
Violence
Ps 73:6 Therefore pride is their necklace; they clothe themselves with violence. *See also* **Est** 3:5–6; **Ps** 86:14
Injustice
Ps 119:78 May the arrogant be put to shame for wronging me without cause . . . *See also* **Ps** 56:2

Oppression
Ps 10:2 In their arrogance the wicked hunt down the weak, who are caught in the schemes they devise. *See also* **Ps** 119:122; **Hab** 2:4–5
Contempt for God
Ps 10:4 In their pride the wicked do not seek him; in all their thoughts there is no room for God. *See also* **2Ki** 19:22

Pride may be accompanied by temporary prosperity
Ps 73:3 . . . I envied the arrogant when I saw the prosperity of the wicked. *See also* **Ps** 10:5

Pride ends in disaster
Pr 16:5 The LORD detests all the proud of heart. Be sure of this: They will not go unpunished.
Pr 16:18 Pride goes before destruction, a haughty spirit before a fall. *See also* **2Sa** 22:28 pp Ps 18:27; **Job** 40:11–12; **Ps** 31:23; 101:5; **Pr** 11:2; 15:25; 26:12; 29:23; **Isa** 2:11–12,17; 13:11; 26:5; **Zep** 3:11; **Mal** 4:1; **Lk** 1:51–52; **1Ti** 3:6

Examples of the proud being humbled
Pharaoh: **Ex** 14:28; **Ne** 9:10
2Ch 26:16
The king of Assyria: **2Ch** 32:21; **Isa** 10:12,16
2Ch 32:25; **Est** 7:10; **Isa** 3:16–17
The king of Babylon: **Isa** 13:19; 14:11–15
Isa 23:9; 25:10–12; 28:1–3
Babylon: **Isa** 47:10–11; **Jer** 50:31–32
Judah and Jerusalem: **Jer** 13:9; **Eze** 7:24
Eze 16:49–50
The king of Tyre: **Eze** 28:5–9,17
Egypt: **Eze** 30:6; 32:12
Da 4:30–33; 5:30; **Am** 6:8; **Zep** 2:15; **Zec** 9:6; 10:11; **Mt** 11:23; **Ac** 12:21–23; **Rev** 18:7–8
See also self-examination, teaching on.

purity
An absence of blemish or stain, especially sin. The state of being morally and spiritually pure, which is seen by Scripture as the result of being the people of God and also as an expected distinguishing mark of the church.

purity, moral and spiritual

Moral and spiritual purity is demanded by God of his people. God calls his people to be holy, just as he is holy.

Divine purity
The purity of God
Hab 1:13 Your eyes are too pure to look on evil; you cannot tolerate wrong . . . *See also* **Job** 4:17; **Ps** 18:26; **1Jn** 1:5
The purity of Jesus Christ
1Jn 3:3 All who have this hope in them purify themselves, just as he [Jesus] is pure. *See also* **Mt** 17:2; **Heb** 7:26

Fellowship with God demands purity
Ps 24:3–4 Who may ascend the hill of the LORD? Who may stand in his holy place? Those who have clean hands and pure hearts . . . **Mt 5:8** "Blessed are the pure in heart, for they will see God." *See also* **Ps** 51:6; 73:1

God's people are to live pure lives
Col 3:5 Put to death, therefore, whatever belongs to your earthly nature: sexual immorality, impurity, lust, evil desires and greed, which is idolatry. *See also* **Lev** 18:30; **Job** 31:1; **Ps** 51:10; **1Co** 5:7–8; 6:15–20; **1Th** 4:3; **Tit** 1:15; 2:5; **Heb** 13:4; **Jas** 1:27; 4:8

Purity is unobtainable by human effort
Because of the sinful human nature
Job 14:4 "Who can bring what is pure from the impure? No-one!" *See also* **Job** 15:14; 25:4; **Ecc** 7:20
Because of the tendency to idolatry
Hos 8:5 "Throw out your calf-idol, O Samaria! My anger burns against them. How long will they be incapable of purity?"
Because of self-deception
Pr 30:12 "those who are pure in their own eyes and yet are not cleansed of their filth;" *See also* **Pr** 20:9
Because of an unwillingness to be cleansed
Eze 24:13 "'Now your impurity is lewdness. Because I tried to cleanse you but you would not be cleansed from your impurity, you will not be clean again until my wrath against you has subsided.'"

Symbols of purification from sin
Ps 51:7 Cleanse me with hyssop, and I shall be clean; wash me, and I shall be whiter than snow. *See also* **Isa** 6:6; **Mk** 1:4; **2Co** 11:2; **2Pe** 3:14

God promises to purify his people
Eze 36:25 "'I will sprinkle clean water on you [Israel], and you will be clean; I will cleanse you from all your impurities and from all your idols.'" *See also* **Zep** 3:9; **Zec** 13:1

Purification through Jesus Christ
Through pardon offered in his death
Heb 9:14 How much more, then, will the blood of Christ, who through the eternal Spirit offered himself unblemished to God, cleanse our consciences from acts that lead to death, so that we may serve the living God! *See also* **Heb** 12:24; **1Jn** 1:7
Through his word
Jn 15:3 "You [the Twelve] are already clean because of the word I have spoken to you." *See also* **Jn** 13:10
Through his presence in resisting temptation
Jas 4:7–8 . . . Resist the devil, and he will flee from you. Come near to God and he will come near to you. Wash your hands, you sinners, and purify your hearts, you double-minded. *See also* **1Pe** 5:9
Through hope built on his promises
Tit 2:12–13 It [the grace of God] teaches us to say "No" to ungodliness and worldly passions, and to live self-controlled, upright and godly lives in this present age, while we wait for the blessed hope—the glorious appearing of our great God and Saviour, Jesus Christ, *See also* **1Jn** 3:3

Purification through judgment
In the OT
Lev 18:28 "'And if you defile the land, it will vomit you out as it vomited out the nations that were before you.'" *See also* **Dt** 13:5; 17:7,12;

Jdg 20:13; **Mal** 3:2–4
In the NT
1Co 5:13 God will judge those outside. "Expel
the wicked person from among you."

Symbols of purity
Whiteness
Da 7:9 ". . . and the Ancient of Days took his
seat. His clothing was as white as snow; the hair
of his head was white like wool . . ."   *See
also* **Ps** 51:7; **Isa** 1:18; **Mt** 17:2 pp **Mk** 9:3; **Mt**
28:3; **Mk** 16:5; **Jn** 20:12; **Rev** 1:14
Light
1Jn 1:7 But if we walk in the light, as he is in
the light, we have fellowship with one another,
and the blood of Jesus, his Son, purifies us from
all sin.   *See also* **Job** 25:5; **Eze** 1:27; **2Co** 6:14;
Eph 5:8–9
Washing
Ps 26:6 I wash my hands in innocence, and go
about your altar, O LORD,   *See also* **Ps** 51:2
Fire
Da 7:9–10 ". . . His [the Ancient of Days']
throne was flaming with fire, and its wheels were
all ablaze. A river of fire was flowing, coming out
from before him . . ."   *See also* **Isa** 33:14; **Eze**
8:2; **Rev** 1:14–15   *See also holiness; immorality;
renewal, people of God; sanctification.*

purity, nature of
The OT recognises a close link between outer
cleanliness and inner purity. In the NT, special
emphasis is placed on inner purity resulting from
spiritual renewal.

Physical cleansing from impurity by
washing or refining
Ge 18:4; **Job** 9:30; **Ps** 12:6

Ritual impurity must be avoided or
cleansed
Lev 10:10–11 "You [Aaron and his sons]
must distinguish between the holy and the
common, between the unclean and the clean, and
you must teach the Israelites all the decrees the
LORD has given them through Moses."   *See also*
Isa 35:8; 52:1,11; **Mk** 7:2,4

Sexual sources of ritual impurity
Childbirth
Lev 12:2 ". . .'A woman who becomes
pregnant and gives birth to a son will be
ceremonially unclean for seven days, just as she is
unclean during her monthly period.'"   *See also*
Lev 12:5; **Lk** 2:22
Sexual intercourse **Ex** 19:15; **Lev** 15:18; **1Sa**
21:4
Seminal emission **Lev** 15:16–17; **Dt** 23:10–11;
1Sa 20:26
Menstruation **Lev** 15:19–20; **2Sa** 11:2–4; **Eze**
18:6
Abnormal discharge **Lev** 15:1–2,25–27; **Mt** 9:20
pp **Mk** 5:25 pp **Lk** 8:43

Other sources of ritual impurity
Dead bodies
Nu 19:11–16 "Whoever touches the dead
body of anyone will be unclean for seven
days . . ."
Unclean creatures
Ge 7:2 "Take with you [Noah] seven of every
kind of clean animal, a male and its mate, and
two of every kind of unclean animal, a male and
its mate,"   *See also* **Lev** 11:24,46–47; **Dt** 14:3;
Hos 9:3
Skin diseases
Lev 13:45 "The person with such an infectious
disease must wear torn clothes, let their hair be
unkempt, cover the lower part of their face and
cry out, 'Unclean! Unclean!'"   *See also* **Mt**
8:2–4 pp **Mk** 1:40–44 pp **Lk** 5:12–14
Mildew Lev 14:36
Contact with a sin offering
Lev 16:26 "The one who releases the goat as
a scapegoat must wash his clothes and bathe
himself with water; afterwards he may come into
the camp."

Cleansing from ritual impurity
Lev 14:8 "The person to be cleansed [from a
skin disease] must wash their clothes, shave off
all their hair and bathe with water; then they will
be ceremonially clean . . ."   *See also* **Lev**
16:26; **Nu** 19:9,17–21; 31:22–23

Contact with God demanded purity

Ex 19:10 And the LORD said to Moses, "Go to the people and consecrate them today and tomorrow. Make them wash their clothes"
See also **Ex** 19:14–15; 30:18–21; **Heb** 10:22

Ritual purity is not required under the new covenant

Mt 15:11 "What goes into your mouth does not make you 'unclean', but what comes out of your mouth, that is what makes you 'unclean'."
pp Mk 7:15   *See also* **Ac** 10:12–15; 21:26; **Ro** 14:14; **Gal** 2:11–12,14–15; **1Ti** 4:4

---

reconciliation, between believers

True restoration of relationships between believers is only possible after they have been reconciled to God through Jesus Christ. Believers are urged to settle differences among themselves in mutual love.

The cause of the breakdown in relationships is sin

Ge 27:41 Esau held a grudge against Jacob because of the blessing his father had given him. He said to himself, "The days of mourning for my father are near; then I will kill my brother Jacob."
The division between Joseph and his brothers: **Ge** 37:4–5,18–20

1Sa 15:12–14; **2Sa** 14:28; **Ac** 15:37–40; **Gal** 2:11

Believers should be reconciled to one another

Mt 5:23–24 "Therefore, if you are offering your gift at the altar and there remember that your brother or sister has something against you, leave your gift there in front of the altar. First go and be reconciled to them; then come and offer your gift."   *See also* **Mt** 5:9,25 pp Lk 12:58; **Mt** 5:44; 18:15–17,21–35; **Jn** 17:20–23; **Ro** 12:18–21; **2Th** 3:14–15

The death of Jesus Christ should bring believers together in peace

Eph 2:14–22 For he [Christ] himself is our peace, who has made the two one and has destroyed the barrier, the dividing wall of hostility, by abolishing in his flesh the law with its commandments and regulations. His purpose was to create in himself one new humanity out of the two, thus making peace, and in this one body to reconcile both of them to God through the cross, by which he put to death their hostility. He came and preached peace to you who were far away and peace to those who were near. For through him we both have access to the Father by one Spirit . . .

The church should display reconciliation

Col 3:12–15 . . . Bear with each other and forgive whatever grievances you may have against one another. Forgive as the Lord forgave you. And over all these virtues put on love, which binds them all together in perfect unity. Let the peace of Christ rule in your hearts, since as members of one body you were called to peace . . .
See also **Ro** 12:18–21; **Eph** 4:32; **2Th** 3:14–15

Examples of reconciliation between people

Ge 33:4 But Esau ran to meet Jacob and embraced him; he threw his arms around his neck and kissed him. And they wept.   *See also* **Ge** 45:1–5; **Jos** 22:10–34; **Lk** 23:12; **Jn** 21:15–17; **Ac** 9:26–28; **1Co** 7:11
See also fellowship; forgiveness; love.

---

renewal

The regeneration or revitalisation that God brings to his people and creation, as part of the process of redemption.

---

renewal, people of God

The transformation by God of the lives of his people, whether corporately or individually, leading to the recovery of lost vitality and purity.

Individual renewal

Isa 40:30–31 . . . those who hope in the LORD will renew their strength. They will soar on wings like eagles; they will run and not grow weary, they will walk and not be faint.

Eph 4:22–24 You were taught, with regard to your former way of life, to put off your old self, which is being corrupted by its deceitful desires; to be made new in the attitude of your minds; and to put on the new self, created to be like God in true righteousness and holiness.   *See also* **Ps** 23:3; 51:10–12; 103:1–5; **Jn** 7:37–39; **Ro** 12:2; **2Co** 4:16; **Col** 3:9–10; **2Ti** 1:6; **Tit** 3:5

Corporate renewal
The renewal of Israel

Eze 37:1–14 "'. . . This is what the Sovereign LORD says to these bones: I will make breath enter you, and you will come to life. I will attach tendons to you and make flesh come upon you and cover you with skin; I will put breath in you, and you will come to life. Then you will know that I am the LORD.'" So I prophesied as I was commanded. And as I was prophesying, there was a noise, a rattling sound, and the bones came together, bone to bone. I looked, and tendons and flesh appeared on them and skin covered them, but there was no breath in them. Then he said to me, "Prophesy to the breath; prophesy, son of man, and say to it, 'This is what the Sovereign LORD says: Come from the four winds, O breath, and breathe into these slain, that they may live.'" So I prophesied as he commanded me, and breath entered them; they came to life and stood up on their feet—a vast army. Then he said to me: "Son of man, these bones are the whole house of Israel. They say, 'Our bones are dried up and our hope is gone; we are cut off.' Therefore prophesy and say to them: This is what the Sovereign LORD says: O my people, I am going to open your graves and bring you up from them; I will bring you back to the land of Israel. Then you, my people, will know that I am the LORD, when I open your graves and bring you up from them. I will put my Spirit in you and you will live, and I will settle you in your own land. Then you will

know that I the LORD have spoken, and I have done it, declares the LORD.'"   *See also* **Jer** 31:31–34; **La** 5:21; **Eze** 11:17–20; 36:24–28; **Joel** 2:28–32

Examples of national renewal

2Ch 34:29–33 . . . The king [Josiah] stood by his pillar and renewed the covenant in the presence of the LORD—to follow the LORD and keep his commands, regulations and decrees with all his heart and all his soul, and to obey the words of the covenant written in this book. Then he made everyone in Jerusalem and Benjamin pledge themselves to it; the people of Jerusalem did this in accordance with the covenant of God, the God of their ancestors. Josiah removed all the detestable idols from all the territory belonging to the Israelites, and he made all who were present in Israel serve the LORD their God. As long as he lived, they did not fail to follow the LORD, the God of their ancestors.   *See also* **Jos** 24:1,14–27; **Ezr** 10:1–4; **Ne** 10:28–29

The new Jerusalem

Isa 65:17–19 "'. . . But be glad and rejoice for ever in what I will create, for I will create Jerusalem to be a delight and its people a joy. I will rejoice over Jerusalem and take delight in my people; the sound of weeping and of crying will be heard in it no more."   *See also* **Rev** 3:12; 21:2–4,10

The church

Mt 9:16–19 "No-one sews a patch of unshrunk cloth on an old garment, for the patch will pull away from the garment, making the tear worse. Neither do people pour new wine into old wineskins. If they do, the skins will burst, the wine will run out and the wineskins will be ruined. No, they pour new wine into new wineskins, and both are preserved." . . . pp **Mk** 2:21–22 pp **Lk** 5:36–39   *See also* **Ac** 2:1–4,42–47   *See also revival; sanctification.*

---

repentance

A change of mind leading to a change of action. It involves a sincere turning from sin to serve God and includes sorrow for, and confession of, sin and where possible restitution. At points, Scripture refers to God changing his plans in response to events.

repentance, examples
Scripture provides examples to illustrate the importance of repentance for individuals and communities.

The repentance of individuals
The call to personal repentance
Ac 2:38 Peter replied, "Repent and be baptised, every one of you, in the name of Jesus Christ for the forgiveness of your sins. And you will receive the gift of the Holy Spirit." *See also* **2Ti** 2:19
Examples of individual repentance Nu 22:31–35; **2Sa** 24:10 pp 1Ch 21:8; **1Ki** 21:27–29; **2Ki** 22:19; **Job** 42:6; **Ps** 51:1–17; **Lk** 15:21; 18:13; **Mt** 26:75 pp Mk 14:72 pp Lk 22:61–62; **Jn** 21:15–17; **Ac** 8:22–24

Corporate repentance
Examples of corporate repentance
Jer 18:7–8 "If at any time I [the LORD] announce that a nation or kingdom is to be uprooted, torn down and destroyed, and if that nation I warned repents of its evil, then I will relent and not inflict on it the disaster I had planned."
Mt 3:1–6 . . . People went out to him [John] from Jerusalem and all Judea and the whole region of the Jordan. Confessing their sins, they were baptised by him in the Jordan River. pp Mk 1:1–6 pp Lk 3:1–6 *See also* **Nu** 21:7; **Jdg** 10:15–16; **1Sa** 7:3–4; **Isa** 19:22; **Ac** 9:32–35
Leaders encouraged corporate repentance
Ezr 10:1 While Ezra was praying and confessing, weeping and throwing himself down before the house of God, a large crowd of Israelites—men, women and children—gathered round him. They too wept bitterly. *See also* **2Ki** 23:1–7; **2Ch** 15:8–15; 30:6–9; **Ezr** 10:10–12; **Jnh** 3:6–8
Corporate repentance within the church
Rev 2:4–5 "Yet I [Jesus] hold this against you [the church in Ephesus]: You have forsaken your first love. Remember the height from which you have fallen! Repent and do the things you did at

first. If you do not repent, I will come to you and remove your lampstand from its place." *See also* **2Co** 7:9–11; **Rev** 2:14–16,20–22; 3:3,19–20

Symbols of repentance
1Ki 21:27 When Ahab heard these words, he tore his clothes, put on sackcloth and fasted. He lay in sackcloth and went around meekly.
Jnh 3:5 The Ninevites believed God. They declared a fast, and all of them, from the greatest to the least, put on sackcloth.
See also **1Sa** 7:6; **Ezr** 8:21; **Ne** 9:1; **Jer** 36:9; **Joel** 1:13–14; 2:12   *See also church; conversion; fasting, reasons; preaching, effects; revival; self-examination.*

repentance, importance
Repentance is of central importance because sin brings God's judgment and fellowship with God is only possible through full and sincere repentance. God, through his servants, calls people to repent as the only way to escape the judgment and receive the forgiveness and restoration which he offers.

The call to repentance
Lk 5:32 "I [Jesus] have not come to call the righteous, but sinners to repentance."
Jas 5:19–20 . . . remember this: Those who turn sinners from the error of their ways will save them from death and cover over a multitude of sins. *See also* **Jer** 25:4–6; **Eze** 33:7–9; **Mk** 1:4 pp Lk 3:3; **Lk** 24:47; **2Ti** 2:24–26

Repentance opens the way for blessing
It is the only way to escape God's judgment
Eze 18:30–32 ". . . Repent! Turn away from all your offences; then sin will not be your downfall. Rid yourselves of all the offences you have committed, and get a new heart and a new spirit. Why will you die, O house of Israel? For I take no pleasure in the death of anyone, declares the Sovereign LORD. Repent and live! *See also* **Job** 36:12; **Jer** 18:7–8; 26:3; **Hos** 11:5; **Jnh** 3:10; **Lk** 3:8–9; **Rev** 2:5
It prepares the way for God's kingdom
Mt 4:17 From that time on Jesus began to

preach, "Repent, for the kingdom of heaven is
near." pp Mk 1:14–15   See also Mt 3:2

It brings forgiveness and restoration

2Ch 7:13–14 ". . . if my people, who are
called by my name, will humble themselves and
pray and seek my face and turn from their wicked
ways, then will I [the LORD] hear from heaven
and will forgive their sin and will heal their land."

Isa 55:7 Let the wicked forsake their ways and
the unrighteous their thoughts. Let them turn to
the LORD, and he will have mercy on them, and
to our God, for he will freely pardon.   See also
Dt 30:1–10; Ne 1:8–9; Job 22:23–25; 36:10–11;
Isa 44:22; Ac 2:38–39; 3:19; 5:31; 11:18

God desires that all people should repent

He wants everyone to be saved

Eze 18:23 "Do I take any pleasure in the
death of the wicked? declares the Sovereign LORD.
Rather, am I not pleased when they turn from
their ways and live?"

His patience with the unrepentant

2Pe 3:9 The Lord is not slow in keeping his
promise, as some understand slowness. He is
patient with you, not wanting anyone to perish,
but everyone to come to repentance.   See also
Isa 65:2; Ro 2:4; Rev 2:21

His discipline encourages repentance

Jer 31:18–20 "I [the LORD] have surely heard
Ephraim's moaning: 'You disciplined me like an
unruly calf, and I have been disciplined. Restore
me, and I will return, because you are the LORD
my God . . .' . . ." . . .   See also Isa
10:20–21; 19:22; Hos 2:6–7; 6:1

Taking God's opportunity for repentance

Isa 55:6 Seek the LORD while he may be
found; call on him while he is near.

Ac 17:30–31 "In the past God overlooked
such ignorance, but now he commands all people
everywhere to repent. For he has set a day when
he will judge the world with justice by the man
he has appointed . . ."   See also Heb 3:13–15;
4:7; Ps 95:7–8

Refusing God's opportunity for repentance

Examples of those who refuse to repent

Jer 35:15 "'Again and again I [the LORD] sent
all my servants the prophets to you. They said,
"Each of you must turn from your wicked ways
and reform your actions; do not follow other gods
to serve them. Then you shall live in the land I
have given to you and your ancestors." But you
have not paid attention or listened to me.'"
See also Jer 5:3; Mt 11:20; 21:32; Rev 9:20–21;
16:9–11

**God confirms those who refuse to repent in
their hardness of heart** Mt 13:14–15 pp Mk
4:11–12 pp Lk 8:9–10; Ac 28:25–27; Isa 6:10

Repentance may not remove the effects of human sin

Nu 14:39–45; 1Sa 15:24–26; 2Sa 12:13–14;
Heb 12:16–17   See also forgiveness.

---

repentance, nature of

Scripture stresses the necessity of repentance from
sin if individuals and communities are to have full
fellowship with God. It also uses the term to refer
to God's relenting of sending judgment on his
people, usually in response to human repentance.

Repentance is a requirement for fellowship with God

2Ki 17:13 The LORD warned Israel and Judah
through all his prophets and seers: "Turn from
your evil ways. Observe my commands and
decrees, in accordance with the entire Law that I
commanded your ancestors to obey and that I
delivered to you through my servants the
prophets."

1Th 1:9 . . . you turned to God from idols to
serve the living and true God,   See also Ps
34:14; Isa 55.7, Ac 14.15; Jas 4:7–10

Repentance involves turning from sin
Sorrow for sin

Ps 51:17 The sacrifices of God are a broken
spirit; a broken and contrite heart, O God, you
will not despise.

2Co 7:8–10 . . . your sorrow led you to

repentance. For you became sorrowful as God intended . . . Godly sorrow brings repentance that leads to salvation and leaves no regret . . . *See also* **Job** 42:6; **Ps** 34:18; **Isa** 57:15; 66:2; **Joel** 2:12–13; **Lk** 18:13

Confession of sin

Lk 15:17–19 ". . . '. . . I [the prodigal son] will set out and go back to my father and say to him: Father, I have sinned against heaven and against you . . .'" *See also* **Lev** 5:5; **Ps** 51:1–3; **Pr** 28:13; **Hos** 14:1–2

Forsaking specific sins Ezr 10:10–11; **Eze** 14:6; **Ac** 15:19–20

Making appropriate restitution Nu 5:6–7; **Lk** 19:8

Repentance involves turning to God
Faith in God

Isa 30:15 This is what the Sovereign LORD, the Holy One of Israel, says: "In repentance and rest is your salvation, in quietness and trust is your strength, but you would have none of it." *See also* **Lk** 22:32; **Ac** 11:21; 20:21; 26:18

Obedience

Eze 18:21–23 "But if the wicked turn away from all the sins they have committed and keep all my [the LORD'S] decrees and do what is just and right, they will surely live; they will not die . . ." *See also* **Mal** 3:7–10

Repentance demonstrated by actions

Ac 26:20 ". . . I [Paul] preached that they should repent and turn to God and prove their repentance by their deeds." *See also* **Isa** 1:16–17; **Da** 4:27; **Mt** 3:8 pp **Lk** 3:8; **Lk** 3:10–14

Repentance must be sincere

Jer 3:10 ". . . Judah did not return to me with all her heart, but only in pretence," declares the LORD.

Jer 24:7 "'I will give them a heart to know me, that I am the LORD. They will be my people, and I will be their God, for they will return to me with all their heart.'" *See also* **1 Ki** 8:46–50 pp **2Ch** 6:36–39; **Ps** 78:34–37; **Hos** 6:1–4

The repentance of God

Jer 26:3 "Perhaps they [Judah] will listen and

each will turn from their evil ways. Then I [the LORD] will relent and not bring on them the disaster I was planning because of the evil they have done." *See also* **Ex** 32:14; **Ps** 106:45; **Hos** 11:8; **Joel** 2:13; **Am** 7:1–6 *See also* *confession of sin; faith; obedience; sin.*

---

respect

An attitude of reverence and deference, reflecting an appreciation of the significance of the person or thing that is esteemed.

---

respect, for environment

Although God created the universe and retains ultimate ownership of it, he has delegated responsibility for the well-being of the earth to the human race. This stewardship includes the care of the animal kingdom and the earth's natural resources.

God's creation is to be respected
The earth belongs to God

Ps 24:1–2 The earth is the LORD's, and everything in it, the world, and all who live in it; for he founded it upon the seas and established it upon the waters. *See also* **Ex** 19:5–6; **Lev** 25:23; **1Ch** 29:14; **Ps** 50:9–12; 89:11; **Hag** 2:8

Responsibility to rule and care for the earth has been delegated to the human race

Ge 1:26–28 Then God said, "Let us make human beings in our image, in our likeness, and let them rule over the fish of the sea and the birds of the air, over the livestock, over all the earth, and over all the creatures that move along the ground." . . . God blessed them and said to them, "Be fruitful and increase in number; fill the earth and subdue it. Rule over the fish of the sea and the birds of the air and over every living creature that moves on the ground." *See also* **Ge** 9:1–3; **Ps** 8:6–8; 115:16; **Heb** 2:8; **Jas** 3:7

God himself maintains a caring supervision of his creation

Mt 6:26–30 "Look at the birds of the air; they do not sow or reap or store away in barns, and yet your heavenly Father feeds them. Are you not much more valuable than they? Who of you by worrying can add a single hour to your life? And why do you worry about clothes? See how the lilies of the field grow. They do not labour or spin. Yet I tell you that not even Solomon in all his splendour was dressed like one of these. If that is how God clothes the grass of the field, which is here today and tomorrow is thrown into the fire, will he not much more clothe you, O you of little faith?" pp Lk 12:24–28   *See also* **Dt** 11:10–15; **Ps** 65:9–13; **Mt** 5:45

Respect for all nature and animals
Dt 20:19 When you lay siege to a city for a long time, fighting against it to capture it, do not destroy its trees by putting an axe to them, because you can eat their fruit. Do not cut them down. Are the trees of the field people, that you should besiege them? *NIV footnote.   See also* **Ex** 23:4–5, 10–11; **Dt** 22:4,6–7; 25:4; **Pr** 12:10

Respect and care for the earth's natural resources
Ex 23:10–11 "For six years you are to sow your fields and harvest the crops, but during the seventh year let the land lie unploughed and unused. Then the poor among your people may get food from it, and the wild animals may eat what they leave. Do the same with your vineyard and your olive grove."   *See also* **Lev** 25:1–7; **Ne** 10:31

respect, for God
God's revelation of himself calls for deference, honour and a response of right living.

Respect for God's name
Ps 29:2 Ascribe to the Lord the glory due to his name; worship the Lord in the splendour of his holiness.   *See also* **Ex** 20:7 pp **Dt** 5:11; **Ex** 23:20–21; **Lev** 18:21; 19:12; 22:31–33; 24:10–16; **Ps** 86:9–11; **Jer** 3:16–17; **Mal** 2:1–2

Respect for God's presence
Ex 3:5–6 "Do not come any closer," God said. "Take off your sandals, for the place where you are standing is holy ground." Then he said, "I am the God of your father, the God of Abraham, the God of Isaac and the God of Jacob." At this,

Moses hid his face, because he was afraid to look at God.   *See also* **Ex** 33:19–23; **Ps** 89:7; **Isa** 6:1–5; **Zep** 1:7; **Zec** 2:13

Respect for God's word
Dt 4:2 Do not add to what I command you and do not subtract from it, but keep the commands of the Lord your God that I give you.   *See also* **Dt** 12:32; **Jos** 1:7–8; **Pr** 30:5–6; **2Pe** 1:19–21; **Rev** 22:18–19

Respect for God's ark and sanctuary
Lev 19:30 " 'Observe my Sabbaths and have reverence for my sanctuary. I am the Lord.' "   *See also* **1Sa** 6:19–20; **2Sa** 6:1–7; **Ecc** 5:1–2; **Hab** 2:20; **Mt** 21:12–13 pp **Mk** 11:15–17 pp **Lk** 19:45–46 pp **Jn** 2:13–17; **Jer** 7:11

Respect for God's servants
1Th 5:12–13 Now we ask you, brothers and sisters, to respect those who work hard among you, who are over you in the Lord and who admonish you. Hold them in the highest regard in love because of their work. Live in peace with each other.   *See also* **Ac** 23:1–5; **Ex** 22:28; **Ac** 28:7–10; **Php** 2:29–30; **1Ti** 5:17–18; **Heb** 13:7,17

Respect for God leads to godly living
Ex 20:20 . . . ". . . the fear of God will be with you to keep you from sinning."   *See also* **2Ch** 6:30–31; **Pr** 16:6; **Heb** 11:7; **1Pe** 1:14–17
See also humility; obedience.

respect, for human beings
Each individual, created in the image of God, should be honoured and esteemed, and this should be worked out in every area of life.

Human beings are to be respected
They are made in the image of God
Ge 9:5–6 ". . . And from each human being, too, I will demand an accounting for the life of another human being. Whoever sheds human blood, by human beings shall their blood be shed; for in the image of God has God made all people."   *See also* **Pr** 14:31; 17:5; **Col** 3:9–11; **Jas** 3:9–10

The bounds of life belong to God

Ex 20:13 "You shall not murder." pp Dt 5:17   *See also* **Ex** 21:22–25; **2Sa** 1:14–15; 4:9–12; **1Ki** 2:31–33; **Ps** 139:13–16

The equality and dignity of human beings is commanded

Dt 1:16–17 And I charged your judges at that time: Hear the disputes between your people and judge fairly, whether the case is between two Israelites or between one of them and an alien. Do not show partiality in judging; hear both small and great alike. Do not be afraid of anyone, for judgment belongs to God . . .   *See also* **Ex** 23:2–3; **Lev** 19:15; **Dt** 16:18–19; **Pr** 24:23–25; 28:21; **Ac** 10:24–28,34–35; **Jas** 2:1–9; **1Pe** 2:17

Respect in the family

Respect for parents is commanded

Ex 20:12 "Honour your father and your mother, so that you may live long in the land the LORD your God is giving you." pp Dt 5:16   *See also* **Lev** 19:3; **Pr** 1:8; **Mal** 1:6; **Mt** 15:4–6 pp Mk 7:10–13; **Mt** 19:19 pp Lk 18:20; **Eph** 6:1–3; **Col** 3:20; **Heb** 12:9

Disrespect for parents is condemned

Dt 27:16 "Cursed is anyone who dishonours father or mother." . . .   *See also* **Ex** 21:17; **Lev** 20:9; **Pr** 30:17; **Isa** 45:10; **2Ti** 3:1–2

Examples of those who respected their parents Ge 9:20–23; 47:11–12; 1Sa 22:3; 1Ki 2:19; 19:20

Jesus Christ: **Lk** 2:51; **Jn** 19:25–27

Respect in marriage

Eph 5:33 However, each one of you also must love his wife as he loves himself, and the wife must respect her husband.   *See also* **Eph** 5:21–25; **Col** 3:18–19; **1Pe** 3:6–7

Respect for children

Mt 18:10 "See that you do not look down on one of these little ones. For I tell you that their angels in heaven always see the face of my Father in heaven."   *See also* **Lev** 20:1–5; **Mt** 18:5–6 pp Mk 9:36–37 pp Lk 9:47–48; **Mt** 19:13–15 pp Mk 10:13–16 pp Lk 18:15–17; **Eph** 6:4; **Col** 3:20–21

Respect for leaders

Leaders must have gained respect

Dt 1:13–15 "Choose some wise, understanding and respected men from each of your tribes, and I will set them over you." . . .   *See also* **1Sa** 9:6; **Pr** 31:23; **1Ti** 3:2–11

Leaders must be given respect

1Sa 26:9–11 . . . ". . . But the LORD forbid that I should lay a hand on the LORD's anointed . . ."   *See also* **1Sa** 24:1–7; **2Ki** 3:14; **Ro** 13:1–7; **1Th** 5:12; **Heb** 13:17

Respect for old age

Lev 19:32 " 'Rise in the presence of the aged, show respect for the elderly and revere your God. I am the LORD."   *See also* **Job** 32:4–7; **La** 5:12; **1Ti** 5:1–2; **Tit** 2:2; **1Pe** 5:5

Respect at the place of work

Dt 24:14–15 Do not take advantage of a hired worker who is poor and needy, whether that worker is an Israelite or an alien living in one of your towns. Pay such workers their wages each day before sunset, because they are poor and are counting on it. Otherwise they may cry to the LORD against you, and you will be guilty of sin.   *See also* **Lev** 19:13; **Eph** 6:5–9; **Col** 3:22–4:1; **1Ti** 6:1–2; **1Pe** 2:18   *See also neighbours, duty to.*

---

rest, spiritual

To be at rest spiritually is to find peace with God through Jesus Christ. This rest is promised to all who put their trust in God and obey him.

The human desire for spiritual rest

La 5:19–22 . . . Why do you [God] always forget us [Israel]? Why do you forsake us so long? Restore us to yourself, O LORD, that we may return; renew our days as of old unless you have utterly rejected us and are angry with us beyond measure.   *See also* **Ps** 55:4–8; **La** 3:25–26; **1Ti** 2:2

Spiritual rest is to be found in God alone

Mt 11:28-30 "Come to me [Jesus], all you who are weary and burdened, and I will give you rest. Take my yoke upon you and learn from me, for I am gentle and humble in heart, and you will find rest for your souls. For my yoke is easy and my burden is light."   *See also* **Ex** 33:14; **Ps** 23:2; 51:12; 62:1–2,5–8; 91:1–13; **Isa** 26:3–4; **Jn** 14:27; **Ro** 5:1; **Gal** 1:3; 5:22; **Col** 1:20

God promises his people spiritual rest

Heb 4:9-11 There remains, then, a Sabbath-rest for the people of God; for those who enter God's rest also rest from their own work, just as God did from his. Let us, therefore, make every effort to enter that rest, so that no-one will fall by following their example of disobedience.   *See also* **Ps** 1:3; 37:7; 116:7; 119:165; 125:1; 131:1–3; **Pr** 29:25; **Isa** 30:15; 32:17–18; 58:11; **Jer** 6:16; 17:7–8; **Jn** 14:1; **Ro** 8:6; **1Pe** 3:4

Spiritual rest is not for the wicked

Ps 1:4-5 Not so the wicked! They are like chaff that the wind blows away. Therefore the wicked will not stand in the judgment, nor sinners in the assembly of the righteous.   *See also* **Ps** 112:10; **Ecc** 2:23; **Isa** 48:22; 57:20–21

God's offer of rest rejected by a faithless people

Isa 28:12 to whom he said, "This is the resting-place, let the weary rest"; and, "This is the place of repose"—but they would not listen. **Jer 6:16** This is what the LORD says: "Stand at the crossroads and look; ask for the ancient paths, ask where the good way is, and walk in it, and you will find rest for your souls. But you said, 'We will not walk in it.'"   *See also forgiveness; peace.*

---

revelation, responses

God requires and imparts a frame of mind that receives and responds to what he has made known of his person, nature and deeds in Scripture, in history and supremely in the person of Jesus Christ.

God commands that his word be heeded

Mk 4:3 "Listen! A farmer went out to sow his seed."   *See also* **Isa** 1:10; **Mk** 4:9; **Rev** 2:7

People do not naturally understand what God has revealed

They fail to recognise God's revelation in Jesus Christ

Mt 11:25-27 At that time Jesus said, "I praise you, Father, Lord of heaven and earth, because you have hidden these things from the wise and learned, and revealed them to little children . . . No-one knows the Son except the Father, and no-one knows the Father except the Son and those to whom the Son chooses to reveal him." pp Lk 10:21–22   *See also* **Jn** 5:37–40; 6:44–45; 10:24–26; 12:37–41; 14:9; **Ro** 9:31–10:4; **1Co** 1:18–25; 2:8; **2Co** 4:4

They fail to understand God's revelation in general

1Co 2:14 The person without the Spirit does not accept the things that come from the Spirit of God but considers them foolishness, and cannot understand them because they are spiritually discerned.   *See also* **Mk** 4:11–12 pp Mt 13:13–15 pp Lk 8:10; **Isa** 6:9–10; **Jn** 8:43–47; **2Co** 3:14–16; **2Th** 2:11–13

God has given his Spirit to illuminate the human mind

He reveals and teaches truth

1Co 2:12-13 We [believers] have not received the spirit of the world but the Spirit who is from God, that we may understand what God has freely given us. This is what we speak, not in words taught us by human wisdom but in words taught by the Spirit, expressing spiritual truths in spiritual words.   *See also* **Jer** 31:31–34; **Mt** 16:17; **Jn** 3:3–10; 14:16–17,25–26; 16:12–15; **Php** 3:15

He reveals through prayer for understanding

Ps 119:18 Open my eyes that I may see wonderful things in your [God's] law.   *See also* **Ps** 119:12,27; **Eph** 1:17–18

Understanding God's revelation carries special responsibility

Lk 12:47–48 ". . . From everyone who has been given much, much will be demanded; and from the one who has been entrusted with much, much more will be asked." *See also* **Mt** 13:11–12; 25:14–30 pp Lk 19:12–27

God's revelation of himself will only be fully understood at the second coming of Jesus Christ

1Co 13:12 Now we [believers] see but a poor reflection as in a mirror; then we shall see face to face. Now I know in part; then I shall know fully, even as I am fully known. *See also* **1Pe** 1:13; **1Jn** 3:2

The consequences of responding to revelation

Repentance

Ac 2:38 Peter replied, "Repent and be baptised, every one of you, in the name of Jesus Christ for the forgiveness of your sins. And you will receive the gift of the Holy Spirit." *See also* **Mt** 4:17; **Ac** 3:19; 26:20; **2Co** 7:10

Faith

Ro 10:17 Consequently, faith comes from hearing the message, and the message is heard through the word of Christ. *See also* **Ro** 10:8–10,14–15; **1Co** 2:4–5

Obedience

Ro 1:5 Through him [Jesus Christ] and for his name's sake, we received grace and apostleship to call people from among all the Gentiles to the obedience that comes from faith. *See also* **Jdg** 2:17; **Phm** 21; **1Pe** 1:2 *See also faith, necessity; life, spiritual; meditation; obedience; repentance; respect, for God.*

revival

The sovereign activity of God whereby he renews his people individually and corporately in vigour, affecting both sincerity of belief and quality of behaviour.

revival, corporate

The experience of God's people both in the OT and NT when prayer is answered and their growth and effectiveness are renewed.

The recurring pattern of apostasy and revival in the OT

Jdg 2:10–19

God is petitioned to revive his people

Ps 80:14–15 Return to us, O God Almighty! Look down from heaven and see! Watch over this vine, the root your right hand has planted, the son you have raised up for yourself. *See also* **Ps** 85:4–7; **Jer** 31:18; **La** 5:21; **Hab** 3:2

Repentance is necessary for revival

God's people are urged to repent

2Ch 30:6 . . . "People of Israel, return to the Lord, the God of Abraham, Isaac and Israel, that he may return to you who are left, who have escaped from the hand of the kings of Assyria." *See also* **Isa** 55:1–3; **Jer** 3:22; **La** 3:40; **Hos** 12:6; 14:1–2; **Zec** 1:3; **Mal** 3:7; **Rev** 2:5,16; 3:2–3

Wholehearted repentance is required

Joel 2:12–13 "Even now," declares the Lord, "return to me with all your heart, with fasting and weeping and mourning." Rend your heart and not your garments. Return to the Lord your God, for he is gracious and compassionate, slow to anger and abounding in love, and he relents from sending calamity. *See also* **Dt** 4:29; 30:2–3; **Jer** 24:7; 29:13–14; **Ac** 19:18–19

Repentance prepares for revival

Isa 59:20 "The Redeemer will come to Zion, to those in Jacob who repent of their sins," declares the Lord. *See also* **Jdg** 10:9–16; **Ezr** 10:1,10–12; **Ne** 1:9; **Eze** 18:30–32

Revival is God's work

Hos 6:2 After two days he [the Lord] will revive us; on the third day he will restore us, that we may live in his presence. *See also* **Ps** 80:3,7,17–19; **Isa** 32:14–17

God promises revival
God promises to revive his people
Eze 11:19 "I will give them an undivided heart and put a new spirit in them; I will remove from them their heart of stone and give them a heart of flesh."   *See also* **Jer** 31:33–34; **Eze** 36:26; **Zec** 10:6

The nations are included in the promise of revival
Isa 2:3 Many peoples will come and say, "Come, let us go up to the mountain of the LORD, to the house of the God of Jacob. He will teach us his ways, so that we may walk in his paths." The law will go out from Zion, the word of the LORD from Jerusalem. pp **Mic** 4:2   *See also* **Isa** 19:22–25; 45:22; 56:6–8; **Zec** 8:20–22

The revival of Israel
Under Hezekiah 2Ki 18:4–6; **2Ch** 29:3–5; 30:1; 31:4,9–10,20–21
Under Josiah 2Ki 23:1–4 pp **2Ch** 34:29–33; **2Ch** 35:1–3

Revival in the NT
Crowds turn to the Lord Mk 1:5; **Jn** 3:26; 4:39; **Ac** 2:41,47; 4:4; 11:21
The Holy Spirit is active in the revival of believers
Ac 4:31 . . . they [the believers] were all filled with the Holy Spirit and spoke the word of God boldly.   *See also* **Ac** 13:9; **2Co** 4:16; **Eph** 5:18
The response of believers in revival
Ro 12:1–2 . . . Do not conform any longer to the pattern of this world, but be transformed by the renewing of your mind . . .   *See also* **Eph** 4:23–24; **Php** 3:13–14; **Col** 3:9–14   *See also* renewal.

---

revival, nature of
Scripture indicates that a number of characteristics precede revival, including repentance, humility and obedience.

Characteristics which precede revival
God's people long for renewal of their lives
Ps 80:18 . . . revive us, and we will call on your name.   *See also* **Ps** 74:22; 80:1–17,19; 85:6

God's people must repent
2Ch 7:14 "if my people, who are called by my name, will humble themselves and pray and seek my face and turn from their wicked ways, then will I hear from heaven and will forgive their sin and will heal their land."   *See also* **1Ki** 8:46–50 pp **2Ch** 6:26–27; **Isa** 64:1–7; **Hos** 5:15; **Ac** 3:19

God's people experience a new awareness of sin
2Ki 22:11 When the king [Josiah] heard the words of the Book of the Law, he tore his robes.   *See also* **Ps** 32:3–5

God's people need to be humble
Isa 57:15 For this is what the high and lofty One says—he who lives for ever, whose name is holy: "I live in a high and holy place, but also with those who are contrite and lowly in spirit, to revive the spirit of the lowly and to revive the heart of the contrite."   *See also* **Ps** 149:4; **Isa** 66:2; **Mic** 6:6–8

God's people are revived through God's initiative
Isa 59:16 He [the LORD] saw that there was no-one, he was appalled that there was no-one to intervene; so his own arm worked salvation for him, and his own righteousness sustained him.   *See also* **Jer** 24:7; 33:6–9; **Tit** 3:5

Characteristic results of revival
People experience inward change
Heb 8:10–12 ". . . I [the LORD] will put my laws in their minds and write them on their hearts. I will be their God, and they will be my people . . ."   *See also* **Jer** 31:33–34; **Eze** 11:19; **Ac** 2:42–47

People live obedient lives
Eze 11:20 ". . . they will follow my decrees and be careful to keep my laws. They will be my people, and I will be their God."   *See also* **Eph** 4:1–3; **1Th** 1:7–8

People are zealous for God's work
Ezr 5:1–2 Now Haggai the prophet and Zechariah the prophet, a descendant of Iddo, prophesied to the Jews in Judah and Jerusalem in the name of the God of Israel, who was over them. Then Zerubbabel son of Shealtiel and Jeshua son of Jozadak set to work to rebuild the

house of God in Jerusalem . . .　*See also* **Hag** 1:12–15

People are generous in giving
Ex 36:5 . . . "The people are bringing more than enough for doing the work the LORD commanded to be done."　*See also* **1Ch** 29:6–9; **2Ch** 31:3–8; **Ac** 11:28–30

People delight in worshipping God
Ezr 3:11 With praise and thanksgiving they [priests and Levites] sang to the LORD: "He is good; his love to Israel endures for ever." And all the people gave a great shout of praise to the LORD, because the foundation of the house of the LORD was laid.　*See also* **Isa** 12:1–6

People are joyful
Ac 13:49–52 The word of the Lord spread through the whole region . . . the disciples were filled with joy and with the Holy Spirit.　*See also* **Isa** 35:1–10; **Ac** 8:5–8　*See also* giving; humility; obedience; repentance; sin; worship.

---

revival, personal
The bringing back of individuals to life or vigour both at the point of personal regeneration through the work of the Holy Spirit and at other times in believers' lives.

Aspects of individual revival
Physical revival
Isa 38:16 . . . You [Lord] restored me [Hezekiah] to health and let me live.　*See also* **Jdg** 15:18–19; **1Sa** 14:27; 30:11–12; **1Ki** 19:7–8; **Job** 33:25; **Ps** 41:3; 116:8–9

Revival of hope
Ge 45:27 . . . the spirit of their father Jacob revived.　*See also* **Ru** 4:14–15

Revival of sanity **Da** 4:26,34,36

Spiritual revival
Ps 23:3 he [the LORD] restores my soul . . .
See also **1Ki** 19:9–15; **Jn** 21:15–19

The Holy Spirit brings regeneration by giving spiritual life to those dead in sin
Eph 2:1–5; **Tit** 3:5–6

Preparation for personal spiritual revival
The Holy Spirit convicts **Jn** 16:8–11; **Ac** 2:37; **1Th** 1:5

Individuals appeal to God
Jer 17:14 Heal me O LORD, and I [Jeremiah] shall be healed . . .　*See also* **Ps** 51:7–12; 119:34–37

Individuals long for God
Ps 42:1–2 As the deer pants for streams of water, so my soul pants for you, O God. My soul thirsts for God, for the living God. When can I go and meet with God?　*See also* **Ps** 63:1

Personal repentance is required
Ps 51:1–4 . . . Wash away all my iniquity and cleanse me from my sin . . .　*See also* **2Ch** 32:26; 33:11–13; **Job** 22:23; **Jer** 15:19

The believer must take responsibility for personal revival
2Ti 1:6 . . . fan into flame the gift of God, which is in you . . .

God is active in bringing about personal revival
Isa 57:15 . . . "I [the LORD] live in a high and holy place, but also with those who are contrite and lowly in spirit, to revive the spirit of the lowly and to revive the heart of the contrite."　*See also* **Ps** 43:3–4; **Isa** 40:31; **Hag** 1:14

God's law may initiate personal revival
Ps 19:7 The law of the LORD is perfect, reviving the soul . . .　*See also* **Ps** 119:130,162

The fruit of personal revival
God receives praise
Ps 40:3 He [the LORD] put a new song in my mouth, a hymn of praise to our God . . .　*See also* **2Sa** 22:50 pp **Ps** 18:49; **Ps** 51:15; 59:16; 61:8

God is obeyed
2Ch 33:15–16 He [Manasseh] got rid of the foreign gods and removed the image from the temple of the LORD, as well as all the altars he had built on the temple hill and in Jerusalem; and he threw them out of the city. Then he restored the altar of the LORD and sacrificed fellowship

offerings and thank-offerings on it, and told Judah to serve the LORD, the God of Israel.   *See also* **Ac** 2:14   *See also conversion; hope; praise.*

sanctification

The process of becoming consecrated to God, which is an integral aspect of being a member of the people of God. This process of being made holy through the work of the Holy Spirit ultimately rests upon the sacrificial death of Jesus Christ, which the OT anticipates and foreshadows.

sanctification, basis of

The process of renewal and consecration by which believers are made holy through the work of the Holy Spirit. Sanctification is the consequence of justification and is dependent upon a person being in a right relationship with God.

Sanctification is grounded in the holiness of God
God is holy
Eze 39:7 "'I will make known my holy name among my people Israel. I will no longer let my holy name be profaned, and the nations will know that I the LORD am the Holy One in Israel.'"   *See also* **Lev** 22:32; **Jos** 24:19; **Ps** 30:4; **Hos** 11:9; **Isa** 6:3; **Rev** 6:10
God demands that his people should reflect his holiness
Lev 19:2 "Speak to the entire assembly of Israel and say to them: 'Be holy because I, the LORD your God, am holy.'"   *See also* **Lev** 11:44–45; 20:7–8; **Heb** 2:11; **1Pe** 1:15–16
Sanctification is the will of God for his people
1Th 4:3 It is God's will that you should be sanctified . . .   *See also* **Eph** 1:4; 2:10; **2Th** 2:13; **1Pe** 1:1–2

The basis for sanctification
God's election of his people 1Co 1:2; Eph 1:4–11; 1Th 5:9
The atoning death of Jesus Christ
Heb 13:12 And so Jesus also suffered outside the city gate to make the people holy through his own blood.   *See also* **Ro** 6:11; 7:4; 8:2; **1Co**

1:30; 6:11; **Eph** 5:25–27; **Heb** 10:10–14; **1Pe** 2:5
The grace of God Lk 1:69–75; Php 2:13; 2Ti 1:9; Heb 12:10
The work of the Holy Spirit Ro 15:16; 2Th 2:13; 1Pe 1:2
The word of God Jn 17:17; Eph 5:25–26; 2Ti 3:16

The need for sanctification
The universal sinfulness of humanity
Isa 64:6 All of us have become like one who is unclean, and all our righteous acts are like filthy rags; we all shrivel up like a leaf, and like the wind our sins sweep us away.   *See also* **Job** 15:14–15; **Ps** 51:5; **Ro** 5:12–19; **Eph** 2:3
Enslavement to evil can only be broken through the death of Jesus Christ
Jn 8:34–36 Jesus replied, "I tell you the truth, everyone who sins is a slave to sin. Now a slave has no permanent place in the family, but a son belongs to it for ever. So if the Son sets you free, you will be free indeed."   *See also* **Ro** 6:16–18; 8:5–7; **Eph** 4:17–24
The need for renewal and growth
2Pe 3:18 But grow in the grace and knowledge of our Lord and Saviour Jesus Christ. To him be glory both now and for ever! Amen.   *See also* **Ro** 12:1–2; **Col** 1:10; **1Th** 4:3–6; **Heb** 6:1–3

The nature of sanctification
A process which has already been initiated 1Co 1:2; 6:11
A process of growth in holiness Ro 12:1–3; 2Co 3:18; Eph 4:15; 1Th 4:3–7; Heb 12:14; 1Pe 2:1 3; 2Pe 3:18
Consecration to God Ex 32:29; 1Ch 29:5; Pr 23:26; Ro 12:1   *See also godliness; holiness; life, spiritual; obedience; renewal.*

sanctification, means and results

Sanctification results from the renewing work of the Holy Spirit and leads to the renewal of believers and their being equipped for ministry in the world.

The means of sanctification
The work of the Holy Spirit
1Co 6:11 . . . you were washed, you were sanctified, you were justified in the name of the Lord Jesus Christ and by the Spirit of our God. *See also* **Ro** 8:9–11; 15:15–16; **1Co** 12:13; **2Co** 1:21–22; **Eph** 1:13–14; **2Th** 2:13; **Tit** 3:4–7; **1Pe** 1:1–2

Meditation on the Scriptures
1Pe 2:2–3 Like newborn babies, crave pure spiritual milk, so that by it you may grow up in your salvation . . . *See also* **Dt** 11:18; **Ps** 119:12–18,48; 143:5–6; **Jn** 17:17; **Col** 3:16; **Jas** 1:25

The active pursuit of holiness and righteousness
1Ti 6:11–12 . . . pursue righteousness, godliness, faith, love, endurance and gentleness. Fight the good fight of the faith. Take hold of the eternal life to which you were called when you made your good confession in the presence of many witnesses. *See also* **2Co** 7:1; **Gal** 5:24; **Eph** 4:1; **1Th** 5:22; **1Pe** 2:9–12; **3Jn** 11

Obedience and self-denial Ro 6:19–22; 8:5–14; **Gal** 2:20; 5:16–24; **1Pe** 2:11

Prayer
Ps 145:18 The LORD is near to all who call on him, to all who call on him in truth. *See also* **Mt** 7:7–8; **Ac** 4:31; **1Ti** 4:4; **Jas** 5:16; **Jude** 20

Confession of sin
1Jn 1:9 If we confess our sins, he is faithful and just and will forgive us our sins and purify us from all unrighteousness. *See also* **Ne** 1:6–9; **Ps** 32:5; 40:11–12; **Pr** 28:13; **Isa** 64:5–7; **Jer** 14:20–22; **La** 3:40

Obstacles to sanctification
A lack of faith Mt 5:13; **Jn** 15:6; **2Co** 12:20–21; **1Ti** 1:18–19

Rebellion against God
Eze 18:24 "But if the righteous turn from their righteousness and commit sin and do the same detestable things the wicked do, will they live? None of the righteous things they have done will be remembered. Because of the unfaithfulness they are guilty of and because of the sins they have committed, they

will die." *See also* **Dt** 32:15–18; **Job** 34:26; **Isa** 65:11–12; **Gal** 1:6–7; 5:7–9; **Heb** 12:15; **Rev** 2:4–5

Satanic temptation
1Pe 5:8–9 Be self-controlled and alert. Your enemy the devil prowls around like a roaring lion looking for someone to devour. Resist him, standing firm in the faith, because you know that your brothers and sisters throughout the world are undergoing the same kind of sufferings. *See also* **Ac** 5:3; **2Co** 2:8–11; **Jas** 4:7

Self-indulgence and greed
Lk 12:15 Then he [Jesus] said to them, "Watch out! Be on your guard against all kinds of greed; life does not consist in the abundance of possessions." *See also* **Lk** 21:34; **Ro** 13:13; **2Co** 12:21; **Eph** 4:19

Yielding to sinful desires
1Pe 1:14 As obedient children, do not conform to the evil desires you had when you lived in ignorance. *See also* **Mk** 4:18–19; **1Co** 10:6–8; **1Pe** 2:11; **2Pe** 2:14–18; **1Jn** 2:16–17

The results of sanctification
Good works
2Co 9:8 And God is able to make all grace abound to you, so that in all things at all times, having all that you need, you will abound in every good work. *See also* **Eph** 2:10; **Col** 1:10; 3:15–17; **2Th** 2:16–17; **Heb** 10:24–25; **Jas** 2:14–26

Becoming like Jesus Christ
1Pe 2:21 To this you were called, because Christ suffered for you, leaving you an example, that you should follow in his steps. *See also* **Jn** 13:15; **Ro** 8:28–30; **1Co** 11:1; **2Co** 3:18; **Gal** 3:27; **1Jn** 3:2–3

Becoming like God Mt 5:48; **Eph** 5:1–2; **Col** 1:21–22

Perfection
Mt 5:48 "Be perfect, therefore, as your heavenly Father is perfect." *See also* **2Co** 13:11; **Col** 1:28

Blamelessness in the sight of God
2Pe 3:14 . . . make every effort to be found spotless, blameless and at peace with him. *See also* **Eph** 1:4; **Col** 1:21–22; **1Th** 5:23

Being able to see God Heb 12:14   *See also*
Christlikeness; discipleship; forgiveness; maturity; self-
denial; sin, avoidance; union with Christ.

---

self-control

Physical and emotional self-mastery, particularly in
situations of intense provocation or temptation.

Self-control is the mark of a wise
person
Pr 29:11 Fools give full vent to their anger, but
the wise keep themselves under control.   *See*
also **Pr** 1:1–5

Self-control is an aspect of Christian
character
Gal 5:22–23 . . . the fruit of the Spirit is . . .
self-control . . .
Tit 2:11–12 . . . the grace of God that brings
salvation has appeared to all people. It teaches us
to say "No" to ungodliness and worldly passions,
and to live self-controlled, upright and godly lives
in this present age,   *See also* **1Ti** 3:2; **Tit** 1:8;
2:2,5–6; **2Pe** 1:5–9

Self-control affects the whole person
Physical self-control
1Co 9:26–27 . . . I [Paul] do not run like
someone running aimlessly; I do not fight like
someone beating the air. No, I beat my body and
make it my slave so that after I have preached
to others, I myself will not be disqualified for the
prize.   *See also* **1Co** 7:36–38; **1Th** 4:3–7
A mental discipline
1Pe 1:13 . . . prepare your minds for action;
be self-controlled; set your hope fully on the grace
to be given you when Jesus Christ is revealed.
See also **1Th** 5:6–8; **1Pe** 4:7; 5:8
Controlled speech
Ps 141:3 Set a guard over my mouth, O Lord;
keep watch over the door of my lips.
Jas 1:19 My dear brothers and sisters, take
note of this: Everyone should be quick to listen,
slow to speak and slow to become angry,   *See*
also **Ps** 17:3; **Pr** 16:23; 21:23; **Ecc** 5:2; **Jas** 3:1–12

Self-control in response to persecution
Mt 5:39–40 ". . . I [Jesus] tell you, Do not
resist an evil person. If someone strikes you on
the right cheek, turn the other cheek also. And if
someone wants to sue you and take your tunic,
hand over your cloak as well." pp Lk
6:27–29   *See also* **1Pe** 2:18–23

Examples of self-control
Ge 39:7–12
David: **1Sa** 24:1–7; 26:7–12; **2Sa** 16:9–10
Job: **Job** 31:1,30
Jesus Christ: **Isa** 53:7; **Mk** 14:61; **Mt** 27:27–30
Paul: **1Co** 4:12–13; 9:24–27

The dangers of a loss of self-control
Pr 18:7 The mouths of fools are their undoing,
and their lips are a snare to their souls.
Jer 14:10 This is what the Lord says about this
people: "They greatly love to wander; they do not
restrain their feet. So the Lord does not accept
them; he will now remember their wickedness and
punish them for their sins."   *See also* **1Sa**
18:10–11; **2Sa** 13:7–14; **Ps** 106:32–33; **Pr** 6:1–3;
29:18; **Ac** 24:25; **Ro** 1:24–31; **1Co** 7:5,9; **Col** 2:23
False teaching was leading to the throwing off of
restraints in the name of the gospel: **2Pe**
2:12–14,18–19; **Jude** 4   *See also discipline;*
immorality; patience; perseverance; self-denial.

---

self-denial

The willingness to deny oneself possessions or
status, in order to grow in holiness and
commitment to God. This practice is commended
and illustrated by Jesus Christ himself, and
underlies Christian fellowship within the church.

The wisdom of self-denial
Pr 23:20–21 Do not join those who drink too
much wine or gorge themselves on meat, for
drunkards and gluttons become poor, and
drowsiness clothes them in rags.   *See also* **Pr**
25:16

Examples of self-denial in order to put God first

Da 1:8 But Daniel resolved not to defile himself with the royal food and wine, and he asked the chief official for permission not to defile himself in this way.

Heb 11:25 He [Moses] chose to be ill-treated along with the people of God rather than to enjoy the pleasures of sin for a short time.   *See also* **Lev** 23:29; **Jer** 35:6; **Da** 10:3; **Lk** 1:15; 7:33 pp **Mt** 11:18

Self-denial is a requirement of following Jesus Christ

Mt 16:24 Then Jesus said to his disciples, "Those who would come after me must deny themselves and take up their cross and follow me." pp **Mk** 8:34 pp **Lk** 9:23

Ac 21:13 Then Paul answered, ". . . I am ready not only to be bound, but also to die in Jerusalem for the name of the Lord Jesus."

Php 3:7 But whatever was to my profit I [Paul] now consider loss for the sake of Christ.

1Pe 2:11 Dear friends, I urge you, as aliens and strangers in the world, to abstain from sinful desires, which war against your soul.   *See also* **Mt** 5:29; 6:10; 9:9 pp **Mk** 2:13–14 pp **Lk** 5:27–28; **Mt** 10:37–38 pp **Lk** 14:26–27; **Mt** 18:8 pp **Mk** 9:43; **Mt** 19:21 pp **Lk** 18:22; **Mt** 19:27 pp **Mk** 10:28 pp **Lk** 18:28; **Mt** 19:29 pp **Mk** 10:29–30 pp **Lk** 18:29–30; **Lk** 5:11; 14:33; 21:34; **Ac** 20:24; **Ro** 6:2,6,11; 8:13; 12:1; 13:14; **1Co** 6:12; 9:25–27; **2Co** 8:5; **Gal** 2:20; 5:16,23; **Col** 3:3,5; **2Ti** 2:21; **Tit** 2:12–13; **Jas** 4:7; **1Pe** 4:2

Self-denial for the sake of others

Ru 2:11 Boaz replied [to Ruth], "I've been told all about what you have done for your mother-in-law since the death of your husband—how you left your father and mother and your homeland and came to live with a people you did not know before."

Php 2:4 Each of you should look not only to your own interests, but also to the interests of others.   *See also* **Ex** 32:32; **Est** 4:16
Self-denial for the sake of those weak in their faith: **Ro** 14:21; 15:1; **1Co** 8:13; 9:23

1Co 10:24,33; 12:15; **Eph** 4:2; 5:21; **Php** 2:17,20–21; **Col** 1:24; **2Ti** 2:10; **Tit** 3:2; **1Pe** 3:8; 5:5

Self-denial and the example of Jesus Christ

Mt 26:39 Going a little farther, he fell with his face to the ground and prayed, "My Father, if it is possible, may this cup be taken from me. Yet not as I will, but as you will." pp **Mk** 14:36 pp **Lk** 22:42

2Co 8:9 For you know the grace of our Lord Jesus Christ, that though he was rich, yet for your sakes he became poor, so that you through his poverty might become rich.   *See also* **Ps** 40:7; **Isa** 53:7; **Mt** 11:29; **Jn** 13:1–17; **Ro** 15:3; **Eph** 5:1–2; **Php** 2:5–8   *See also discipleship; cost; fasting; self-control.*

---

self-examination

Reflection on one's own character, motives and actions, in order to judge whether they are truly in accordance with Christian values.

---

self-examination, examples

Scripture provides numerous examples of self-examination, and its results. In particular, self-examination is often portrayed as leading to repentance.

Self-examination in the experience of Israel

Self-examination at the entry into the promised land Jos 7:1–26; 24:14

Self-examination during the war with the Philistines 1Sa 14:24–47

Self-examination at the time of the exile Jer 31:18–20

Self-examination after returning from exile in Babylon Ne 8:9; Hag 1:5–12; 2:15–19

Self-examination by other nations
Jnh 3:1–10

Self-examination in the experience of individuals

King David
Ps 51:3-6 For I [David] know my transgressions, and my sin is always before me. Against you, you only, have I sinned and done what is evil in your sight, so that you are proved right when you speak and justified when you judge. Surely I was sinful at birth, sinful from the time my mother conceived me. Surely you desire truth in the inner parts; you teach me wisdom in the inmost place.   *See also* **2Sa** 12:1-13; **Ps** 32:3-5

Job
Job 42:1-6 . . . ". . . Surely I [Job] spoke of things I did not understand, things too wonderful for me to know . . ."

The psalmists
Ps 119:59 I have considered my ways and have turned my steps to your statutes.   *See also* **Ps** 42:5,11; 43:5

The lost son
Lk 15:17-20 "When he came to his senses, he said, 'How many of my father's hired servants have food to spare, and here I am starving to death! I will set out and go back to my father and say to him: Father, I have sinned against heaven and against you. I am no longer worthy to be called your son; make me like one of your hired servants.' So he got up and went to his father . . ."

The disciples
Mt 26:22 They were very sad and began to say to him one after the other, "Surely not I, Lord?" pp Mk 14:19
Judas Mt 26:25; 27:3-5   *See also repentance.*

---

self-examination, teaching on
Self-examination should take place on the basis of God's revelation of himself and the example he sets believers in Jesus Christ. It is especially important before confessing one's sins.

The importance of self-examination
Hag 1:5 Now this is what the LORD Almighty says: "Give careful thought to your ways."
See also **Ps** 4:4; 77:6; **Hag** 1:7; 2:15,18; **1Co** 11:28; **2Co** 13:5; **Heb** 3:12

A lack of self-examination leads to pride and self-delusion
1Co 11:28-29 We ought to examine ourselves before we eat of the bread and drink of the cup. For those who eat and drink without recognising the body of the Lord eat and drink judgment on themselves.   *See also* **Mt** 7:5; **Jn** 8:7; **Ro** 2:1-4

Self-examination is not easy because of humanity's fallen nature
Ps 19:12-14 Who can discern their errors? Forgive my hidden faults. Keep your servant also from wilful sins; may they not rule over me. Then will I be blameless, innocent of great transgression. May the words of my mouth and the meditation of my heart be pleasing in your sight, O LORD, my Rock and my Redeemer.
See also **Jer** 17:9

God helps believers in their self-examination
Ps 26:2 Test me, O LORD, and try me, examine my heart and my mind;   *See also* **Job** 7:17-18; 13:9,23; **Ps** 11:4-5; 139:23-24; **Pr** 5:21; **Jer** 17:10; 20:12

The purpose of self-examination is to lead people to God and amendment of life
La 3:40-42 Let us examine our ways and test them, and let us return to the LORD. Let us lift up our hearts and our hands to God in heaven, and say: "We have sinned and rebelled and you have not forgiven."   *See also* **Ps** 42:5,11; 43:5; **Jas** 1:23-25

Self-examination is especially important when ministering to others
Gal 6:1 Brothers and sisters, if someone is caught in a sin, you who are spiritual should restore that person gently. But watch yourself, or you also may be tempted.   *See also* **Ro** 14:4; **Gal** 6:3-4; **1Ti** 4:16; **Jas** 3:1   *See also confession of sin; meditation; sin, forgiveness of.*

self-respect

A sense of personal worth and dignity. Scripture points to the need for believers to ground their self-respect in God himself, rather than trusting in the opinion and valuation of other individuals or society as a whole.

Self-respect is often assumed
Mt 22:39 ". . . 'Love your neighbour as yourself.'" pp Mk 12:31 *See also* **Mt** 7:12; 19:19; **Ro** 12:3; **Eph** 5:29

Examples of those who had self-respect
Job 12:3 "But I [Job] have a mind as well as you [Job's friends]; I am not inferior to you. Who does not know all these things?" *See also* **Job** 10:16; **Pr** 31:25; **Php** 3:4

The basis of self-respect
A relationship with God
Ps 139:13-14 For you [O Lord] created my inmost being; you knit me together in my mother's womb. I praise you because I am fearfully and wonderfully made; your works are wonderful, I know that full well. *See also* **Ps** 30:6; **1Co** 3:16-17; 6:12-20; **2Co** 6:16; **Eph** 2:22; **1Ti** 4:4
Equality in God's community
Jas 1:9-10 Believers in humble circumstances ought to take pride in their high position. But those who are rich should take pride in their low position, because they will pass away like a wild flower. *See also* **1Co** 12:22-25
A clear conscience and faithfulness to God
2Co 1:12 Now this is our boast: Our conscience testifies that we have conducted ourselves in the world, and especially in our relations with you, in the holiness and sincerity that are from God. We have done so not according to worldly wisdom but according to God's grace. *See also* **Jn** 7:18; **Gal** 6:4; **Heb** 13:18

God's strength is a source of self-respect
Da 10:19 "Do not be afraid, O man highly esteemed," he [one who looked like a man] said. "Peace! Be strong now; be strong." When he spoke to me, I [Daniel] was strengthened and said, "Speak, my lord, since you have given me strength." *See also* **Ex** 15:2; **2Sa** 22:33; **Ps** 71:5; 89:17; 118:14; **2Ti** 4:17

Self-respect results from disciplined living
Job 4:6 "Should not your piety be your confidence and your blameless ways your hope?" *See also* **Pr** 20:3; **1Th** 4:4; **Tit** 2:2

Self-respect can be lost through humiliation
Jer 31:19 "'After I [Jeremiah] strayed, I repented; after I came to understand, I beat my breast. I was ashamed and humiliated because I bore the disgrace of my youth.'" *See also* **2Sa** 10:1-5 pp **1Ch** 19:1-5; **2Sa** 13:1-22; **Da** 4:33

Self-respect can rest on wrong foundations
Gal 6:3 If any of you think you are something when you are nothing, you deceive yourselves. *See also* **Dt** 8:17-18; **Job** 20:6-7; **Php** 3:4-7

Ways in which self-respect can be undermined
By others Job 30:1-15
By the effects of sin and the work of Satan
Mk 5:2-5 pp **Lk** 8:27-29; **Mk** 5:25-28 pp **Mt** 9:20-22 pp **Lk** 8:43-48; **Lk** 15:13-16; 17:12-13
By unwise spiritual zeal Gal 6:1; **1Ti** 5:1-2; **Jude** 22 *See also* pride; respect; self-control.

---

servanthood in believers
Servanthood as an expression of subservience is an integral aspect of a person's relationship with God.

Servants of God in the OT
Abraham
Ge 18:5 Let me [Abraham] get you [three men] something to eat, so you can be refreshed and then go on your way—now that you have come to your servant." "Very well," they

answered, "do as you say."   *See also* **Ge**
26:24; **Dt** 9:27; **Ps** 105:6,42

Moses
Ex 14:31 And when the Israelites saw the great
power the LORD displayed against the Egyptians,
the people feared the LORD and put their trust in
him and in Moses his servant.   *See also* **Nu**
12:7–8; **Dt** 34:5; **Jos** 1:1–2,7,13,15; 8:31,33;
11:15; 22:2,4–5; **2Ki** 18:12; **2Ch** 1:3; **Heb** 3:5;
Rev 15:3

Joshua
Jdg 2:8 Joshua son of Nun, the servant of the
LORD, died at the age of a hundred and ten.
See also **Jos** 24:29

David
2Sa 3:18 ". . . For the LORD promised David,
'By my servant David I will rescue my people
Israel from the hand of the Philistines and from
the hand of all their enemies.'"   *See also* **2Sa**
7:5 pp 1Ch 17:4; **2Sa** 7:8 pp 1Ch 17:7; **2Sa**
7:18–20,25; **1Ch** 21:8; **Ps** 78:70; 89:3,20; 132:10;
Eze 34:23–24; **Lk** 1:69; **Ac** 4:25–26

Jesus Christ and servanthood
Jesus Christ's teaching on servanthood
Mt 6:24 "No-one can be a slave to two
masters. Either you will hate the one and love the
other, or you will be devoted to the one and
despise the other. You cannot be a slave to both
God and Money." pp Lk 16:13   *See also* **Mt**
25:31–46; **Jn** 12:26; 13:13–17; 15:15,20
Parables on servanthood Mt 20:1–16; 24:45–51
pp Lk 12:42–46; **Mt** 25:14–30 pp Lk 19:12–27; **Lk**
12:35–40; 17:7–10

Servants of God in the NT
Ac 16:17 She followed Paul and the rest of us,
shouting, "These men are servants of the Most
High God, who are telling you the way to be
saved."   *See also* **Ac** 2:18; 4:29; **2Pe** 1:1;
Jude 1

Paul as a servant
A servant of God
Ro 15:17 Therefore I [Paul] glory in Christ
Jesus in my service to God.   *See also* **Ro** 1:9;
2Co 6:4; **2Ti** 1:3

A servant of Jesus Christ
Ro 1:1 Paul, a servant of Christ Jesus, called to
be an apostle and set apart for the gospel of
God—   *See also* **Gal** 1:10; **Php** 1:1
A servant of the gospel
Eph 3:7 I [Paul] became a servant of this gospel
by the gift of God's grace given me through the
working of his power.   *See also* **Col** 1:23
A servant of the church
2Co 4:5 For we [Paul and Timothy] do not
preach ourselves, but Jesus Christ as Lord, and
ourselves as your servants for Jesus' sake.
See also **2Co** 13:4; **Col** 1:24–25

Christian servanthood
Gifts of service
1Pe 4:10 Each of you should use whatever gift
you have received to serve others, faithfully
administering God's grace in its various forms.
See also **Ro** 12:7; **1Co** 12:5; **Eph** 4:12; **1Pe** 2:16
Examples of service
Ro 12:11 Never be lacking in zeal, but keep
your spiritual fervour, serving the Lord.   *See also*
2Co 9:12–13; **Eph** 6:6–7; **Col** 3:22–24; **Rev** 2:19
Christian leadership entails service
1Pe 5:2 Be shepherds of God's flock that is
under your care, serving as overseers—not
because you must, but because you are willing, as
God wants you to be; not greedy for money, but
eager to serve;   *See also* **Ac** 6:2–4
The office of deacon was seen as a serving role: **1Ti**
3:10,12–13   *See also discipleship; ministry.*

---

sin
Primarily a wrong relationship with God, which
may express itself in wrong attitudes or actions
towards God himself, other human beings,
possessions or the environment. Scripture stresses
that this condition is deeply rooted in human
nature, and that only God is able to break its
penalty, power and presence.

---

sin, avoidance
God calls his people to avoid sin, and through
Jesus Christ gives them the inner power to be
victorious over it.

God's people are to resist sin

1Pe 2:11 Dear friends, I urge you, as aliens and strangers in the world, to abstain from sinful desires, which war against your soul. *See also* **Ps** 97:10; **Pr** 4:23–27; **1Co** 15:34; **Eph** 4:25–5:20; **Jas** 1:21

The Christian life is a constant struggle against sin

Heb 3:13 . . . so that none of you may be hardened by sin's deceitfulness. *See also* **Ac** 20:28; **Ro** 7:14–25; **Eph** 6:10–18; **1Pe** 5:8–9

God helps his people to resist sin
Release from sin through Jesus Christ's death
1Pe 2:24 He himself bore our sins in his body on the tree, so that we might die to sins and live for righteousness; by his wounds you have been healed. *See also* **Ro** 6:1–7; **Gal** 2:20; 5:24; **Col** 2:11–12

The avoidance of sin through new life in Jesus Christ
1Jn 3:9 Those who are born of God will not continue to sin, because God's seed remains in them; they cannot go on sinning, because they have been born of God. *See also* **2Co** 5:17; **1Pe** 1:23; **1Jn** 3:6; 5:18

Believers co-operate with Jesus Christ to avoid sin

Php 2:12–13 . . . continue to work out your salvation with fear and trembling, for it is God who works in you to will and to act according to his good purpose.

Believers are to put to death what is sinful in them
Col 3:5 Put to death, therefore, whatever belongs to your earthly nature: sexual immorality, impurity, lust, evil desires and greed, which is idolatry. *See also* **Ro** 6:11–14; 8:13

Believers are to exchange sinful for righteous behaviour
Ro 13:12–14 The night is nearly over; the day is almost here. So let us put aside the deeds of darkness and put on the armour of light . . . *See also* **Eph** 4:22–24; **Col** 3:7–10; **1Ti** 6:11; **2Ti** 2:22

Believers are to allow the Spirit to inform and direct their conduct

Ro 12:2 Do not conform any longer to the pattern of this world, but be transformed by the renewing of your mind. Then you will be able to test and approve what God's will is—his good, pleasing and perfect will. *See also* **Ro** 8:5–8; **Gal** 5:16–25

Practical steps for overcoming sin and temptation
Meditation on Scripture
Ps 119:11 I have hidden your word in my heart that I might not sin against you. *See also* **Ps** 18:22–23; **Mt** 4:1–11 pp Lk 4:1–13; **2Ti** 3:16–17

Prayerful dependence upon God
Mt 6:13 "'And lead us not into temptation, but deliver us from the evil one.'" pp Lk 11:4 *See also* **Ps** 19:13; **Mt** 26:41; **1Co** 10:13; **Heb** 4:15–16

Active seeking of the good
Ro 6:19 . . . Just as you used to offer the parts of your body in slavery to impurity and to ever-increasing wickedness, so now offer them in slavery to righteousness leading to holiness. *See also* **Ps** 34:14; **Isa** 1:16–17; **Am** 5:14–15; **1Th** 5:22; **3Jn** 11

Incentives for avoiding sin
The fear of God
Pr 16:6 . . . through the fear of the LORD evil is avoided. *See also* **Ex** 20:20; **Pr** 3:7; 8:13
The holiness of God
1Pe 1:15–16 But just as he who called you is holy, so be holy in all you do; for it is written: "Be holy, because I am holy." *See also* **Lev** 11:44–45; 19:2; 20:7; **1Co** 6:18–20; **1Th** 4:7
The expectation of Jesus Christ's return
1Pe 4:7 The end of all things is near. Therefore be clear minded and self-controlled so that you can pray. *See also* **2Co** 5:9–10; **1Th** 5:4–6; **2Pe** 3:10–14
A consideration of the consequences of sin
Gal 6:7–8 Do not be deceived: God cannot be mocked. People reap what they sow. Those who sow to please their sinful nature, from that nature

will reap destruction; those who sow to please the Spirit, from the Spirit will reap eternal life.   *See also* **Mk** 9:42–48; **Ro** 6:21–23; **Heb** 6:7–8; 10:26–31

The need to be a good witness to unbelievers
1Pe 2:15 For it is God's will that by doing good you should silence the ignorant talk of foolish people.   *See also* **1Pe** 3:1–2,15–16

The role of others in avoiding sin
Bad company is to be avoided
1Co 15:33 Do not be misled: "Bad company corrupts good character."   *See also* **Dt** 7:1–4; **Ps** 1:1; **Pr** 1:10; **1Co** 5:1–13

A good example is to be followed
1Co 11:1 Follow my [Paul's] example, as I follow the example of Christ.   *See also* **Php** 3:17; 4:9; **Heb** 12:1–3; **1Pe** 4:1–3

Believers are to support one another
Jas 5:19–20 My brothers and sisters, if one of you should wander from the truth and someone should bring that person back, remember this: Those who turn sinners from the error of their ways will save them from death and cover over a multitude of sins.   *See also* **Mt** 18:15–17; **Gal** 6:1–2; **1Ti** 5:20; **Heb** 3:12   *See also fellowship; holiness; sanctification; temptation; watchfulness.*

sin, deliverance from
The gospel reveals the purpose and power of God to deal with sin and all of its effects. Scripture uses a range of images to express the comprehensiveness of salvation.

God's removal of sin
Atonement for sin
Isa 6:7 With it [a live coal] he touched my mouth and said, "See, this has touched your lips; your guilt is taken away and your sin atoned for."   *See also* **Ex** 32:30; **Lev** 4:27–31; **Pr** 16:6; **Ro** 3:25; **Heb** 2:17

Forgiveness of sin
Mic 7:18 Who is a God like you, who pardons sin and forgives the transgression of the remnant of his inheritance? You do not stay angry for ever but delight to show mercy.
Ac 13:38 "Therefore, my brothers and sisters, I

want you to know that through Jesus the forgiveness of sins is proclaimed to you."   *See also* **1Ki** 8:35–36; **2Ch** 30:18–20; **Ps** 103:2–3; **Isa** 33:24; 55:7; **Joel** 3:21; **Mt** 26:27–28; **Lk** 24:46–47; **Eph** 1:7; **1Jn** 1:9

Cancellation of a debt
Mt 6:12 " 'Forgive us our debts, as we also have forgiven our debtors.' "   *See also* **Mt** 18:21–35; **Lk** 7:41–50

A covering over of sin
1Pe 4:8 Above all, love each other deeply, because love covers over a multitude of sins.   *See also* **Ps** 32:1; 85:2; **Jas** 5:20

The taking away of sin
Ps 103:12 as far as the east is from the west, so far has he removed our transgressions from us.   *See also* **2Sa** 12:13; **Isa** 6:6–7; **Zec** 3:4; **Jn** 1:29; **Heb** 9:28; **1Jn** 3:5

Remembering sin no more
Isa 43:25 "I [the LORD], even I, am he who blots out your transgressions, for my own sake, and remembers your sins no more."   *See also* **Ps** 25:7; **Jer** 31:33–34; **2Co** 5:19

God's deliverance for the sinner
The salvation of the sinner
1Ti 1:15 Here is a trustworthy saying that deserves full acceptance: Christ Jesus came into the world to save sinners—of whom I am the worst.   *See also* **Ps** 28:8–9; **Mt** 1:21; **Lk** 19:9–10; **Jn** 3:17; **Heb** 7:25

The image of healing
Lk 5:31–32 Jesus answered them [Pharisees and teachers of the law], "It is not the healthy who need a doctor, but the sick. I have not come to call the righteous, but sinners to repentance."   pp **Mt** 9:12 pp **Mk** 2:17   *See also* **2Ch** 7:14; **Isa** 53:5; 57:18–19; **Hos** 14:4; **1Pe** 2:24

The image of cleansing
Ps 51:2 Wash away all my iniquity and cleanse me from my sin.   *See also* **Lev** 16:30; **Eze** 36:25; **Jn** 13:1–11; **Heb** 10:22; **Ac** 22:16; **1Jn** 1:9

Redemption by God
Ps 130:8 He himself will redeem Israel from all their sins.   *See also* **Isa** 44:22; **Tit** 2:14; **1Pe** 1:18–19

Justification before God

Gal 2:16 ". . . a person is not justified by observing the law, but by faith in Jesus Christ. So we, too, have put our faith in Christ Jesus that we may be justified by faith in Christ and not by observing the law, because by observing the law no-one will be justified." *See also* **Isa** 53:11; **Ro** 3:24–26; 4:5,25; 5:16–19; 8:33

Freedom from condemnation

Ro 8:1 Therefore, there is now no condemnation for those who are in Christ Jesus, *See also* **Jn** 3:18; 8:3–11; **Ro** 8:34

Peace with God

Ro 5:1 Therefore, since we have been justified through faith, we have peace with God through our Lord Jesus Christ, *See also* **Isa** 53:5; **Lk** 2:14; **Eph** 2:17

Reconciliation with God

2Co 5:18 All this is from God, who reconciled us to himself through Christ . . . *See also* **Ro** 5:9–11; **Col** 1:19–20

Sanctification to God

Heb 10:10 And by that will, we have been made holy through the sacrifice of the body of Jesus Christ once for all. *See also* **1Co** 6:11; **Eph** 5:25–26; **Col** 1:22

Freedom from sin and the sinful nature

Ro 7:24 What a wretched man I am! Who will rescue me from this body of death?

1Pe 2:24 He himself bore our sins in his body on the tree, so that we might die to sins and live for righteousness . . . *See also* **Ro** 6:1–18; 8:1–9; **Gal** 5:24

A transition from death to life

Col 2:13 When you were dead in your sins and in the uncircumcision of your sinful nature, God made you alive with Christ . . . *See also* **Lk** 15:22–24; **Eph** 2:4–5

Receiving eternal life

Ro 6:23 For the wages of sin is death, but the gift of God is eternal life in Christ Jesus our Lord. *See also* **Jn** 3:16,36 *See also eternal life; freedom; peace.*

sin, effects of

Sin affects every level of human existence, including the sinner's relationship with God, with other human beings and with the environment.

The effects of sin on individuals

Lack of peace of mind

Isa 57:20–21 But the wicked are like the tossing sea, which cannot rest, whose waves cast up mire and mud. "There is no peace," says my God, "for the wicked." *See also* **Job** 15:20–35; **Ps** 38:5–8; **Pr** 13:15–22; **La** 1:20–21

Bondage to a continuing habit of sin

Jn 8:34 . . . ". . . everyone who sins is a slave to sin." *See also* **Pr** 5:22; **Ro** 6:16; **2Ti** 2:16

Physical death

1Co 15:56 The sting of death is sin . . . *See also* **Ge** 2:17; 3:19; **Pr** 21:16; **Ro** 5:12–14; 6:21–23; **1Co** 15:22; **Jas** 1:15

The sinful life is equivalent to death

Eph 2:1 As for you, you were dead in your transgressions and sins, *See also* **Ro** 7:9,13; 8:10; **Col** 2:13

The effects of sin on the sinner before God

Uncleanness

Isa 64:6 All of us have become like one who is unclean, and all our righteous acts are like filthy rags . . . *See also* **Ps** 106:39; **Isa** 6:5; **Jer** 2:22; **La** 1:8; **Mt** 15:18–20 pp **Mk** 7:20–23

Guilt

Ezr 9:6 . . . "O my God, I am too ashamed and disgraced to lift up my face to you, my God, because our sins are higher than our heads and our guilt has reached to the heavens." *See also* **Ge** 3:10; **Ps** 38:3–4; 44:15; **Isa** 59:12–13; **Jer** 3:25; 14:20

Separation from God

Isa 59:2 But your iniquities have separated you from your God; your sins have hidden his face from you, so that he will not hear. *See also* **Dt** 31:18; **Isa** 1:15; 64:7; **Eze** 8:6; **Hos** 5:6; **Mic** 3:4; **Eph** 2:12

The effects of sin on Israel

Pr 14:34 Righteousness exalts a nation, but sin is a disgrace to any people. *See also* **Jos** 7:1–16; **1Ki** 8:33–40; **Isa** 1:4–9; **Ro** 1:21–32

The effects of sin on the world
The ground cursed
Ge 3:17-18 . . . ". . . Cursed is the ground because of you; through painful toil you will eat of it all the days of your life. It will produce thorns and thistles for you, and you will eat the plants of the field." *See also* **Jer** 12:13; **Ro** 8:20-22

The land polluted
Lev 18:25 " 'Even the land was defiled; so I punished it for its sin, and the land vomited out its inhabitants.' " *See also* **Ge** 4:10-12; **Nu** 35:33-34; **Ps** 106:38; **Isa** 24:4-6; **Jer** 3:1

---

sin, forgiveness of
Sinners must respond to God's offer of forgiveness through faith in Jesus Christ.

The conviction of sin
La 1:20 "See, O LORD, how distressed I am! I am in torment within, and in my heart I am disturbed, for I have been most rebellious. Outside, the sword bereaves; inside, there is only death."
Jn 16:8-9 "When he [the Counsellor] comes, he will convict the world of guilt in regard to sin and righteousness and judgment: in regard to sin, because people do not believe in me [Jesus];" *See also* **1Ki** 8:38-40; **Isa** 6:5; **Eze** 33:10-11; **Ac** 16:29

The inward response of faith
Ac 16:31 . . . "Believe in the Lord Jesus, and you will be saved . . ." *See also* **Mk** 1:14-15; **Jn** 3:36; 5:24; **Ac** 13:38-39; 16:25-34; **Ro** 3:22-26; 10:8-10; **Eph** 2:8

The outward response of baptism
Ac 22:16 " 'And now what are you waiting for? Get up, be baptised and wash your sins away, calling on his [Jesus'] name.' " *See also* **Mk** 1:4-5 pp **Mt** 3:1-6 pp **Lk** 3:2-6; **Ac** 2:38; 8:36; **Col** 2:11-12; **1Pe** 3:21

Confession of sin
Pr 28:13 Those who conceal their sins do not prosper, but those who confess and renounce them find mercy.

1Jn 1:9 If we confess our sins, he is faithful and just and will forgive us our sins and purify us from all unrighteousness. *See also* **Lev** 16:20-22; 26:40-42; **2Sa** 12:13; **Ps** 32:3-5; **La** 3:40; **Lk** 15:17-20; **Ac** 19:18

Repentance
Turning towards God
Ac 3:19 "Repent, then, and turn to God, so that your sins may be wiped out . . ." *See also* **2Ch** 6:36-39; **Isa** 55:7; **Eze** 18:21; **Mt** 3:1-2 pp **Mk** 1:4 pp **Lk** 3:2; **Ac** 17:30; **2Co** 7:10; **1Th** 1:9

Turning away from sin
Jn 8:11 . . . "Then neither do I condemn you [the woman caught in adultery]," Jesus declared. "Go now and leave your life of sin." *See also* **Jer** 4:3-4; **Lk** 19:1-10; **Jn** 5:14; **Ro** 6:11-14; **1Pe** 2:11

The making of restitution
Lk 19:8 But Zacchaeus stood up and said to the Lord, "Look, Lord! Here and now I give half of my possessions to the poor, and if I have cheated anybody out of anything, I will pay back four times the amount." *See also* **Lev** 6:1-7; **Nu** 5:6-8; **Pr** 6:30-31; **Eze** 33:12-16

The forgiveness of others
Lk 11:4 " 'Forgive us our sins, for we also forgive everyone who sins against us . . .' " pp **Mt** 6:12 *See also* **Mt** 6:14-15; 18:21-35; **Mk** 11:25; **Eph** 4:32; **Col** 3:13 *See also baptism; confession of sin; conversion; faith; forgiveness, Jesus Christ's ministry; repentance.*

---

speech
The human capacity to express oneself and communicate with others through the spoken word. God addresses humans through the spoken word, and supremely in and through Jesus Christ.

---

speech, negative
The sinfulness of fallen human nature can express itself in speech, provoking God's displeasure and causing enmity and division amongst people.

Evil speech comes from a corrupt heart
Mt 12:33-35 ". . . out of the overflow of the heart the mouth speaks. Good people bring good things out of the good stored up in them, and evil people bring evil things out of the evil stored up in them." *See also* **Pr** 2:12-15; 24:1-2; **Mt** 15:10-11 pp **Mk** 7:14-15; **Lk** 6:43-45

Evil speech is a feature of a corrupt society
Mic 6:12-13 "Her [Jerusalem's] rich people are violent; her inhabitants are liars and their tongues speak deceitfully. Therefore, I have begun to destroy you, to ruin you because of your sins." *See also* **Isa** 6:5; 59:1-4,12-15; **Jer** 9:1-9; **Ro** 1:29-32; **2Ti** 3:1-5

Evil speech provokes God's displeasure
Pr 12:22 The LORD detests lying lips, but he delights in those who are truthful. *See also* **Pr** 6:16-19

Kinds of evil speech
Profaning God's name
Ex 20:7 "You shall not misuse the name of the LORD your God, for the LORD will not hold anyone guiltless who misuses his name." pp **Dt** 5:11 *See also* **Ex** 22:28; **Lev** 19:12; **Ps** 139:19-20
Lies and deceit
Ps 5:9 Not a word from their [my enemies'] mouth can be trusted; their heart is filled with destruction. Their throat is an open grave; with their tongue they speak deceit. *See also* **Ps** 36:3; 52:1-4; 62:4; **Pr** 14:5,25; 15:4; 17:20
Foolish boasting
Ps 94:4 They pour out arrogant words; all the evildoers are full of boasting. *See also* **Ps** 10:2-6; 12:3-4; **Isa** 10:12-14; **2Th** 2:3-4; **Jas** 4:13-16; **2Pe** 2:17-18
Ridicule and insults
Pr 11:12 Those who lack judgment deride their neighbours, but those who have insight hold their tongues. *See also* **1Sa** 17:41-44; **2Ki** 2:23-24; **Ne** 2:19; **Pr** 9:7; **La** 2:15-16; **Mt** 5:22; 27:39-44 pp **Mk** 15:29-32 pp **Lk** 23:35-39; **Jn** 9:28-29
Criticism and complaint
Nu 12:1-15 Miriam and Aaron began to talk against Moses because of his Cushite wife, for he had married a Cushite. "Has the LORD spoken only through Moses?" they asked. "Hasn't he also spoken through us?" And the LORD heard this . . . *See also* **Nu** 16:1-50; **1Sa** 17:28; **Pr** 19:13; 21:9,19; 25:24; **Ac** 11:2-3; **Php** 2:14-15
Slander
Lev 19:16 "'Do not go about spreading slander among your people . . .'" *See also* **1Ki** 21:1-14; **Pr** 10:18; **Jas** 4:11
Cursing
Ex 21:17 "Anyone who curses father or mother must be put to death." *See also* **2Sa** 16:5-8; **Pr** 20:20; **Jas** 3:9-10
Gossip
Pr 16:28 The perverse stir up dissension, and gossips separate close friends. *See also* **Pr** 11:13; 17:9; 20:19
Obscenity
Eph 5:4 Nor should there be obscenity, foolish talk or coarse joking, which are out of place, but rather thanksgiving. *See also* **Col** 3:8

Evil speech is silenced
By God's actions
Ps 107:41-42 But he [the LORD] lifted the needy out of their affliction and increased their families like flocks. The upright see and rejoice, but all the wicked shut their mouths. *See also* **Ps** 63:11; **Eze** 16:63
By believers' blameless lives
1Pe 2:15 For it is God's will that by doing good you should silence the ignorant talk of foolish people. *See also* **Tit** 2:7-8

---

speech, positive
The way in which believers speak should reflect their calling as Christians. Christian speech should be sincere, godly and honouring to God.

The desire for godly speech
In oneself
Ps 19:14 May the words of my mouth and the meditation of my heart be pleasing in your sight, O LORD, my Rock and my Redeemer. *See also* **Ps** 17:3; 39:1; 141:3

In others

Eph 4:29-31 Do not let any unwholesome talk come out of your mouths, but only what is helpful for building others up according to their needs, that it may benefit those who listen . . .   *See also* **Pr** 4:24; **Ecc** 5:6; **Eph** 5:4; **Col** 3:8-10; **1Pe** 3:9-10; **Ps** 34:12-13

Characteristics of godly speech in relation to God

It gives glory to God

Heb 13:15 Through Jesus, therefore, let us continually offer to God a sacrifice of praise—the fruit of lips that confess his name.   *See also* **Ps** 34:1; 35:28; 51:15; **1Pe** 2:9

It gives thanks and praise to God

Col 3:17 And whatever you do, whether in word or deed, do it all in the name of the Lord Jesus, giving thanks to God the Father through him. *See also* **Dt** 8:10; **1Ch** 16:4,7-8,34-36; **Ps** 100:4; 118:1,19,21,28-29; **Joel** 2:26; **Mk** 8:6-7; **Col** 2:7; **1Th** 5:18; **Jas** 3:9-10

It confesses Jesus Christ as Lord

Ro 10:9-10 . . . if you confess with your mouth, "Jesus is Lord," and believe in your heart that God raised him from the dead, you will be saved. For it is with your heart that you believe and are justified, and it is with your mouth that you confess and are saved.   *See also* **Mt** 10:32-33 pp Lk 12:8-9; **Mt** 16:16; **1Co** 12:3

Characteristics of godly speech in relation to others

It is gentle, gracious and tactful

Col 4:6 Let your conversation be always full of grace, seasoned with salt, so that you may know how to answer everyone.   *See also* **Jdg** 8:1-3; **Pr** 10:32; 15:1; 16:24; **Ecc** 10:12; **Da** 2:14-16; **1Pe** 3:15

It is kind

Pr 12:25 Anxiety weighs down the heart, but a kind word cheers it up.   *See also* **Ge** 50:19-21; **Job** 4:3-4; **1Co** 4:13; **2Ti** 2:24-25

It is instructive and edifying

Col 3:16 Let the word of Christ dwell in you richly as you teach and admonish one another with all wisdom, and as you sing psalms, hymns and spiritual songs with gratitude in your hearts to God.   *See also* **Pr** 12:18; 15:2,4,7; 20:15; 25:11-12; 31:26; **Mal** 2:7; **Eph** 4:15,29

It is prudent and restrained

Pr 17:27 Those who have knowledge use words with restraint, and those who have insight are even-tempered.   *See also* **Pr** 15:28; 18:13; **Ecc** 5:2; 9:17; **Jas** 1:19

It is honest and unadorned

Mt 5:37 "Simply let your 'Yes' be 'Yes', and your 'No', 'No'; anything beyond this comes from the evil one."   *See also* **Ps** 15:2-3; 141:5; **Pr** 24:26; 27:5-6,9; 28:23

It is truthful and sincere

Zec 8:16 "These are the things you are to do: Speak the truth to each other, and render true and sound judgment in your courts;"   *See also* **Ex** 20:16 pp **Dt** 5:20; **Pr** 12:17,19,22; **Mal** 2:6; **2Co** 2:17; 4:2; 6:7; **Eph** 4:25

It is wise

Ps 37:30 The mouths of the righteous utter wisdom, and their tongues speak what is just. *See also* **Pr** 10:13,31; 13:14; **Ac** 6:10

It will speak of God and his works

Dt 6:6-9 These commandments that I [Moses] give you today are to be upon your hearts. Impress them on your children. Talk about them when you sit at home and when you walk along the road, when you lie down and when you get up . . .   *See also* **Ps** 40:9-10; 145:7; **Mal** 3:16

Jesus Christ's speech was perfect and unique

Jn 7:46 "No-one ever spoke the way this man [Jesus] does," . . .   *See also* **Mt** 7:28-29; 13·54 pp Mk 6:2; **Lk** 4:22; **1Pe** 2:22-23; **Isa** 53:9

Speech as a means of blessing people

Nu 6:22-27 The LORD said to Moses, "Tell Aaron and his sons, 'This is how you are to bless the Israelites. Say to them: "The LORD bless you and keep you; the LORD make his face shine upon you and be gracious to you; the LORD turn his face towards you and give you peace." ' So they will put my name on the Israelites, and I will bless them."   *See also* **Ge** 1:22,28; **Dt** 21:5; **1Ch** 23:13   *See also faithfulness, relationships; praise; thankfulness.*

spiritual gifts

Although all believers have received the gift of the Holy Spirit, Scripture points to God giving individuals certain special gifts of a spiritual nature for the fulfilling of specific tasks.

spiritual gifts, nature of

In both the OT and the NT God graciously pours out gifts on his people. They are to be welcomed and used for the good of all.

OT examples of God giving special gifts

God's gracious provision from above

Joel 2:23–24 Be glad, O people of Zion, rejoice in the LORD your God, for he has given you the autumn rains in righteousness. He sends you abundant showers, both autumn and spring rains, as before. The threshing-floors will be filled with grain; the vats will overflow with new wine and oil.   *See also* **Ex** 16:4,8,13–14; **Dt** 11:14; **1Ki** 17:6; **Job** 5:10; **Isa** 55:10

Distribution of land to tribes

Jos 13:6–7 ". . . Be sure to allocate this land to Israel for an inheritance, as I [the LORD] have instructed you, and divide it as an inheritance among the nine tribes and half of the tribe of Manasseh."   *See also* **Eze** 47:21

The future promise of spiritual gifts

Joel 2:28–29 "And afterwards, I will pour out my Spirit on all people. Your sons and daughters will prophesy, your old men will dream dreams, your young men will see visions. Even on my servants, both men and women, I will pour out my Spirit in those days."   *See also* **Ac** 2:17–18

In his earthly ministry Jesus Christ offers supernatural gifts

Mt 11:28 "Come to me, all you who are weary and burdened, and I will give you rest."   *See also* **Mt** 16:19; **Lk** 10:19; **Jn** 4:14; 6:51

Spiritual gifts linked with grace

Ro 12:6 We have different gifts, according to the grace given us . . .   *See also* **Mt** 10:8; **1Co** 4:7

Specific reference to spiritual gifts

1Co 12:1 Now about spiritual gifts, brothers and sisters, I do not want you to be ignorant.   *See also* **Ro** 1:11; **1Co** 14:1,12,37

Diverse gifts, one giver

1Co 12:4–6 There are different kinds of gifts, but the same Spirit. There are different kinds of service, but the same Lord. There are different kinds of working, but the same God works all of them in everyone.   *See also* **Ro** 12:6–8; **1Co** 7:7,17; 12:8–11,27; **Eph** 4:11; **Heb** 2:4; **1Pe** 4:10–11

The purpose of spiritual gifts is to build up the church

1Co 14:12 . . . Since you are eager to have spiritual gifts, try to excel in gifts that build up the church.   *See also* **1Co** 12:7; 14:2–5,17–19,26,31; **Eph** 4:16

The body of Christ benefits from these varied gifts

1Co 12:12 The body is a unit, though it is made up of many parts; and though all its parts are many, they form one body. So it is with Christ.   *See also* **1Co** 12:14–31; **Ro** 12:4–6

Encouragement to aspire to the greater spiritual gifts 1Co 12:31; 14:1

The importance of love in exercising spiritual gifts

1Co 13:1 If I speak in human or angelic tongues, but have not love, I am only a resounding gong or a clanging cymbal.   *See also* **Ro** 12:5–9; **1Co** 14:1

Warnings about spiritual gifts

1Co 14:39 Therefore, my brothers and sisters, be eager to prophesy, and do not forbid speaking in tongues.   *See also* **1Co** 14:37; **1Th** 5:19–20   *See also mercifulness.*

spiritual gifts, responsibility

A spiritual gift may be intended to equip its recipient for a specific function or appointment. Those who are equipped in this way need the enabling power of God's spirit to carry out their appointed tasks.

OT examples of God's gifts or appointments

God appoints prophets

Jer 1:5 "Before I formed you [Jeremiah] in the womb I knew you, before you were born I set you apart; I appointed you as a prophet to the nations."

God appoints Israel's kings

1Sa 15:11 "I am grieved that I have made Saul king . . ." . . .   *See also* **2Sa** 7:8; 12:7

God appoints the Persian king Cyrus

Isa 45:1 "This is what the LORD says to his anointed, to Cyrus, whose right hand I take hold of . . ."   *See also* **Isa** 41:2

God empowers leaders and kings with his Spirit

Nu 27:18 So the LORD said to Moses, "Take Joshua son of Nun, a man in whom is the spirit, and lay your hand on him."   *See also* **Jdg** 3:10; 6:34; 11:29; 13:25; 14:6,19; 15:14; **1Sa** 10:6,10; 11:6; 16:13–14

The Spirit is given to the servant of the LORD

Isa 42:1 "Here is my servant, whom I uphold, my chosen one in whom I delight; I will put my Spirit on him and he will bring justice to the nations."   *See also* **Isa** 61:1

Jesus Christ is endowed with the Holy Spirit

Mt 3:16–17 As soon as Jesus was baptised, he went up out of the water. At that moment heaven was opened, and he saw the Spirit of God descending like a dove and lighting on him. And a voice from heaven said, "This is my Son, whom I love; with him I am well pleased." pp Mk 1:10 11 pp Lk 3:21–22   *See also* **Jn** 1:32–33; **Ac** 10:38

The apostles are endowed with the Holy Spirit

Ac 1:8 "But you [the apostles] will receive power when the Holy Spirit comes on you; and you will be my witnesses . . ."

Spiritual gifts given to the church

Eph 4:11 It was he [Christ] who gave some to be apostles, some to be prophets, some to be evangelists, and some to be pastors and teachers.   *See also* **1Co** 12:28

Many functions within the church yet unity is preserved

Eph 4:4–7 There is one body and one Spirit— just as you were called to one hope when you were called—one Lord, one faith, one baptism . . .   *See also* **1Co** 12:4–11

All Christians are appointed to build up the church

Eph 4:15–16 Instead, speaking the truth in love, we will in all things grow up into him who is the Head, that is, Christ. From him the whole body, joined and held together by every supporting ligament, grows and builds itself up in love, as each part does its work.   *See also* **1Co** 12:12

The experience of spiritual gifts

Associated with the laying on of hands

2Ti 1:6–7 For this reason I remind you to fan into flame the gift of God, which is in you through the laying on of my hands. For God did not give us a spirit of timidity, but a spirit of power, of love and of self-discipline.   *See also* **Nu** 8:10; 27:18; **Dt** 34:9; **Ac** 6:6; **1Ti** 4:14; 5:22

Associated with prayer and fasting

Ac 14:23 Paul and Barnabas appointed elders for them [new disciples] in each church and, with prayer and fasting, committed them to the Lord . . .   *See also* **Ac** 13:3

Spiritual gifts must not to be neglected

1Ti 4:14 Do not neglect your gift, which was given you [Timothy] through a prophetic message when the body of elders laid their hands on you. *See also* **Lk** 19:11–26

---

spiritual growth

Scripture uses a number of images to emphasise that believers are meant to grow in their faith, understanding, holiness and commitment. It also provides advice on how this may be achieved.

---

spiritual growth, means of

God has provided various means by which believers may grow spiritually.

God supplies the resources for spiritual growth

Php 2:13 . . . it is God who works in you to will and to act according to his good purpose.

2Pe 1:3 His [Jesus'] divine power has given us everything we need for life and godliness through our knowledge of him who called us by his own glory and goodness.   *See also* **Jn** 1:16; 4:14; 15:2,5; **1Co** 10:13; **2Co** 3:18; 9:10; **Gal** 5:22–23; **Php** 1:6; **Col** 2:19; **Jas** 1:17; 4:6; **Jude** 24

God's people must make efforts to grow spiritually

Php 2:12 . . . continue to work out your salvation with fear and trembling,

2Pe 1:5–9 . . . make every effort to add to your faith goodness; and to goodness, knowledge; and to knowledge, self-control; and to self-control, perseverance; and to perseverance, godliness; and to godliness, mutual affection; and to mutual affection, love . . .

See also **Ro** 6:19; **2Co** 7:1; **Gal** 5:16,25; **Eph** 5:15–16; 6:11–13; **1Ti** 4:7; 6:11–12; **2Ti** 1:6; **2Pe** 3:14; **1Jn** 3:3; **Jude** 20

Specific means of spiritual growth
Death to self-interest
Col 3:5 Put to death, therefore, whatever belongs to your earthly nature: sexual immorality, impurity, lust, evil desires and greed, which is idolatry. *See also* **Mt** 16:24 pp **Mk** 8:34 pp **Lk** 9:23; **Ro** 6:6,12; 8:13; **Eph** 4:22; **Col** 3:9; **1Pe** 1:14; 2:11
The Scriptures
2Ti 3:16–17 All Scripture is God-breathed and is useful for teaching, rebuking, correcting and training in righteousness, so that God's servant may be thoroughly equipped for every good work.   *See also* **Jos** 1:8; **Ps** 19:7–8; 119:9–11; **Jn** 17:17; **Eph** 6:17; **Col** 3:16; **1Pe** 2:2; **1Jn** 2:14
Prayer
Mt 6:13 " 'And lead us not into temptation, but deliver us from the evil one." pp **Lk** 11:4
Col 4:2 Devote yourselves to prayer, being watchful and thankful.   *See also* **1Ch** 16:11; **Mt** 7:11 pp **Lk** 11:13; **Mt** 26:41 pp **Mk** 14:38 pp **Lk** 22:46; **Jn** 16:24; **Ac** 4:29–31; **Eph** 6:18; **1Th** 5:17; **Jas** 1:5

Focusing on Jesus Christ
Heb 3:1 Therefore, holy brothers and sisters, who share in the heavenly calling, fix your thoughts on Jesus, the apostle and high priest whom we confess.   *See also* **Mt** 11:29; **Jn** 13:15; **Ro** 15:5; **Php** 2:5; **Heb** 12:2–3; **1Pe** 2:21; **1Jn** 2:6

The role of the Holy Spirit in spiritual growth
Eph 3:16–18 I pray that out of his glorious riches he may strengthen you with power through his Spirit in your inner being, so that Christ may dwell in your hearts through faith. And I pray that you, being rooted and established in love, may have power, together with all the saints, to grasp how wide and long and high and deep is the love of Christ,   *See also* **Eph** 1:13–14,17; 2:19–22
Christian leadership
Eph 4:11–13 It was he [Christ] who gave some to be apostles, some to be prophets, some to be evangelists, and some to be pastors and teachers, to prepare God's people for works of service, so that the body of Christ may be built up until we all reach unity in the faith and in the knowledge of the Son of God and become mature, attaining to the whole measure of the fulness of Christ.   *See also* **1Co** 4:16; 11:1; **Php** 1:25; 3:17; **Heb** 13:7,17; **1Pe** 5:2–3
Faith in God
Eph 6:16 . . . take up the shield of faith, with which you can extinguish all the flaming arrows of the evil one.   *See also* **Heb** 11:6; **1Jn** 5:4
Suffering and testing
Ro 5:3–4 . . . we also rejoice in our sufferings, because we know that suffering produces perseverance; perseverance, character; and character, hope.   *See also* **Job** 23:10; **Ps** 119:67; **Zec** 13:9; **Heb** 12:10–11; **1Pe** 1:6–7; **Jas** 1:2–4
Perseverance
Heb 12:1 . . . let us throw off everything that hinders and the sin that so easily entangles, and let us run with perseverance the race marked out for us.   *See also* **Php** 3:12–14; **1Ti** 4:15
Cultivating wholesome thinking
Php 4:8 Finally, brothers and sisters, whatever is

true, whatever is noble, whatever is right, whatever is pure, whatever is lovely, whatever is admirable—if anything is excellent or praiseworthy—think about such things.

God will bring the spiritual growth of believers to completion
1Jn 3:2 Dear friends, now we are children of God, and what we will be has not yet been made known. But we know that when he appears, we shall be like him, for we shall see him as he is.   *See also* **Eph** 5:25–27; **Php** 1:6; **Jude** 24–25; **Rev** 21:2   *See also commitment; faith; perseverance; prayer; spiritual gifts.*

---

spiritual growth, nature of
Having given spiritual life to his people, God expects them to grow to maturity.

God desires the spiritual growth of his people
Mt 5:48 "Be perfect, therefore, as your heavenly Father is perfect."

Heb 6:1 . . . let us leave the elementary teachings about Christ and go on to maturity, not laying again the foundation of repentance from acts that lead to death, and of faith in God,   *See also* **2Co** 13:9–11; **Eph** 1:4; 2:10; 3:17–19; **Php** 3:12; **1Th** 4:1,7; **2Ti** 1:9

Christlikeness is the goal of spiritual growth
Ro 8:29 . . . those God foreknew he also predestined to be conformed to the likeness of his Son, that he might be the firstborn among many brothers and sisters.   *See also* **Eph** 4:13–15; **Php** 2:5; **1Jn** 3:2–3

Aspects of spiritual growth
Growth in grace
2Pe 3:18 . . . grow in the grace and knowledge of our Lord and Saviour Jesus Christ. To him be glory both now and for ever! Amen.   *See also* **Pr** 4:18; **1Pe** 2:1–3
Growth in faith
2Th 1:3 We [Paul, Silas and Timothy] ought always to thank God for you, brothers and sisters,

and rightly so, because your faith is growing more and more, and the love every one of you has for each other is increasing.   *See also* **2Co** 10:15
Growth in love
1Th 3:12 May the Lord make your love increase and overflow for each other and for everyone else, just as ours does for you.   *See also* **Ro** 5:5; **1Co** 14:1; **Php** 1:9; **1Th** 4:9–10; **Heb** 10:24; **1Jn** 4:7–21; 5:1–3
Growth in understanding
Ps 119:27 Let me understand the teaching of your precepts; then I will meditate on your wonders.

1Co 14:20 Brothers and sisters, stop thinking like children. In regard to evil be infants, but in your thinking be adults.   *See also* **Ps** 119:97–99; **Ro** 12:2; 16:19; **1Co** 13:11; **Eph** 1:17–19; **Php** 1:9–10; **Col** 1:9; **Heb** 5:14
Growth in holiness
2Co 7:1 . . . let us purify ourselves from everything that contaminates body and spirit, perfecting holiness out of reverence for God.   *See also* **Eph** 5:25–26; **Heb** 2:11; 10:10–14; 12:14; 13:12; **1Pe** 1:15–16
Growth in fruitfulness
Jn 15:16 "You [the disciples] did not choose me [Jesus], but I chose you and appointed you to go and bear fruit—fruit that will last . . ."   *See also* **Mt** 13:23 pp **Mk** 4:20 pp **Lk** 8:15; **Jn** 15:2,8; **Php** 1:11; **Col** 1:10
Growth in contentment
Php 4:11–12 . . . I [Paul] have learned to be content whatever the circumstances . . .   *See also* **1Ti** 6:6; **Heb** 13:5

Examples of spiritual growth
In individuals 1Sa 2:26; **Lk** 1:80
Jesus Christ: **Lk** 2:40,52
Paul: **Ac** 9:22; **1Co** 9:26–27; **Php** 3:12–14
Ac 18:26; **Phm** 11; **3Jn** 2–3
In the church Ac 9:31; 11:26; 16:5; **2Co** 10:15; **Col** 1:6; **1Th** 2:13; **2Th** 1:3   *See also abiding in Christ; Christlikeness; church; purpose; discipleship; fruit, spiritual; holiness; maturity, spiritual; sanctification; spirituality.*

spiritual warfare

The struggle against the forces of evil, which is a constant feature of the life of faith. Scripture locates the origins of spiritual warfare in the rebellion of Satan and his angels against God and affirms the hope of God's final victory over such forces through Jesus Christ's death and resurrection.

spiritual warfare, armour

The armour of God refers to the resources that Christians possess for defending themselves against the attacks of the world, the flesh and the devil.

God is the believer's strength and shield

Ps 28:7-8 The LORD is my strength and my shield; my heart trusts in him, and I am helped. My heart leaps for joy and I will give thanks to him in song. The LORD is the strength of his people . . . *See also* **Ge** 15:1; **Dt** 33:29; **Ps** 3:3; 7:10; 119:114

Believers should be rightly clothed for battle

Ro 13:12-14 The night is nearly over; the day is almost here. So let us put aside the deeds of darkness and put on the armour of light. Let us behave decently, as in the daytime, not in orgies and drunkenness, not in sexual immorality and debauchery, not in dissension and jealousy. Rather, clothe yourselves with the Lord Jesus Christ, and do not think about how to gratify the desires of the sinful nature. *See also* **Eph** 4:22-24; **Col** 3:9,12-14; **1Pe** 4:1

Believers should put on the full armour of God
The belt of truth
Eph 6:14 Stand firm then, with the belt of truth buckled round your waist . . .
The importance of sound teaching: a good understanding of God's truth counters Satan's deceit: **Ps** 119:95,116; **Eph** 4:14-15; **Col** 2:8; **2Ti** 1:13-14; **1Pe** 1:13
The breastplate of righteousness
Eph 6:14 Stand firm then . . . with the

breastplate of righteousness in place,
Assurance that believers are righteous in God's sight will counter Satan's accusations: **Pr** 4:23; 13:6; **Isa** 61:10; **Zec** 3:1-4
The gospel of peace
Eph 6:15 and with your feet fitted with the readiness that comes from the gospel of peace.
The peace of God reassures and gives confidence in times of trouble: **Jn** 14:27; 16:33; **Php** 4:6-7
The shield of faith
Eph 6:16 In addition to all this, take up the shield of faith, with which you can extinguish all the flaming arrows of the evil one.
Exercising faith draws strength from God, guards against deception and helps overcome temptation: **Ro** 1:17; **Hab** 2:4; **1Pe** 5:9; **1Jn** 5:4
The helmet of salvation
Eph 6:17 Take the helmet of salvation . . .
The expectation of future glory encourages the Christian soldier and helps overcome despair: **1Th** 5:8-9; **Tit** 2:11-14; **1Jn** 3:3

The Christian's spiritual weapons
2Co 10:4 The weapons we fight with are not the weapons of the world. On the contrary, they have divine power to demolish strongholds.
The sword of the Spirit
Eph 6:17 Take . . . the sword of the Spirit, which is the word of God.
The Scriptures give readiness and confidence in battle and a sure defence against the evil one: **Ps** 119:11; **2Ti** 3:16-17; **Heb** 4:12
The armour of God is worn with prayer
Eph 6:18 And pray in the Spirit on all occasions with all kinds of prayers and requests. With this in mind, be alert and always keep on praying for all the saints.
Prayer ensures that believers recognise their need to turn to God and depend on him alone: **Ps** 55:16-18; **Heb** 4:16; **Jas** 5:16 *See also equipping, spiritual; faith; hope, as confidence; peace, experience; witnessing, and Holy Spirit.*

spiritual warfare, causes
Spiritual warfare has its origin in a rebellion of many angels against God. Satan is seen as the prince of this world, leading an array of forces

opposed to God. Although disarmed by Jesus Christ on the cross, they remain a powerful threat to the church and to individual believers.

Satan and his angels fall

2Pe 2:4 . . . God did not spare angels when they sinned, but sent them to hell, putting them into gloomy dungeons to be held for judgment; *See also* **Isa** 14:12–15; **Eze** 28:12–19; **1Ti** 3:6; **Jude** 6

Satan and his angels comprise a well-organised army

Eph 6:12 For our struggle is not against flesh and blood, but against the rulers, against the authorities, against the powers of this dark world and against the spiritual forces of evil in the heavenly realms.   *See also* **Col** 1:13

Satan and his angels will ultimately be fully disarmed by Jesus Christ

Col 2:15 And having disarmed the powers and authorities, he [Christ] made a public spectacle of them, triumphing over them by the cross.
Rev 12:7–9 And there was war in heaven. Michael and his angels fought against the dragon, and the dragon and his angels fought back. But he was not strong enough, and they lost their place in heaven . . .   *See also* **Mk** 3:27 pp **Mt** 12:29; **Lk** 10:18; **Jn** 12:31; **Heb** 2:14; **1Jn** 3:8

Satan persecutes the church

Rev 12:13 When the dragon saw that he had been hurled to the earth, he pursued the woman who had given birth to the male child.   *See also* **Rev** 2:10; 13:7

Satan opposes the gospel

2Co 4:4 The god of this age has blinded the minds of unbelievers, so that they cannot see the light of the gospel of the glory of Christ, who is the image of God.   *See also* **Mt** 13:19 pp **Mk** 4:15 pp **Lk** 8:12; **Mt** 13:38–39; **1Th** 2:2,18
Examples of opposition to the first Christians
Ac 6:8–14; 7:54–58; 8:1–3
Opposition to Paul and his companions: **Ac** 13:6–12,44–45; 17:13; 18:6,12

Violent hostility to Paul and his companions: **Ac** 9:23; 14:5,19; 16:16–24; 17:5–6; 19:23–29; 20:3; 21:27–36

Jewish plots against Paul in Jerusalem: **Ac** 23:12–15; 25:3

Satan attacks individual believers

Rev 12:17 Then the dragon was enraged at the woman and went off to make war against the rest of her offspring—those who obey God's commandments and hold to the testimony of Jesus.   *See also* **Job** 2:7; **Lk** 22:31–32; **2Ti** 3:12; **1Pe** 5:8   *See also jealousy; persecution.*

spiritual warfare, conflict

The warfare believers must fight is spiritual, personal, intense and continual. It calls for courage, determination and prayer, and therefore believers must stand in God's strength and use the armour he has provided.

General descriptions of spiritual conflict
It is spiritual

Eph 6:12 For our [believers'] struggle is not against flesh and blood, but against the rulers, against the authorities, against the powers of this dark world and against the spiritual forces of evil in the heavenly realms.   *See also* **Zec** 4:6; **2Co** 10:3–4; **Gal** 5:17; **1Pe** 2:11

It is personal

Lk 22:31–32 "Simon, Simon, Satan has asked to sift you as wheat. But I [Jesus] have prayed for you, Simon, that your faith may not fail . . ."   *See also* **Ro** 7:23; **2Ti** 3:12; 4:18

It is strenuous

Heb 12:4 In your struggle against sin, you have not yet resisted to the point of shedding your blood.   *See also* **Jn** 16:33; **Php** 1:27–30; **1Pe** 4:12–13

It is continual

Eph 6:13 Therefore put on the full armour of God, so that when the day of evil comes, you may be able to stand your ground, and after you have done everything, to stand.   *See also* **2Ti** 2:3; **Heb** 3:13; **Rev** 12:10

How believers are to fight
With courage
1Co 16:13 Be on your guard; stand firm in the faith; be courageous; be strong.   *See also* **Jos** 1:9; 10:25; **2Ch** 32:6–8
With determination
1Ti 6:12 Fight the good fight of the faith. Take hold of the eternal life to which you were called . . .   *See also* **2Th** 1:4; **Heb** 10:23; **1Pe** 5:9–10
With watchfulness
1Pe 5:8 Be self-controlled and alert. Your enemy the devil prowls around like a roaring lion looking for someone to devour.   *See also* **1Co** 16:13; **Gal** 6:1; **Eph** 6:18
With prayer
Eph 6:18 And pray in the Spirit on all occasions with all kinds of prayers and requests. With this in mind, be alert and always keep on praying for all the saints.   *See also* **Ex** 17:11; **Mt** 6:13 pp Lk 11:4; **Mt** 26:41 pp Mk 14:38 pp Lk 22:46; **Ac** 12:5; **2Th** 3:2
Standing in God's strength
Eph 6:10 Finally, be strong in the Lord and in his mighty power.   *See also* **1Sa** 17:45; **2Sa** 22:40; **Ps** 18:32–36; 118:8; **Eph** 3:16; **Php** 4:13; **2Ti** 2:1
Using the armour of God
Eph 6:11 Put on the full armour of God so that you can take your stand against the devil's schemes.   *See also* **Ro** 13:12–14; **2Co** 10:4; **Eph** 6:13–17   *See also perseverance; suffering, encouragements in; watchfulness, believers.*

---

spiritual warfare, enemies
Christians are at war with the world, the flesh and the devil. Satan empowers the world to attack believers externally, persecuting, deceiving and seducing them. Internally, sinfulness frustrates the efforts of believers to serve God fully.

The world is an enemy
Jas 4:4 You adulterous people, don't you know that friendship with the world is hatred towards God? Anyone who chooses to be a friend of the world becomes an enemy of God.   *See also* **Ro** 12:2; **1Jn** 2:15–17; 5:4

The world hates Christians
Jn 15:19–20 "If you belonged to the world, it would love you as its own. As it is, you do not belong to the world, but I have chosen you out of the world. That is why the world hates you . . ."   *See also* **Mt** 5:10–12 pp Lk 6:22; **Jn** 16:2; 17:14; **1Pe** 4:12–16; **1Jn** 3:13; **Rev** 13:7
The world has its own false teaching and religion
Col 2:8 See to it that no-one takes you captive through hollow and deceptive philosophy, which depends on human tradition and the basic principles of this world rather than on Christ.   *See also* **1Ti** 4:1; **2Ti** 4:3–4; **1Jn** 4:1; **2Jn** 7–11; **Jude** 3–4; **Rev** 13:11; 19:20
The world seeks to seduce Christians
1Jn 2:16 For everything in the world—the cravings of sinful people, the lust of their eyes and the boasting of what they have and do—comes not from the Father but from the world.   *See also* **Lk** 12:15,19; **2Ti** 4:10; **Tit** 2:12; **Heb** 11:24–25; **Rev** 17:1–5

Sinful human nature is an enemy
Gal 5:17 For the sinful nature desires what is contrary to the Spirit, and the Spirit what is contrary to the sinful nature. They are in conflict with each other, so that you do not do what you want.

1Pe 2:11 Dear friends, I urge you, as aliens and strangers in the world, to abstain from sinful desires, which war against your soul.   *See also* **Ro** 6:12; 7:14–23; 8:13; **Gal** 5:24; **Col** 3:5; **Heb** 12:4; **Jas** 4:1

The devil is an enemy
1Pe 5:8 . . . Your enemy the devil prowls around like a roaring lion looking for someone to devour.   *See also* **Mt** 13:39 pp Mk 4:15 pp Lk 8:12; **Jn** 17:15; **2Th** 3:3; **Rev** 2:10; 12:17
He seeks to tempt Christians
1Th 3:5 . . . I was afraid that in some way the tempter might have tempted you and our efforts might have been useless.   *See also* **Ge** 3:1–6; **Heb** 2:18; 4:15
He seeks to deceive
2Co 11:3 But I am afraid that just as Eve was

deceived by the serpent's cunning, your minds may somehow be led astray from your sincere and pure devotion to Christ.

Rev 12:9 The great dragon was hurled down— that ancient serpent called the devil, or Satan, who leads the whole world astray . . . *See also* **Ge** 3:13; **2Co** 2:11; 4:4; 11:4; **Rev** 20:3

He constantly seeks to accuse believers

Rev 12:10 . . . ". . . For the accuser of our brothers and sisters, who accuses them before our God day and night, has been hurled down." *See also* **Job** 1:9–11; **Zec** 3:1   *See also flesh, sinful nature; life, spiritual; sin, avoidance; temptation, resisting.*

---

spirituality

The quality of life generated and nourished by the Spirit of God, in which believers experience the power and presence of God in their lives. True spirituality comes from living under the control of the Holy Spirit and is evidenced by the fruit of the Spirit, spiritual maturity and growth in holiness.

The foundations of spirituality

The need for spiritual renewal 1Co 2:14; **Ro** 7:14; **Jude** 19

Believers have been renewed spiritually

Jn 3:5–8 Jesus answered, "I tell you [Nicodemus] the truth, no-one can enter the kingdom of God without being born of water and the Spirit. Flesh gives birth to flesh, but the Spirit gives birth to spirit . . ." *See also* **Ro** 8:11; **Tit** 3:5; **1Pe** 1:3,23

Faith

Heb 11:6 And without faith it is impossible to please God, because anyone who comes to him must believe that he exists and that he rewards those who earnestly seek him. *See also* **Jn** 6:53–58; 14:1; 20:31; **Ac** 16:31; **Ro** 10:9–10

A longing for God

Ps 27:8 My heart says of you, "Seek his face!" Your face, LORD, I will seek. *See also* **Ps** 119:2; 143:5–6; **Php** 3:10–14

The nature of spirituality
Living under the Spirit's control

Ro 8:5–9 Those who live according to the sinful nature have their minds set on what that nature desires; but those who live in accordance with the Spirit have their minds set on what the Spirit desires . . . You, however, are controlled not by the sinful nature but by the Spirit, if the Spirit of God lives in you. And if anyone does not have the Spirit of Christ, that person does not belong to Christ. *See also* **Ro** 8:12–13; **Gal** 5:16–17; **Eph** 5:18

Reflecting Jesus Christ's character

2Co 3:18 And we, who with unveiled faces all reflect the Lord's glory, are being transformed into his likeness with ever-increasing glory, which comes from the Lord, who is the Spirit. *See also* **Ro** 8:29; **1Jn** 3:2–3

Intimacy with God through the Spirit

Ro 8:14–16 . . . For you did not receive a spirit that makes you a slave again to fear, but you received the Spirit of adoption. And by him we cry, "*Abba*, Father." . . . *See also* **Gal** 4:6

Evidence of spirituality
Bearing spiritual fruit

Gal 5:22–23 But the fruit of the Spirit is love, joy, peace, patience, kindness, goodness, faithfulness, gentleness and self-control. Against such things there is no law. *See also* **Mt** 7:17; **Jn** 15:5–8; **Ro** 14:17; **Eph** 5:8–9

Love for one another

1Jn 4:7 Dear friends, let us love one another, for love comes from God. Everyone who loves has been born of God and knows God. *See also* **Jn** 13:34–35; **1Co** 13:1–4; **Col** 3:12

Spiritual maturity

1Co 3:1–3 Brothers and sisters, I [Paul] could not address you as spiritual but as worldly—mere infants in Christ . . . *See also* **1Co** 14:20; **Heb** 5:13–14

Showing concern for weaker believers

Gal 6:1 Brothers and sisters, if someone is caught in a sin, you who are spiritual should restore that person gently. But watch yourself, or you also may be tempted. *See also* **Ro** 14:1–3,19–21; **1Co** 8:9–13

Understanding spiritual truths
1Co 2:9–13 . . . We have not received the spirit of the world but the Spirit who is from God, that we may understand what God has freely given us . . . *See also* **Jn** 14:17; 16:13–15; **1Co** 2:15–16

Holiness
Tit 2:12 It [God's grace] teaches us to say "No" to ungodliness and worldly passions, and to live self-controlled, upright and godly lives in this present age, *See also* **Ro** 12:1–2; **1Co** 6:19–20; **Gal** 5:24; **Col** 3:1–2

Obedience Jn 15:10; **1Jn** 2:2–6; 5:2–3

Aids to spirituality
Co-operation with the Spirit
Gal 5:25 Since we live by the Spirit, let us keep in step with the Spirit. *See also* **Ac** 7:51; **Eph** 4:30; **1Th** 5:19

Meditation on God's word Jos 1:8; **Jn** 17:7; **2Ti** 3:15–17

Spending time with God Lk 6:12; **Mk** 1:35; **Ac** 4:13

Encouragement of others
Heb 10:24 And let us consider how we may spur one another on towards love and good deeds. *See also* **Col** 3:16; **1Th** 2:11–12

Tests and trials
Jas 1:2–4 . . . you know that the testing of your faith develops perseverance. Perseverance must finish its work so that you may be mature and complete, not lacking anything. *See also* **Ro** 5:3–4; **1Pe** 1:6–7

Examples of spirituality
Ge 5:24; 6:9
Moses: **Nu** 12:3,6–8
David: **1Sa** 13:14; **Ac** 13:22
Stephen: **Ac** 6:5,8

Ac 11:24 *See also Christlikeness; fellowship, with God; holiness; life, spiritual; maturity, spiritual; sanctification; spiritual growth.*

---

suffering
The experience of pain or distress, both physical and emotional. Scripture is thoroughly realistic about the place of suffering in the world and in the lives of believers. To become a Christian is not to escape from suffering, but to be able to bear suffering with dignity and hope.

---

suffering, and hardship
Scripture provides examples of types of hardship which people may expect to encounter.

Different kinds of hardship
Poverty
Pr 10:15 The wealth of the rich is their fortified city, but poverty is the ruin of the poor. *See also* **Dt** 15:11; **Job** 24:5–11; **Mt** 26:11 pp **Mk** 14:7; **Jn** 12:8

Hunger and thirst
Ps 107:4–5 Some wandered in desert wastelands, finding no way to a city where they could settle. They were hungry and thirsty, and their lives ebbed away. *See also* **Ge** 41:53–57; **Ex** 15:22–24; 16:2–3; 17:1–3; **Nu** 11:4–6; **1Ki** 17:7–12; **Ne** 5:1–5; **Mt** 4:2 pp **Lk** 4:2

Hard labour
Ge 3:17–19 To Adam he [God] said, "Because you listened to your wife and ate from the tree about which I commanded you, 'You must not eat of it,' Cursed is the ground because of you; through painful toil you will eat of it all the days of your life. It will produce thorns and thistles for you, and you will eat the plants of the field. By the sweat of your brow you will eat your food until you return to the ground, since from it you were taken; for dust you are and to dust you will return." *See also* **Ge** 31:38–42; **2Ch** 10:3–4; **Ecc** 2:21–22; **1Th** 2:9

Oppression
Job 35:9 "People cry out under a load of oppression; they plead for relief from the arm of the powerful." *See also* **Ex** 1:11; 2:23; 5:8–9; **2Ki** 4:1; **Ps** 12:5; 31:9–13; **Ecc** 4:1; **Jer** 6:6; **Am** 3:9; **Jas** 5:4

Danger
Ne 4:21–23 So we [Jews] continued the work with half the men holding spears, from the first light of dawn till the stars came out. At that time I also said to the people, "Have every man and his helper stay inside Jerusalem at night, so that

they can serve us as guards by night and as workers by day." Neither I nor my brothers nor my men nor the guards with me took off our clothes; each had his weapon, even when he went for water.   *See also* **Ex** 18:8; **1Ki** 2:26; **1Ch** 11:15–19; **Ac** 27:27–44

Examples of those who suffered hardship
Israel
Dt 28:47–48 Because you did not serve the LORD your God joyfully and gladly in the time of prosperity, therefore in hunger and thirst, in nakedness and dire poverty, you will serve the enemies the LORD sends against you. He will put an iron yoke on your neck until he has destroyed you.   *See also* **Dt** 8:15; 26:6–7
David was oppressed by his enemies
Ps 132:1 O LORD, remember David and all the hardships he endured.
Paul suffered in serving the Lord
2Co 6:4–5 Rather, as servants of God we commend ourselves in every way: in great endurance; in troubles, hardships and distresses; in beatings, imprisonments and riots; in hard work, sleepless nights and hunger;

God's people must endure hardship
The example of Jesus Christ 2Co 8:9
The suffering of believers
Ac 14:21–22 They [Paul and Barnabas] preached the good news in that city and won a large number of disciples. Then they returned to Lystra, Iconium and Antioch, strengthening the disciples and encouraging them to remain true to the faith. "We must go through many hardships to enter the kingdom of God," they said.   *See also* **1Co** 4:11–13; **2Co** 1:8–9; 11:23–29; **Php** 4:11–14; **2Ti** 2:3; **Heb** 10:34; 11:37–38; 12:7; **Rev** 2:3
The need for faith, courage and endurance 2Co 1:9; **Heb** 3:6; 10:36; **Jas** 1:12; **Rev** 1:9; 14:12

God helps his people through hardship
He provides for them Dt 8:16; 1Ki 17:2–9; 2Co 1:10; **Php** 1:19; 4:19
He comforts them with his love Ro 8:35–39; 2Co 1:3–4; **Heb** 13:5

He sets heaven before them Rev 7:16–17
See also work.

suffering, encouragements in
Believers are encouraged by the loving care and faithful promises of God and by the example, support and prayers of fellow believers. The prospect of heaven helps them to endure.

The encouragement of God's love
The care of the Father
Ps 103:13 As a father has compassion on his children, so the LORD has compassion on those who fear him;   *See also* **Ps** 86:17; **Isa** 50:10; 64:8–9; **Lk** 18:6–7; **Jn** 16:27; 17:11,15; **Ro** 8:32; **2Co** 1:3
The sympathetic understanding of Jesus Christ
Heb 2:18 Because he himself suffered when he was tempted, he is able to help those who are being tempted.   *See also* **Isa** 40:11; 42:3; 53:5; **Lk** 4:18; **Isa** 61:1; **Jn** 14:27; 16:22; **Ro** 8:35–39; **Heb** 4:15; 7:25; 12:3
The comfort of the Spirit
Jn 14:16–17 ". . . I [Jesus] will ask the Father, and he will give you another Counsellor to be with you for ever—the Spirit of truth. The world cannot accept him, because it neither sees him nor knows him. But you know him, for he lives with you and will be in you."   *See also* **Lk** 11:13; **Ro** 5:5; 8:26; **Gal** 5:22–23; **Eph** 3:16; **1Pe** 4:14
The promises of God
Ps 119:50 My comfort in my suffering is this: Your promise preserves my life.

Ro 8:28 And we know that in all things God works for the good of those who love him, who have been called according to his purpose.

2Co 12:9 But he [the Lord] said to me, "My grace is sufficient for you, for my power is made perfect in weakness." Therefore I will boast all the more gladly about my weaknesses, so that Christ's power may rest on me.   *See also* **Isa** 41:10; 43:2–3; **Mt** 6:31–33; **Ro** 15:4; **Php** 4:7; **1Pe** 5:10

The encouragement of the fellowship of believers
Examples from the past
Heb 12:1 Therefore, since we are surrounded by such a great cloud of witnesses, let us throw off everything that hinders and the sin that so easily entangles, and let us run with perseverance the race marked out for us.   *See also* **Ps** 102:17–18; **Jer** 20:11; **Php** 4:11; **Heb** 11:25–26; **Jas** 5:10–11
Support from other believers
1Th 5:11 Therefore encourage one another and build each other up, just as in fact you are doing.   *See also* **Ru** 2:13; **Job** 42:11; **Ac** 28:15; **Ro** 16:4; **2Co** 7:6–7; **Php** 4:14; **Col** 4:11; **1Th** 2:11–12; 4:18; **2Ti** 4:9,11; **Phm** 13; **Heb** 10:25

The encouragement of looking ahead
The assurance of victory
Ro 8:37 No, in all these things we are more than conquerors through him who loved us. *See also* **Ro** 16:20; **1Co** 15:20,25,55–57; **1Th** 4:16–17
The prospect of glory
Ro 8:18 I consider that our present sufferings are not worth comparing with the glory that will be revealed in us.   *See also* **Job** 19:25–26; **Isa** 65:17; **2Co** 4:17–5:1; **2Th** 1:6–7; **2Pe** 3:13; **Jude** 24–25; **Rev** 7:16–17; 21:1–4   *See also fellowship; peace, experience.*

---

suffering, nature of
Since the fall, human beings have suffered in various ways. Scripture provides insights into the nature and place of suffering both in the world and in the lives of believers.

Suffering began with the fall
Ge 2:17; 3:16–19; **Ro** 5:12

Suffering is universal
Job 5:7; 14:1

Different kinds of suffering
Physical pain and illness
Ge 48:1 . . . Joseph was told, "Your father is ill." . . .   *See also* **2Ki** 20:1 pp 2Ch 32:24 pp Isa 38:1; **Job** 2:7; **Ps** 42:10; **Mt** 8:6; 17:15; **Lk** 4:38; **Ac** 28:8; **2Ti** 4:20; **Jas** 5:14
Emotional stress
Ps 55:4–5 My heart is in anguish within me; the terrors of death assail me. Fear and trembling have beset me; horror has overwhelmed me. *See also* **Ge** 35:18; **Pr** 12:25; **Jn** 11:32–35; **Php** 2:27
Spiritual suffering
Ps 22:1 My God, my God, why have you forsaken me? Why are you so far from saving me, so far from the words of my groaning? *See also* **Mt** 27:46 pp Mk 15:34
The prospect of death
Ge 3:19 ." . . dust you [Adam] are and to dust you will return."   *See also* **Ecc** 12:7

Major causes of suffering
The disorder in creation
Ge 3:17 . . . ". . . Cursed is the ground because of you [Adam]; through painful toil you will eat of it all the days of your life."   *See also* **Ge** 12:10; **Joel** 1:4; **Mt** 24:7 pp Lk 21:11; **Ro** 8:22; **Rev** 11:13
Human cruelty
Ps 54:3 Strangers are attacking me; ruthless people seek my life—people without regard for God . . .
Murder: **Ge** 4:8; **Ex** 1:16,22; **1Ki** 21:19; **Mt** 2:16 **Ge** 49:5–7
Oppression: **Ex** 1:11; **Am** 2:6–7; 4:1; **Mal** 3:5 **2Ki** 6:25; 19:17; **2Ch** 10:13–14; **Job** 1:14–15,17; **Am** 1:3,13; **Jas** 5:4–6; **Rev** 6:4
Family troubles
Ps 27:10 Though my father and mother forsake me, the LORD will receive me.   *See also* **1Sa** 1:7; **2Sa** 16:11; **Job** 19:14–19; **Mal** 2:14; **Mt** 10:36; **Jas** 1:27
Old age
Ps 71:9 Do not cast me away when I am old; do not forsake me when my strength is gone. *See also* **Ecc** 12:1–7
Satan's activity
1Jn 5:19 . . . the whole world is under the control of the evil one.   *See also* **Job** 1:12; 2:6–7; **Lk** 13:16; **2Co** 12:7; **Rev** 2:10; 20:7–8

Aggravations to suffering
Memories Job 29:2
Fears Job 3:25; **Heb** 2:15
Resentment Job 2:9

Sin and suffering
They are not necessarily related
Jn 9:3 "Neither this man [who was born blind]
nor his parents sinned," said Jesus, "but this
happened so that the work of God might be
displayed in his life."   *See also* **Job** 2:3; **Lk** 13:2
They are sometimes closely related
Ro 1:18 The wrath of God is being revealed
from heaven against all the godlessness and
wickedness of those who suppress the truth by
their wickedness,   *See also* **Ge** 6:5–7; **Nu** 14:33;
Dt 28:15; **Ps** 107:17; **Eze** 23:49; **Ac** 5:5,10; **Ro**
1:27; **1Co** 11:29–30; **Jude** 7; **Rev** 2:22
God's final judgment
Mt 25:41 ". . . 'Depart from me, you who are
cursed, into the eternal fire prepared for the devil
and his angels.'"   *See also* **Da** 12:2; **Mt** 8:12;
Mk 9:48; **Isa** 66:24; **Rev** 20:15

Effects of suffering
Hardness of heart
Rev 16:9 . . . they cursed the name of God,
who had control over these plagues, but they
refused to repent and glorify him.   *See also* **Ex**
7:22; **Rev** 9:20–21
Repentance 2Ch 33:12; Lk 15:17–18
Blessing
Ps 119:71 It was good for me to be afflicted
so that I might learn your decrees.   *See also* **Isa**
38:17   *See also* sin.

suffering, of believers
Believers ought to expect to suffer as an
inevitable part of their calling. To believe is not to
evade suffering; it is to face it with new
confidence and hope. Rightly approached, suffering
develops the character of believers, equips them
for more effective service, draws believers closer to
Jesus Christ and prepares them for eternal life.

Believers must expect suffering
Jesus Christ foretold it
Mt 10:22 "Everyone will hate you because of

me, but those who stand firm to the end will be
saved." pp **Mk** 13:13   *See also* **Mt** 10:17;
23:34; 24:9; **Lk** 21:16–17
The apostles foretold it
Ac 14:22 . . . "We must go through many
hardships to enter the kingdom of God," . . .
2Ti 3:12 In fact, everyone who wants to live a
godly life in Christ Jesus will be persecuted,
See also **Php** 1:29; **1Jn** 3:13; **Rev** 2:10
The experience of the OT shows it Ro 8:36;
Heb 11:25–26,32–38
The experience of the NT shows it Ac 4:3;
5:40; 9:29; 12:1–3; **2Co** 11:23–29; **Gal** 3:4; **1Th**
2:2,14; **1Pe** 4:4; **Heb** 10:32–34

Suffering for Jesus Christ is commendable
Mt 5:10–12 "Blessed are those who are
persecuted because of righteousness, for theirs is
the kingdom of heaven . . ." pp **Lk** 6:20–23
See also **Ac** 5:41; **2Ti** 1:8; **1Pe** 2:19; 3:17;
4:12–16

Suffering is profitable
It affirms believers' adoption
Heb 12:7 Endure hardship as discipline; God is
treating you as children. For what children are not
disciplined by their parents?   *See also* **Jn** 15:19;
17:14; **Ro** 8:17; **Gal** 6:17; **2Th** 1:4–5
It is the price of godliness
Heb 12:11 No discipline seems pleasant at the
time, but painful. Later on, however, it produces a
harvest of righteousness and peace for those who
have been trained by it.   *See also* **Ps** 119:67,71;
Isa 38:17; **Jn** 15:2; **1Pe** 1:6–7
It is a condition of service
2Co 4:10 We always carry around in our body
the death of Jesus, so that the life of Jesus may
also be revealed in our body.
Col 1:24 Now I [Paul] rejoice in what was suffered
for you, and I fill up in my flesh what is still lacking
in regard to Christ's afflictions, for the sake of his
body, which is the church.   *See also* **Ps** 126:5–6;
Ac 9:16; 20:23–24; **1Co** 4:9–13; **2Co** 1:3–5; **Gal**
4:19; **Php** 3:18; **Col** 2:1; **2Ti** 1:11–12; 2:3,10
It develops trust
2Co 1:9 Indeed, in our hearts we [Paul and

Timothy] felt the sentence of death. But this happened that we might not rely on ourselves but on God, who raises the dead. *See also* 1Pe 4:19

It develops character

Ro 5:3–4 . . . we know that suffering produces perseverance; perseverance, character; and character, hope. *See also* Heb 5:8; Jas 1:3

It deepens fellowship

1Co 12:26 If one part suffers, every part suffers with it; if one part is honoured, every part rejoices with it. *See also* Ro 12:15; 2Co 1:7; 8:2; Gal 4:14–15; 6:2

It draws believers to the Lord

Php 3:8 . . . I [Paul] consider everything a loss compared to the surpassing greatness of knowing Christ Jesus my Lord, for whose sake I have lost all things. I consider them rubbish, that I may gain Christ

Php 3:10 I [Paul] want to know Christ and the power of his resurrection and the fellowship of sharing in his sufferings, becoming like him in his death, *See also* Job 42:5; 2Co 4:8–10; 12:9–10; 1Pe 4:13

It prepares believers for heaven 2Co 4:16–5:4 *See also* Christlikeness; holiness; persecution; spiritual growth.

---

teachableness

A quality in those who desire to learn, present in the disciples of Jesus Christ and seen in Christ's relationship to his Father. Unwillingness to receive the truth leads to spiritual darkness.

The importance of teachableness
For spiritual growth

Heb 12:5–12 . . . Moreover, we have all had human parents who disciplined us and we respected them for it. How much more should we submit to the Father of our spirits and live! Our parents disciplined us for a little while as they thought best; but God disciplines us for our good, that we may share in his holiness . . . *See also* Heb 5:11–14

For a life of obedience

Php 4:9 Whatever you have learned or received or heard from me [Paul], or seen in me—put it

into practice. And the God of peace will be with you. *See also* Jas 1:25; Rev 3:3

For discerning God's guidance

Pr 3:5–6 Trust in the Lord with all your heart and lean not on your own understanding; in all your ways acknowledge him, and he will make your paths straight. *See also* Ps 25:4–5; Ro 12:2

The requirements for teachableness
Eagerness to learn

Pr 18:15 The heart of the discerning acquires knowledge; the ears of the wise seek it out.

Isa 50:4–5 The Sovereign Lord has given me an instructed tongue, to know the word that sustains the weary. He wakens me morning by morning, wakens my ear to listen like one being taught . . . *See also* 2Ch 26:3–5; Ps 27:11; 43:3; 86:11; 119:9–11; 139:23–24; 143:8–10

Willingness to learn

From God: Ex 15:26; Dt 5:27

From God's representatives: Ex 20:18–19; Dt 18:15; 31:12; Ne 8:3,9

From godly parents: Ps 34:11; Pr 4:10–13,20–21; 8:32–33; 13:1; 23:22–23

From the wise: Pr 1:5; 19:20; 22:17; 25:12

From Jesus Christ: Mt 12:42 pp Lk 11:31; Mt 17:5 pp Mk 9:7 pp Lk 9:35; Jn 10:27

From the Holy Spirit: Lk 12:11–12; Rev 2:7

Readiness to ask for help

Ac 8:30–31 . . . "Do you understand what you are reading?" Philip asked. "How can I," he [an Ethiopian eunuch] said, "unless someone explains it to me?" So he invited Philip to come up and sit with him. *See also* Mk 4:10; 9:11,28; 10:10; 13:4; Lk 3:12; 11:1

Readiness to pray for wisdom

Jas 1:5 If any of you lacks wisdom, you should ask God, who gives generously to all without finding fault, and it will be given to you. *See also* 2Ch 20:12; Ps 143:8–10

Readiness to pray for spiritual insight

Eph 1:17–19 I keep asking that the God of our Lord Jesus Christ, the glorious Father, may give you the Spirit of wisdom and revelation, so that you may know him better . . . *See also* Eph 3:16–19; Col 1:9

Humility
1Co 3:18–20 Do not deceive yourselves. If any of you think they are wise by the standards of this age, you should become "fools" so that you may become wise. For the wisdom of this world is foolishness in God's sight. As it is written: "He catches the wise in their craftiness"; and again, "The Lord knows that the thoughts of the wise are futile." *See also* **Job** 6:24; **Pr** 11:2; **Mt** 11:29; 18:3–4; **1Co** 8:1–2; **Jas** 1:21

Living by truth already known
Jn 8:31–32 To the Jews who had believed him, Jesus said, "If you hold to my teaching, you are really my disciples. Then you will know the truth, and the truth will set you free." *See also* **2Pe** 1:5–8

Jesus Christ was willing to be taught by the Father
Jn 15:15 "I [Jesus] no longer call you servants, because servants do not know their master's business. Instead, I have called you friends, for everything that I learned from my Father I have made known to you." *See also* **Jn** 5:30; 8:26–28

Hindrances to teachableness
The activity of the devil
2Co 4:4 The god of this age [Satan or the devil] has blinded the minds of unbelievers, so that they cannot see the light of the gospel of the glory of Christ, who is the image of God. *See also* **2Ti** 2:25–26

Not having the Holy Spirit
1Co 2:14 The person without the Spirit does not accept the things that come from the Spirit of God but considers them foolishness, and cannot understand them because they are spiritually discerned.

Unwillingness to be taught
Isa 48:17–18 This is what the LORD says—your Redeemer, the Holy One of Israel: "I am the LORD your God, who teaches you what is best for you, who directs you in the way you should go. If only you had paid attention to my commands, your peace would have been like a river, your righteousness like the waves of the sea. *See*

also **Ps** 32:9; 81:11–12; **Mt** 13:14–15 pp Mk 4:12 pp Lk 8:10; **Isa** 6:9–10; **Lk** 11:52; 16:31; 19:41–44; **Jas** 1:22–24

Reliance on the wisdom of the world
1Co 1:19–20 For it is written: "I [the Lord] will destroy the wisdom of the wise; the intelligence of the intelligent I will frustrate." . . . *See also* **Isa** 29:14; **Ro** 1:21–23; **2Co** 10:4–5

Being afraid to ask questions
Mk 9:32 But they [the disciples of Jesus] did not understand what he meant and were afraid to ask him about it. pp Lk 9:45

---

temptation
Pressure to yield to influences that can lead people away from God and into sin.

temptation, and Christ
Jesus Christ, like every other human being, knew temptation. However, he never yielded to it. The sinlessness of Christ refers to his obedient refusal to give in to temptation. It does not mean that he did not experience temptation himself.

The temptation of Jesus Christ
Mk 1:13 . . . he [Jesus] was in the desert for forty days, being tempted by Satan . . . pp Mt 4:1–10 pp Lk 4:1–13

The temptation to avoid the cross
Mt 16:21–23 From that time on Jesus began to explain to his disciples that he must go to Jerusalem and suffer many things at the hands of the elders, chief priests and teachers of the law, and that he must be killed and on the third day be raised to life. Peter took him aside and began to rebuke him. "Never, Lord!" he said. "This shall never happen to you!" Jesus turned and said to Peter, "Get behind me, Satan! You are a stumbling-block to me; you do not have in mind the concerns of God, but human concerns." pp Mk 8:31–33 *See also* **Mt** 26:36–44 pp Mk 14:32–42 pp Lk 22:40–46; **Mt** 27:39–44 pp Mk 15:31–32 pp Lk 23:36–37 pp Lk 23:39

The temptation to please the crowd

Lk 11:16 Others tested him by asking for a sign from heaven.　*See also* **Mt** 12:38–39 pp Lk 11:29; **Jn** 2:18; 6:30

The significance of the temptation of Jesus Christ

Believers can identify with Jesus Christ in his temptation

Heb 2:18 Because he [Jesus] himself suffered when he was tempted, he is able to help those who are being tempted.

Believers can have confidence in the face of temptation

Heb 4:15–16 For we do not have a high priest who is unable to sympathise with our weaknesses, but we have one who has been tempted in every way, just as we are—yet was without sin. Let us then approach the throne of grace with confidence, so that we may receive mercy and find grace to help us in our time of need.

temptation, resisting

Being tempted is not in itself a sin. Sin arises when believers give in to temptation. Scripture urges believers to resist temptation, and gives them encouragement to face it.

Encouragement to those facing temptation

Jas 1:12 Blessed are those who persevere under trial, because when they have stood the test, they will receive the crown of life that God has promised to those who love him.　*See also* **Ro** 8:37; **Heb** 2:18; 4:15–16; **Jas** 1:2–3; 1Jn 4:4

Finding in God and his word resources to overcome temptation

Da 11:32 "With flattery he [the king of the North] will corrupt those who have violated the covenant, but the people who know their God will firmly resist him."　*See also* **Pr** 2:1–2,12–15; **Mt** 6:13 pp Lk 11:4; 1Ti 6:11–12; **Jas** 4:7

Practical suggestions for overcoming temptation

Overcoming temptation through prayer

Mt 26:41 "Watch and pray so that you will not fall into temptation. The spirit is willing, but the body is weak." pp Mk 14:38 pp Lk 22:40　*See also* **Mt** 18:8–9; 1Co 7:5

Overcoming temptation through personal discipline Heb 12:4,7; 2Pe 3:17

Encouragements to resist temptation

Gal 6:1 . . . But watch yourself, or you also may be tempted.

1Th 5:22 Avoid every kind of evil.　*See also* **Pr** 1:10–15; **Ro** 6:12–14

Examples of those who did not give in to temptation

Job 1:22 In all this, Job did not sin by charging God with wrongdoing.　*See also* **Ge** 39:7–10; **Job** 2:10; **Jer** 35:5–6; **Da** 1:8

Jesus Christ resisted temptation

Mt 4:4 Jesus answered, "It is written: 'People do not live on bread alone, but on every word that comes from the mouth of God.' " pp Lk 4:4　*See also* **Mt** 4:7 pp Lk 4:12; **Mt** 4:10 pp Lk 4:8　*See also obedience, to God; purity, moral and spiritual; sanctification; self-control; watchfulness, believers.*

temptation, sources

Temptation comes from a number of sources but not from God.

Temptation arising from sinful human nature

Eph 2:1–3 As for you, you were dead in your transgressions and sins, in which you used to live when you followed the ways of this world and of the ruler of the kingdom of the air, the spirit who is now at work in those who are disobedient. All of us also lived among them at one time, gratifying the cravings of our sinful nature and following its desires and thoughts . . .

Jas 1:14 . . . each of you is tempted when, by your own evil desire, you are dragged away and enticed.　*See also* **Mt** 5:29–30 pp Mk 9:43–47; **Mt** 6:23; **Ro** 7:18–23

Temptation from other people

2Pe 2:18 For they [false teachers] mouth empty, boastful words and, by appealing to the lustful desires of sinful human nature, they entice people who are just escaping from those who live in error.   *See also* **Ge** 3:6; **Pr** 5:3–6

Temptation from Satan

Ge 3:1 Now the serpent was more crafty than any of the wild animals the LORD God had made. He said to the woman, "Did God really say, 'You must not eat from any tree in the garden'?"
See also **1Ch** 21:1; **Mt** 4:1 pp Mk 1:13 pp Lk 4:2; **Mk** 4:15 pp Lk 8:12; **1Co** 7:5; **1Th** 3:5

Temptation from the world

1Jn 2:16 For everything in the world—the cravings of sinful people, the lust of their eyes and the boasting of what they have and do—comes not from the Father but from the world.
See also **Mt** 13:22 pp Mk 4:19 pp Lk 8:14

Attractions which lead to temptation
Money

1Ti 6:9–10 Those who want to get rich fall into temptation and a trap and into many foolish and harmful desires that plunge people into ruin and destruction. For the love of money is a root of all kinds of evil. Some people, eager for money, have wandered from the faith and pierced themselves with many griefs.
Power Dt 8:17–18; **2Ch** 26:16
Lust Pr 6:25; 7:21
Pride Pr 11:2

Temptation does not come from God

Jas 1:13 When tempted, no-one should say, "God is tempting me." For God cannot be tempted by evil, nor does he tempt anyone;
See also **Mt** 6:13 pp Lk 11:4   *See also flesh, sinful nature; world.*

---

temptation, universal

Scripture makes clear that all human beings are subject to temptation. It provides examples of individuals who have faced and yielded to such influences.

The inevitability of temptation to do wrong

1Co 10:13 No temptation has seized you except what is common among people . . .
See also **Pr** 7:21–23; **Mt** 13:20–21 pp Mk 4:16–17 pp Lk 8:13; **Lk** 17:1; **Ro** 7:15; **1Co** 10:12; **2Co** 11:3; **1Pe** 1:6

Examples of those who were tempted
Adam and Eve tempted

Ge 3:6–7 When the woman saw that the fruit of the tree was good for food and pleasing to the eye, and also desirable for gaining wisdom, she took some and ate it. She also gave some to her husband, who was with her, and he ate it. Then the eyes of both of them were opened, and they realised that they were naked; so they sewed fig leaves together and made coverings for themselves.
Esau tempted Ge 25:29–34
Achan tempted Jos 7:21
Samson tempted Jdg 14:16–17
David tempted 2Sa 11:2–4
Solomon tempted 1Ki 11:1,4
Gehazi tempted 2Ki 5:20–23
Peter tempted Mt 26:69–75 pp Lk 22:55–62 pp Jn 18:16–18 pp Jn 18:25–27

Help for those facing temptation

Ro 8:31 What, then, shall we say in response to this? If God is for us, who can be against us?   *See also* **Jos** 1:5; **Ro** 8:37–39; **Heb** 4:15–16; 13:5; **1Jn** 2:1; 4:4; **Rev** 3:10   *See also faith, testing of.*

---

thankfulness

Heartfelt gratitude to God, expressed in response to his love and mercy.

Thankfulness for God's goodness

Ps 100:4–5 Enter his gates with thanksgiving and his courts with praise; give thanks to him and praise his name. For the LORD is good and his love endures for ever; his faithfulness continues through all generations.   *See also* **1Ch** 16:8,34–35; **2Ch** 7:3–6; **Ezr** 3:10–11; **Ps** 68:19;

106:1; 116:12–14; 136:1–3,26; **Isa** 63:7; **1Th**
5:18; **Heb** 12:28

Thankfulness for deliverance
From adversity
Ps 35:9–10 Then my soul will rejoice in the
LORD and delight in his salvation. My whole being
will exclaim, "Who is like you, O LORD? You
rescue the poor from those too strong for them,
the poor and needy from those who rob
them."   *See also* **Ps** 31:7–8,21–23; 44:6–8;
66:8–9,16–20; 103:1–5
From slavery in Egypt
Ex 15:20–21 Then Miriam the prophet, Aaron's
sister, took a tambourine in her hand, and all the
women followed her, with tambourines and
dancing. Miriam sang to them: "Sing to the LORD,
for he is highly exalted. The horse and its rider he
has hurled into the sea."   *See also* **Ex** 15:1–18;
Ps 105:1–45; 136:1–26
From the power of death
1Co 15:53–57 . . . "Where, O death, is your
victory? Where, O death, is your sting?" The
sting of death is sin, and the power of sin is the
law. But thanks be to God! He gives us the
victory through our Lord Jesus Christ.

Thankfulness for answered prayer
1Sa 2:1–10 Then Hannah prayed and said:
"My heart rejoices in the LORD; in the LORD my
horn is lifted high. My mouth boasts over my
enemies, for I delight in your deliverance . . ."
See also **Ps** 30:1–12; 66:16–20; 138:1–5; **Jn** 11:40

Thankfulness for others
Phm 4 I [Paul] always thank my God as I
remember you [Philemon] in my prayers,   *See
also* **Ne** 11:17; **Ro** 1:8; **Php** 4:6; **Col** 1:10; 4:2;
1Ti 2:1; **2Ti** 1:3

Thankfulness for Jesus Christ
2Co 9:15 Thanks be to God for his indescribable
gift [Christ]!   *See also* **Lk** 2:25–32,36–38; **Col**
2:6; 3:15–17

Thankfulness for God's provision
Mt 14:19 And he [Jesus] directed the people to

sit down on the grass. Taking the five loaves and
the two fish and looking up to heaven, he gave
thanks and broke the loaves . . . pp Mk 6:41 pp
Lk 9:16 pp Jn 6:11   *See also* **Ps** 147:7–9; **Mt**
15:36 pp Mk 8:6; **Mt** 26:26–27 pp Mk 14:22–23
pp Lk 22:17–19; **Lk** 24:30; **Ac** 27:35; **Ro** 14:6; **1Ti**
4:3

Means of expressing thankfulness to God
In song
Eph 5:19–20 Speak to one another with
psalms, hymns and spiritual songs. Sing and make
music in your heart to the Lord, always giving
thanks to God the Father for everything, in the
name of our Lord Jesus Christ.   *See also* **Ps**
69:30; 95:2; 96:1; **Isa** 55:12
In music Ps 27:6; 92:1–3
In dance Ps 149:3
In worship Ps 95:2; 100:4; **Heb** 12:28   *See also*
hospitality; life, believers' experience; praise; prayer,
answers; worship, elements.

---

tithing
The practice of offering to God a tenth of the
harvest of the land and of livestock, as holy to
the LORD. The idea is also used in a more general
sense, meaning offering one-tenth of one's income
to the Lord.

Tithing was practised before the giving of the OT law
Ge 14:18–20 Then Melchizedek king of Salem
brought out bread and wine. He was priest of
God Most High, and he blessed Abram, saying,
"Blessed be Abram by God Most High, Creator of
heaven and earth. And blessed be God Most High,
who delivered your enemies into your hand."
Then Abram gave him a tenth of everything.
See also **Ge** 28:22; **Heb** 7:1–3

Tithing under the law
Tithing extends to all kinds of produce and livestock
Lev 27:30–32 " 'A tithe of everything from
the land, whether grain from the soil or fruit from

the trees, belongs to the LORD; it is holy to the LORD. If you redeem any of your tithe, you must add a fifth of the value to it. The entire tithe of the herd and flock—every tenth animal that passes under the shepherd's rod—will be holy to the LORD.'"   *See also* **2Ch** 31:5–6; **Ne** 10:35–38; 13:12

All tithes were paid to the Levites Nu 18:21–24; **Ne** 10:37–38; **Heb** 7:5

Tithes were to be paid in a designated place Dt 12:5–6; 14:22–29; 26:2

Levites offered a tenth to the LORD Nu 18:25–29; **Ne** 10:39

Uses of the tithe
Support of the Levites
Nu 18:21 "I [the LORD] give to the Levites all the tithes in Israel as their inheritance in return for the work they do while serving at the Tent of Meeting."   *See also* **2Ch** 31:4

The tithe meal
Dt 14:23 Eat the tithe of your grain, new wine and oil, and the firstborn of your herds and flocks in the presence of the LORD your God at the place he will choose as a dwelling for his Name, so that you may learn to revere the LORD your God always.

A three-yearly gift to the poor
Dt 14:28–29 At the end of every three years, bring all the tithes of that year's produce and store it in your towns, so that the Levites (who have no allotment or inheritance of their own) and the aliens, the fatherless and the widows who live in your towns may come and eat and be satisfied, and so that the LORD your God may bless you in all the work of your hands.

Tithing of minor items must not lead to neglect of major matters
Mt 23:23 "Woe to you, teachers of the law and Pharisees, you hypocrites! You give a tenth of your spices—mint, dill and cummin. But you have neglected the more important matters of the law—justice, mercy and faithfulness. You should have practised the latter, without neglecting the former."   *See also* **Lk** 11:42; 18:9–14

Freewill offerings were made in addition to the tithe
They were given freely
Ex 36:3 They received from Moses all the offerings the Israelites had brought to carry out the work of constructing the sanctuary. And the people continued to bring freewill offerings morning after morning.   *See also* **Lev** 7:12–18; **Nu** 15:3; **Ezr** 1:4; **Ps** 54:6; **Eze** 46:12

They were given according to ability
Dt 16:10 Then celebrate the Feast of Weeks to the LORD your God by giving a freewill offering in proportion to the blessings the LORD your God has given you.   *See also* **Dt** 16:17; **Ac** 11:29; **1Co** 16:2; **2Co** 8:12

Blessing promised to those who tithe
Mal 3:10 "Bring the whole tithe into the storehouse, that there may be food in my house. Test me in this," says the LORD Almighty, "and see if I will not throw open the floodgates of heaven and pour out so much blessing that you will not have room enough for it."   *See also* **Pr** 3:9–10

Failure to tithe and abuses of the tithe
Mal 3:8–10 "Will a mere mortal rob God? Yet you rob me. But you ask, 'How do we rob you?' In tithes and offerings. You are under a curse—the whole nation of you—because you are robbing me. Bring the whole tithe into the storehouse, that there may be food in my house. Test me in this," says the LORD Almighty, "and see if I will not throw open the floodgates of heaven and pour out so much blessing that you will not have room enough for it."   *See also* **Lev** 27:33; **1Sa** 8:15,17; **Ne** 13:10   *See also giving; money.*

unbelief, and life of faith
Believers may go through periods of doubt and indecision, especially on account of difficulties in trusting God or accepting certain aspects of his will for them.

General examples of unbelief in believers
Abraham
Ge 17:17 Abraham fell face down; he laughed and said to himself, "Will a son be born to a man a hundred years old? Will Sarah bear a child at the age of ninety?" *See also* **Ge** 15:8
Sarah Ge 18:13–14
Moses Nu 11:21–22
Gideon Jdg 6:12–13,17,36–40
Elisha's servant 2Ki 4:42–44
Zechariah Lk 1:20
John the Baptist Mt 11:3

The unbelief of Jesus Christ's disciples
Unbelief concerning Jesus Christ's power over the natural world
Mt 8:24–26 . . . The disciples went and woke him [Jesus], saying, "Lord, save us! We're going to drown!" He replied, "You of little faith, why are you so afraid?" Then he got up and rebuked the winds and the waves, and it was completely calm. pp Mk 4:38–40 pp Lk 8:23–25
Mt 14:26 When the disciples saw him [Jesus] walking on the lake, they were terrified. "It's a ghost," they said, and cried out in fear. pp Mk 6:49
Mt 14:29–31 . . . Peter got down out of the boat, walked on the water and came towards Jesus. But when he saw the wind, he was afraid and, beginning to sink, cried out, "Lord, save me!" Immediately Jesus reached out his hand and caught him. "You of little faith," he said, "why did you doubt?"
Mt 16:8–10 . . . Jesus asked, "You of little faith, why are you [his disciples] talking among yourselves about having no bread? Do you still not understand? Don't you remember the five loaves for the five thousand, and how many basketfuls you gathered? Or the seven loaves for the four thousand, and how many basketfuls you gathered?" pp Mk 8:17–21 *See also* **Mk** 6:37 pp Jn 6:7; **Mk** 6:52; **Mt** 15:33 pp Mk 8:4; **Jn** 11:39; **Ac** 12:15–17
Unbelief concerning Jesus Christ's resurrection
Mk 16:14 Later Jesus appeared to the Eleven as they were eating; he rebuked them for their

lack of faith and their stubborn refusal to believe those who had seen him after he had risen.
Lk 24:25 He [Jesus] said to them [two disciples on the way to Emmaus], "How foolish you are, and how slow of heart to believe all that the prophets have spoken!" *See also* **Mk** 16:9–13; **Lk** 24:11,37–41; **Jn** 20:25
Unbelief concerning Jesus Christ's power to heal
Mt 17:17 "O unbelieving and perverse generation," Jesus replied, "how long shall I stay with you? How long shall I put up with you? Bring the boy here to me." pp Mk 9:19 pp Lk 9:41 *See also* **Mt** 17:19–20

Encouragements in overcoming unbelief
Mk 9:24 Immediately the boy's father exclaimed, "I do believe; help me overcome my unbelief!"
Jn 14:11 "Believe me [Jesus] when I say that I am in the Father and the Father is in me; or at least believe on the evidence of the miracles themselves." *See also* **Mt** 11:4–6; **Jn** 10:37–38; 20:30–31; **Ro** 4:20 *See also doubt; faith; hope.*

understanding
God-given perception of the nature and meaning of things, resulting in sound judgment and decision-making; in particular the ability to discern spiritual truth and to apply it to human disposition and conduct.

The source of understanding
Understanding belongs to God
Job 12:13 "To God belong wisdom and power; counsel and understanding are his."
Ps 136:5 who by his [the LORD's] understanding made the heavens, *His love endures for ever. See also* **Ps** 147:5; **Pr** 3:19; **Jer** 15:15; 51:15
Understanding is a gift from God
Pr 2:6 For the LORD gives wisdom, and from his mouth come knowledge and understanding.
Isa 29:24 "Those who are wayward in spirit will gain understanding; those who complain will accept instruction." *See also* **1Ki** 4:29; **Job**

38:36; **Isa** 32:3–4; **Da** 1:17; 2:21,30; 9:22; **Ro** 15:21; **Isa** 52:15

Understanding spiritual truth
Understanding truth about God
1Jn 5:20 We know also that the Son of God has come and has given us understanding, so that we may know him who is true . . . *See also* **Pr** 2:5; 9:10; **Isa** 40:21,28; 43:10; **Jer** 9:24; **Jn** 10:38; **Ro** 1:20

Understanding God's purposes Dt 9:6; **1Ch** 28:19; **Job** 34:10–11; **Ps** 73:16–17; **Isa** 57:1–2; **Jer** 9:12–13

God's purpose in bringing judgment: **Jer** 23:20; 30:24 **Da** 8:15–16

God's will regarding his people: **Eph** 5:17; **Col** 1:9

Understanding God's word
Ps 119:73 Your hands made me and formed me; give me understanding to learn your commands.

Lk 24:45 Then he [Jesus] opened their [the disciples'] minds so they could understand the Scriptures. *See also* **Ne** 8:8,12; **Ps** 119:27,125; **Mt** 24:15 pp **Mk** 13:14; **Lk** 24:27; **Ac** 8:30–31; **Jn** 12:16

Understanding Jesus Christ's teaching Mt 13:11 pp **Mk** 4:11 pp **Lk** 8:10; **Mt** 16:12; 17:13; **Mk** 4:33; 8:17; **Jn** 2:22

Understanding God's salvation
Eph 1:18 I [Paul] pray also that the eyes of your heart may be enlightened in order that you may know the hope to which he [God] has called you, the riches of his glorious inheritance in the saints, *See also* **Isa** 41:20; **Ro** 13:11; **Eph** 1:9; 3:4,17–19; **Col** 2:2; **Phm** 6

Human understanding is limited
Job 36:26 "How great is God—beyond our understanding! The number of his years is past finding out."
Job 37:5 "God's voice thunders in marvellous ways; he does great things beyond our understanding."
Pr 3:5 Trust in the Lord with all your heart and lean not on your own understanding; *See also* **Job** 26:14; 36:29; 42:3; **Pr** 20:24; **Ecc** 11:5; **Isa** 40:13–14; 55:8–9; **1Co** 13:12

Gaining understanding
Through faith
Heb 11:3 By faith we understand that the universe was formed at God's command, so that what is seen was not made out of what was visible. *See also* **Mt** 16:8–9

Through God's Spirit
1Co 2:12 We have not received the spirit of the world but the Spirit who is from God, that we may understand what God has freely given us. *See also* **1Ch** 28:12; **Job** 32:8; **Isa** 11:2; **Jn** 14:26; 16:13–15; **1Co** 2:14; **Eph** 1:17

Through God's word
Ps 119:130 The unfolding of your [the Lord's] words gives light; it gives understanding to the simple. *See also* **Dt** 4:6; **Ps** 111:10; **Da** 9:2; **Jn** 20:9

Through wise teaching
Ps 49:3 My mouth will speak words of wisdom; the utterance from my heart will give understanding. *See also* **Job** 8:8–10; **Pr** 1:2; 4:1; 15:32; **Ecc** 12:9

Lack of understanding of spiritual truth
Not knowing God
Isa 1:3 "The ox knows its master, the donkey its owner's manger, but Israel does not know, my [the Lord's] people do not understand." *See also* **Dt** 32:28–29; **Isa** 27:11; **Jer** 4:22; **Ro** 10:19; **Dt** 32:21

Lack of understanding due to hardened hearts
Dt 29:4 But to this day the Lord has not given you [Israel] a mind that understands or eyes that see or ears that hear.
Isa 6:9–10 He [the Lord] said, "Go and tell this people: 'Be ever hearing, but never understanding; be ever seeing, but never perceiving.' Make the heart of this people calloused; make their ears dull and close their eyes. Otherwise they might see with their eyes, hear with their ears, understand with their hearts, and turn and be healed." *See also* **Job** 17:4; **Isa** 44:18; 48:8; **Jer** 5:21; **Eze** 12:2; **Mt** 13:13–15 pp **Mk** 4:11–12 pp **Lk** 8:10; **Mk** 6:52; **Jn** 12:40; **Ac** 28:26–27; **Eph** 4:18

Not understanding God's purposes Ps 82:5;
92:6–7; Isa 5:13; 19:12; Mic 4:12; Lk 12:56;
1Co 2:8
Not understanding Jesus Christ's teaching Mt
13:19
By Jesus Christ's disciples: Mk 4:13; 9:32; Jn
4:32–33; 8:27; 11:13; 16:18
Lk 2:50
By some Jews: Jn 2:20–21; 6:51–52; 8:43
Jn 4:11

Understanding people and situations
1Ch 12:32; Est 1:13; Job 13:1; Pr 20:5; Jn
7:24

Understanding languages
Ge 11:7; Dt 28:49; Ps 81:5; Isa 36:11; Ac
2:6; 1Co 14:2

Those who have understanding
The wise Dt 32:29; 1Ki 4:29; Pr 8:14; Hos 14:9
Good leaders
Jer 3:15 "Then I [the LORD] will give you
shepherds after my own heart, who will lead you
with knowledge and understanding."   *See also*
Dt 1:13; 1Ch 22:12; 2Ch 30:22; Pr 28:2
Bad leaders, by contrast, lack judgment: Pr 28:16; Isa
56:11

The results of understanding
Seeking God
Ps 14:2 The LORD looks down from heaven on
the human race to see if there are any who
understand, any who seek God.   *See also* Ps
53:2; Ro 3:11
Obedience
Ps 119:34 Give me [the psalmist]
understanding, and I will keep your [the LORD's]
law and obey it with all my heart.   *See also* Ne
10:28; Ps 32:9; 119:100; Pr 28:7
Taking the right path
Pr 2:9 Then you will understand what is right
and just and fair—every good path.   *See also*
Ps 119:104; Pr 15:21
Life Ps 119:144; Pr 16:22
Sensible living Job 28:28; Pr 11:12; 12:11;
13:15; 17:27; Jas 3:13

The results of a lack of understanding
Foolish behaviour Pr 6:32; 7:7; 17:18; 18:1–2;
24:30–31; Hos 4:11
Death Pr 10:21; 21:16; Hos 4:14   *See also*
discernment.

---

union with Christ
The sharing of believers in the life of Jesus Christ
by faith, allowing them to share in all the benefits
and riches that result from his person and work.

---

union with Christ, nature of
The nature of the union of Jesus Christ with
believers is explained using a number of central
images. The NT stresses the reality, closeness and
considerable benefits of this union.

A covenantal relationship
OT background
Isa 54:5–8 "For your [Israel's] Maker is your
husband—the LORD Almighty is his name—the
Holy One of Israel is your Redeemer; he is called
the God of all the earth . . ." . . .   *See also*
Jer 3:14; 31:32; Hos 2:7,16
In the NT
Eph 5:31–32 "For this reason a man will leave
his father and mother and be united to his wife,
and the two will become one flesh." This is a
profound mystery—but I am talking about Christ
and the church.

A relationship deepened through the
incarnation
Jn 1:14 The Word became flesh and made his
dwelling among us. We have seen his glory, the
glory of the One and Only, who came from the
Father, full of grace and truth.   *See also* Ro 8:3;
2Co 5:21; Gal 4:4; Php 2:7–8; 1Ti 3:16; Heb
2:14–18

A relationship personally entered
through faith
Jn 3:16 "For God so loved the world that he
gave his one and only Son, that whoever believes
in him shall not perish but have eternal life."
See also Jn 1:12; 2:11; 7:38; Ac 16:31; Ro 3:22;
8:1; 10:9–10; 2Co 5:17; Gal 2:16

A relationship enriched through the sacraments

Baptism

Ro 6:3-5 Or don't you know that all of us who were baptised into Christ Jesus were baptised into his death? We were therefore buried with him through baptism into death in order that, just as Christ was raised from the dead through the glory of the Father, we too may live a new life. If we have been united with him like this in his death, we will certainly also be united with him in his resurrection.

Gal 3:27 for all of you who were baptised into Christ have clothed yourselves with Christ.   *See also* **Mt** 28:19; **Ro** 6:8; **Col** 2:11-12

The Lord's Supper Mt 26:26-28 pp Mk 14:22-24 pp Lk 22:17-20; **1Co** 10:16; 11:23-29

A relationship that affects every aspect of life

1Co 6:17 But whoever is united with the Lord is one with him in spirit.   *See also* **Jn** 15:1-8; 17:20-26; **Ro** 8:9-11; **1Co** 6:19-20; **Gal** 2:20

It is a mysterious relationship

Col 1:27 To them [the saints] God has chosen to make known among the Gentiles the glorious riches of this mystery, which is Christ in you, the hope of glory.   *See also* **Eph** 5:32   *See also abiding in Christ; baptism; Christlikeness; life, spiritual; Lord's Supper.*

union with Christ, significance

The union between Jesus Christ and believers is the basis for all exhortation to faithful, holy living, as well as to sharing in all his benefits.

For the believer

Identification with Jesus Christ

Mt 10:40 "Anyone who receives you [apostles] receives me [Jesus], and anyone who receives me receives the one who sent me."   *See also* **Mt** 18:5; 25:40; **Eph** 1:1; **Php** 1:1

The experience of being in Christ

Ro 8:10 But if Christ is in you [believers], your body is dead because of sin, yet your spirit is alive because of righteousness.

2Co 5:17 . . . if anyone is in Christ, there is a new creation: the old has gone, the new has come!   *See also* **Jn** 14:20; **2Co** 13:5; **Gal** 2:20; **Eph** 3:14-19; **Col** 1:27

Conformity to Jesus Christ

Col 3:1-4 Since, then, you [believers] have been raised with Christ, set your hearts on things above, where Christ is seated at the right hand of God. Set your minds on things above, not on earthly things. For you died, and your life is now hidden with Christ in God. When Christ, who is your life, appears, then you also will appear with him in glory.   *See also* **Mt** 16:24 pp Mk 8:34 pp Lk 9:23; **Ro** 6:5; **1Co** 6:15-17; **2Co** 4:10; **Eph** 2:6; **Php** 3:10-11; **1Pe** 4:13; **1Jn** 2:6,28; 3:24; 5:20

Righteousness in Christ

Ro 4:23-25 The words "it was credited to him" were written not for him [Abraham] alone, but also for us, to whom God will credit righteousness—for us who believe in him who raised Jesus our Lord from the dead. He was delivered over to death for our sins and was raised to life for our justification.

2Co 5:21 God made him who had no sin to be sin for us, so that in him we might become the righteousness of God.   *See also* **Ro** 1:17; **1Co** 1:30

Blessing in Christ

Eph 1:3-14 Praise be to the God and Father of our Lord Jesus Christ, who has blessed us in the heavenly realms with every spiritual blessing in Christ . . .

For the church

In persecution

Ac 9:3-5 As he [Saul] neared Damascus on his journey, suddenly a light from heaven flashed around him. He fell to the ground and heard a voice say to him, "Saul, Saul, why do you persecute me?" "Who are you, Lord?" Saul asked. "I am Jesus, whom you are persecuting," he replied.   *See also* **Ac** 22:6-8; 26:14

In service

1Co 12:12 The body is a unit, though it is made up of many parts; and though all its parts are many, they form one body. So it is with Christ.   *See also* **Ro** 12:4-8; **1Co** 12:27; **Eph**

1:22–23; 5:28–30; **Col** 3:15   *See also church, nature of; commitment, to Christ; discipleship; faith; godliness; persecution, attitudes; sanctification.*

waiting on God

Being prepared to look patiently towards God for his guidance and accept the timing he proposes. Waiting on God can lead to an atmosphere of expectation and confidence in God and a realisation of the unreliability of one's own judgment.

Waiting on God is something that is commanded

Hos 12:6 But you must return to your God; maintain love and justice, and wait for your God always.   *See also* **Ps** 27:14; 37:7,34; 123:2; **Isa** 30:18

Reasons for waiting on God

Jer 14:22; **Ps** 25:5; 145:15–16

Waiting on Christ

Jas 5:7–8 Be patient, then, brothers and sisters, until the Lord's coming. See how the farmer waits for the land to yield its valuable crop, patiently waiting for the autumn and spring rains. You too, be patient and stand firm, because the Lord's coming is near.   *See also* **Lk** 12:35–40; **1Co** 1:7; 4:5; **Tit** 2:13; **Heb** 9:28; **Jude** 21

The benefits of waiting on God
It leads to expectancy

Ps 5:3 In the morning, O Lord, you hear my voice; in the morning I lay my requests before you and wait in expectation.   *See also* **Ro** 8:23; **1Co** 4:5; **Gal** 5:5; **Tit** 2:13

It leads to hope

Ps 33:20 We wait in hope for the Lord; he is our help and our shield.   *See also* **Ps** 130:5; **Isa** 51:5; **Mic** 7:7

It leads to trust

Isa 8:17 I will wait for the Lord, who is hiding his face from the house of Jacob. I will put my trust in him.

It leads to patience

Ro 8:23–25 Not only so, but we ourselves, who have the firstfruits of the Spirit, groan inwardly as we wait eagerly for our adoption, the redemption of our bodies. For in this hope we were saved. But hope that is seen is no hope at all. Who hopes for what one already has? But if we hope for what we do not yet have, we wait for it patiently.   *See also* **La** 3:24–26; **Rev** 6:9–11

Examples of people who waited on God

Ge 49:18; **Ps** 39:7; **Isa** 8:17; **Mic** 7:7; **Mk** 15:43; **Lk** 2:25   *See also hope; patience; prayer, persistence.*

watchfulness

The state of being alert and expectant; watching over someone in one's care or waiting for the arrival of someone important or for some significant event. Scripture lays particular emphasis on the need to watch for the second coming of Jesus Christ.

watchfulness, believers

Alertness to dangers and blessings in the Christian life, and also to opportunities to do good.

Watchfulness for dangers

1Pe 5:8 Be self-controlled and alert. Your enemy the devil prowls around like a roaring lion looking for someone to devour.   *See also* **Pr** 4:23
The danger of false teaching

Mt 7:15 "Watch out for false prophets. They come to you in sheep's clothing, but inwardly they are ferocious wolves."   *See also* **Ps** 94:8; **Pr** 8:33–34; **Mt** 24:4–5; **Mk** 8:15; **Ro** 16:17; **1Co** 16:13
The danger of temptation

Mt 26:41 "Watch and pray so that you will not fall into temptation. The spirit is willing, but the body is weak." pp **Mk** 14:38   *See also* **Dt** 4:15; **1Ki** 2:4; **Lk** 12:15; 17:1–3; **1Co** 10:12; **Gal** 6:1; **2Jn** 8
The danger of neglecting the word of God

Dt 4:9 Only be careful, and watch yourselves

closely so that you do not forget the things your
eyes have seen or let them slip from your heart
as long as you live. Teach them to your children
and to their children after them.   *See also* **Jos**
22:5; **1Ki** 2:3; **Heb** 2:1; 12:25; **2Pe** 1:19
The danger of damage to the Lord's work Ne
4:9; 7:3
The danger of speaking sinfully Ps 39:1; 141:3;
Pr 13:3; 21:23; **Jas** 1:26; 3:5–8; **1Pe** 3:10

Watchfulness for blessings
Ps 25:15; 59:9; 123:1–2; 130:5–6; **Isa** 40:9;
Mic 7:7; **Lk** 2:25,36–38

Watchfulness and prayer
Col 4:2–3 Devote yourselves to prayer, being
watchful and thankful. And pray for us, too, that
God may open a door for our message, so that
we may proclaim the mystery of Christ, for which
I am in chains.   *See also* **Mt** 26:41 pp Mk
14:38; **Mk** 13:33 fn; **Lk** 21:36; **Eph** 6:18; **1Pe** 4:7

Watchfulness for the return of Jesus Christ
Mt 24:42–44 "Therefore keep watch, because
you do not know on what day your Lord will
come. But understand this: If the owner of the
house had known at what time of night the thief
was coming, he would have kept watch and
would not have let his house be broken into. So
you also must be ready, because the Son of Man
will come at an hour when you do not expect
him."   *See also* **Mt** 25:1–13; **Mk** 13:32–37; **Lk**
12:35–40; 21:32–36; **1Th** 5:4–8; **Rev** 16:15

Watchfulness for opportunities to serve the Lord
1Pe 3:15 . . . Always be prepared to give an
answer to everyone who asks you to give the
reason for the hope that you have. But do this
with gentleness and respect,   *See also* **Eph**
5:15–16; **Col** 4:5–6
Meeting the needs of others
Eph 6:18 And pray in the Spirit on all occasions
with all kinds of prayers and requests. With this in
mind, be alert and always keep on praying for all the
saints.   *See also* **Mt** 26:36–40; **Gal** 6:10; **Tit** 3:1

Contrast with the watchfulness of unbelievers with evil intent
Ps 37:32 The wicked lie in wait for the
righteous, seeking their very lives;   *See also* **1Sa**
18:9; 19:11; **Ps** 10:8; **Jer** 20:10; **Mt** 26:16; **Mk**
3:2; **Ac** 9:24

Warning against neglect of watchfulness
Rev 3:2–3   *See also hope; obedience; self-
examination; servanthood in believers; temptation.*

---

witnessing
The task of declaring what has happened,
especially in relation to the life, death and
resurrection of Jesus Christ. Believers are given the
responsibility of proclaiming the good news of
Jesus Christ to the world at all times and in all
places.

---

witnessing, and Holy Spirit
Christian witnessing is made effective through the
empowering, strengthening and guiding of the Holy
Spirit. Witnessing is an aspect of spiritual warfare,
and believers need supernatural aid to face
Satan's opposition.

The Holy Spirit supports believers in witnessing
Ac 5:31–32 "God exalted him [Jesus] to his
own right hand as Prince and Saviour that he
might give repentance and forgiveness of sins to
Israel. We are witnesses of these things, and so
is the Holy Spirit, whom God has given to those
who obey him."   *See also* **Jn** 15:26–27

The Holy Spirit empowers effective witness
Ac 1:8 "But you [the disciples] will receive
power when the Holy Spirit comes on you; and
you will be my [Jesus'] witnesses in Jerusalem,
and in all Judea and Samaria, and to the ends of
the earth."
1Co 2:1–5 When I came to you, brothers and
sisters, I did not come with eloquence or superior
wisdom as I proclaimed to you the testimony

about God . . . My message and my preaching were not with wise and persuasive words, but with a demonstration of the Spirit's power, so that your faith might not rest on human wisdom, but on God's power.   *See also* **Lk** 4:14–19; 24:48–49

He confirms the testimony of believers 1Th 1:5; **Heb** 2:3–4

He convinces people of their need Jn 16:7–11

He brings people to new birth Jn 3:5–8

The Holy Spirit guides believers in witnessing

Ac 8:39–40 . . . the Spirit of the Lord suddenly took Philip away . . . [Philip] appeared at Azotus and travelled about, preaching the gospel in all the towns until he reached Caesarea.   *See also* **Ac** 8:29–35; 16:6–7

Witnessing and spiritual warfare

Rev 12:11 "They [God's people] overcame him [the accuser] by the blood of the Lamb and by the word of their testimony; they did not love their lives so much as to shrink from death. *See also* **Eph** 6:15–17

Witnessing and persecution
Witnessing results in persecution

Rev 1:9 I, John, your brother and companion in the suffering and kingdom and patient endurance that are ours in Jesus, was on the island of Patmos because of the word of God and the testimony of Jesus.   *See also* **Ac** 4:17; 5:40; 7:54–60; 22:22–25; **Eph** 6:19–20; **Col** 4:3–4; **2Ti** 1:8; **Rev** 2:12–13; 6:9; 17:6

Supernatural help to face persecution

Mt 10:18–20 "On my [Jesus'] account you [the disciples] will be brought before governors and kings as witnesses to them and to the Gentiles. But when they arrest you, do not worry about what to say or how to say it. At that time you will be given what to say, for it will not be you speaking, but the Spirit of your Father speaking through you." pp Mk 13:9–11 pp Lk 21:12–15

Ac 7:55 But Stephen, full of the Holy Spirit, looked up to heaven and saw the glory of God,

and Jesus standing at the right hand of God. *See also* **Ac** 5:18–19; 18:9–10

Witness is promoted by persecution Ac 8:1–5; **Php** 1:12–14   *See also persecution; spiritual warfare; suffering, of believers.*

witnessing, approaches

Scripture provides teaching, supported by examples, concerning when believers should witness, the methods they are to use, and the manner of doing it.

When and where to witness
In the home and family

Mk 5:18–19 As Jesus was getting into the boat, the man who had been demon-possessed begged to go with him. Jesus did not let him, but said, "Go home to your family and tell them how much the Lord has done for you, and how he has had mercy on you." pp Lk 8:38–39   *See also* **2Ki** 5:1–3; **Jn** 1:41

To individuals

Jn 1:40–42 Andrew, Simon Peter's brother . . . had followed Jesus. The first thing Andrew did was to find his brother Simon and tell him, "We have found the Messiah" (that is, the Christ). And he brought him to Jesus . . .   *See also* **Jn** 4:7–26; **Ac** 8:30–35

To assembled groups

Ac 17:17 So he [Paul] reasoned in the synagogue with the Jews and the God-fearing Greeks, as well as in the market-place day by day with those who happened to be there.   *See also* **Ac** 5:42; 16:13; 19:8–9

Methods of witnessing
Sharing personal testimony

Jn 4:29 "Come, see a man [Jesus] who told me everything I [a Samaritan woman] ever did. Could this be the Christ?"   *See also* **Ac** 22:3–8

Explaining the Scriptures

Ac 8:30–35 . . . Then Philip began with that very passage of Scripture and told him [the Ethiopian eunuch] the good news about Jesus. *See also* **Isa** 53:7–8; **Ps** 119:172; **Ac** 17:1–3,10–12

Using prophetic gifts
1Co 14:24–25 But if an unbeliever or someone who does not understand comes in while everybody is prophesying, such people will be convinced by all that they are sinners and will be judged by all, and the secrets of their hearts will be laid bare. So they will fall down and worship God, exclaiming, "God is really among you!"

Answering questions
Col 4:6 Let your conversation be always full of grace, seasoned with salt, so that you may know how to answer everyone.   *See also* **Jn** 9:8–11,15–17,24–25; **1Pe** 3:15

Through writing
Jn 20:31 But these are written that you may believe that Jesus is the Christ, the Son of God, and that by believing you may have life in his name.   *See also* **Lk** 1:1–4

Through holy living
Mt 5:16 "In the same way, let your light shine before others, that they may see your good deeds and praise your Father in heaven."   *See also* **1Pe** 3:1–2

Through acts of devotion
Mt 26:6–7 While Jesus was in Bethany in the home of Simon the Leper, a woman came to him with an alabaster jar of very expensive perfume, which she poured on his head as he was reclining at the table. pp Mk 14:3   *See also* **Lk** 7:36–38; **Jn** 12:1–3

The manner of witnessing
With love
Mk 10:21 Jesus looked at him [the rich young man] and loved him . . .   *See also* **Php** 1:15–17

With urgency
2Co 5:20 We are therefore Christ's ambassadors, as though God were making his appeal through us. We implore you on Christ's behalf: Be reconciled to God.   *See also* **Eze** 33:7–9

Fearlessly
Eph 6:19–20 Pray also for me [Paul], that whenever I open my mouth, words may be given me so that I will fearlessly make known the mystery of the gospel, for which I am an ambassador in chains. Pray that I may declare it fearlessly, as I should.   *See also* **Ac** 4:29

Clearly and courteously
1Pe 3:15 . . . Always be prepared to give an answer to everyone who asks you to give the reason for the hope that you have. But do this with gentleness and respect,   *See also* **Ac** 26:1–3; **Col** 4:4–6   *See also gentleness; holiness; love; respect.*

---

witnessing, importance
Sharing the good news about God and Jesus Christ with others is a work to which some believers have a special calling, but in which all believers are to take part.

Witnessing is sharing the truth of God
Ps 145:10–12 All you have made will praise you, O LORD; your saints will extol you. They will tell of the glory of your kingdom and speak of your might, so that all people may know of your mighty acts and the glorious splendour of your kingdom.

Lk 24:46–48 He [Jesus] told them [his disciples], "This is what is written: The Christ will suffer and rise from the dead on the third day, and repentance and forgiveness of sins will be preached in his name to all nations, beginning at Jerusalem. You are witnesses of these things."   *See also* **1Ch** 16:7–9; **Ps** 71:15; **Mt** 27:54 pp Mk 15:39 pp Lk 23:47; **Jn** 1:35–36; 4:29

Believers are commanded to witness
Mt 28:18–19 Then Jesus came to them [the disciples] and said, "All authority in heaven and on earth has been given to me. Therefore go and make disciples of all nations, baptising them in the name of the Father and of the Son and of the Holy Spirit,"   *See also* **Isa** 12:4–5; **Mt** 24:14 pp Mk 13:10; **Ac** 1:8; 9:15–16

Special ministries of witnessing
By the prophets
Jn 1:6–8 There came a man who was sent from God; his name was John. He came as a witness to testify concerning that light, so that through him all might believe . . .   *See also* **Jer**

1:4–9; **Eze** 33:7–9; **Jnh** 1:2,9; **Jn** 1:15,29,36; **Ac** 10:43

By Jesus Christ
Jn 18:37 . . . ". . . for this I [Jesus] came into the world, to testify to the truth . . ."
See also **Jn** 3:31–34; **Rev** 1:5; 3:14

By the apostles
Ac 4:33 With great power the apostles continued to testify to the resurrection of the Lord Jesus . . .   *See also* **Ac** 2:32; 10:39–42; 13:30–31; **1Jn** 1:1–3

By Christian leaders
2Ti 1:8 . . . do not be ashamed to testify about our Lord . . .   *See also* **Ac** 8:5; **Eph** 4:11

Witnessing is a task for all God's people
1Pe 2:9 But you are a chosen people, a royal priesthood, a holy nation, a people belonging to God, that you may declare the praises of him who called you out of darkness into his wonderful light.
1Pe 3:15 . . . Always be prepared to give an answer to everyone who asks you to give the reason for the hope that you have . . .   *See also* **Ps** 26:6–7; 107:1–2
All of the people of Israel are called to be God's witnesses: **Isa** 43:10,12; 44:8
Isa 52:7; **Ac** 8:4

Witnessing is a major aspect of Christian living
Ro 10:9–10 . . . if you confess with your mouth, "Jesus is Lord," and believe in your heart that God raised him from the dead, you will be saved. For it is with your heart that you believe and are justified, and it is with your mouth that you confess and are saved.   *See also* **Mt** 10:32–33 pp **Mk** 8:38 pp **Lk** 12:8–9; **2Co** 4:13; **1Jn** 2:23; 4:15

Examples of witnessing to Jesus Christ
Mt 16:16 pp **Mk** 8:29 pp **Lk** 9:20; **Lk** 2:16–17; **Jn** 1:40–42,49; 11:27; 20:28; **Ac** 8:37 fn

Witnessing recounts personal experience
Isa 63:7 I will tell of the kindnesses of the LORD, the deeds for which he is to be praised, according to all the LORD has done for us—yes, the many good things he has done for the house of Israel, according to his compassion and many kindnesses.   *See also* **Ps** 66:16; **Jer** 51:10; **Da** 4:2; **Mt** 9:27–31; **Mk** 1:40–45; **Jn** 9:25; **Ac** 4:20

Witnessing to the resurrection of Jesus Christ
Ac 2:32 "God has raised this Jesus to life, and we are all witnesses of the fact."   *See also* **Lk** 24:33–35; **Ac** 5:30–32; **1Co** 15:3–7   *See also evangelism; preaching.*

work

Work was ordained by God as a means of fulfilment, service and praise. It is to be supplemented by rest, following the pattern of God's creation of the world. Despite the effects of sin, work can still be honouring to God.

work, and rest

In creation, God has established a pattern of work and rest that is to be a model for believers.

Work and rest built into creation
Ex 20:11 "For in six days the LORD made the heavens and the earth, the sea, and all that is in them, but he rested on the seventh day. Therefore the LORD blessed the Sabbath day and made it holy."   *See also* **Ge** 2:1–3; **Ps** 104:19–23

The pattern of work and rest confirmed in the OT
By Sabbath observance **Ex** 20:10 pp **Dt** 5:14; **Lev** 23:3
By observing holy festivals **Ex** 12:16; **Lev** 16:29; 23:6–8 pp **Nu** 28:17–18; **Lev** 23:28–31 pp **Nu** 29:7; **Lev** 23:35–36,39 pp **Nu** 29:12; **Est** 9:17–19

Work and rest in the ministry of Jesus Christ
Mk 6:30–32 The apostles gathered round Jesus and reported to him all they had done and taught. Then, because so many people were coming and going that they did not even have a chance to eat, he said to them, "Come with me by yourselves to a quiet place and get some rest." . . .   *See also* **Jn** 4:6

Wisdom needed to balance work and rest
To avoid idleness Pr 6:9–11; 10:4–5; 14:23; 20:13; 24:30–34
To avoid overwork Ex 18:13–24; **Ps** 127:2; **Lk** 10:38–42

Work and rest are both potential means of glorifying God
1Co 10:31 So whether you [Corinthian Christians] eat or drink or whatever you do, do it all for the glory of God.   *See also* **Ecc** 2:24; **Col** 3:17

Work and rest will be perfectly fulfilled in heaven
Rev 14:13 . . . ". . . Blessed are the dead who die in the Lord from now on." . . . "they will rest from their labour, for their deeds will follow them."
Rev 22:3 . . . his [God's] servants will serve him.

---

work, and the fall
Human work, which was once a pleasure, became a burden only on account of human disobedience.

Work is under God's judgment
Ge 3:17–19 To Adam he said, "Because you listened to your wife and ate from the tree about which I commanded you, 'You must not eat of it,' Cursed is the ground because of you; through painful toil you will eat of it all the days of your life. It will produce thorns and thistles for you, and you will eat the plants of the field. By the sweat of your brow you will eat your food until you return to the ground, since from it you were taken; for dust you are and to dust you will return."   *See also* **Ge** 5:29

Work is often frustrating
Ecc 2:22–23 What do people get for all the toil and anxious striving with which they labour under the sun? All their days their work is pain and grief; even at night their minds do not rest. This too is meaningless.   *See also* **Ecc** 2:11,18; 4:8; 5:16–17

Work may exploit rather than enhance society
Through dishonesty Lev 19:35; **Dt** 25:13; **Hos** 12:7
Through oppression Ex 1:11–14; **1Ki** 12:4,10–14

Work may be undervalued or overvalued
Some people avoid work to their cost Pr 6:6–11; 13:4; 19:15; 24:30–34; **Ecc** 10:18; **2Th** 3:10–11
Some people overwork to their cost Ex 18:17–18; **Ps** 127:2; **Lk** 10:41–42; 12:15–21
See also disobedience.

---

work, ordained by God
God ordained work as the normal routine of living. Every legitimate human task, therefore, is of intrinsic worth, however menial it may seem, and is potentially a means of glorifying God.

Work is ordained by God
Ge 1:27–28 . . . God created human beings . . . male and female he created them. God blessed them and said to them, "Be fruitful and increase in number; fill the earth and subdue it. Rule over the fish of the sea and the birds of the air and over every living creature that moves on the ground."   *See also* **Ex** 20:9 pp Dt 5:13; **Ps** 104:23

God's purposes in ordaining work
That people should be self-supporting
Ge 3:19 "By the sweat of your brow you will eat your food . . ."   *See also* **Ps** 128:2; **1Th** 4:12

That people should find self-fulfilment
Ecc 2:24 People can do nothing better than to eat and drink and find satisfaction in their work. This too, I see, is from the hand of God, *See also* **Pr** 14:23; **Ecc** 3:22; 5:19

That people should serve others
Eph 4:28 Those who have been stealing must steal no longer, but must work, doing something useful with their own hands, that they may have something to share with those in need.   *See also* **Pr** 31:15; **1Th** 2:9; **1Ti** 5:8

That people should glorify God
Col 3:17 And whatever you [Colossian Christians] do, whether in word or deed, do it all in the name of the Lord Jesus, giving thanks to God the Father through him.   *See also* **1Co** 10:31; **Eph** 6:5–8 pp Col 3:22–24

Consequences of viewing work as God's ordinance

Work is seen as a moral duty
Tit 3:14 Our people must learn to devote themselves to doing what is good, in order that they may provide for daily necessities and not live unproductive lives.   *See also* **Pr** 6:6; **Ecc** 9:10; **1Th** 4:11; **2Th** 3:7–12

Any legitimate work may be seen as God's calling
Ge 2:15 The LORD God took the man and put him in the Garden of Eden to work it and take care of it.   *See also* **Ex** 31:1–6; 35:30–35; **Ps** 78:70–71; **Mt** 13:55 pp Mk 6:3; **Ro** 13:6; **1Co** 7:17,20–24

Work is seen as a stewardship from God himself
Col 3:23–24 Whatever you [Colossian Christians] do, work at it with all your heart, as working for the Lord, not for human masters, since you know that you will receive an inheritance from the Lord as a reward. It is the Lord Christ you are serving. *See also* **Mt** 25:14–30 pp Lk 19:12–27; **Eph** 6:5–8

Criticism of those who will not work
2Th 3:10–11 For even when we were with you, we gave you this rule: "Anyone who will not work shall not eat." We hear that some

among you are idle. They are not busy; they are busybodies.

world

Scripture understands "the world" in a number of senses. It initially refers to the world as God's good creation. However, that same world has now fallen into sin, with the result that it can be a threat to believers. Believers are called to live in the world, maintaining contact with it, while remaining distinct from it, and avoiding being contaminated by it.

world, behaviour in

Human behaviour in the world is now characterised by self-centredness as a result of sin. Believers are called upon to renounce such sinful behaviour.

Human passion in the world is expressed in various ways

In physical desires
1Jn 2:15–16 Do not love the world or anything in the world. If you love the world, the love of the Father is not in you. For everything in the world—the cravings of sinful people, the lust of their eyes and the boasting of what they have and do—comes not from the Father but from the world.   *See also* **Ex** 20:17; **Pr** 27:20; **Lk** 12:15; 21:34; **Jas** 4:4; **2Pe** 2:18–20

In indulgence
Jas 5:1 Now listen, you rich people, weep and wail because of the misery that is coming upon you.

Jas 5:5 You have lived on earth in luxury and self-indulgence. You have fattened yourselves in the day of slaughter.   *See also* **Job** 21:7–13; **Ps** 73:2–3; **2Ti** 4:10

In intellectual pursuits
Col 2:8 See to it that no-one takes you captive through hollow and deceptive philosophy, which depends on human tradition and the basic principles of this world rather than on Christ. *See also* **Gal** 4:3–5; **Eph** 2:3

In a weak will
Ex 23:2 "Do not follow the crowd in doing

wrong. When you give testimony in a lawsuit, do not pervert justice by siding with the crowd," See also **Job** 31:34; **Ro** 6:17–19

Though remaining in the world, believers are not of the world
Jn 17:6–19

Believers are to renounce the passions of the world
Through a renewed mind
Ro 12:2 Do not conform any longer to the pattern of this world, but be transformed by the renewing of your mind . . . See also **Gal** 1:4; **Eph** 4:23; **Col** 3:5–10
Through obedience
1Pe 1:14–15 As obedient children, do not conform to the evil desires you had when you lived in ignorance. But just as he who called you is holy, so be holy in all you do; See also **2Co** 10:2–5; **Gal** 5:24; 6:15; **Eph** 5:17; **Tit** 2:12; **Jas** 1:27; **2Pe** 1:4
Through having spiritual priorities
Lk 12:29–31 "And do not set your heart on what you will eat or drink; do not worry about it. For the pagan world runs after all such things, and your Father knows that you need them. But seek his kingdom, and these things will be given to you as well." pp Mt 6:31–33 See also **Mt** 10:39; **Lk** 14:26–27; 17:33; **Jn** 12:24–26; **1Ti** 6:6
Through growing to maturity
1Co 3:1 Brothers and sisters, I [Paul] could not address you as spiritual but as worldly—mere infants in Christ. See also **Heb** 5:12; 6:1–3

The futility of worldly pursuits
They bring no lasting material gain
1Ti 6:7 For we brought nothing into the world, and we can take nothing out of it. See also **Job** 1:21; **Ps** 49:17; **Ecc** 5:15; **1Ti** 6:17–19
They bring no spiritual gain
Mk 8:36–37 "What good is it for you to gain the whole world, yet forfeit your soul? Or what can you give in exchange for your soul?" pp Lk 9:25 See also **Job** 20:4–5; **Ps** 17:14; **Lk** 16:25–26 See also discipleship; love, and the world; maturity; obedience.

worship

The praise, adoration and reverence of God, both in public and private. It is a celebration of the worthiness of God, by which honour is given to his name.

worship, acceptable attitudes

True worship is not the mechanical repetition of rituals, but should be wholehearted and reverent. It should be based upon trustful and obedient lives, in that obedience is itself to be seen as an act of worship.

Worship should be in accordance with God's commands
Ge 22:2 Then God said, "Take your son, your only son, Isaac, whom you love, and go to the region of Moriah. Sacrifice him there as a burnt offering on one of the mountains I will tell you about." See also **Ge** 12:1,7–8; **Dt** 30:16–20; **1Sa** 15:22; **Ps** 40:6–8; **Jer** 7:2; **Da** 3:28; **Ac** 13:2; **Ro** 12:1

Worship should not be mechanical
Jn 4:23–24 "Yet a time is coming and has now come when the true worshippers will worship the Father in spirit and truth, for they are the kind of worshippers the Father seeks. God is spirit, and his worshippers must worship in spirit and in truth." See also **Heb** 10:1

Worship should give God the honour due to him
1Ch 16:29 pp Ps 96:8–9

Worship of mere human devising is unacceptable
Isa 29:13 The Lord says: "These people come near to me with their mouth and honour me with their lips, but their hearts are far from me. Their worship of me is based on merely human rules which they have been taught." See also **Lev** 10:1; **Mt** 15:7–9 pp Mk 7:6–7; **Php** 3:3; **Col** 2:23

Worship should be orderly and reverent

1Co 14:40 But everything should be done in a fitting and orderly way.   *See also* **1Ch** 16:37–42; **1Ki** 18:30–39; **1Co** 14:26

Worship should be grounded in godly and obedient living

Mic 6:6–8 With what shall I come before the LORD and bow down before the exalted God? Shall I come before him with burnt offerings, with calves a year old? Will the LORD be pleased with thousands of rams, with ten thousand rivers of oil? Shall I offer my firstborn for my transgression, the fruit of my body for the sin of my soul? He has showed you, O people, what is good. And what does the LORD require of you? To act justly and to love mercy and to walk humbly with your God.

Ro 12:1 Therefore, I [Paul] urge you, brothers and sisters, in view of God's mercy, to offer your bodies as living sacrifices, holy and pleasing to God—this is your spiritual act of worship.   *See also* **Ps** 15:1–5; 24:3–4; **1Ti** 2:10

The proper attitude of worshippers
Preparation for worship

1Co 11:28 We ought to examine ourselves before we eat of the bread and drink of the cup.   *See also* **Lev** 16:3–4; **2Sa** 12:20; **2Ch** 7:1; **Mt** 2:11

Wholeheartedness

Dt 6:5 Love the LORD your God with all your heart and with all your soul and with all your strength.   *See also* **Ex** 34:14; **Dt** 10:12; **Jos** 22:5; **1Sa** 12:24; **Ps** 27:4; **Mt** 22:37 pp **Mk** 12:30; **Lk** 10:27

Confidence in approaching God

Heb 10:22–23 let us draw near to God with a sincere heart in full assurance of faith, having our hearts sprinkled to cleanse us from a guilty conscience and having our bodies washed with pure water. Let us hold unswervingly to the hope we profess, for he who promised is faithful.
See also **Ge** 4:4; **Jas** 4:8; **Heb** 7:19; 11:4   *See also holiness; obedience; prayer, as praise and thanksgiving; prayer, practicalities.*

worship, elements

Praise and thankfulness are important elements of worship, which also includes confession of sin, the reading of Scripture and music.

Worship with awe

Dt 10:12 And now, O Israel, what does the LORD your God ask of you but to fear the LORD your God, to walk in all his ways, to love him, to serve the LORD your God with all your heart and with all your soul,   *See also* **Lev** 10:1–3; **2Ch** 7:3; **Ps** 2:11; 68:35; 96:9; **Ecc** 5:1

Worship includes trust

Ps 4:5 Offer right sacrifices and trust in the LORD.   *See also* **Ps** 37:7; **Heb** 11:6

Worship includes praise

Ps 22:22 I will declare your name to my people; in the congregation I will praise you.
Ps 107:32 Let them exalt him in the assembly of the people and praise him in the council of the elders.
Heb 13:15 Through Jesus, therefore, let us continually offer to God a sacrifice of praise—the fruit of lips that confess his name.   *See also* **2Ch** 31:2; **Ne** 9:5–6; **Ps** 150:1–6; **Heb** 2:12; **Rev** 7:11–12

Worship includes thanksgiving

Ps 100:4 Enter his gates with thanksgiving and his courts with praise; give thanks to him and praise his name.
Rev 11:16–17 And the twenty-four elders, who were seated on their thrones before God, fell on their faces and worshipped God, saying: "We give thanks to you, Lord God Almighty, the One who is and who was, because you have taken your great power and have begun to reign."   *See also* **2Ch** 7:3; **Ps** 50:14,23; **Eph** 5:19–20; **Php** 4:6; **Rev** 7:11–12

Worship with joy

Ps 95:1 Come, let us sing for joy to the LORD . . .   *See also* **Ps** 27:6; 43:4; 100:2; **Lk** 24:52–53; **Ac** 2:46–47

Worship includes the confession of Jesus Christ as Lord

Heb 13:15 Through Jesus, therefore, let us continually offer to God a sacrifice of praise—the fruit of lips that confess his name.

Worship includes confession of sin

Hos 14:2 Take words with you and return to the Lord. Say to him: "Forgive all our sins and receive us graciously, that we may offer the fruit of our lips."   *See also* **Lev** 16:21; **Ne** 9:2; **Ps** 66:18

Worship includes the reading of God's word

Col 3:16 Let the word of Christ dwell in you richly as you teach and admonish one another with all wisdom, and as you sing psalms, hymns and spiritual songs with gratitude in your hearts to God.

1Ti 4:13 Until I come, devote yourself to the public reading of Scripture, to preaching and to teaching.   *See also* **Ne** 8:5–6; 9:3

Worship includes music and song

Ps 95:2–3 Let us come before him [the Lord] with thanksgiving and extol him with music and song. For the Lord is the great God, the great King above all gods.   *See also* **2Sa** 6:5; **Ps** 100:2; **Eph** 5:19–20

Worship includes dance

Ps 149:3 Let them praise his name with dancing and make music to him with tambourine and harp.   *See also* **Ex** 15:20; **Ps** 30:11   *See also confession of sin; faith.*

---

worship, of God

God alone is worthy of worship; the worship of other gods is forbidden. In the NT worship is offered to the Son of God.

God alone is to be worshipped
He alone is worthy of worship

1Ch 16:25 For great is the Lord and most worthy of praise; he is to be feared above all gods.   *See also* **Ps** 48:1; 96:4–5; 145:3; **2Sa** 22:4

The worship of God the Father

Jn 4:23 "Yet a time is coming and has now come when the true worshippers will worship the Father in spirit and truth, for they are the kind of worshippers the Father seeks."   *See also* **Php** 2:11

The worship of God the Son

Mt 2:11 On coming to the house, they [the Magi] saw the child with his mother Mary, and they bowed down and worshipped him. Then they opened their treasures and presented him with gifts of gold and of incense and of myrrh.

Mt 14:33 Then those who were in the boat worshipped him [Jesus], saying, "Truly you are the Son of God."

Jn 20:28 Thomas said to him [Jesus], "My Lord and my God!"   *See also* **Mt** 28:16–17; **Jn** 9:35–38; **Php** 2:9–11; **Heb** 1:6; **Rev** 5:8–14

Angels worship God

Ps 103:20 Praise the Lord, you his angels, you mighty ones who do his bidding, who obey his word.

Ps 148:1–2 Praise the Lord. Praise the Lord from the heavens, praise him in the heights above. Praise him, all his angels, praise him, all his heavenly hosts.   *See also* **Ps** 29:1–2; **Isa** 6:1–4; **Eze** 10:1–18; **Rev** 4:8–9

The worship of other gods forbidden

Ex 20:3 "You shall have no other gods before me." pp Dt 5:7

2Ki 17:35–36 When the Lord made a covenant with the Israelites, he commanded them: "Do not worship any other gods or bow down to them, serve them or sacrifice to them. But the Lord, who brought you up out of Egypt with mighty power and outstretched arm, is the one you must worship. To him you shall bow down and to him offer sacrifices."   *See also* **Ex** 34:14; **Dt** 6:13–14; **Ne** 9:6; **Ps** 86:9–10; 97:7; **Ac** 10:25–26; 14:13–18

The worship of angels forbidden

Col 2:18 Do not let anyone who delights in false humility and the worship of angels disqualify you for the prize . . .   *See also* **Rev** 19:9–10; 22:8–9

worship, reasons

The supreme reason for human existence is to worship God for his love, greatness and saving deeds.

To worship is a divine command

Mt 4:10 Jesus said to him, "Away from me, Satan! For it is written: 'Worship the Lord your God, and serve him only.'" pp Lk 4:8   *See also* **Dt** 6:13; **Ex** 23:25; **2Ki** 17:36; **1Ch** 16:29; **Ps** 22:23; 29:2; 68:26; 113:1; 117:1; 148:11–13; 150:6; **1Ti** 2:8; **Rev** 14:7

God's people are to be a worshipping people

1Pe 2:9 But you are a chosen people, a royal priesthood, a holy nation, a people belonging to God, that you may declare the praises of him who called you out of darkness into his wonderful light.   *See also* **Ex** 19:5–6; **Ps** 105:1–6; **Isa** 43:21; **Rev** 1:5–6

Worship is the response of God's people

To God's love

Ex 4:31 . . . And when they [the elders of the Israelites] heard that the LORD was concerned about them and had seen their misery, they bowed down and worshipped.   *See also* **Dt** 6:5; 12:7; 26:10–11; **2Ch** 7:3; **Ps** 95:6–7; 117:1–2; 138:2

To God's holy presence

1Ch 16:29 . . . Bring an offering and come before him; worship the LORD in the splendour of his holiness. pp Ps 96:8–9   *See also* **Ex** 33:10; **Lev** 10:3; **Jos** 5:13–15; **Ps** 29:2; 99:5; **Rev** 4:8; 15:4

To God's greatness

Ps 95:1–3 Come, let us sing for joy to the LORD; let us shout aloud to the Rock of our salvation. Let us come before him with thanksgiving and extol him with music and song. For the LORD is the great God, the great King above all gods.   *See also* **Ex** 3:12; **Ps** 22:27–28; 66:1–4; 96:1–3; **Rev** 15:3–4

To the deeds of God

Ge 8:20 Then Noah built an altar to the LORD and, taking some of all the clean animals and clean birds, he sacrificed burnt offerings on it. *See also* **Ge** 12:7

The signs and wonders in Egypt and Sinai: **Ex** 4:29–31; 12:27; 15:1,20

Ezr 3:10–11; **Isa** 19:21; **Da** 3:28; **Mt** 9:7–8 pp Mk 2:12 pp Lk 5:25–26; **Ac** 3:8

To the fear of God

Ps 22:23 You who fear the LORD, praise him! All you descendants of Jacob, honour him! Revere him, all you descendants of Israel!

Heb 12:28 Therefore, since we are receiving a kingdom that cannot be shaken, let us be thankful, and so worship God acceptably with reverence and awe,   *See also* **Ps** 2:11; **Ac** 10:2   *See also praise; thankfulness.*

Index

SHARE THE WORD

An ideal second Bible for evangelistic use

Designed to help equip Christians to witness in fulfilment of the great commission:

. . . Therefore go and make disciples of all nations, baptising them in the name of the Father and of the Son and of the Holy Spirit, and teaching them to obey everything I have commanded you.
Matthew 28:18-20 (NIV)

A complete NIV Bible featuring easy-to-use guides, written by youthworker Lindsay Shaw, to help every Christian become confident in sharing the good news with others and give practical advice about caring for new believers.

The only full Bible containing witness material like that found in popular paperbacks for evangelism training. A must-have for evangelical Christians of all ages.

SECTIONS INCLUDE
* Why is God so interested in mission?
* Not for the squeamish?
* Who do you know?
* Know your message
* Turning point
* Insider faith
* Doing what comes naturally
* Reaching people from other faiths
* Meeting Jesus in the Gospels
* Growth groups
* Too much to swallow?
* Resources

It's more important than ever for ordinary Christians to know how to share their faith in an articulate, attractive, non-embarassing, natural way . . . Lindsay Shaw has produced a remarkable set of guidelines which distil a tremendous amount of experience and wisdom into a few vital pages, and roots everything he says in the words of Scripture. Here you will learn not only the secrets of making Christianity intelligible to your friends, but also how to lead them to Christ and even nurture them through the first critical stages of new life. I'm glad to commend this sensible practical and amazingly comprehensive guide.
John Allan, Executive Editor, Youthwork magazine

NIV SHARE THE WORD EDITION   Paperback 129mm × 131mm
ISBN 0 340 68669 3

For further details of this edition or any other NIV Bible please contact your local bookshop.

NIV APPLICATION COMMENTARY SERIES

From biblical text . . . to contemporary life

An indispensable tool for every pastor and teacher who seeks to make the Bible's timeless message speak to this generation. Billy Graham

This exciting and unique new commentary has 2 functions:
* to discuss the meaning of the text in its biblical context
* to apply its meaning to contemporary situations

Volumes feature: introduction, outline, bibliography, NIV text presented one passage at a time with detailed commentary, scripture index and subject index.

Each passage is discussed in three sections:
Original Meaning gives the biblical context.
Bridging Contexts provides a bridge between the biblical world and today by focusing on both the timely and the timeless aspects of the text.
Contemporary Significance enables the reader to apply what they have learned.

Available titles:		*ISBN number*	General Editor: Terry Muck
Mark	David E. Garland	0 340 69450 5	Hardback
Luke	Darrell Block	0 340 67104 1	232mm × 152mm
1 Corinthians	Craig Blomberg	0 340 65197 0	US text
Galatians	Scot McKnight	0 340 65198 9	
Ephesians	Klyne Snodgrass	0 340 67108 4	
Philippians	Frank Thielman	0 340 67112 2	
Hebrews	George H. Guthrie	0 340 71388 7	
James	David Nystrom	0 340 69452 1	
1 Peter	Scot McKnight	0 340 67105 X	
2 Peter, Jude	Douglas J. Moo	0 340 69451 3	
Letters of John	Gary Burge	0 340 67106 8	

Ideal for Bible study groups who want to apply the Bible to their lives and the wider world.

it [brings] the ancient and powerful Word of God into the present so that it can be heard and believed with all the freshness of a new day.
Eugene H. Peterson, Regent College.

This series dares to go where few scholars have gone before—into the real world of biblical application faced by pastors and teachers every day. This is everything a good commentary series should be.
Leith Anderson, Pastor, Wooddale Church, USA.

For further details, please contact your local bookshop.